Game Programming for Teens, Second Edition

Maneesh Sethi

THOMSON
COURSE TECHNOLOGY
Professional ■ Technical ■ Reference

ISBN: 1-59200-834-8
Library of Congress Catalog Card Number: 2005923913
Printed in Canada
05 06 07 08 09 WC 10 9 8 7 6 5 4 3 2 1

THOMSON
COURSE TECHNOLOGY™
Professional ■ Technical ■ Reference

Thomson Course Technology PTR,
a division of Thomson Course Technology
25 Thomson Place
Boston, MA 02210
http://www.courseptr.com

Publisher and General Manager, Thomson Course Technology PTR:
Stacy L. Hiquet

Associate Director of Marketing:
Sarah O'Donnell

Manager of Editorial Services:
Heather Talbot

Marketing Manager:
Heather Hurley

Senior Acquisitions Editor:
Emi Smith

Senior Editor:
Mark Garvey

Marketing Coordinator:
Jordan Casey

Project Editor:
Jenny Davidson

Technical Reviewer:
Jonathan Harbour

Thomson Course Technology PTR Editorial Services Coordinator:
Elizabeth Furbish

Copyeditor:
Kezia Endsley

Interior Layout Tech:
Jill Flores

Cover Designer:
Mike Tanamachi

CD-ROM Producer:
Brandon Penticuff

Indexer:
Sharon Shock

Proofreader:
Sara Gullion

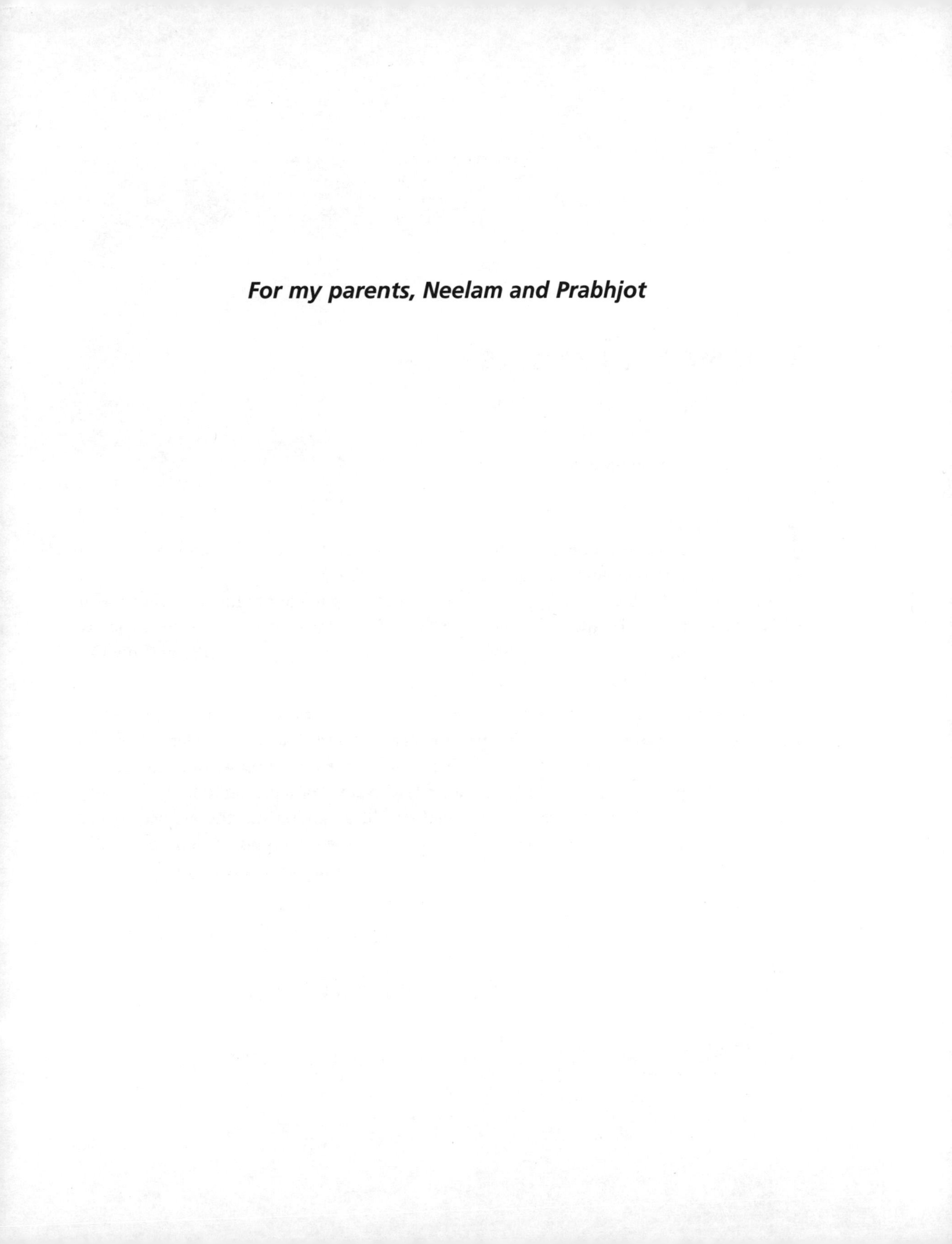

For my parents, Neelam and Prabhjot

Acknowledgments

Jeez, there are so many people to thank. This feels like I'm accepting an Oscar™: I'm afraid the band will start playing and usher me off the stage. Anyway, first of all thank you André LaMothe for giving me a chance and taking me out to lunch. I will get you back for that one day. Thank you everyone at Premier Press: my production editor Jenny Davidson, my copy editor, Kezia Endsley, my acquisitions editor, Emi Smith, and my CD editor, Brandon Penticuff.

Thanks go out to Adam Hepworth, who spent a lot of his "busy" day helping read my text and correcting a lot of errors. To all of my brothers and sisters, Rachi, who offered her help even though she was across an ocean, Nagina, whose love and support (and numerous phone calls) helped carry me through, and Ramit, who gave me a person to look up to and who helped me through the thick and thin (as well as giving me the chance to use "abeyance" in a sentence). Thanks for being here and giving me support when I needed it. To my mom and dad: I couldn't have done this without you. I love you so much.

Finally, thanks to Edgar L. Ibarra (Feo) for his artwork and Thomas Stenbäck for his work on the CD's music. Also, to Ari Feldman, for allowing me to use his sprite library on the CD.

Also, for contributing a demo program to the book, thanks to Jason Brasier and Edgar Ibarra for *Rockfall* and Marcus "Eikon" Smith for *Galaxiga.*

And to everyone whose name I forgot, you know who you are. Thanks!

About the Author

Maneesh Sethi is a high school student in California who will be enrolled at Stanford University in 2006. Maneesh has worked with Web design and development since he was in fifth grade and was the founder and head designer of Standard Design, a Web site design company. Maneesh has taught game programming on TechTV's *Call for Help* and at game programming conferences such as the XGDX. He is the author of *Game Programming for Teens (First Edition)* and *Web Design for Teens*, both published by Course PTR, and *How to Succeed as a Lazy Student.*

Besides game programming, Maneesh enjoys playing games (of course), sports such as tennis and basketball, and of course, sleep. Learn more about Maneesh, as well as his award-winning T-shirts and iPod sock case at www.maneeshsethi.com.

Contents

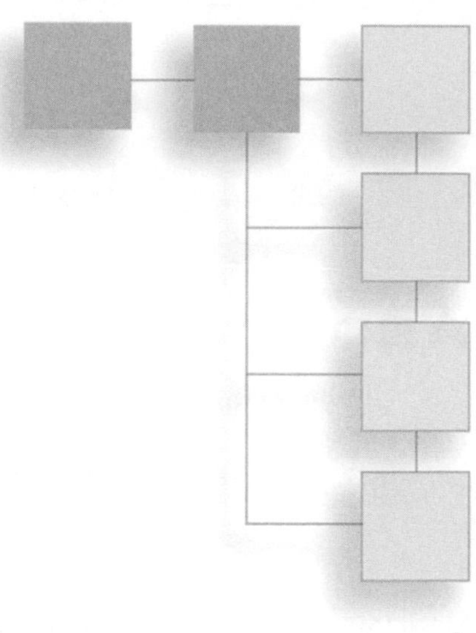

Part II: Getting Graphical 105

Introduction

Hey, reader. Thanks for buying my book. I am really thankful for it.

What is programming? Programming, according to Dictionary.com, is "a set of coded instructions that enables a machine, especially a computer, to perform a desired sequence of operations." In other words, programming allows you to make your computer do whatever you want it to do. Programming is used in everything related to the computer, but there are many distinct flavors of programming. This book teaches *game programming.*

Game programming is very different from the other types of programming. When you turn on your computer, you often see static programs—programs that sit there and wait for you to do something. Not with games. Games are running constantly, and they don't need the player to do anything to keep it running.

Of course, does this mean that game programming is a bit tougher than other styles of programming? Yes and no. Although game programming can be difficult at times, this book strives to turn the difficult into second nature. We use a language of programming called BASIC, which, as you can probably guess, is pretty darn basic.

What's in the Book?

This book is meant to be a guide to teach any beginner how to design and develop games. Inside the book you will find a wealth of knowledge all written in mind to help you reach the goal of making a game. Each chapter builds on the previous chapters and makes the book seem like a staircase—you move up step by step. The last chapter helps use all of your culminated knowledge in the production of a final game.

Part I discusses the BlitzPlus language. During this time, the book does not discuss graphical programs, but instead uses text-based to get the language points across.

Part II teaches the reader all about graphics within games. There is such information as varying colors, loading and displaying images, making scrolling backgrounds, and things like that.

Part III examines other related parts to game programming. The reader can learn how to use keyboard input, sounds, and music, and take into account artificial intelligence. This part also creates the final game that the book has been leading up to.

Part IV contains all the appendixes for the book. You will find all of the scan codes (for handling input), a list of Web sites to further your knowledge in the field, and what is on the CD.

Who Are You?

I suppose you can answer this question better than I, but let me tell you what I am looking for in a reader. First of all, I am guessing that you are either a teenager who is interested in game programming or a parent who is interested in having your child learn game programming. That is pretty much all that is required: interest. This book is not set up to be difficult. It helps introduce the reader into the world of game programming.

There are literally very few requirements. All you really need is a basic knowledge of math, like addition, subtraction, multiplication, and division. If you know those techniques, you are pretty much set! I also suggest that the reader asks his or her parent for help whenever necessary. I use some rudimentary algebra, but those instances are few and far between, and should be easy to comprehend.

You don't need to have any knowledge of other programming languages. Not that it won't help if you do, of course. If you do know any other languages, you can learn from this book as well. But, *Game Programming for Teens, Second Edition* teaches the language of game programming along with the ability to actually implement games.

If you are the parent of a child who wants to learn programming, this book is the way to go. General programming is a long and boring subject, but game programming allows your child to create things that are *fun.* Help your child with programming while he or she reads this book, as well. Not only will you both learn programming, but who knows, it may strengthen the bond between parent and child (this comes from my psychologist side).

Who Am I?

Hey everybody, I am Maneesh Sethi. I am a high school student, and the reason I am writing this book is because I believe that, because I am a teenager myself, I would be the best one to help other teens learn about programming. I began programming in 1999 in C and

C++. Two years ago I discovered BlitzPlus and I have studied it ever since. BlitzPlus seems to be the easiest way for any novice to begin writing games, and I want to help the reader progress as fast as possible. The Web site for this book is located on www.maneeshsethi.com, and you can e-mail me with any questions (before or after you buy the book) at maneesh@maneeshsethi.com. I love to get e-mails!

Conventions Used in This Book

note

Notes provide additional information on a feature, extend an idea on how to do something, or illustrate a cool fact.

caution

Cautions warn you of potential problems and tell you what *not* to do.

tip

Tips give you some pertinent information on a better, faster, or easier way of doing something.

Let's Get Ready to Rumble…

If you are still browsing this book in the bookstore, now would be the time to take it home. The bookstore would probably appreciate it if you buy it first (so would I!).

The first part quickly teaches you all of the intricacies of the BlitzPlus programming language.

And so we begin…

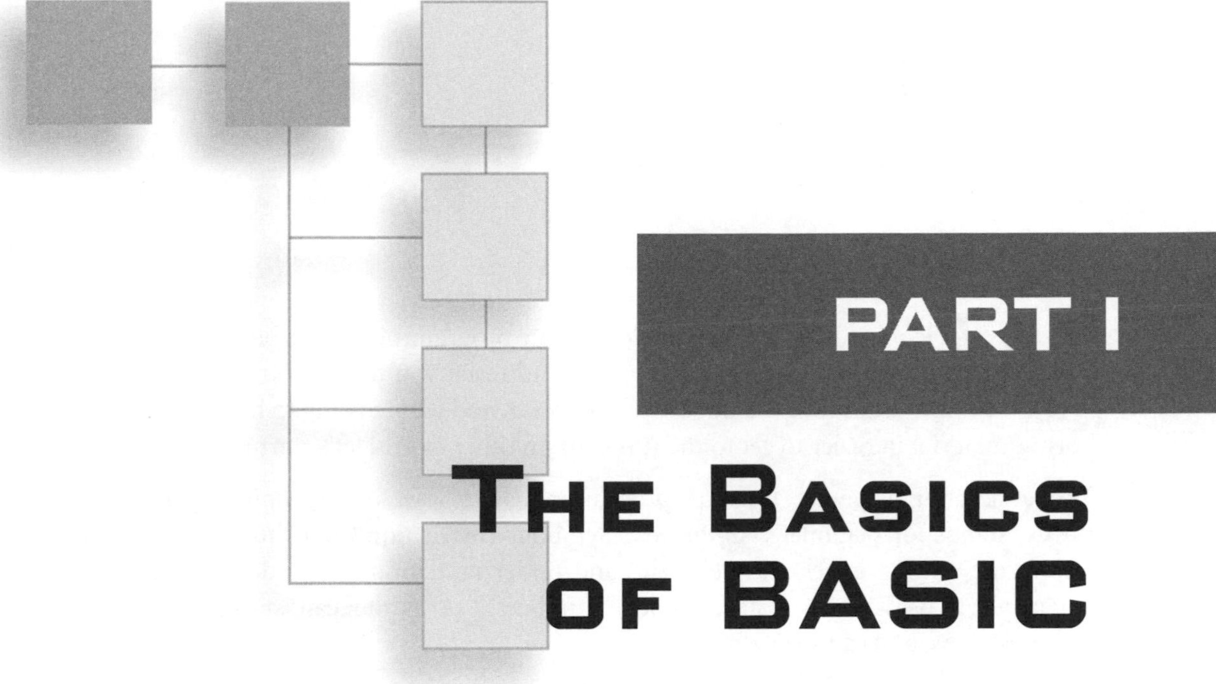

PART I

The Basics of BASIC

Welcome to the amazing world of game programming! This book will show you the ins and outs of video games and teach you to develop your own. Game programming is a huge topic, however, and we are going to hurry through the boring material in order to get to the fun stuff. In other words, let's start right away!

The easiest language for learning programming (at least in my opinion) is BASIC. BASIC stands for **B**eginner's **A**ll Purpose **S**ymbolic **I**nstruction **C**ode, but that's not really important. BASIC is very easy to write and understand, and it's modeled after human language (it uses words instead of just numbers), so if you can speak English, you shouldn't have a hard time with BASIC.

We will be using a program called BlitzPlus in this book. BlitzPlus is built to use a modified version of BASIC in its programming. We begin with a short history of BASIC, just to get the ball rolling on the language.

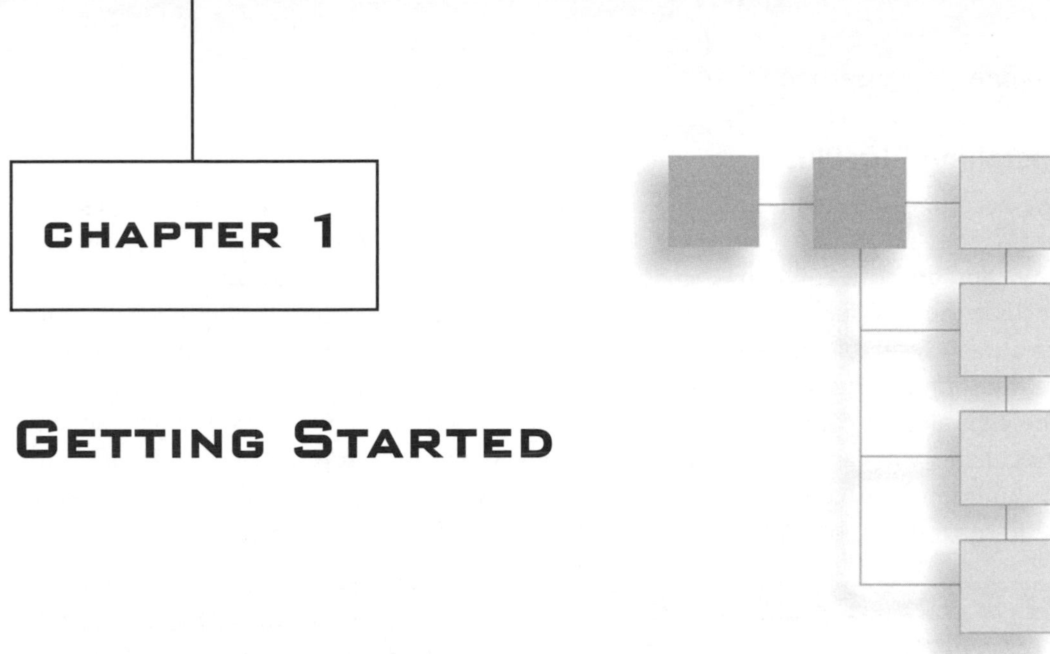

Chapter 1

Getting Started

A Brief History of BASIC

The language of BASIC was first developed in 1964 by J. Kemeny and T. Kurtz at Dartmouth College. It was designed to be a very easy language to understand, translate, and write. It was also meant to be the first step toward writing programs for tougher languages.

In the 1970s two people, Paul Allen and Bill Gates, decided to develop a BASIC language for the new Altair Personal Computer. The developers of the Altair showed a lot of interest in the BASIC language, and Gates and Allen licensed it.

Bill Gates and Paul Allen put BASIC onto other types of computers. By 1980, BASIC was moved to Atari, Commodore, and Apple computers as well as the Altair. Bill Gates developed an operating system called DOS (Disk Operating System) with a BASIC interpreter. This allowed any user that owned DOS to write programs in BASIC.

Microsoft, headed by Gates, realized how popular BASIC was and decided to write a compiler for it that did not require DOS. QuickBasic, the first standalone BASIC compiler, was born. Soon after, Microsoft decided to focus on graphics, and developed Visual Basic, which created graphical programs using BASIC as a core language.

BlitzPlus, the program we are using in this book, was developed by Mark Sibly, and is geared toward the game developer. BlitzPlus is very easy to learn and understand due to its BASIC nature, and is a good way to learn game programming without having to worry about extra code that has almost nothing to do with the actual game itself.

Installing BlitzPlus

We need to get BlitzPlus onto our computers so that we can start writing games as soon as possible. BlitzPlus is a compiler, so it takes your code and turns it into a program that any computer can run. However, the demo version that is included on the CD does not include the compiler, but only the interpreter. Unlike a compiler, an interpreter does not create an executable file that can be run on any computer; instead, it only runs from within the compiler. In other words, the programs you write will only be able to be run from the compiler on your computer. If you want to compile the program into a standalone executable, you can purchase the full BlitzPlus package from http://www.blitzbasic.com. In addition, you can download new versions of BlitzPlus from http://www.maneeshsethi.com (this book's Web site). The BlitzPlus installer is shown in Figure 1.1.

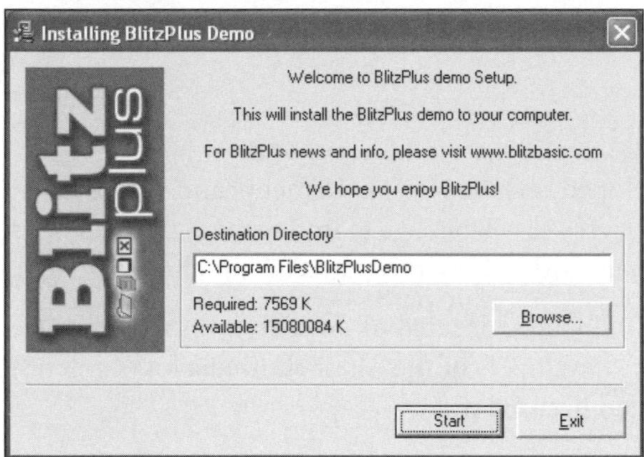

Figure 1.1
BlitzPlus installer.

Okay, first things first. To install this program, put the CD into your CD-ROM drive, and run BlitzPlus-Demo.exe. BlitzPlus will ask you where you want to install the program. Choose a directory (the default one is a good choice), and press install. When the installation finishes, click OK, launch the program, and you're done! You now have a full BASIC interpreter on your computer.

note

The BlitzPlus demo has one annoying part—the demo runs only 30 times before it locks up and requires you to purchase it. For this reason, I have included on the CD a demo for the old version of BlitzPlus, BlitzBasic. You can install this by choosing BlitzBasicDemo.exe when loading the CD. The BlitzBasic demo will run most of the BlitzPlus code, although you may need to make a few small modifications. BlitzBasic has no time limit, however, and will allow you to continue to write code for as long as you like.

Understanding the IDE

BlitzPlus can seem a little daunting at first. The program has a lot of menus and icons, but you can master them with a little effort. The first thing you see when you open the program is the documentation window, pictured in Figure 1.2. If you need to find tutorials or sample programs, this is the place to do it. After you have read through anything that interests you, open a new document, by selecting File>New or the New icon.

note

The > (arrow) symbol means a selection from a menu. In other words, File>New instructs you to open the File menu and select New. You can access the menus at the top of the program, right above the main toolbar.

Figure 1.2
The Documentation window.

What you see now, as in Figure 1.3, is considered the IDE. IDE means Integrated Development Environment, and it is an area in which you can write and compile your programs in the same workspace.

Each of the windows, toolbars, and menus are necessary for game programming, so a good explanation of each might be helpful.

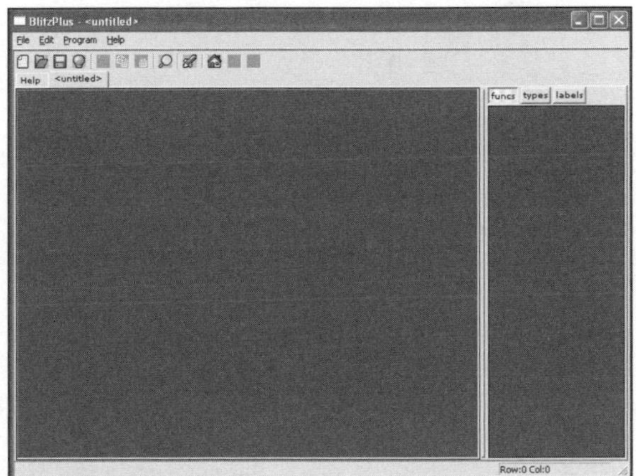

Figure 1.3
The BlitzPlus IDE.

Windows and Panels

The main window takes up most of the program space and it is the most important part of BlitzPlus. This window is where the actual code from the game is typed. The keywords and important parts of your program will be highlighted when you type in this area. If you want to see an example, type the word **End**, so that your screen looks like the one pictured in Figure 1.4. You will notice that as soon as you complete the word and press the spacebar, it becomes a different color. This highlight feature helps in reading and understanding your program.

Figure 1.4
Highlighted code.

Take a look to the right of the screen. Although not pictured in the previous figure, the only visible panel located on the right is under buttons labeled *funcs*, *types*, and *labels*. Each of these buttons displays separate info on the panel. Funcs shows which functions you have created, Types shows your defined types, and Labels shows any existing labels. These descriptions probably don't mean much to you now, but by the end of this book you will understand what they do.

Toolbars

The main toolbar (shown in Figure 1.5) is simply a set of shortcut icons. It allows you to perform actions quickly without having to search through the menus for the command. Table 1.1 briefly describes each icon going from left to right.

Figure 1.5
The main toolbar.

Table 1.1 Main Toolbar Shortcut Icons

Icon	Description
New	Opens a new blank BlitzPlus document.
Open	Allows you to open an existing file from the disk.
Save	If your program has been saved previously, the Save icon quick-saves the open document; if not, Save asks for a file name and a location to save the file to.
Close	Closes a single document.
Cut, Copy, and Paste	The Cut command saves highlighted text to the clipboard but deletes the highlighted text, the Copy command saves the highlighted text to the clipboard but leaves the highlighted text untouched, and Paste places saved text in the clipboard in the document.
Find	Allows you to search for a certain word or certain words in an opened document.
Run	Compiles and runs an open document.
Pause, Continue, Step Over, Step Into, Step Out, End	Advanced debug tools.
Home, Back, Forward	All three commands allow you to enter and navigate through the BlitzPlus documentation. Unless you are in the documentation window, Back and Forward will be grayed out.

Menus

The menu toolbar allows you to exercise the full power of BlitzPlus. The main toolbar looks like Figure 1.6. Buried within each menu are many helpful and useful commands. Table 1.2 shows the most important.

Figure 1.6
BlitzPlus menus.

Table 1.2 BlitzPlus Menu Commands

Command	Description
Program>Check for errors	This command allows you to error-check your code without compiling and running it.
Program>Debug Enabled?	If this feature is enabled, you will be able to run your program in a small window (instead of the program taking the entire screen) and debugging your program becomes much easier.

The First Game: KONG

All right, now you will be able to see what a full game looks like. This is basically a simple *Pong* clone, and it is easy to control and play. The idea of this game is to score more points than your opponent by hitting the ball past his side of the table. To play, either run demo01-01.exe from the CD or compile the code.

To compile the code yourself, you need to find demo01-01.bb on the CD. After finding it, copy it to your computer and open it through the BlitzPlus compiler. To open it, find the File menu on the top of the compiler and choose Open. Navigate to demo01-01.bb and press Enter. The code should now appear inside your compiler.

To actually compile, find the Program menu in BlitzPlus. Select Program>Run Program, and the game will compile and run! If you get a window asking you to save the file, choose a directory to save it in or just press Cancel, and the program will run. You have just compiled your first program!

Feel free to examine the code; although it may seem very weird and hard to understand now, you will soon be able to figure out this code easily.

Table 1.3 lists the keys you will use for this game.

Okay, let's actually take a look at the code. Read it, but don't worry if some of it is hard to understand. This is the first program you have seen, and it isn't easy. You will learn how to actually write this code throughout the book.

Table 1.3 Keys Used in KONG

Key	Action
Up Arrow	Move player up
Down Arrow	Move player down
Escape	Exit game
P	Pause and Unpause

```
;demo01-01.bb - A Complete game of KONG

;Set up graphics mode
Graphics 800,600

;Seed the random generator (make random numbers actually random)
SeedRnd(MilliSecs())

;Create a back buffer
SetBuffer BackBuffer()
;Set the handle to the center of images
AutoMidHandle True


;CONSTS
;The following are key code constants
Const UPKEY = 200   ;Up
Const DOWNKEY = 208  ;Down
Const PAUSEKEY = 25  ;P


Const HUMANSPEED = 7 ;The human's max speed
Const COMPUTERSPEED = 6 ;The computer's max speed


;TYPES
;The player type: both the human and the opponent
Type player
     Field y,score     ;y position and score
End Type

;The ball type: for the ball
Type ball
     Field x,y,xv,yv     ;x, y coordinates, and x, y velocity
End Type
```

```
;IMAGES
;The picture of the human player
Global player1image = LoadImage("player1.bmp")

;The picture of the computer player
Global player2image = LoadImage("player2.bmp")

;The picture of the ball
Global ballimage = LoadImage("ball.bmp") ;Load the ball image

;TYPE INITIALIZATION

;Create a ball
Global ball.ball = New ball
;Create the human
Global player1.player = New player
;Create the computer
Global player2.player = New player
```

This is the end of the declaration section of the code. This part sets up the important variables for the program as well as the types and images. (Don't worry; you will be introduced to all of this as the book progresses.)

After the declaration, we begin the initialization. Initialization is the process of setting up everything that will be used in the program—in this section, the initialization section sets up the beginning score values and the players' position on the screen.

```
;INITIALIZATION

Text 400,300,"Ready...Set"
;Wait for one second
Delay(1000)
Text 420,330,"GO!!!"
Flip
;Delay for 1/5 of a second
Delay(200)

;Initialize the level
InitializeLevel()


;Set initial scores
player1\score = 0
player2\score = 0
```

The initialization section sets up some important variables for the game, such as the score and the player variables. These variables keep track of how the player is doing and where he or she is located.

After initialization, the actual loop begins:

```
;MAIN LOOP
While Not KeyDown(1)

;Clear the screen
Cls

;Draw the ball
DrawImage (ballimage,ball\x,ball\y)
;Draw the human
DrawImage (player1image, 60, player1\y)
;Draw the computer
DrawImage (player2image, 740, player2\y)

;Test what user pressed
TestKeyboard()
;What should AI do?
TestAI()
;Draw the HUD
DrawScore()

Flip

Delay 20

Wend ;END OF MAIN LOOP
```

What Is a Frame?

I am about to reference the word *frame* a bunch of times in a few moments, and you should know what it means. A frame is the screen at any given moment. A game can be compared to an animated film—both are made up of a bunch of different pictures that, when put together, create animation. The frames blend together so quickly that the objects on the screen appear to be moving. An average game runs at 30 frames per second, which means 30 pictures on the screen are blended together each and every second.

This is the end of the main loop. To put it bluntly, the main loop is the entire game. Every frame of a game is a single iteration of the main loop. By the way, a loop causes some code to be repeated over and over until some condition becomes false. Here, the condition is that the Esc key has not been pressed. Usually, the main loop is a `while` loop, shown here in the line

```
While Not KeyDown(ESCKEY)
```

At this point, the actual game loop has been completed, so we must now define the functions. A function is called with its name followed by parentheses; for example, `InitializeLevel()`. Functions are like little helpers that perform specific activities that we want to do over and over. If you look at the main loop, you will see that most of these functions are called from there, and some others are called from within other functions.

```
;INITIALIZELEVEL()
;Sets up starting values
Function InitializeLevel()

;Put ball in center of the screen
ball\x = 400
ball\y = 300

;Make the ball move in a random direction
ball\xv = Rand(2,6)
ball\yv = Rand(-8,8)

;Place the players in their correct position
player2\y = 300
player1\y = 300
End Function
```

This function sets up the starting values for the players and the ball. The ball is in the center of the screen and it is directed toward the right of the screen (to the computer player's side) with a small variation on how high or low it goes. The human player is near the left edge of the screen, and the computer player is near the right.

```
;DRAWSCORE()
;Draws the HUD in the top right
Function DrawScore()
;Write the human score
Text 700,0,"Player 1: " + player1\score
;Write the computer's score
Text 700,30,"Player 2: " + player2\score
End Function
```

This is probably the simplest function in this program because all it does is draw the scores on the top right of the screen.

```
;TESTKEYBOARD()
;Moves player up and down based on keyboard
Function TestKeyboard()

;If player hits up, move him up
If KeyDown(UPKEY)
     player1\y = player1\y - HUMANSPEED
EndIf

;If player presses down, move him down
If KeyDown(DOWNKEY)
     player1\y = player1\y + HUMANSPEED
End If

;if player presses Pause, pause the game
If KeyHit(PAUSEKEY)
     ;make screen blank
     Cls

     Text 400,300,"Press 'P' to Unpause Game"

     Flip

     ;wait for player to unpause
     While Not KeyHit(PAUSEKEY)
     Wend

EndIf

End Function
```

This function determines what keys the user pressed, if any. If it doesn't make sense to you, try reading the following pseudocode:

What Is Pseudocode?

Big word, huh? Pseudocode is a very helpful device in game programming because it takes hard-to-understand concepts and turns them into human language. Pseudocode is the program code put into easier-to-understand terms. Basically, to convert code into pseudocode, simply change each line of code into human language. However, pseudocode does not have all the detail that real code does, so although it is good for understanding concepts, it isn't a good idea to try and put it back into a program. Within this book, pseudocode appears in italics.

```
If (player presses up)
       Move player up


If (player presses down)
       Move player down


If (player presses 'P')
       Pause the game
```

Pretty easy to understand, don't you think? Refer back to the actual code to see the correlation.

Next, look at the function `TestAI()`.

```
;TESTAI()
;Updates ball and score and enemy
Function TestAI()

;If ball is above computer, move computer up
If ball\y > player2\y
     player2\y = player2\y + COMPUTERSPEED

;if ball is lower than computer, move computer down
ElseIf ball\y < player2\y
     player2\y = player2\y - COMPUTERSPEED
     EndIf

;If ball hits human player, reflect it away from him and vary its velocity and direc-
tion
If ImagesOverlap(ballimage,ball\x,ball\y,player1image,60,player1\y)
     ball\xv = -ball\xv + Rand(-4,4)
```

```
	ball\yv = ball\yv + Rand(-4,4)

;If ball hits computer, reflect it away from computer and vary its velocity and direc-
tion
ElseIf ImagesOverlap(ballimage,ball\x,ball\y,player2image,740,player2\y)
	ball\xv = -ball\xv + Rand(-4,4)
	ball\yv = ball\yv + Rand(-4,4)

;If ball hits top wall, reflect it downwards
ElseIf ball\y <= 0
	ball\yv = -ball\yv + Rand (-1,1)
	ball\xv = ball\xv + Rand (-1,1)

;If ball hits bottom wall, reflect it upwards
ElseIf ball\y >= 600
	ball\yv = -ball\yv + Rand (-1,1)
	ball\xv = ball\xv + Rand (-1,1)

;if ball hits left wall, computer has scored so computer gets one more point
ElseIf ball\x <= 0
	player2\score = player2\score + 1   ;computer scores
	Text 400,300,"Player 2 Scores!!!"
	Flip
	;wait two seconds
	Delay(2000)

	;reset level
	InitializeLevel()

;If ball hits right wall, human scored so give him a point
ElseIf ball\x >= 800
	player1\score = player1\score + 1   ;human scores
	Text 400,300,"Player 1 Scores!!!"
	Flip
	;wait 2 secs
	Delay(2000)
	;reset level
	InitializeLevel()
EndIf
```

```
    ;update ball's position on screen
    ball\x = ball\x + ball\xv
    ball\y = ball\y + ball\yv

End Function
```

This one is a lot harder to understand. `TestAI()` changes the position of the ball based on its direction variables and changes the position of the computer's paddle based on the position of the ball. It also increments the score if either team hits the ball past the opposing paddle. If you are having trouble understanding this function, maybe the following pseudocode will clear it up:

```
If (ball is above computer)
        Move computer up

OR if (ball is below computer)
        Move computer down


If (ball hits player's paddle)
        Change direction of ball

OR if (ball hits computer's paddle)
        Change direction of ball

OR if (ball hits top wall)
        Change direction of ball

OR if (ball hits bottom wall)
        Change direction of ball

OR if (ball hits left wall)
        Score a point for computer
        Reset the level

OR if (ball hits right wall)
        Score a point for the player
        Reset the level
```

Once again, if you want to have a better perspective of this game, run demo01-01.bb off the CD.

caution

Because of margin constraints, some of the lines of code may have spread over two lines or more. In a real game, all of the code must be on one line, or else it won't run. For example, if I had written something like the following line

```
ElseIf ImagesOverlap(ballimage,ball\x,ball\y,player2image,740,player2\y)  ;This
tests to see if the ball has collided with player 2's image.
```

Typing it into the compiler with the line break would not work. It must be on the same line, even though the margins in the book made it appear broken up.

Figures 1.7 and 1.8 show the KONG title screen and main screen, respectively.

Figure 1.7
KONG title screen.

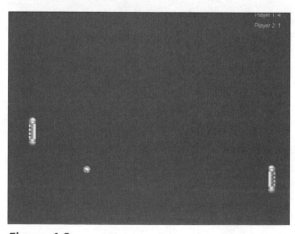

Figure 1.8
KONG main screen.

Compiling the Code

Compiling the code is a very simple procedure. Just open the file (demo01-01.bb) off the CD in BlitzPlus (or type it into the workspace), save the file (File>Save) onto your computer, and select Program>Run Program, as shown in Figure 1.9.

Well, that isn't what you would call a full game. I did not add any special effects or sounds because they aren't very important at this point. The idea is to get a feel for what code looks like and how it is written. You will notice that the meanings of most of the functions are easy to understand because of the function names. This helps in understanding the program.

Let me summarize the main parts of a game. The game consists of:

- The initialization section
- The main loop
- The shutdown

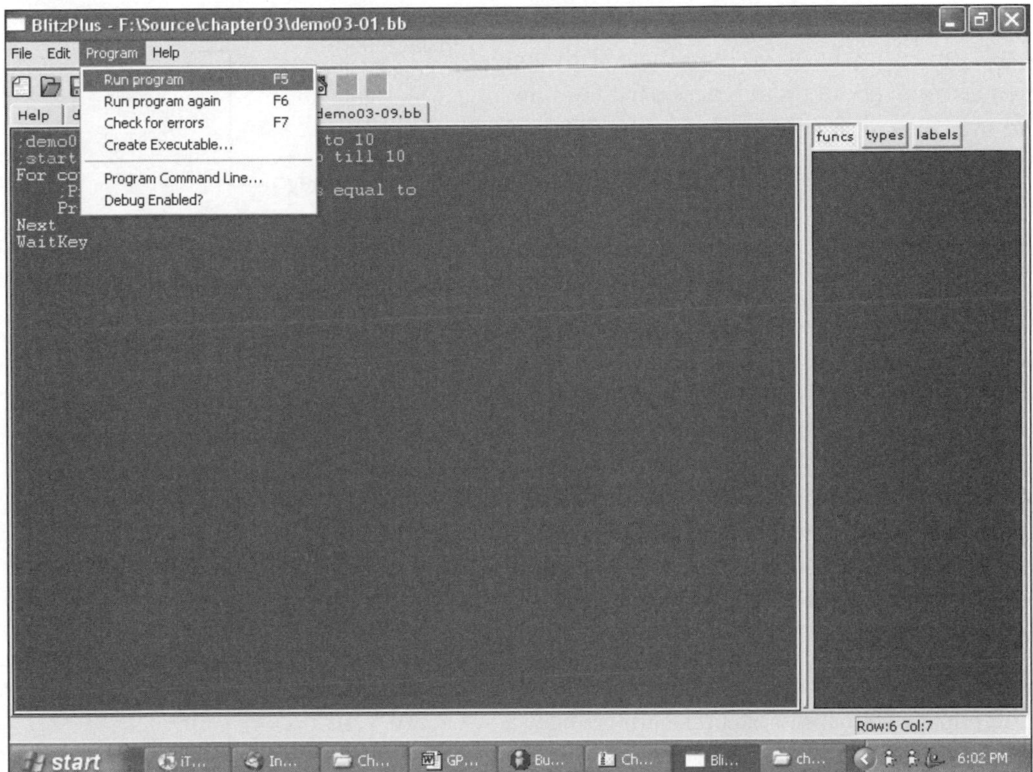

Figure 1.9
Compiling the game.

Initialization sets up variables and functions that are used throughout the game. Declaration is part of initialization and is used to set up variables that will be used later in the program. The game loop is what you see on the screen. Each *iteration* (an iteration is each time the program runs through the loop) of the loop is one frame of the game. Usually, there are at least 30 frames, or iterations, per second. See Figure 1.10 for a description of initialization, the game loop (also known as the main loop), and shutdown in KONG.

The shutdown sequence is the final part of the game, and it runs just before and during the end of the game. It closes all open files, deletes any running variables, and quits the game.

Of course, there are a few other important parts to any game, but I will go over them with you when learning about them is necessary. For now, read over the commented code (on the CD) and try to understand what in heck is going on. If you follow the functions, it shouldn't be too hard.

> **The Day that Maneesh Got Embarrassed**
>
> In March of 2004, I was on a show called "Call for Help" on TechTV. I decided to demonstrate this game, KONG, on the show, because it was an easy to understand and play game. Turns out I made a bad choice. During the game, some of the random-ization code got messed up, so the ball bounced up and down and up and down repeatedly. My game actually crashed on TV!
>
> You can see the segment on TechTV on my Web site, http://www.maneeshsethi.com. Just promise not to laugh!

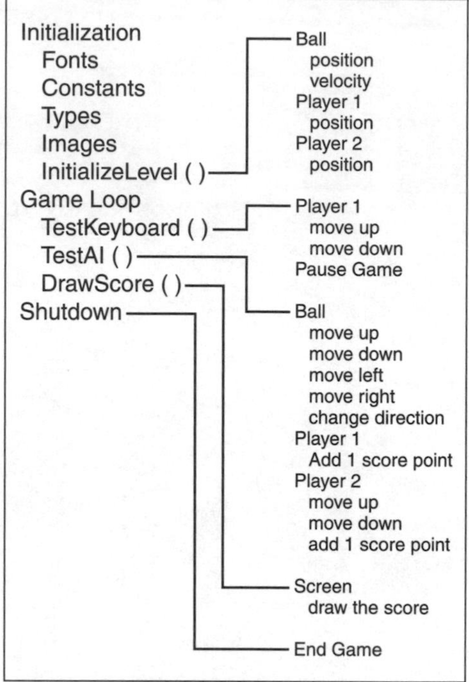

Figure 1.10
Initialization, game loop, and shutdown.

Summary

We have certainly covered a lot of ground in this chapter! So far, we have learned about the history of BASIC, we have installed BlitzPlus, we have learned the important features of the program, and we have written, read, and played our first game. One important thing: *Do not* be disheartened by the length or complexity of the sample code. This game is not a tough one, and although it seems long now, it will be relatively simple to write by the time you finish this book.

In this chapter, we went over the following concepts:

- The history of BASIC
- Installing the BlitzPlus program
- Creating our first game
- Compiling our first game

The next chapter will introduce you to the fundamentals of BASIC; it will discuss common operators and operations. If you've made it this far, the next chapter should be a cinch.

Just sit back, relax, and enjoy the ride.

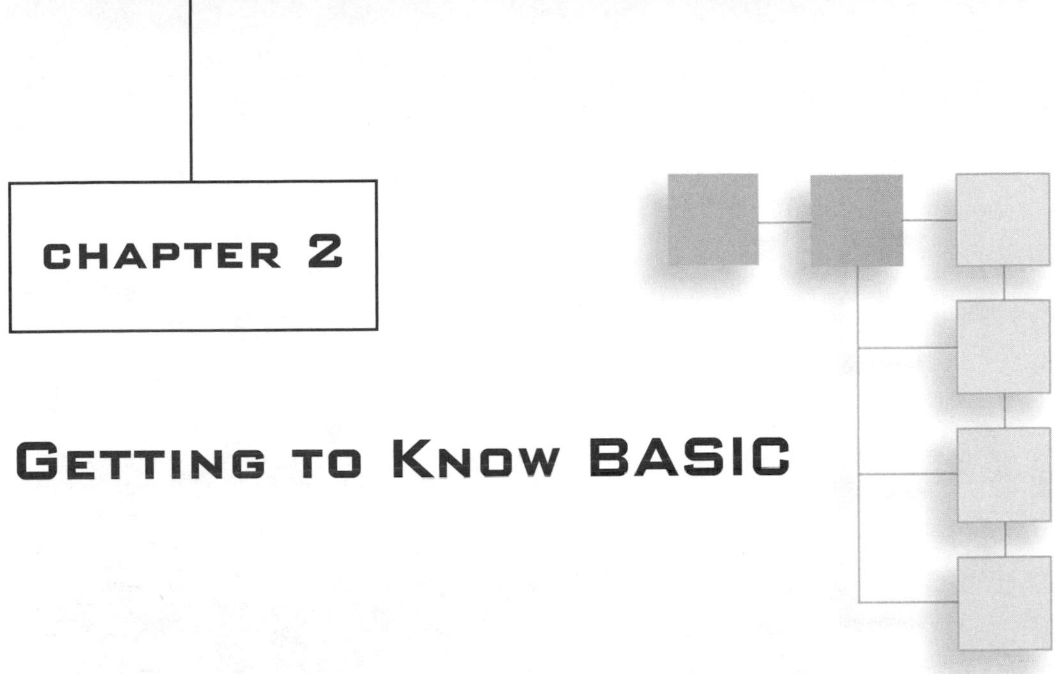

Getting to Know BASIC

This chapter examines the simple and fundamental aspects of the BASIC language. There will be very few graphics involved in this chapter, so everything you do can be viewed on the screen in text format.

I suggest taking what you learn about general BASIC programming from this chapter and writing your own sample programs. Although you will not be able to make graphical programs, you will be able to make simple text-based programs. Sample programs help cement ideas that you learn into your mind, so it will be much easier to remember them. The next chapters build heavily on the concepts you learn here, so make sure you understand the fundamentals explained in this chapter before moving on to the next chapters.

In this chapter, you will learn how to use variables, input, and conditionals. Ready?

Hello, World!

Okay, before you go any further, you're going to write your first program. This is a common one for first-time programmers to write in any computer programming language, most likely because it is so simple. This program simply displays the text `Hello, World!` on the screen. That's right, no graphics, no special effects, just pure, hardcore text.

Let's go over how to compile the following code. Type what follows into your BlitzPlus compiler or open demo02-01.bb (see Figure 2.1). Next, select Program>Run Program and watch the magic.

If you decide to type the code into the compiler, make sure that the workspace into which you are typing is blank first. Only the code should be displayed in the main window of the BlitzPlus compiler.

If you don't want to compile the code, you can also run this program from the CD. Figure 2.2 shows the executed Hello World program.

```
;demo02-01.bb - Displays text "Hello World"
Print "Hello, World!"

;Wait for five seconds
Delay 5000
```

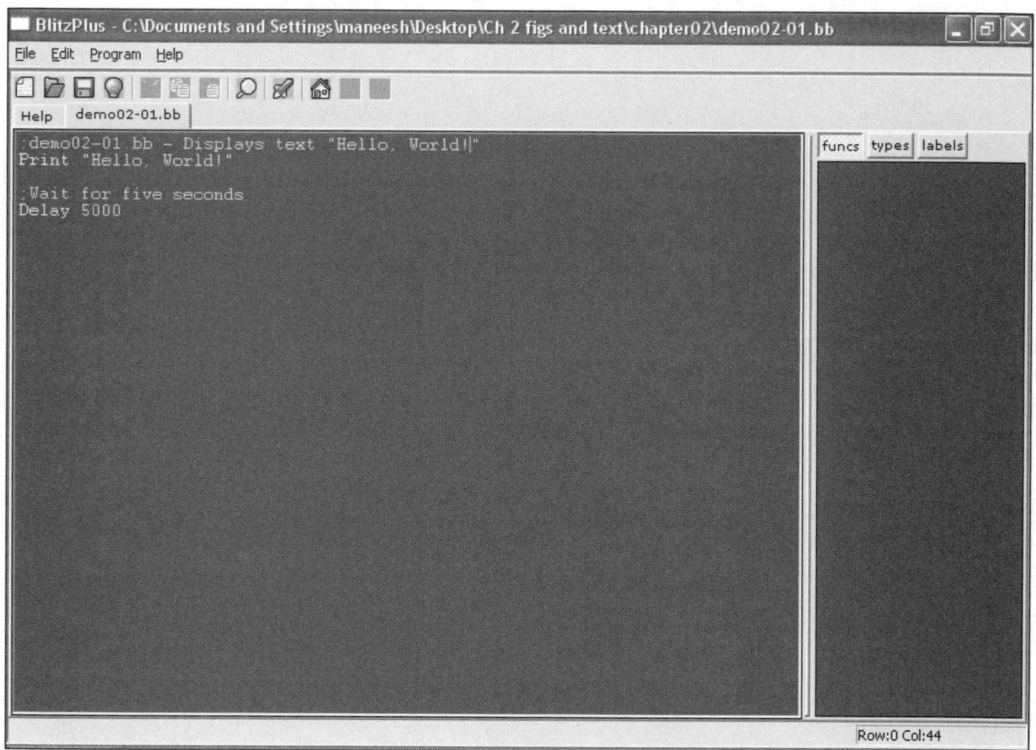

Figure 2.1 The Hello World program in BlitzPlus.

Although this program may seem very simple, it is a big hurdle you have just crossed. You just created a file, typed in the code, compiled it, and ran it as a program. Congratulations!

Let's analyze this program a bit (although there isn't much to analyze). First of all, the line

```
;demo02-01.bb - Displays text "Hello, World!"
```

is a comment. A comment is any text that is written after a semicolon (;). The comment ends at the end of the line. A comment does not have to occupy its own line; it can be written after some actual program code. For example, this line

```
Print "This is code" ;This is a comment.
```

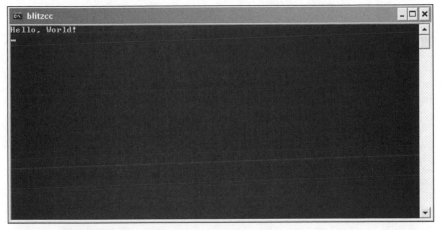

Figure 2.2 The executed Hello World program.

consists of two parts: a line of code and a comment. Comments are used to help you understand the code; the compiler does not understand or care about information in comments. The compiler automatically ignores any comments. Figure 2.3 demonstrates how comments look inside a compiler.

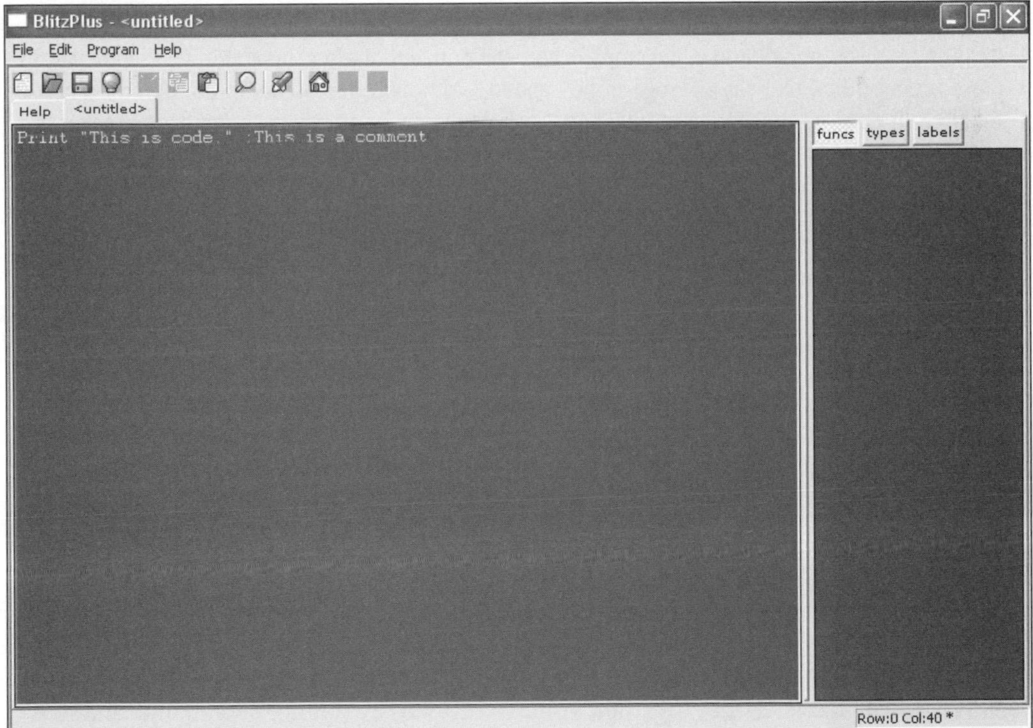

Figure 2.3 Comments in a compiler.

tip

You might be wondering, "If it is my code, why would I need a comment to understand it? I wrote it, so I understand it!" The problem with this assumption is twofold: one, you may decide to share the code with someone after you write the program, and two, you could forget how your program works and spend a lot of time trying to figure out what some parts do. More than once I have forgotten to comment my code, and the results were not good. I had to spend quite some time trying to understand a little bit of code I had written only a few months earlier. Anyway, the moral of the story is *always comment your code.*

The next line of code is the meat of the program.

```
Print "Hello, World!"
```

This line prints the text string `"Hello, World!"` on the screen (a text string is simply a set of characters) and begins a new line. To see what I mean by new line, add another `Print` command to the code. You will see that the new text is written below the old text.

Note the quotes around `"Hello, World!"` Quotes are necessary around any part of a string. The quotes identify to the program that what is being typed is a set of letters and numbers, not a variable name. If you leave off the quotes, you will get an error.

note

If you type this program into your compiler, you will notice that after running it, your compiler displays a dialog box that says, "Program has ended." Although this occurs in the demo version of BlitzPlus, it does not happen in the full version. If you want to rid any program of the dialog box, just type `End` where you want the program to end. `End` exits the program without displaying any dialog boxes. Try it out on demo02-01.bb by adding `End` somewhere in the source file.

I usually like to provide the function declaration for easy reference when calling functions. A *function declaration* describes any parameters taken in by the function as well as the function name. The function declaration for `Print` is:

```
Print [string$]
```

note

Notice the square brackets ([]) on the left and right of the `[string$]` variable. These brackets mean that the variable is optional and not required. If the variable is required but omitted, you will receive an error and not be able to compile your code.

As you can see, the function's name is `Print` and the only parameter is `[string$]`. A string is just a series of characters put together; you can think of a sentence as a string. The string would be the entire sentence lined up together, including the spaces and punctuation.

First of all, `Print` is a function. Functions (which are described in more detail later) come in two flavors: user-defined and compiler-defined. User-defined functions are written by the programmer (`TestKeyboard()` from the Chapter 1 game is an example) and compiler-defined functions are embedded in the compiler and are available for use in a program. `Print` is an example of a compiler-defined function.

See Table 2.1 for a description of the Print parameters.

Table 2.1 Parameters for Print

Parameter	Description
`string$`	A text string followed by a new line that will be displayed onscreen. If `string$` is omitted, only a new line will be printed.

The final line calls the function `Delay`.

```
Delay millisecs%
```

This function simply pauses for the given amount of time before proceeding. In this program, I had the program pause for 5000 milliseconds, or five seconds. If you remove this line from the program, the program will end before the user can read `Hello, World!`.

One question remains: What is that dollar sign and the percent sign doing after the parameters to the functions? That brings you to the next topic, variables.

Variables

Variables are intrinsic to almost every program written. A variable is just that: "variable". This means that the value of a variable can change. For example, say you were running a program that uses a high score that is stored in a variable. When the high score changes, the high score variable changes to reflect the new score.

Declaring Variables

Variables are very easy to use because they can be used as regular numbers. However, unlike numbers, variables must first be declared. When a variable is declared, the program knows that the variable exists, and you can use it in your program.

There are three types of variables in BASIC: integer variables, floating point variables, and string variables. See Table 2.2 for a description of the types of variables.

Table 2.2 Description of Variable Types

Parameter	Description
`integer%`	Fixed-point variables with no decimal places.
`float#`	Floating-point variables with decimal places allowed.
`string$`	A text string.

note

When variables are created, they are automatically assumed to be integers, or whole numbers in other words. Therefore, the percent sign on all integer variables is unnecessary and from now on, they will mostly be omitted from the code.

Each type of variable is defined in a similar way. Simply type the name of the variable you want to define followed by the type symbol (`%`, `#`, or `$`). For example,

```
highscore% = 100
pi# = 3.14159
myname$ = "Maneesh Sethi"
```

Using Variables

You are now ready to write a few programs using variables. These programs should demonstrate a few important points about variables.

```
;demo02-02.bb - Adds two cool numbers

;VARIABLES
favnum = 314
coolnum = 13

;Print the two variables
Print "I like " + favnum + " And I like " + coolnum
;Print the variables added together)
Print "These numbers added together are " + (favnum + coolnum)
;Delay for 5 seconds
Delay 5000
```

The output is shown in Figure 2.4.

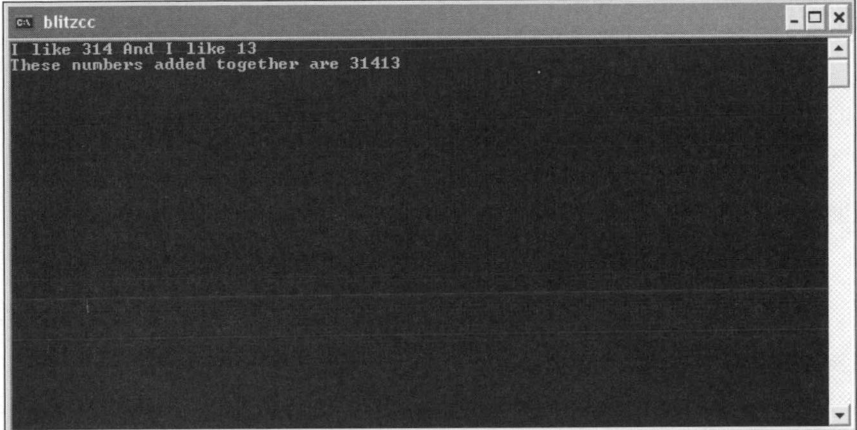

Figure 2.4 The demo02-02.bb program.

Well, this is certainly interesting. Let's check it out. First, a comment is written to describe the program. This is good practice and should be used on most programs. Next, I initialized two variables: `favnum` and `coolnum`. Then, I called the `Print` function. The string variable begins with the static text `"I like"` and then displays `favnum`. To display `favnum`, you use the concatenation operator (+). The concatenation operator links separate strings together; in this case, it displays the variable `favnum`. It finishes out the first `Print` statement by displaying `"And I like"` + the variable `coolnum`.

The next `Print` statement displays `"These numbers added together are"` and shows 327, which is equal to 314 + 13. However, try removing the parentheses around `favnum` and `coolnum`, like in Figure 2.5. A strange answer comes up when these parentheses are removed: 31413!

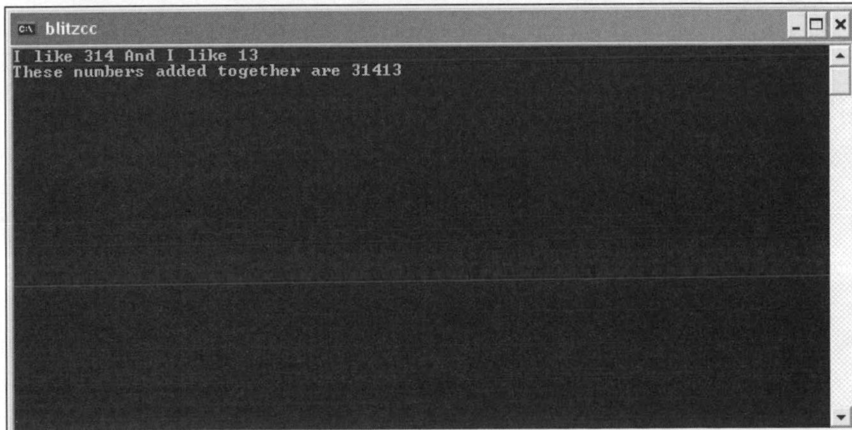

Figure 2.5 Demo02-02.bb without parentheses.

The reason for this strange answer is that without the parentheses, the addition operator (+) is interpreted as the concatenation operator due to the context in which it is used. Because there are no parentheses, the operator simply adds the string "13" to the end of the string "314" and displays it as a string rather than an integer. The only way to fix this problem is to use parentheses.

Here is an example using only string variables.

```
;demo02-03.bb - adds strings together
string1$ = "I "
string2$ = "like "
string3$ = "programming!"
;concatenate the strings
completestring$ = string1$ + string2$ + string3$
;print 'em out
Print completestring$
Delay 5000
```

In this program, a set of single words are created and joined together in the `completestring$` variable using the concatenation operator. As you can see in Figure 2.6, "I " + `"like "` + `"programming!"` becomes `"I like programming!"`.

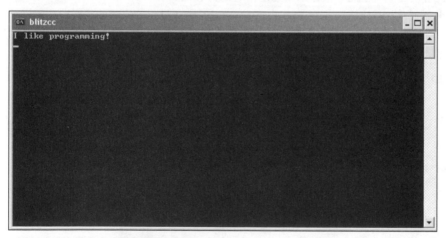

Figure 2.6 The demo02-03.bb program.

Input

Finally, you understand how variables work. Now, let's use those variables to get input from the user of the program. Using input, you can recognize what keys the user presses, or you might have the user answer a question. Either way, most input is stored in a variable. Figure 2.7 shows the output of this program.

```
;demo02-04.bb asks user's name and shows it
;get the user's name
name$ = Input$("Hi! May I know your name please? ")
Print "Hi " + name$ + "."

;Wait five seconds
Delay 5000
```

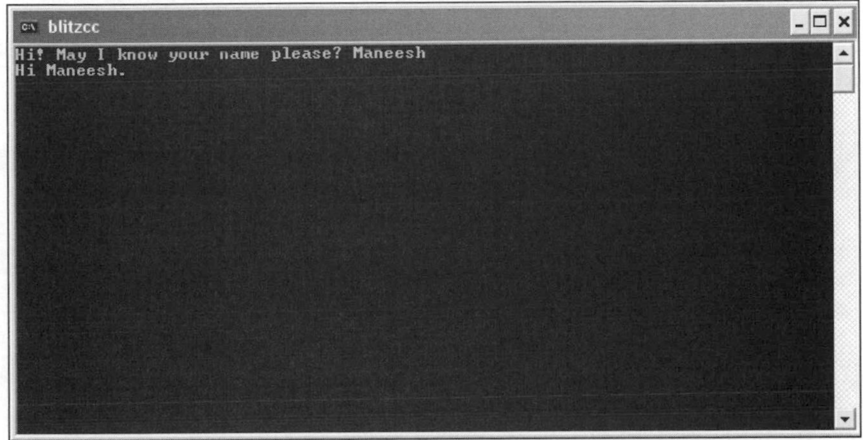

Figure 2.7 The demo02-04.bb program.

The first line is a comment that tells what the program does. The second line takes in the input, and the third and final line displays what the user entered.

`Input$` is declared as this:

```
Input$(prompt$)
```

caution

> Notice that the function name, `Input$`, has a `$` sign attached to the end. This symbol signifies the return type of the function. Because it is a string, the function only returns strings. What this means is that if you request the user to put in numbers to add together, such as 2 + 2, the value returned will be `"2 + 2"`, NOT 4. Of course, if the user typed in 4, the function would return 4.

`Input$` is the name of the function. Table 2.3 explains that `prompt$` is a string that is displayed to the computer before taking the input value. `prompt$` is usually used to ask the user to provide you with the info you want so that the user will know what to tell the program. Notice that there are parentheses around `prompt$` in the function. Parentheses are required; if you fail to place them in the program, the program will not compile. Also, notice that there are no brackets around `prompt$`. This means that the variable is required. If you want to have a blank `prompt$`, use "" (two quotation marks) as your prompt.

Table 2.3 Input$()'s Parameter

Parameter	Description
`prompt$`	The string displayed to the user before allowing the user to enter an input value.

In the previous program, `name$` is set equal to the `Input$` command. When the Input$ command receives an answer from the user, it is stored in the `name$` variable. If you left this line looking like this:

```
Input$("Hi! May I know your name please? ")
```

without including a variable, the response that the user made would be simply thrown away. Using `Input$` without a variable is not a good idea.

`Input$` only returns strings (that's why a `$` is added to the function name). However, if the variable you use to retrieve the user input is an integer instead of a string, the value will be interpreted as an integer. Therefore, if you ask the user "How old are you?" and the variable you use to retrieve the value is an integer, the variable will contain whatever the user types in.

Okay, you now have the basics of input down. However, this input function isn't very useful so far. Who wants a program that tells them their own name? This brings me to the next topic: conditionals.

Conditionals

Conditionals are a very important part of any program. Conditionals allow your program to think. With them, any program can make choices and decisions. Before you can fully understand conditionals, however, you must first learn about the BlitzPlus idea of truth and falsehood.

Truth and Falsehood

BlitzPlus has a different idea about what is true and what is false than we humans do. To a human, some things may be partly true, but to a computer, any expression is either true or false. Although parts of an expression can be different than the rest, the entire expression is only evaluated as one or the other.

BlitzPlus (and computers in general) believes that zero is false and any other value (nonzero value) is true, although the true value is usually one. This makes programming a much easier job.

To determine whether something is true or false, you use the relational and logical operators. These operators check one statement against another to see whether the aspect of their relationship that is being checked is true or false. Table 2.4 lists all of the relational and logical operators.

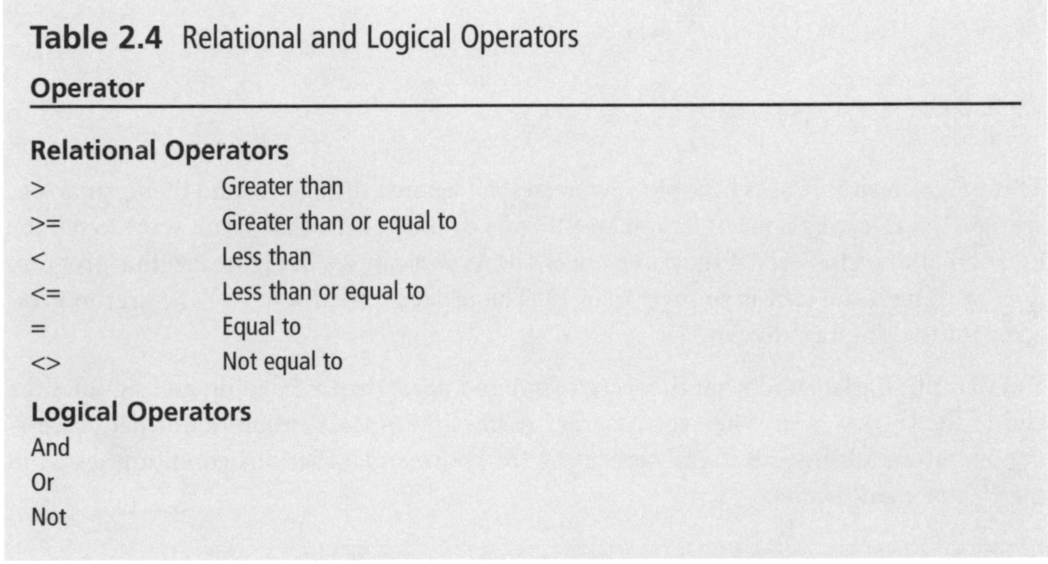

Table 2.4 Relational and Logical Operators

Operator	
Relational Operators	
>	Greater than
>=	Greater than or equal to
<	Less than
<=	Less than or equal to
=	Equal to
<>	Not equal to
Logical Operators	
And	
Or	
Not	

Using Table 2.4 as a guide, you can see that if, say, variable A is equal to 14 and variable B is equal to 12, `A>B` will return True, because 14 is a larger number than 12.

If...Then

The first conditional you will learn is the `If` statement. The `If` statement has a very basic declaration:

```
If
```

The idea of an `If` statement is that it allows your program to make choices. You pass an expression into the `If` statement by following the `If` command with the expression:

```
If expression is true Then
;Do something
Endif
```

As you can see, the `If` statement is followed by an expression. If the expression is true, the code between the `If` and `EndIf` commands is executed. If not, nothing happens.

```
;demo02-05.bb - Tests if you are old enough to vote

;Find out how old the user is
age = Input$("How old are you? ")
;if older or equal to 18, print out confirmation that user is allowed to vote.
If age >= 18 Then
     Print "You are legally allowed to vote!"
EndIf
;Wait five seconds
Delay 5000
```

This program simply asks how old you are, tests it against the age 18, and then prints `"You are legally allowed to vote!"` if you are 18 years or older. But what if you want to tell the user something else, even if they aren't over 18? As you can see in Figure 2.8, this program does nothing if the user is younger than 18. The program then waits for the user to press a key for the program to exit.

You may not understand what the `EndIf` command does. `The EndIf` command signifies the end of the `If...Then` test. When the program reaches the `EndIf`, it resumes normal processing of commands instead of only executing the commands when the condition tested in the `If` statement is met.

Figure 2.8 The demo02-05.bb program.

If...Then...Else

Perhaps you want the program to test if the user is younger than 18. You could rewrite the program by adding another `If` statement to check if the user is younger than 18, but there is another easier (and better) way: Use the `Else` statement.

```
;demo02-06.bb - Tests if you are old enough to vote

;Ask how old the user is
age = Input$("How old are you? ")

;if older or equal to 18 then let them vote
If age >= 18 Then
     Print "You are legally allowed to vote!"

;if younger than 18, do not let them vote

Else Print "Sorry, you need To be a few years older."
EndIf

;Wait five seconds
Delay 5000
```

Figure 2.9 shows the output.

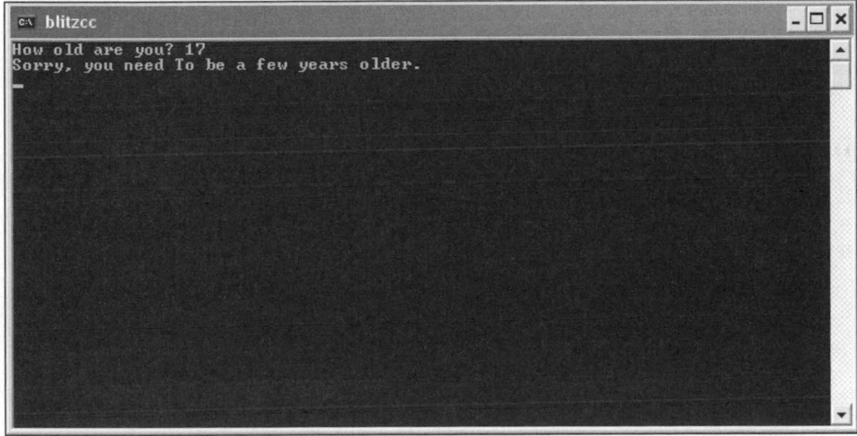

Figure 2.9 The demo02-06.bb program.

This time, the program tests the user's age, but if it is less than 18, it prints out the sentence under the `Else` statement.

There is also one other effective use of the `If...Else` conditional. You can combine the two to create `Else If`.

```
;demo02-07.bb Tests if you are old enough to vote
age = Input$("How old are you? ")
If age = 18 Then
       Print "You can now vote."
Else If age > 18
       Print "You've been able to vote for a while."
Else If age < 18
       Print "Sorry, you will have to wait a few years to vote."
EndIf
WaitKey
```

Figure 2.10 shows the output.

Figure 2.10 The demo02-07.bb program.

caution

This program will only work if the user enters an integer. If the user enters a string, the variable will always be zero. You can fix this problem using a loop or `Goto`, which will be explained soon.

This program tests all three user possibilities.

Sometimes, you might want to test a large number of possibilities, and using `If...Then` can be awkward. A conditional statement was made to fix this problem: `Select...Case`.

Select...Case

`Select...Case` makes working with a large number of values much easier. The best way to demonstrate is with an example.

```
;demo02-08.bb - tests the keys pressed

x = Input$("Enter 1 to say hi, or 0 to quit. ")

Select x
     Case 1
          Print "Hi!"
     Case 0
          End
     Default
          Print "Huh?"
End Select

;Wait five seconds
Delay 5000
```

In this listing, the program asks the user to enter either one or zero. It then either writes `"Hi!"` or quits the program. The default case is a catch-all command; if the user enters neither one nor zero, the default code is displayed.

note

> If you haven't observed it already, notice that I have been indenting my code in a very easy to understand and logical manner. This makes reading and understanding code much easier, and I highly recommend that you do the same.

In this case, `Select...Case` isn't very necessary. Because there are only two cases, it is just as easy to use an `If...Else`. However, when the programs get more complex, `Select...Case` becomes a more useful tool.

By the way, the declaration for `Select...Case` is

```
Select variable
```

Easy enough, huh?

Logical Operators

Logical operators are a base for expressions and conditional statements. You can view all of the BlitzPlus logical operators in Table 2.5. It lists all of the conditions that make the logical operators true and false.

Table 2.5 Logical Operator Truth Table

P	Q	P AND Q	P OR Q	NOT P
0	0	0	0	1
0	1	0	1	1
1	1	1	1	0
1	0	0	1	0

The `AND` operator is true only if both its parameters are true; the `OR` operator is true if one or more of its parameters are true; and the `NOT` operator is true only if its parameter is false. Here is an example of the `AND` operator.

```
;demo02-09.bb - Shows use of the And operator

;find out how old the user is
age = Input$("How old are you? ")
;find out if the user lives in america
location = Input$("Do you live in America? (1 For yes, 2 For no) ")

;Write out the proper string depending on the user's age and locations
If age >= 18 And location = 1 Then
     Print "Congrats, you are eligible to vote!"
Else
     Print "Sorry, you can't vote."
EndIf

;Wait five seconds
Delay 5000
```

The output is shown in Figure 2.11.

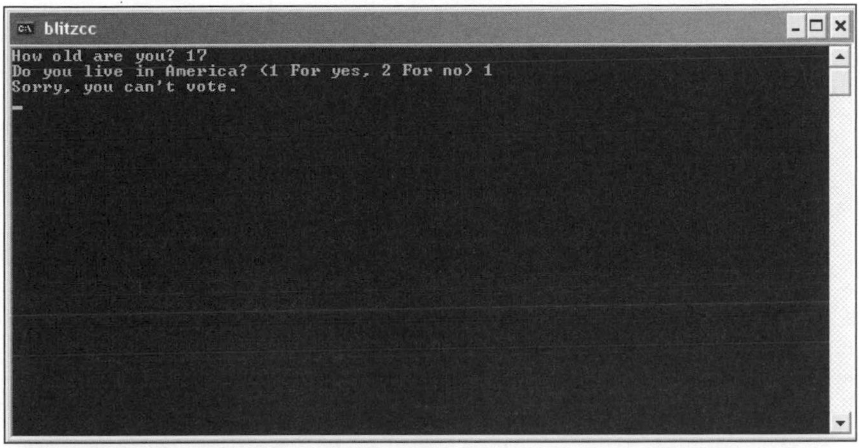

Figure 2.11 The demo02-09.bb program.

The NOT Operator

The NOT operator is a little bit different than the other two logical operators. Instead of two operands, it only takes one. And instead of returning a value based on the other two operands, it only returns the opposite of the operand it is working on.

Remember that because false is zero and true is one, the only value NOT will return is one or zero. If you write

```
Not 0
```

your answer will be one, and conversely if you write

```
Not 1
```

your answer will be zero.

The Goto Command

Before writing a full-fledged game, I want to introduce you to the concept of Goto. Goto is a very simple command, but it can be misused very easily, so I recommend using Goto as sparingly as possible. Almost always, if something can be done by using Goto, it can be done in another way.

Goto works like this: you add a label somewhere in your code, and Goto jumps to that label. (See Figure 2.12.) The best illustration of this is a sample program.

```
;demo02-10.bb - Demonstrates use of Goto
.label
Print "Hello"
```

```
selection = Input("Enter 1 if you want me to repeat 'Hello' ==> ")
If (selection = 1)
	Goto label
EndIf
End
```

The output is shown in Figure 2.13.

note

Notice that I did not include `WaitKey` in this program. Because the program repeats and then ends with an `End` command, the `WaitKey` is not necessary.

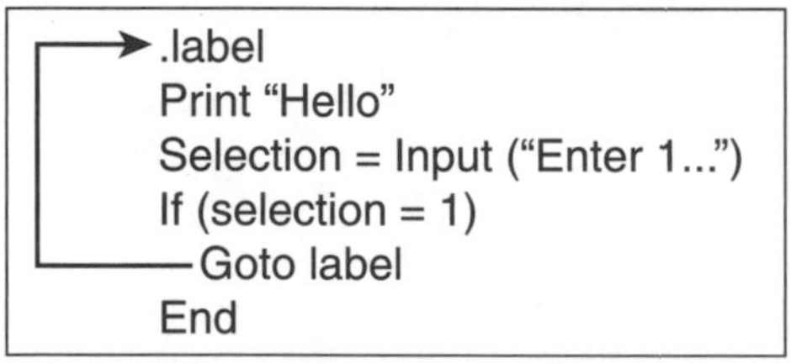

```
.label
Print "Hello"
Selection = Input ("Enter 1...")
If (selection = 1)
Goto label
End
```

Figure 2.12 Using `Goto`.

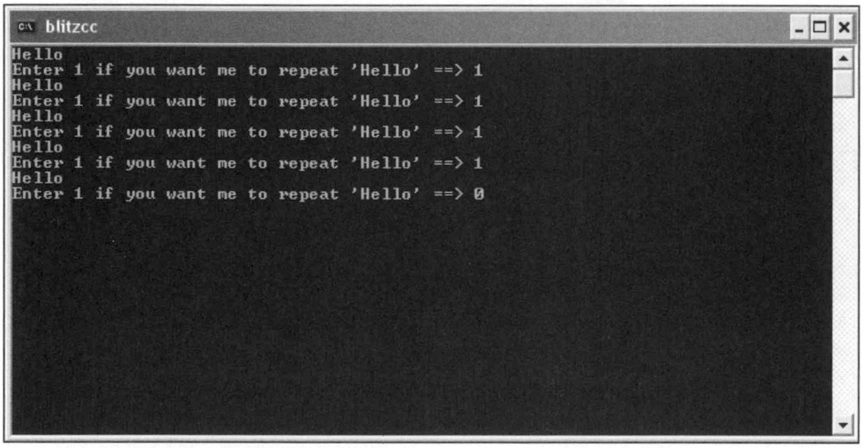

```
blitzcc
Hello
Enter 1 if you want me to repeat 'Hello' ==> 1
Hello
Enter 1 if you want me to repeat 'Hello' ==> 1
Hello
Enter 1 if you want me to repeat 'Hello' ==> 1
Hello
Enter 1 if you want me to repeat 'Hello' ==> 1
Hello
Enter 1 if you want me to repeat 'Hello' ==> 0
```

Figure 2.13 The demo02-10.bb program.

As you can see in Figure 2.12, calling `Goto` starts the program back at the top. This is accomplished by putting `.label` at the top of the program. You can make `Goto` move anywhere by simply moving the line `.label`. Notice that when you define the label, you put a period (.) before it. When you call it from `Goto`, however, you discard the period.

A Text-Based Guessing Game

Now, let's put all of what you learned in this chapter and create your first guessing game! Basically, the users enter a number, and you will tell them if they are too high or too low. You will allow the users to guess until they figure it out. In order to make this game work, you will be using a loop in this game. If you cannot understand what the loop's function is, it is explained in the next chapter.

First you need to create an initialization section. It will look something like this.

```
;demo02-11.bb - Try to guess the number
Print "Welcome to the Guessing Game!"
AppTitle "Guessing Game!"
;Seed the random generator...don't worry, it will be explained later
SeedRnd MilliSecs()

;Pick a number between 1 and 100
numbertoguess = Rand(1,100)

;The num of guesses the user has used
numofguesses = 0
```

The first line, after `Print`, calls the function `AppTitle`. This changes the name in the heading bar, so that instead of the program being named "Blitz Runtime Window," it will be named "Guessing Game!".

The randomizer works like this: `numbertoguess` is assigned to a random number, which is returned by `Rand`. `Rand` returns a number between what is given; here, it returns a number between 1 and 100. This section prints out introduction text, sets up the guessing number, and declares some variables.

Next you set up the loop and the test to make sure the player guessed a number between 1 and 100.

```
;set the beginning of loop label
.loopbegin
	;Find out the user's guess
	guess = Input$("Guess a number ")

	;If player guesses outside of range, tell him to guess again
	If guess > 100 Or guess < 1
		Print "Pick a number between 1 and 100, silly!"
		;Go back to the beginning
		Goto loopbegin

	EndIf
```

The first line of this code sets up a label to go back to the loop later. Next, the loop begins, the player is asked for input, and the number is tested to see if it is within the correct range. If not, the player is sent back to the beginning of the loop.

Now, you insert the code to test and see if the player has guessed correctly.

```
;Add a guess to the guess counter
numofguesses = numofguesses + 1

;If the guess is too low, go back to beginning
If guess < numbertoguess Then
       Print "The number was too low."
       Goto loopbegin
;If guess is too high, go back to the beginning
Else If guess > numbertoguess Then
       Print "The number was too high."
Goto loopbegin
EndIf
```

The first line adds one to the user's number of guesses. Then, the code is tested to see if the user has guessed too high, too low, or just right. If the player has guessed just right, the code just continues through to the end of the program without going back to the beginning of the loop.

Finally, you enter the last section of code.

```
Print "You guessed the number " + numbertoguess + " in " + numofguesses  + " tries!"

;Wait five seconds
Delay 5000
```

This program can be run off the CD. It is named demo02-11.bb. Figure 2.14 shows the output of the complete Guessing Game.

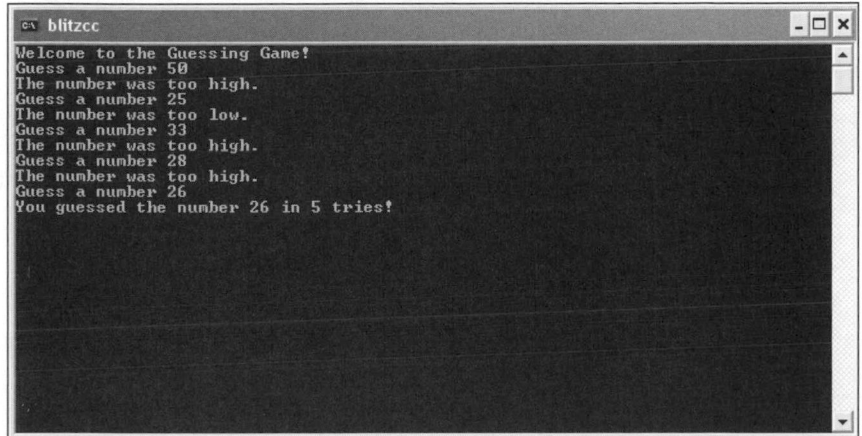

Figure 2.14 The complete Guessing Game.

Summary

This has been a tough chapter for you as well as me. I hope that you remember most of what I have told you so far. I suggest you write a few sample programs using everything taught in this program before you head on to the next chapter; it will help solidify the information in your head.

This chapter covered the following concepts:

- The Hello, World! program
- Variables
- Input
- Conditionals

The next chapter discusses loops, functions, arrays, and types. I hope you're ready!

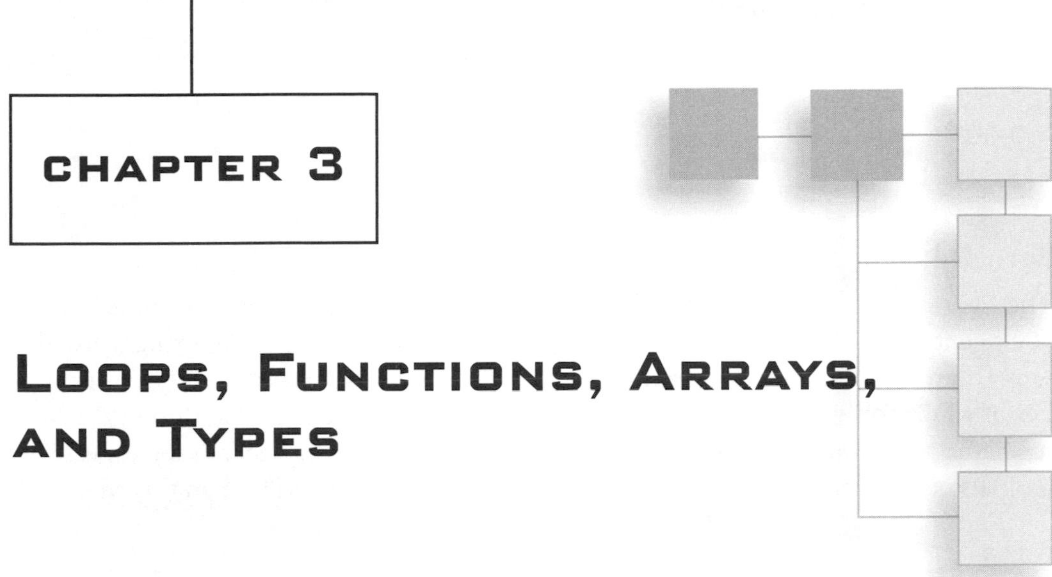

Loops, Functions, Arrays, and Types

We are finally moving up to the tough stuff. This chapter introduces the important and interesting subjects of loops, functions, arrays, and types. All of these are essential to any computer game program.

In this chapter, I'm going to explain each of the processes separately, and then create a simple game that incorporates them all. By the time you get there, you will know how to use loops, functions, arrays, and types.

Understanding Loops

A *loop* is a block of code that is repeated over and over until a condition is met. For example, the main game loop is repeated over and over until the player quits or wins the game. We can use `goto`, a command that we learned in the previous chapter, as a loop. If you remember the demo02-10.bb program, a set of commands was repeated until the user wanted them to stop. Loops work exactly like this: a set of commands is repeated over, and over, and over, until a condition is met—either the user wants to exit the loop or the loop is executed a specific number of times. Figure 3.1 shows a sketch of a loop.

Loops are used for many repetitive tasks in computer programs. In a space shooter game, for example, we have to use a loop to check every bullet against the enemy ships. We will also use loops to update the artificial intelligence (AI) for each of the ships.

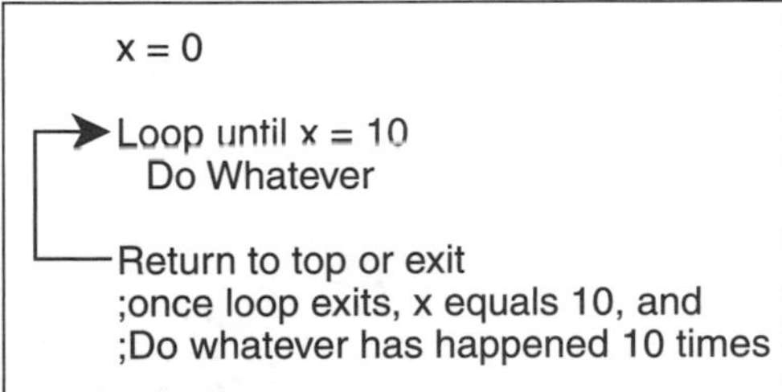

x = 0
Loop until x = 10
Do Whatever
Return to top or exit
;once loop exits, x equals 10, and
;Do whatever has happened 10 times

Figure 3.1 The loop.

There are three types of loops, and although they are somewhat interchangeable, each has a specific style and it is best if they are used in the proper situation. The three types of loops are

- For...Next
- While...Wend
- Repeat...Until

For...Next

The For...Next loop steps through a block of code a set number of times. In other words, you use it when you know how many times the loop should iterate. You might use this loop when you want the player to move up exactly 10 spaces. Because you know the number of times you want the player to move up, you might have each iteration of the loop move the player up one space and have the loop go through its commands ten times. This loop also can update the info of a set of types (types are explained later in this chapter).

note

Before we move on, I want to discuss the concept of iterations. As you know, a loop processes a number of commands over and over again, starting at the top, going to the bottom, and moving back to the top again. An *iteration* occurs when all of the commands have been processed one full time. When the loop finishes the last statement of the loop, but has not returned to the top of the loop, it has completed one iteration. When it returns to the top, the second iteration begins, and so on.

For...Next loops are always used as follows:

```
For variable = beginning_number To ending_number [Step step_amount]
      ;Perform actions
Next
```

As you can see, a For...Next loop begins with For and ends with Next. The To command defines how many times the loop performs its actions. Step_amount, which is optional, defines how much is added to beginning_number each time. If you omit Step, beginning_number is incremented by 1 each time the loop is traversed.

Let's examine a code example:

```
;demo03-01.bb - counts from 1 to 10
;start counter at one and loop till 10
For counter = 1 To 10
     ;Print whatever counter is equal to
     Print counter
Next

;Delay for five seconds
Delay 5000
```

Figure 3.2 shows the output.

Figure 3.2 The demo03-01.bb program.

This program simply prints the numbers 1 to 10 on the screen. The first line after the entry comment begins the `For…Next` loop. It declares `counter` and initializes it to 1. The `To` command tells the compiler how many iterations the loop will go through. Here, it says it will count from one to ten.

The next line simply prints the value of `counter`, which adds one to its count every iteration of the loop. The final line of the loop returns the code to the beginning of the loop and raises `counter` by 1.

You can change the step amount of the loop if you want. The step amount is how much is added to the variable on each iteration of the loop. By default, the step amount is 1.

To change the step amount, simply add the command `Step` after the `To` command like this:

```
;demo03-02.bb - Counts backwards using step amounts
;start counter at 5 and loop till 0 by -1.2
For counter# = 5.0 To 0.0 Step -1.2
     ;Print value of counter
     Print counter
Next

;Delay for five seconds
Delay 5000
```

The output is shown in Figure 3.3.

Figure 3.3 The demo03-02.bb program.

caution

> Make sure to double-check your loops to ensure you did not make them never-ending. If this program had been written with the step value as 1.2 (as opposed to −1.2), the program would have looped forever and never ended. Fortunately, Blitz Basic normally catches this error and simply skips the loop.

This program might seem a little strange, but I wrote it as such in order to make a few points. First, the counter variable is a floating-point variable (a variable with decimal places). The starting value is 5.0 and the ending value is 0.0. The step value is −1.2.

The step value causes the program to count down instead of counting up. On the first iteration of the loop, the counter variable is 5.0. Then it decreases to 3.8, and so on.

Let's look at the values for this loop. Table 3.1 explains the values of the counter variable, the step amount, and the output throughout the program. As you can see, the first iteration of the `For...Next` loop does not decrease the `Step` amount; instead, the `Step` amount begins being subtracted beginning with the second iteration.

Table 3.1 Demo02-02.bb's Variable Values

Iteration	Counter#/Output	Step
1	5.0	−1.2
2	3.8	−1.2
3	2.6	−1.2
4	1.4	−1.2
5	0.2	−1.2

Now is a good time to introduce *float trimming*. If you look at the output of the demo03-02.bb sample (see Figure 3.3), you will notice that there are six digits after the decimal place. Six digits after the decimal is the default value. Because only one of the digits is significant, why leave the extra five sitting there? Trimming in this context is removing the trailing zeroes from a float value.

In order to trim the trailing zeroes, we have to follow two steps. First, we must convert the floating variable (which has decimal places) into a string. Next, we remove all the unnecessary digits. Then, we are free to display the string.

Let's try it:

```
;demo03-03.bb - Counts using step amounts
For counter# = 5.0 To 0.0 Step -1.2
        Print Left$( Str counter, 3)
Next

;Delay for five seconds
Delay 5000
```

Figure 3.4 shows the output.

note

Notice that this example uses 3 as the length variable. The reason is because the number is converted to a string, and the decimal is part of it. The example keeps the number before the decimal, the decimal, and one number after the decimal.

Figure 3.4 The demo03-03.bb program.

This program begins the same way as the previous program did: it creates a `For...Next` loop that begins with 5.0 and decreases by 1.2 until it reaches 0.0. The next line prints the newly trimmed version of counter's value. Let's examine this statement.

The `Print` statement writes out each float value with one digit after the decimal place. The first thing it does is call the `Left$()` function. `Left$()` is declared as

```
Left$ (string$, length)
```

In this case, the `string$ variable` was

```
Str counter
```

The `Str` function takes an integer or float and converts it to a string. It then returns the created string. Because the return value is a string, we can use it in place of the `string$` variable. The `length` variable is set to `3` to include the number and only one decimal point. Table 3.2 describes the parameters.

Table 3.2 Left$'s Parameters

Parameter	Description
`string$`	The string you want to trim
`length`	The number of letters you want to include

While...Wend

The next type of loop is the `While...Wend` loop. This loop is very much like the `For...Next` loop, but it is normally used to test variable conditions. In other words, the `While...Wend` loop is normally used when you aren't sure when to exit the loop.

`While` loops are the most common main loops in games. The main loop (also known as the *game* loop) is a loop that runs over and over until the game is over. Because it cannot be determined *exactly* when to end a game, the `While...Wend` loop is a perfect choice.

```
;demo03-04.bb - Waits for a key and then exits
Graphics 640,480
Text 0,0, "This program is worthless."
Text 0,12,"Press escape to exit."
Flip
;Wait until user presses 1 to Escape
While Not KeyDown(1)
Wend
End
```

note

You might notice some strange functions in this program, such as `Flip` and `Graphics`. To check for `KeyDown()`, you have to be in graphics mode, and the `Graphics` command does that. You will learn more about this in Part 2; for now, just pretend it isn't there.

Figure 3.5 shows the output of this program.

Figure 3.5 The demo03-04.bb program.

This program simply displays some text and asks you to quit. Almost a waste of time, huh? Well, at least it demonstrates `While…Wend` and it introduces a new function, `KeyDown()`.

The `While…Wend` loop begins like this:

```
While Not KeyDown(1)
```

This line of code sets up a `While` loop that exits only when the user presses the Esc key. The loop continues until the user presses the Esc key. `KeyDown()`, which is declared as

```
KeyDown(scancode)
```

determines whether Esc has been pressed.

Here, the number 1 is used as the *scan code.* A scan code is a code generated by pressing any key on a keyboard. Each key has its own separate scan code. Esc has the scan code of 1. You can see a list of all of the scan codes in Appendix A.

`KeyDown` returns 1 (true) if the key has been pressed and 0 (false) if the key has not been pressed. Because we want the `While...Wend` loop to continue until the key has been pressed, we invert the return value by including `NOT`. Therefore, if the player does not press Esc, the `KeyDown` returns 0. The `NOT` command inverts this to a 1, and the `While...Wend` loop continues to the next iteration.

Now is a good time to introduce the basic game loop. This loop only ends when the user presses Esc. If the user loses, a function is called that will end the program. Note that this code *will not* work. It will only call functions that don't exist (functions are introduced later in this chapter).

```
;Basic Game loop
While Not KeyDown(1)
      PerformLogic()
      Animation()
      If playerlost Then
         GameOver()
      EndIf
Wend
```

This game loop is basically the most simplified version possible. Unless the player loses or presses Esc, the loop continues to iterate. The `PerformLogic()` function probably updates the AI for the game and `Animation()` probably draws and animates everything onscreen. If the `playerlost` variable is set to 1 (most likely by the `PerformLogic()` function), the `GameOver()` function is called and the game is over.

You should always strive to keep your main loop as simple as possible. It should not perform more operations than necessary. You will learn how to delegate operations to smaller and more efficient functions soon in this chapter.

Repeat...Until

The final Blitz Basic loop is the `Repeat...Until` loop. This loop is almost exactly like the `While...Wend` loop, except that the condition is written after the closing statement (`Until`) instead of the opening statement (`Repeat`).

Doesn't seem like a big difference, huh? The only time you use this type of loop is when you know for sure that the loop should be executed at least once. This is evident in situations that involve displaying menus and testing for keys.

```
;demo03-05.bb  - Closes program after player presses ESC.
Graphics 640,480
Text 0,0, "Why did you open this program?"
Flip
;y is the variable that judges the location of the text
y=12
Repeat
     ;Print text
     Text 0,y, "Press Esc to exit."
     ;wait a sec
     Delay 1000
     Flip

     ;Move next line of text down
     y=y+12

;repeat until user hits esc
Until KeyHit(1)
Text 0,y, "Program is ending."
Flip
```

The output is shown in Figure 3.6.

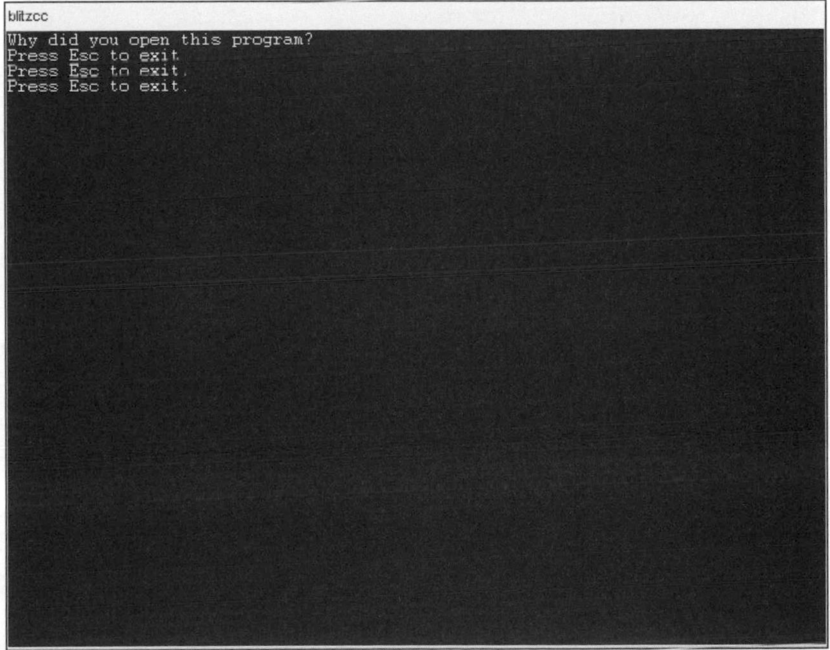

Figure 3.6 The demo03-05.bb program.

This program simply writes "Press Esc to exit" to the screen until the user presses Esc. It introduces two main functions: Delay and KeyHit().

`Delay` pauses the program's execution for a set number of milliseconds. `Delay` is declared as

```
Delay milliseconds
```

where `milliseconds` is the number of milliseconds you want to delay the program for. This program delays the execution for one second (1000 milliseconds).

The other new function introduced is `KeyHit()`.

```
KeyHit(scancode)
```

`scancode` is the code for the key that might be pressed. This function determines if the key was pressed. If the key was pressed, it returns true; if not, it returns false.

The `y` variable tracks the location of the `Text` command. Each time, the `y` variable is incremented by 12, moving the text down one line.

The reason that the text is moved down 12 pixels is because the font size of the text is size 12. Moving the text down 12 pixels is equivalent to making a new line in the program. The condition for exiting the `Repeat...Until` loop is the opposite of `While...Wend` and `For...Next` loops. Instead of continuing to iterate the loop only as long as the condition is true, the `Repeat...Until` loop continues only when the condition is false. Take extra precautions to make sure you do not create a never-ending loop.

note

You might wonder about the difference between the new function `KeyHit()` and the previously introduced function `KeyDown()`. The fact is, there is very little difference. `KeyDown()` determines if the button is down at the time of the test, whereas `KeyHit()` determines if it has been down since the last `KeyHit()` was checked. You can see the difference in any game. If you use `KeyDown()`, you can hold down a key to make it work repeatedly; if you use `KeyHit()`, you have to press the button every time you use it.

Because the program used `Repeat...Until`, the "Press Esc to exit" line will always be shown, even if you press Esc before the loop begins. If you ever write a program that utilizes menus (most RPG [*Role-Playing Game*] games do), you should use a `Repeat...Until` loop.

Okay, I have now thoroughly discussed each of the loops. I hope that you are now an expert on how, as well as when, to use all three of the types of loops. Now on to an extremely important subject: functions.

Understanding Functions

Functions are integral to any program. Even in the programs you have been writing so far, you have used functions such as `Print` and `Delay`, and you have even written your own implicit main function. This section teaches you how to write your own functions that will make understanding and writing your program much easier and simpler.

Functions are small snippets of code that usually perform a single task. All programs consist of at least one function: `main`. Although `main` isn't actually defined, it still exists within the program.

Every line of code written so far (with the exception of the ones in Chapter 1) has been written in the function `main`. This function is the starting point and ending point of every Blitz Basic program. Figure 3.7 shows an example of the `main` function in action. Because the `main` function is never formally declared, I always write a comment telling myself where it begins. I suggest you do the same.

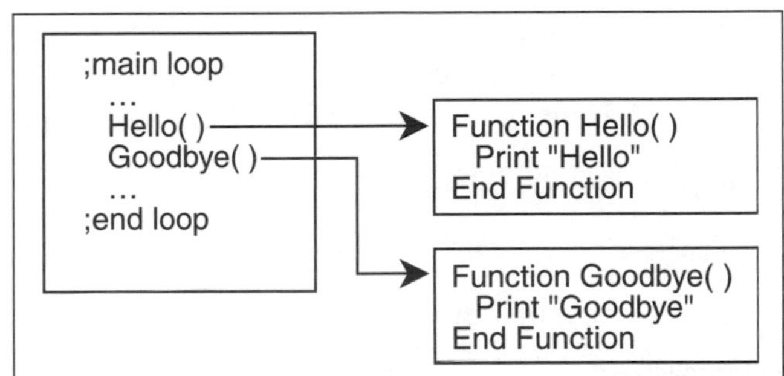

Figure 3.7 A function example.

`Main` calls two types of programs to do its work: user-defined and program-defined functions. *User-defined functions* are those that are written by the programmer, such as `TestAI()` in the Chapter 1 game. All of these functions must be defined before they are used. *Program-defined functions* are defined within the compiler, like the function `Print`. All of these have already been written; all you have to do is call them with the proper parameters.

A parameter is a piece of information sent to the function to tell it what to do. For example, the `string$` variable is a parameter to the `Print` function. This variable tells `Print` what you want printed to the screen.

You can send parameters to your own functions as well, but make sure that you declare the parameters in advance. If your function is called with an extra parameter, your code will not compile.

To use any function, you first must declare it. The function declaration is usually written directly before the function code.

```
Function functionname([parameter variable,…])
```

Looks kind of complex, huh? Let's make this easy. First type **Function**. This is required for every function declaration. Now, pick a function name (make sure it describes what the function does; for example, if it counts, call it *Count*). Now, add an open parenthesis. Add as many parameter variables as you need, each separated by a comma. Finally, add an ending parenthesis.

Here is an example

```
Function ConvertFtoC (fvalue)
```

This function most likely converts a Fahrenheit value to a Celsius value. You can see that by looking at the function's name. Make sure yours are easy to understand too.

Next, you write the actual function code.

```
Return (5.0/9.0 * (fvalue - 32))
```

Remember that the * sign means multiplication and the / sign means division. This code returns the Celsius value of the variable sent. A return value is any number or string returned by a called function. For example, on the `KeyHit()` function, either a one or a zero is returned. Here, the returned value is the Celsius equivalent to the Fahrenheit number.

Finally, we end the function.

```
End Function
```

We now need a main function call to actually use this function.

```
Print "Welcome to our FtoC converter"
fvalue = Input$("What Fahrenheit value do you wish to convert?")
cvalue = ConvertFtoC(fvalue)
Print fvalue + " Fahrenheit = " + cvalue + " Celsius."
```

This section of code is the actual main program. It starts off by introducing the program and receiving the Fahrenheit value to convert. Next it calls `ConvertFtoC()` and stores its value in the variable `cvalue`. Finally it prints the results.

Let's put all these parts together now.

```
;demo03-06.bb - Converts Fahrenheit to Celsius

;MAIN PROGRAM
Print "Welcome to our FtoC converter"
;get Fahrenheit and put it in fvalue
fvalue = Input$("What Fahrenheit value do you wish to convert?")

;Convert fvalue to Celsius
cvalue = ConvertFtoC(fvalue)
```

```
;print results
Print fvalue + " Fahrenheit = " + cvalue + " Celsius."

;Delay for five seconds
Delay 5000

;END OF MAIN PROGRAM

Function ConvertFtoC(fvalue)
	;convert value and return it
	Return 5.0/9.0 * (fvalue - 32)
End Function
```

Figure 3.8 shows the output of this program.

```
Welcome to our FtoC converter
What Fahrenheit value do you wish to convert?314
314 Fahrenheit = 157 Celsius.
```

Figure 3.8 The demo03-06.bb program.

And that's all there is to functions. Well, almost…

Scope Considerations

There are two possible scopes in Blitz Basic: global and local. *Global variables* are visible throughout the program, in every function and every line of code. *Local variables* are valid only in the function in which they are defined. This means that a variable defined within one function is not valid in another.

What Is Scope?

Scope is kind of hard to understand, so to help, I went to http://www.dictionary.com and looked up scope. Here is what it said:

"The scope of an identifier is the region of a program source within which it represents a certain thing. This usually extends from the place where it is declared to the end of the smallest enclosing block (begin/end or procedure/function body). An inner block may contain a redeclaration of the same identifier, in which case the scope of the outer declaration does not include (is "shadowed" or "occluded" by) the scope of the inner."

What? If you finished reading that (20 bucks says you gave up after "program source within which it represents a certain thing"), you are probably as lost as you were before.

Scope is a range of operation from where variables can be referenced. The fact that there are two kinds of scopes allows programmers to create programs that have two or more variables with the same name. You can have one variable with the name `variablex` in the global scope (otherwise known as the main program) and another variable named `variablex` in the function `HiIAmAFunction()`. Even though every other part of the program, including other functions, will use the global scope's version of variablex, `HiIAmAFunction()` will use its separate, more specialized, version of `variablex`.

By the way, Scope is also a mouthwash.

Let me show you an example of scoping. Note that this code will not work. It is only used to demonstrate scope problems.

```
;CallMe() - Broken
CallMe()
Print x

Function CallMe()
      x = 314
End Function
```

The example output is shown in Figure 3.9.

As you can see, this program calls `CallMe()` and `x` is assigned to 314. Then it tries to print `x`, but it ends up printing 0! What gives?

You guessed it—scope. This function calls `CallMe()` and has `x` assigned to 314. But when it returns back to `main`, the 314 has been flushed from memory. Although `x` is equal to 314 in `CallMe()`, it is equal to 0 in `main`.

Figure 3.9 The broken `CallMe()` program.

There are a few ways to fix this. One way is to have `CallMe()` return a value like this:

```
CallMe()
Print "x is equal to " + CallMe()

Function CallMe()
	x = 314
	Return x
End Function
```

In this example, `CallMe()` returns the `x` value, which is printed by `main`.

The other way to solve this problem is to use global variables. Global variables have global scope and are visible throughout the program. This means that the scope of `x` in `CallMe()` will be the same as the scope of `x` in `main`.

To create a global variable, simply precede the variable with the `Global` command.

```
;demo03-07.bb - Fixed CallMe()
Global x
CallMe()
Print "x is equal to " + x

;Delay five seconds
Delay 5000

Function CallMe()
	x = 314
End Function
```

The example output is shown in Figure 3.10.

Figure 3.10 The fixed `CallMe()` program.

note

Notice that I wrote `Global x` in the `main` program rather than the function `CallMe()`. This is because you can only create global variables in the main program. If you want to use global scope, you must create the variable in the main program. By the way, the act of creating a variable without actually setting the variable is called *declaring*. Making the variable equal to something is called *defining* it.

This time, we make `x` global. Then, when we assign 314 to `x`, `x` is equal to 314 in every function, and not just in `CallMe()`.

What Is Portable Code?

Porting is an important concept, because in the long run, it can save you a lot of time. In English, for something to be portable, it must be able to easily move around. Think of that *Game Boy Advance* you saw at Wal-mart a few days ago. Portable code is easy to move around. Portable code is independent code that doesn't rely upon global variables for information. This allows you to cut and paste functions from one program to another. Take the demo03-06.bb, the Fahrenheit-to-Celsius calculator. That is a very portable function because you can rip that program right out and use it in another program, if the need ever arises. Because the function does not rely on any global variables, you have nothing more to set up. When the function does rely on global variables, it is extremely hard to cut and paste code from one program to another, simply because global variables usually do not exist in two different programs.

Global variables are common in games, but you should try to use them as little as possible for a few reasons. First, because every function has access to them, it is very easy to change the variable by accident. Second, using global variables makes functions less portable. If a function only uses parameters and local variables, it can be ported to other programs by just copying and pasting. If it uses global variables, you have to go through the code and change any references to global variables that don't exist in the new program. Although it doesn't seem like a big deal now, it can be a big pain to have to search through functions when you decide to add them to a new program.

By the way, another way to create a local variable is to add the keyword `Local` before a variable, such as:

```
Local x
```

If you add the `Local` keyword to `x` in the previous program

```
x = 314
```

the `x` variable in `main` will once again equal zero. This is because the local scope takes precedence over the global scope. Therefore, the local version of `x` is initialized to 314, while the global version is left unaffected.

There is no difference between

```
Local variable
```

and

```
variable
```

if there is no declared global variable. In other words, when you declare a local variable, you can omit the `Local` keyword (although you might want to keep it just for clarity and style).

When to Use Functions

Functions are necessary to programming. You know that you have to use them, but when should you do so?

Use functions whenever you have to perform a task. I know that this is a vague statement to make, but you should have at least a few functions for anything but the most trivial of programs.

Usually, the main function should do little, if any, work. The tasks should be handed to functions. If the task can be subdivided into two or more tasks, be sure to create the extra functions. You can always call functions from within another function.

Here is an example: say you are creating a spaceship game and you have a function to draw everything onscreen. You should probably make separate functions for drawing each part of the game: a separate function for drawing the ships and the bullets. It is possible to subdivide those even more. If you wanted to, you could create separate functions for drawing the bullets from the player and bullets from the enemy. Two more functions would draw the player and the enemy ships.

Basically, if you see a place where a function could be useful, write it. It takes hardly any more code than just putting the task in the `main` function and it makes your code much more portable, not to mention readable.

Understanding Arrays

One large problem in programming is the creation of a large number of variables. Think about how long it would take to create 10 variables of the same type right now. It might look something like this:

```
variable0 = 314
variable1 = 314
variable2 = 314
variable3 = 314
variable4 = 314
variable5 = 314
variable6 = 314
variable7 = 314
variable8 = 314
variable9 = 314
```

Seems like a waste of time, huh? But imagine if you had to create a thousand variables. That might take forever!

As you might have guessed, Blitz Basic has a way to remedy this problem. The solution is to use a feature called an *array*. Arrays are basically sets of variables with almost the same name. An array looks like any other variable, except it appends a subscript (a number within parentheses) to the end of the variable name.

Imagine an array as a single-column box that contains separate places to place jars (see Figure 3.11). Each jar contains a number. In this case, each jar contains the number 314, but you can change these numbers. You can access the number through the array counter, which looks like `variable(0)` or `variable(1)`. Basically, each jar is independent of the other jars, but they are all packaged in the same box. In arrays, the box represents the array, the jars are the individual array variables, and the numbers are the variable data.

Any variable that is part of an array is written something like this:

```
variablename(subscript#)
```

Here, the name of the array is `variablename` and the `subscript#` (it is always an integer, never a string) is equal to the amount of array variables you want to generate.

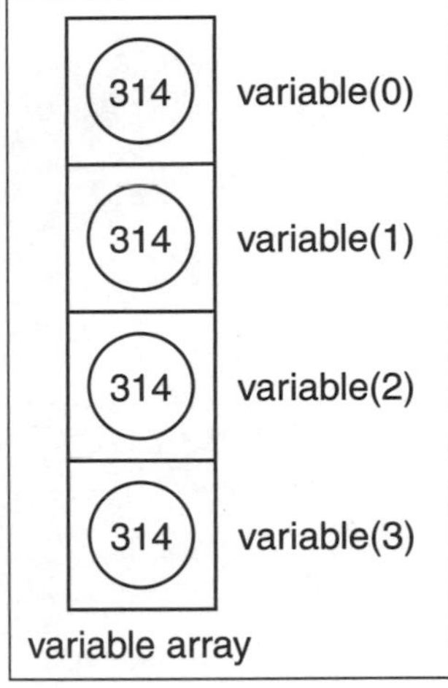

Figure 3.11
Box to array comparison.

Now we actually have to create the array. Let's use the variables from the previous example.

```
Dim variable(10) ;Declare array

variable(0) = 314
variable(1) = 314
variable(2) = 314
variable(3) = 314
variable(4) = 314
variable(5) = 314
variable(6) = 314
variable(7) = 314
variable(8) = 314
variable(9) = 314
```

Doesn't seem any simpler, does it? That's because I created the array in the longer way. However, using a `For...Next` loop, we can condense this into a much shorter procedure.

note

You might be wondering what the `Dim` command means. `Dim` literally means "dimension", and it simply creates memory space that will be used later. You must use the `Dim` command to declare arrays before using them.

```
;demo03-08.bb - initializes 10 vars to 314
Dim variable(10) ;Declare array

For i=0 To 10
        variable(i) = 314
        Print variable(i)
Next
WaitKey
```

The output is shown in Figure 3.12.

This does the same thing and more (it prints out the variable as well), but it is a heck of a lot shorter! This time, the array is declared just as in the previous example. Next, a `For...Next` loop iterates through each variable and sets it equal to 314! Easy, huh?

Figure 3.12 The demo03-08.bb program.

note

Make sure you notice that all of the variables begin with 0. Computers count differently than humans because they start counting with 0 rather than 1. In other words, the 10th variable in declaration of `array(10)` is `array(9)`. In other words, when you declare an array, you are telling the computer how many elements the array should have, plus one. However, because computers always count from 0, you access the array elements beginning with 0 and ending with *n*, where *n* is equal to the size of the array. For example, if you take an array declared as `array(5)`, the array would contain the elements `array(0)`, `array(1)`, `array(2)`, `array(3)`, `array(4)`, and `array(5)`. So an array that had five elements would be accessed with the numbers; 0, 1, 2, 3, 4, and 5—no more, no less. I often use less than the maximum amount of units, however, so I use 0-4 on an `array(5)`declaration.

To see how the box and jar example fits in with this program, see Figure 3.13.

All right, how about one more example of functions? This program will set a series of variables to an increasing number. From there, the user can choose to add, subtract, multiply, or divide two of the numbers. It's sort of like a mini calculator.

```
;demo03-09.bb - Allows user to perform math operations of 1-100

;op1 and op2 are global so they can be accessed from all functions
;op1 contains first operand, op2 contains second
Global op1
Global op2
Dim array(100) ;0 - 100
InitializeArray()
```

```
;continue is 1 as long as program is running
continue = 1


While continue ;as long as the computer wants to play
	;Get the first operand
	op1 = Input("What is the first number? ")
	;Get the second operand
	op2 = Input("And the second? ")

	; what does the user want to do?
	operator$ = Input("Enter +, -, *, or / ")
	;Print the answer
	PrintAnswer(operator$)

	;Find out if user wants to continue
	continue = Input("Enter 1 to continue or 0 to quit ")

	;Insert a new line
	Print ""
Wend
End
```

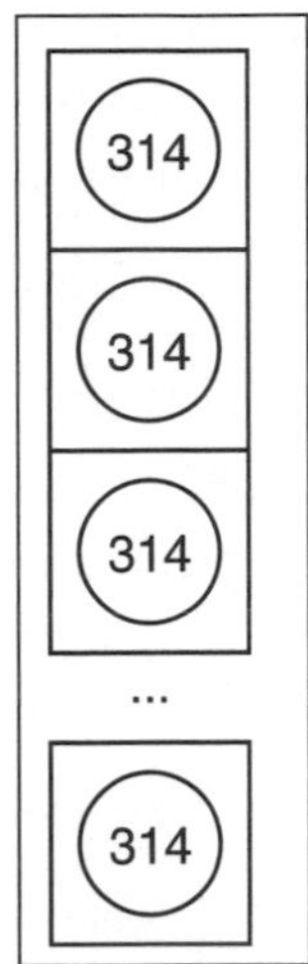

Figure 3.13 Demo03-08.bb box and jar example.

This ends the initialization and the main loop sections of the calculator program. The program begins by creating two global variables: `op1` and `op2`. These are the two numbers that will be added together. For example, in the expression 3 + 14, 3 represents `op1` and 14 represents `op2`.

Next, it creates the array. The array has 101 elements, and therefore, it goes from `array(0)` to `array(100)` (remember that arrays begin counting from 0). After the array declaration, `InitializeArray()` is called.

The `continue` variable is then created. This variable determines whether the program is still running. As long as `continue` is not equal to 0, the game loop continues to run.

The main loop begins next. First, it receives the variables `op1` and `op2` from the user. After that, it asks for `operator`. `operator` gives the users a choice of what operation they want to perform (addition, subtraction, multiplication, or division).

The loop then calls `PrintAnswer()` to print the answer. Finally, the loop asks the users if they would like to go through the program again. If the user chooses yes, `continue` remains as 1 and the game loop starts from the top. If not, the program exits.

This program has two user-defined functions: `PrintAnswer()` and `InitializeArray()`. Let's take a look at each of them.

```
;This Function sets up the array
Function InitializeArray()
For i=0 To 100
      array(i) = i
Next
End Function
```

This function simply creates the array that is used in the following calculations. Each array element contains its respective number. Therefore, the 14th element (array(13)) is equal to 13. After the numbers 0 through 100 have been initialized, they are all sent back to the main loop to go through the rest of the input.

The next user-defined function is PrintAnswer().

```
;This function prints the answer to the expression
Function PrintAnswer(operator$)
Print op1 + " " + operator$ + " " + op2 +
" is equal to " + FindAnswer(operator$)
End Function
```

This function simply writes out what the user wants to do. If the user wants to add 13 and 31, this function writes out "13 + 31 is equal to 44." You might be wondering how it gets the answer. That is accomplished by the final user-defined function: FindAnswer().

```
;This function performs the math based on the user input
Function FindAnswer(operator$)
      Select operator
            Case "+"
                  Return array(op1) + array(op2)
            Case "-"
                  Return array(op1) - array(op2)
            Case "*"
                  Return array(op1) * array(op2)
            Case "/"
                  Return array(op1) / array(op2)

      End Select
End Function
```

Note that if op1 or op2 is larger than 100 or less than 0, the program will not function.

The output is shown in Figure 3.14.

By the way, one thing about this program. The program will crash if op2 is set to 0 and operator$ is division. This is because it is impossible to divide any number by 0. As you can see, this function begins with a Select statement. The Select command chooses an action based on which operator is being used. If the user chooses to multiply something, the function returns `op1` times `op2`. The return value is then printed to the screen in the `PrintAnswer()` function.

```
What is the first number? 10
And the second? 12
Enter +, -, *, or / +
10 + 12 is equal to 22
Enter 1 to continue or 0 to quit
```

Figure 3.14 The demo03-09.bb calculator program.

note

If you happen to try dividing two numbers that aren't evenly divisible, you will get the correct number, but the decimal place will be missing. That is because this program uses integers. Try modifying this program so it uses floating-point variables instead.

Figures 3.15 and 3.16 portray the array as a box and demonstrate how two numbers are added.

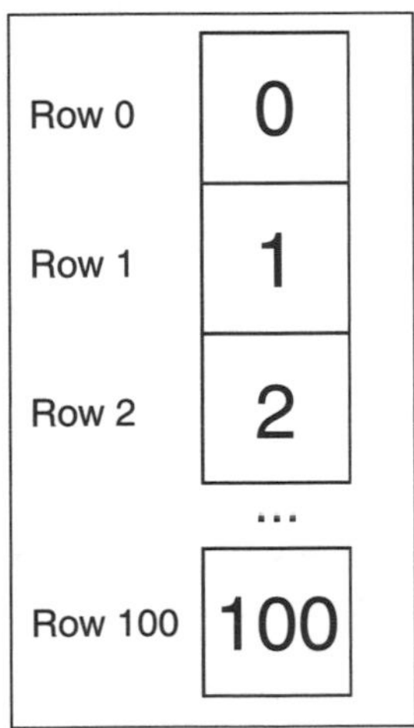

Figure 3.15
The array box.

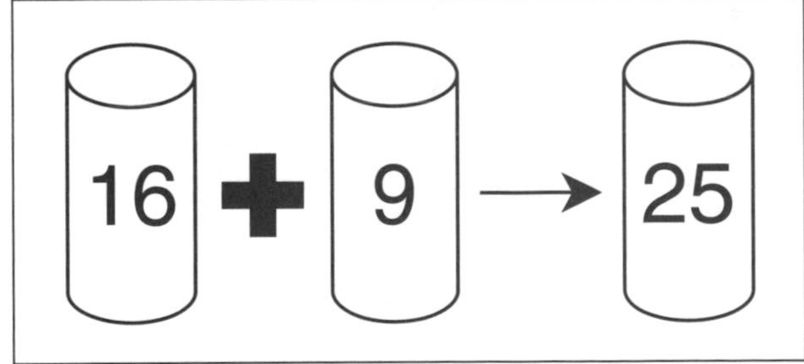

Figure 3.16 Adding two jars.

Multi-Dimensional Arrays

Multi-dimensional arrays are very similar to regular arrays, except that, well, they have more than one dimension. In essence, the main difference is that a multi-dimensional array has more than one subscript. An easy way to visualize a multi-dimensional array is to use the box example again. However, instead of only having one column, it has two or more, as shown in Figure 3.17.

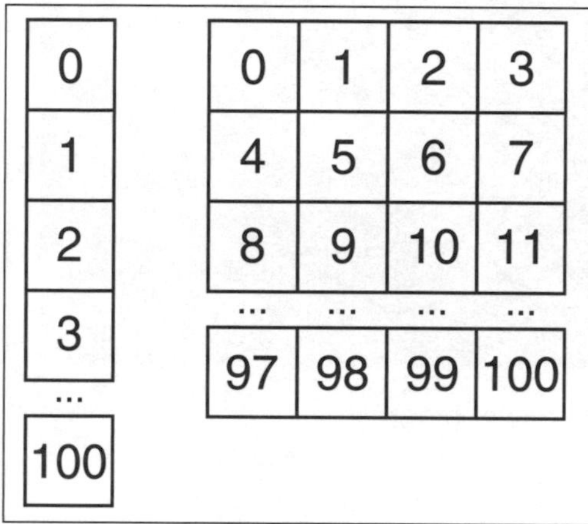

Figure 3.17 Single and multi-dimensional arrays.

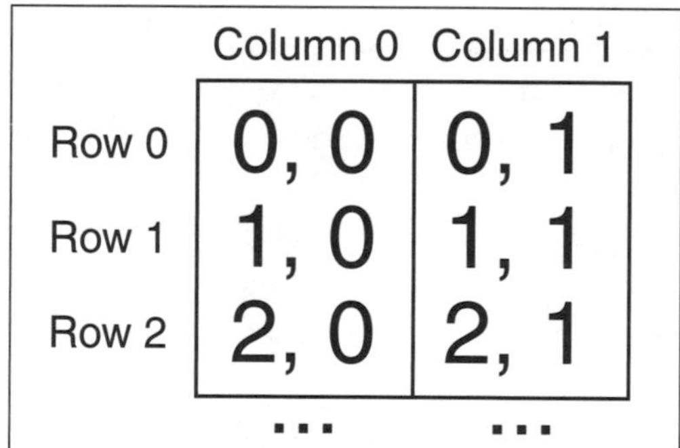

Figure 3.18 The two-dimensional bullet array.

Multi-dimensional arrays are used in situations in which you need sets of variables within the array set. For example, you might create an array of bullets. You could then create an array with two dimensions, and place the bullets shot by the player in one dimension, and the bullets shot by the enemy in the other. This is demonstrated in Figure 3.18.

Okay, let's make a multi-dimensional array. This process is very similar to making a single-dimensional array; you only have to add another subscript into the declaration.

```
Dim bullets(2,100)
```

This command creates an array of bullets with two parts. The first part determines who shot the bullet and the second part determines which bullet it was. Each column contains 100 bullets.

Now, to actually use the array, you only have to add the second subscript to the variable call like this:

```
bullets(0,23)
```

This command calls the 24th bullet from the player. Remember, because the computer begins counting at 0, the subscript 23 is the 24th element of the array.

All right, let's make a program. This simply draws out 25 asterisks (*) and 25 plus signs (+). It doesn't do much, but you will understand how you can use arrays when you learn about types in the next section. Figure 3.19 portrays the info in a table.

```
;demo03-10.bb - Draws out 25 '*'s and 25 '+'s

;create the array
Dim starsplusses$(2,24)

;initialize the array. The first dimension will
contain *'s and the second will contain +'s
For rows = 0 To 1
    For columns=0 To 24
          Assign either + or *, depending on
the return value of FindChar$()
          starsplusses$(rows,columns) = Find-
Char$(rows)
    Next
Next
```

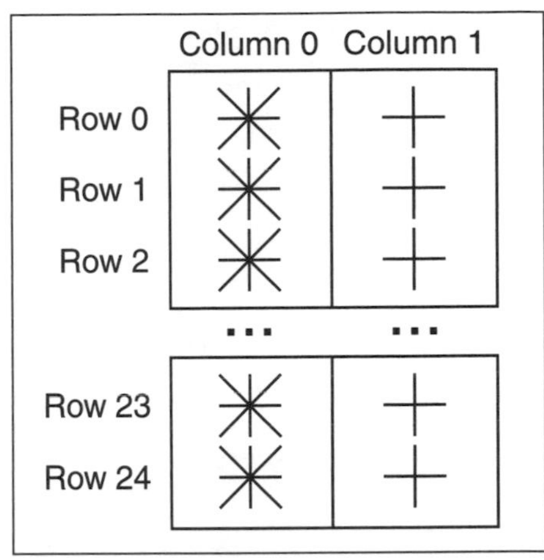

Figure 3.19 The `starsplusses$` array.

This first fragment begins by creating the `starsplusses$` array. Because its subscript is (2,25), it will contain a total of 50 objects. How did I get this number? I simply multiplied the first subscript by the second subscript: 2*25 = 50.

The next section of the code initializes the array. It runs two `for` loops within each other. In multi-dimensional arrays, two `for` loops are commonly used. The first loop runs throughout the first subscript and the second loop runs throughout the second subscript. The outer loop, `For i = 0 To 1`, counts from 0 to 1. The second `for` loop counts from 0 to 24. The line

```
starsplusses$(rows,columns) = FindChar$(rows)
```

determines what each element is set equal to with the help of the `FindChar$()` function.

`FindChar$()` is a user-defined function. It looks like this:

```
;FUNCTION FINDCHAR$(i)
;returns * or +
Function FindChar$(i)
       If i = 0
              Return "*"
       Else If i = 1
              Return "+"
       EndIf
End Function
```

If the initialization loop calls this function with the row number being 0, the array element becomes an asterisk (star). If the function is called with the row being 1, the array element is a plus sign. Therefore, the array has two rows of 25 characters—one row is made up of stars, the other is made up of plusses.

Next, you have to display the array.

```
;display the array
For rows = 0 To 1
	For columns = 0 To 24
		;Write each value to the screen
		Write starsplusses$(rows,columns)
	Next
	;write a new line after each row
	Print ""
Next
;Delay five seconds
Delay 5000
```

Once again, this function has two `for` loops running within each other. The outer loop counts by rows and the inner loop counts by columns. Every element is drawn to the screen. When the loop gets to the end of the first row, a new line is printed so it can print out the next row.

A new function, `Write`, is introduced here. `Write` has the same prototype as `Print`:

```
Write string$
```

In fact, these two functions are extremely similar. The only difference between `Write` and `Print` is that `Write`, unlike `Print`, does not automatically print out a new line after the line is written. This is extremely useful when trying to write out the contents of the array because you don't want a new line after each element. Figure 3.20 shows what demo03-10.bb looks like when `Write` is substituted for `Print`.

Figure 3.20 Demo03-10 without `Write`.

Figure 3.21 shows the demo03-10.bb program.

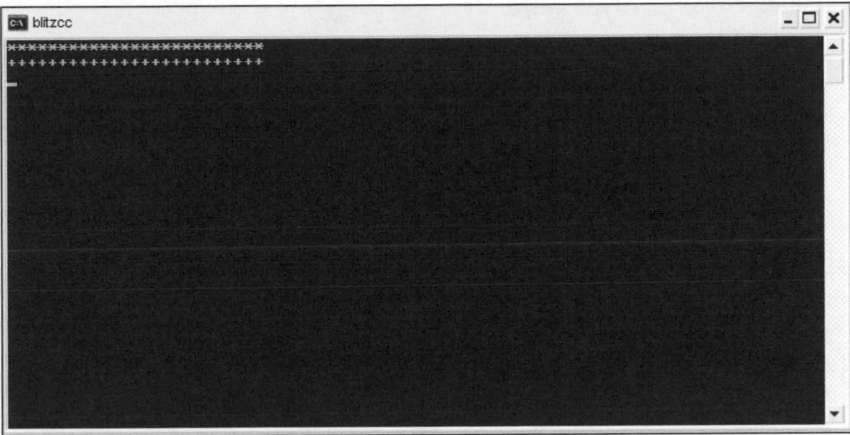

Figure 3.21 The demo03-10.bb program.

Using Types

The entire chapter has been leading up to *types*, because they are a very important and useful part of the Blitz Basic language. Types are simply a set of related data. That might sound a lot like the definition of an array, but with types, you can have different names for each of the variables, as well as different data types (string, integer, and floating point).

Here is an example. Imagine you have a player ship. The computer needs to know where to put the ship. For this example, we are going to put the ship at the coordinates 100, 100 (if you don't understand coordinates, they will be explained soon). You could do something like this:

```
playerx = 100
playery = 100
```

Seems pretty easy, eh? What if you wanted to add a hit counter? You have to create another variable.

```
playerhits = 3
```

That's three variables. If you wanted to make it possible for the ship to move up and down, you would need two more variables. That's a total of five variables!

The best way to remedy this problem is to use types. A type can take all of these unorganized variables and attach them to a single type name, like in Figure 3.22. Here is the creation of a ship type:

Unattached	Attached Type player
Player x	x
Player y	y
Player hits	hits
Player x = 0	Player\x = 0
Player y = 0	Player\y = 0
Player hits = 0	Player\hits = 0

Figure 3.22
Unattached and attached variables.

```
Type Ship
       Field x,y ;the ship's location
       Field hits ;ship's hit points
End Type
```

To create a new type, add the keyword `Type` before the name of the type. Next, create the individual fields. Each field is a separate variable that is part of the type. Each `Field` variable can be an integer, a floating point, or a string.

Now you have declared the type, and you have to create a variable that can hold this new data type. The procedure to do this is a little different from defining a variable with one of the built-in types (strings, integers, and floats are the built-in types). To create this new variable, or *instance* as it is called, use the following syntax.

```
player.ship = New ship
```

Wow, that looks bizarre. Let's break it down piece by piece. The first thing that you see is the word `player` to the left of the decimal point. This word refers to the name of the variable you are creating. After the decimal point, you see the word `ship`. This is the type you want the variable associated with. This variable will now have all of the same fields as the `ship` type, declared previously. To finish off the process, we provide the proper fields by setting `player.ship` equal to `New ship`.

This creates the new player ship. You could create an enemy ship by simply changing the name of `player` to `enemy`. Creation of a new type almost always uses this base:

```
instancename.typename = New typename
```

Now that we have organized all the loose variables by putting them in a type and creating an instance of the type, we can set the field variables.

```
player\x = 100
player\y = 100
player\hits = 3
```

Not too bad, huh? To access one of the variables, just use this formula.

```
instancename\variablename
```

Now you can create, define, and access types. Let's get to an example and see how this baby works. To write this program, I am going to use the function `Text`, which is declared as

```
Text x,y,string$,[centerx],[centery]
```

Refer to Table 3.3 to see what each parameter means. `Text` allows you to draw text on the screen, just like `Print`, but it also provides the capability for the programmer to choose the exact coordinate position that will appear.

Table 3.3 Text's Parameters

Parameter	Description
x	The x coordinate of the text
y	The y coordinate of the text
`string$`	The string you want printed
`[centerx]`	Set to true if you want the text horizontally centered
`[centery]`	Set to true if you want the text vertically centered

This program uses `Text` to draw the players on the screen and to show their hit points. You will also be able to decrease the player's hit points and move them around. This is a pretty basic and simple game. Also, the ship will be represented by the characters <-*->. Table 3.4 describes the keys used in this game.

Table 3.4 Demo03-11.bb's Keys

Key	Function
Left arrow	Moves the ship left
Right arrow	Moves the ship right
Up arrow	Moves the ship up
Down arrow	Moves the ship down
Spacebar	Decreases the ship's hit points by one
Esc	Exits the game

```
;demo03-11.bb - Draw a ship which can be moved and killed

Graphics 400,300

;CONSTANTS
Const STARTHITPOINTS = 3
Const SHIP$ = "<-*->"
Const ESCKEY = 1, SPACEBAR = 57, UPKEY = 200,
LEFTKEY = 203, DOWNKEY = 208, RIGHTKEY = 205
Const STARTX = 200, STARTY = 150
```

This is the first part of the program. It begins by setting the graphics mode. Next, it designates which variables are constants. *Constants*, as you remember, are variables whose values don't change throughout the game. If you want to make a change to any of these variables, feel free to do so. The difference will be reflected throughout the entire program. It probably isn't a good idea to change the key constants (such as ESCKEY, SPACEBAR, and so on) because doing so just causes some problems—you will have to search for the correct key.

All of the constants are listed in Table 3.5.

Table 3.5 demo03-11.bb's Constants

Constant	Default Value	Description
STARTHITPOINTS	3	The number of times you can decrease the hit points (by pressing spacebar) before the game ends.
SHIP$	"<-*->"	The characters that make up the player. Because there are no images, the player is simply a text string. Change this value to change how the player looks.
ESCKEY	1	The key code for Esc.
SPACEBAR	57	The key code for the spacebar.
UPKEY	200	The key code for the up arrow.
LEFTKEY	203	The key code for the left arrow.
DOWNKEY	208	The key code for the down arrow.
RIGHTKEY	205	The key code for the right arrow.
STARTX	200	The starting x position for the ship.
STARTY	150	The starting y position for the ship.

Okay, let's keep going.

```
;TYPES
Type Ship
        Field x,y
        Field hitpoints
        Field shipstring$
End Type
```

This section defines all of the types used in the program. Here, only one is defined—`Ship`. The `Ship` type groups all of the variables necessary to draw the ship on the screen. Table 3.6 lists all of the fields of the `Ship` type.

Table 3.6 demo03-11.bb's Types

Field	Description
x	The x coordinate of the ship. The field is first initialized to the x value given in `STARTX`.
y	The y coordinate of the ship. The field is first initialized to the y value given in `SSTARTY`.
`hitpoints`	The number of hit points remaining on the ship. The field is first initialized to the hit point value given in `STARTHITPOINTS`.
`shipstring$`	The actual look of the ship. This field is first initialized to the string value `SHIP$`.

Next we move to the initialization of the program.

```
;INITIALIZATION SECTION
Global cont = 1
Global player.ship = New ship
player\x = STARTX
player\y = STARTY
player\hitpoints = STARTHITPOINTS
player\shipstring = SHIP$
```

The initialization section defines all of the variables that will be used in the program. It also initializes the fields of the `Ship` type. The first variable, `cont`, is used in the game loop as the variable that determines whether the game continues playing. As long as the user wants to continue, `cont` is equal to 1.

The line

```
Global player.ship = New ship
```

creates an instance of the `Ship` type with the name `player`. Therefore, any fields that are in the ship type can now be accessed via `player`. The rest of the initialization section sets up the `player` type by assigning its fields to their respective constants.

caution

Be careful to not confuse the "/" operator and the "\" operator. A forward slash "/" indicates division. A backward slash "\" indicates that you are accessing something from a type.

Next, move on to the game loop.

```
;Game loop
While cont = 1
	Cls
	Text player\x, player\y, player\shipstring$

	TestInput()
	DrawHUD()
Wend
;End of loop
```

The game loop is short, as it should be. It begins by testing the `cont` variable. If `cont` is equal to 1, the game runs; if not, the game exits. After that, the loop clears the screen by calling `Cls`. Without calling `Cls`, the screen would exhibit streaks, like in Figure 3.23. After that, the player is drawn to the screen at the given position. The loop then tests the input by calling `TestInput()` and draws the HUD by calling `DrawHUD()`. The HUD is the *heads-up display*, or the area of the screen that explains some values that are being used in the game.

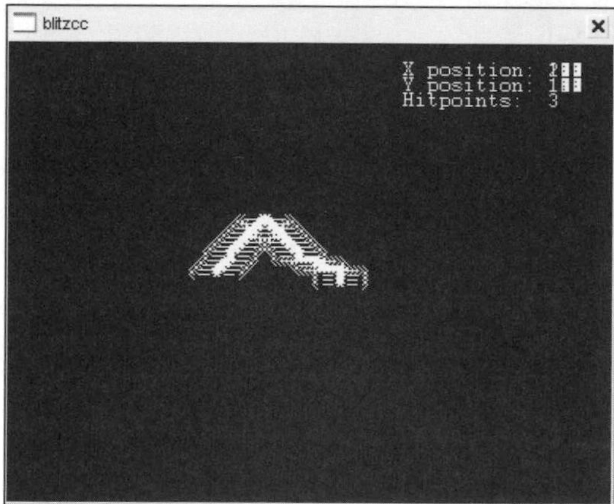

Figure 3.23 The main loop without `Cls`.

```
;TestInput() changes the direction or hit points of the player
Function TestInput()
;If player presses left, move him left.
If KeyHit(LEFTKEY)

       player\x = player\x - 3
       If player\x <= 0
              player\x = 10
       EndIf
EndIf

;If player presses right, move him right.
If KeyHit(RIGHTKEY)
       player\x = player\x + 3

       If player\x >= 385
              player\x = 380
       EndIf
EndIf

;If player presses up, move him up.
If KeyHit(UPKEY)

       player\y = player\y - 3
       If player\y <= 0
              player\y = 10
       EndIf
EndIf

;If player presses down, move him down.
If KeyHit(DOWNKEY)

       player\y = player\y + 3
       If player\y >= 285
              player\y = 280
       EndIf
EndIf

;If player presses spacebar, remove a hit point

If KeyHit(SPACEBAR)
```

```
		player\hitpoints = player\hitpoints - 1
		If player\hitpoints <= 0
			cont = 0
		EndIf

EndIf

;If player presses Esc, set cont to 0, and exit the game
If KeyHit(ESCKEY)
	cont = 0
EndIf
```

The TestInput() function is very long, but also very simple. It simply tests the keys that the user has pressed and updates the variables based on the input. Starting from the top, if the player presses the left arrow, the player moves three pixels to the left. If the player happens to move the character too far (off the screen), the ship's position is moved back to the right. If the user presses the right arrow, he moves left a little. The same happens if the user moves the ship too far up or down—the ship is repositioned back on the screen.

If the player presses the spacebar, the hit point counter decreases by one. The program then tests the counter to determine if the player has 0 hit points. If so, cont is set to 0, and the game is exited on the next frame.

The last test determines if the user pressed Esc. If so, cont is set to 0, and the game exits on the next frame.

```
;DrawHUD() draws user's info in top Right of the screen
Function DrawHUD()
	Text 260, 10, "X position: " + player\x
	Text 260, 20, "Y position: " + player\y
	Text 260, 30, "Hitpoints: " + player\hitpoints
End Function
```

The final function in the program, DrawHUD(), simply writes out the ship's information to the screen. The x and y coordinate positions and remaining hit points are drawn in the top-right section of the screen.

note

> You might notice a major slowdown on your computer when you run this program. That is because we are running a mini-game without using page flipping. Don't worry, I will teach you how to fix this problem in Part 2 of this book.

Figure 3.24 shows how the loop works and Figure 3.25 is a screenshot of the actual program.

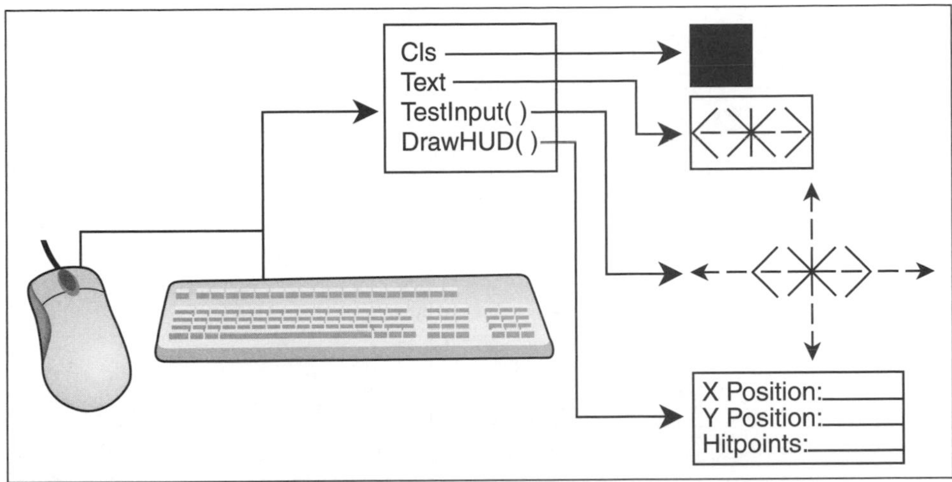

Figure 3.24 The main game loop.

Coordinate Systems

I'm going to leave the concept of types for a moment to talk about coordinate points. Coordinates explain where on the screen something is. They are shown in the format of x, y. For example, something that is at coordinate 314, 13 has an x position of 314 and a y position of 13.The coordinate plane looks like Figure 3.26. The origin, or 0 value of both the x and y direction, is at the top-left part of the screen. X increases from the origin right, and y increases from the origin down. When you want to get to coordinate position 314, 13, for example, you move from the origin 314 spaces to the right and 13 spaces down.

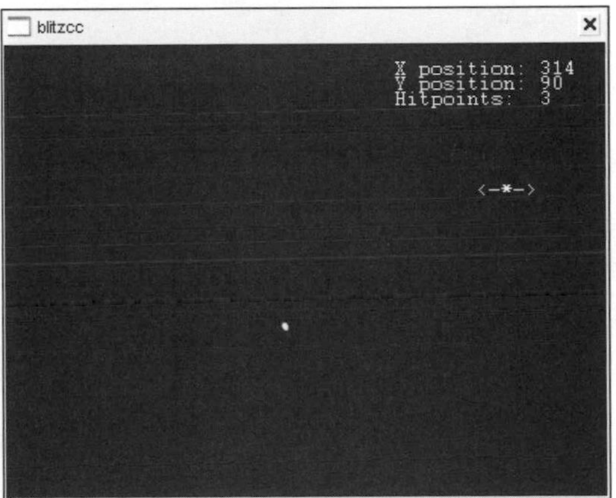

Figure 3.25 The demo03-11.bb program.

Each position is a single pixel on the screen. A *pixel* is the smallest measurement of a computer screen. Each pixel is a different color, and the pixels fitted together create an image. To see the size of a single pixel on your machine, run demo03-12.bb (see Figure 3.27). The tiny white dot in the center is a single pixel. Small, huh?

When you want to plot an object to the screen, you plot it to a certain pixel position. Usually the top-left corner of the object is drawn to that pixel position. So, as in Figure 3.28, if you want to write some text to a certain position, the top left of the text is at the selected pixel. If you write with the `Text` command, you can also center the text.

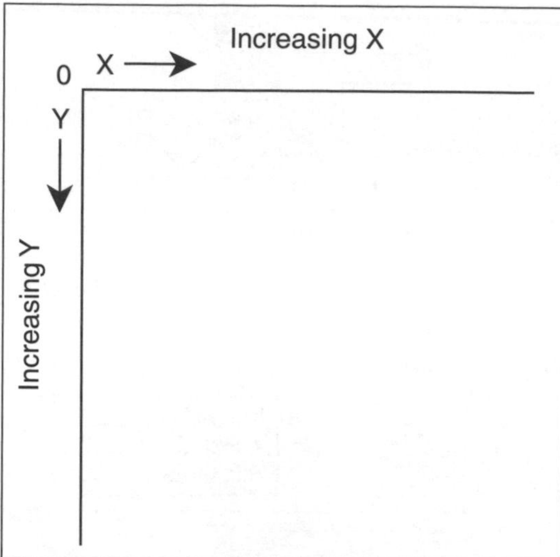

Figure 3.26 A coordinate system.

Figure 3.27 A single pixel.

For...Each...Next

Types have been specifically designed to work well with loops. In fact, there is a new kind of loop that only works with types. It is called the `For...Each...Next` loop.

The `For...Each...Next` loop allows you to create sets of types and perform actions on them as a whole. For example, using a `For...Each...Next` loop, you could create a set of enemy ships from one call. Using the type:

```
Type ship
    Field x,y
    Field hitpoints
End Type
```

You now create a bunch of enemy ships—say, 100:

```
SeedRnd MilliSecs()
For enemycounter = 0 To 99 ;100 new ships
              enemy.ship = New ship
              enemy\x = Rand(1,640)
              ememy\y = Rand (1,480)
              ememy\hitpoints = 3
Next
```

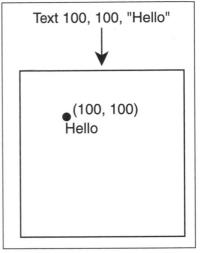

Figure 3.28
Drawing objects at pixel locations.

Well, we have just created 100 different enemy ships. Now, to test all of the enemies, we need to use the `For...Each...Next` loop. This loop tests every member of a certain type; this makes it easy to create a bunch of copies of an enemy and get rid of them when you're done. Refer to Figure 3.29 to see how the `For...Each...Next` loop looks in memory. This specific loop tests each enemy's hit points to make sure they are really alive. If not, the program deletes the enemy.

note

> It might seem like we are creating the same enemy over and over again. In actuality, we are creating a whole bunch of enemies with the same name. Using the `For...Each...Next` loop, you can quickly and easily test and modify every enemy ship.

```
For enemyships.ship = Each ship
       If hitpoints <= 0
              Delete enemyships
       EndIf
Next
```

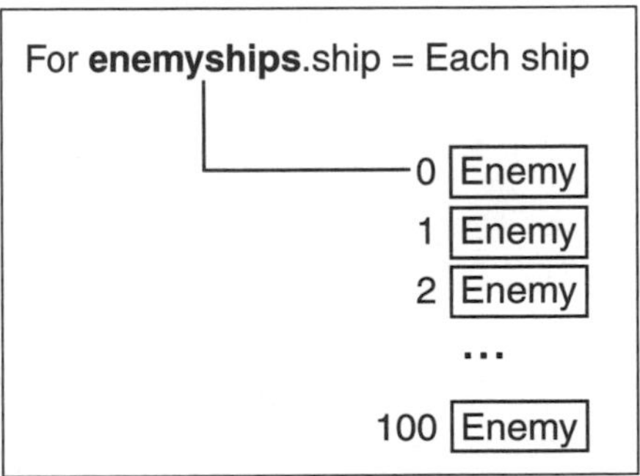

Figure 3.29 The `enemyships` in memory.

Pretty easy, if I do say so myself! This code snippet tests every one of the ships and deletes them if their hit point counter is equal to or less than 0. To see how the For...Each...Next loop works in memory, check out Figure 3.30.

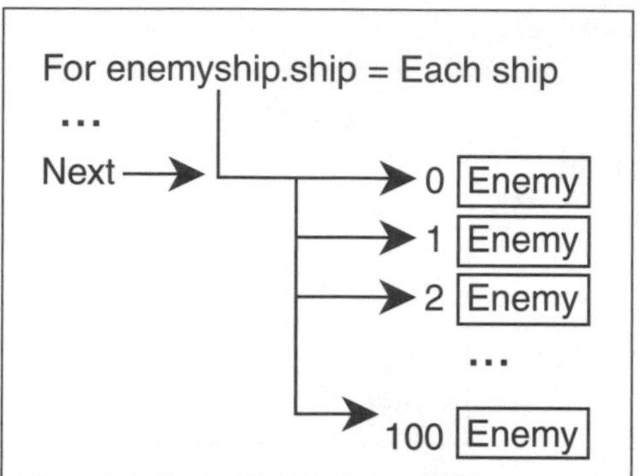

Figure 3.30 The `enemyships` loop in memory.

tip

You might wonder why the program determines if the hit point count is equal to *or less than* 0. Because the ship is always deleted at 0, why test for less than 0? The reason is, sometimes a tiny error leaks through, and a ship could be assigned a −1 hit point count (this might happen if the ship was hit twice in the same frame). In cases like these, it's better to be safe than sorry. The moral: always test for unlikely conditions.

You can easily change this loop to interact with the enemy ship's x and y values. For example, if you add an x or y direction, you can make the enemies move randomly. You might update the type to look something like this:

```
Type ship
        Field x,y
        Field directionx, directiony
        Field hitpoints
End Type
```

Next, inside the initialization loop, you randomize the direction values (a positive number for `directionx` moves the enemy right, and a positive number for `directiony` moves the enemy down).

```
enemy\directionx = Rand(-3,3)
enemy\directiony = Rand(-3,3)
```

And finally, you would add code in the final loop to move the enemy around:

```
enemy\x = enemy\x + enemy\directionx
enemy\y = enemy\y + enemy\directiony
```

note

If you put all this code in a program and watch the enemy ships, you might notice that the ships leave streaks behind them. This is because their previous position was not deleted. If you want to fix this problem, simply add the command `Cls`, clear screen, to the beginning of the game loop.

Congratulations, you have created animation!

Putting It All Together: Textanoid!

Okay, now, using all we have learned, you can put it together and make a game. This game is a simple text-based copy of *Arkanoid* that uses all of the processes discussed in this long chapter.

Because we will be using text, the basic game commands are run by the `Text` and `KeyDown` commands. Basically, the idea of the game is to get rid of all the blocks by hitting them with the ball. The players control a paddle, which can move left or right. Player attempts to keep the ball from hitting the bottom wall of the game board. Each time the player clears the field of blocks, the player will reach a new level. Theoretically, you can go on to an infinite level (because the difficulty never increases), but I'm betting the player will get bored before then.

The full source of the game can be found on the CD under the name demo03-13.bb. This game might be hard to understand for a beginning programmer; however, I am going to help you through the tough parts of the code. Let's start off with the defined types.

```
;TYPES
Type paddle ;the player type
	Field x,y ;coordinates
End Type

Type ball
	Field x,y
	Field directionx, directiony
End Type
```

The output is shown in Figure 3.31.

These types define the player and the ball in the game. The x and y coordinates are simply the position of each object on the screen, but the `directionx` and `directiony` variables might seem strange.

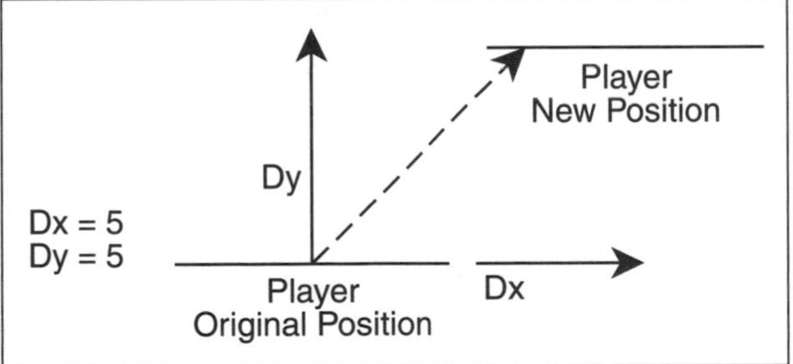

Figure 3.31
How `DirectionX` and `DirectionY` work.

note

Notice that I decided not to make a block type. I felt that it would be easier to create it as an array. For an exercise, try to make and use a block type in the program.

The *direction* variables define how the ball moves—the `directionx` defines the left and right movement and the `directiony` variable defines the up and down movement. Referring to Figure 3.31, you can see that as `directionx` moves the paddle left, `directiony` moves the paddle up. The end result is a new position that is above and to the left of the original position.

Next up is the constants section:

```
;Constants
Const BLOCKSTRING$ = "XXXXXXX"
Const PADDLESTRING$ = "---------"
Const BALLSTRING$ = "O"
Const BLOCKROWS = 3
Const BLOCKCOLUMNS = 6
Const BLOCKXGAP = 85
Const BLOCKYGAP = 32
Const BLOCKXORIGIN = 16
Const BLOCKYORIGIN = 8
Global BLOCKHEIGHT = FontHeight()
Global BLOCKWIDTH = Len(BLOCKSTRING$) * FontWidth()
Global PADDLEHEIGHT = FontHeight()
Global PADDLEWIDTH = Len(PADDLESTRING$) * FontWidth()
Global BALLHEIGHT = FontHeight()
Global BALLWIDTH = Len(BALLSTRING$) * FontWidth()
Const STARTX = 300
Const STARTY= 340
Const ESCKEY = 1, LEFTKEY = 203, RIGHTKEY = 205
```

Refer to Table 3.7 to see what each constant means. By the way, the function `FontHeight()` (which is used in each of the height variables) returns the height in pixels of the selected font (you will learn how to change the font later). The `FontWidth()` function returns the width of one character of the selected font. The `Len` function returns the number of characters in a string. Figure 3.32 shows what `FontWidth()` and `Len` would return on a sample string.

caution

> Unfortunately, due to some error in the BlitzPlus demo, `FontWidth()` does not work. You have to find the width of the font manually in this case. However, `FontHeight()` works fine. Hopefully this error will be fixed in a new demo. I will let you know if there is any new way to fix this error on my Web site, http://www.maneeshsethi.com.

Table 3.7 Textanoid!'s Constants

Variable	Description
BLOCKSTRING	Defines what each block looks like
PADDLESTRING	Defines what the paddle looks like
BALLSTRING	Defines what the ball looks like
BLOCKROWS	The number of rows of blocks
BLOCKCOLUMNS	The number of columns of blocks
BLOCKXGAP	The number of pixels between each column
BLOCKYGAP	The number of pixels between each row
BLOCKXORIGIN	The number of pixels from the top-left corner of the window to the first column
BLOCKYORIGIN	The number of pixels from the top-left corner of the window to the first row
BLOCKHEIGHT	The height of each block
BLOCKWIDTH	The width of each block
PADDLEHEIGHT	The height of the paddle
PADDLEWIDTH	The width of the paddle
BALLHEIGHT	The height of the ball
BALLWIDTH	The width of the ball
STARTX	The starting x coordinate of the player
STARTY	The starting y coordinate of the player
ESCKEY	The key code for the Esc button
LEFTKEY	The key code for the left arrow
RIGHTKEY	The key code for the right arrow

note

You might be wondering why the HEIGHT and WIDTH variables are global and not constant. The reason is that a constant value can never be variable. The FontHeight() function can return a different value, and therefore it is variable. Because I need to use the HEIGHT and WIDTH variables throughout the program, I made them global.

Figure 3.32 Len and FontWidth().

Okay, next is the initialization section.

```
;Initialization
SeedRnd MilliSecs()
Global score = 0
Global blockhits = 0
Global level = 1
Dim blocks(BLOCKROWS, BLOCKCOLUMNS)

Global ball.ball = New ball
Global player.paddle = New paddle
NewLevel()
```

Let's discuss this section. First the `SeedRnd` command seeds the random generator. Next, this section creates the `score`, `blockhits`, and `level` variables. `score` is the points the player has accumulated, `blockhits` tells how many times the player has hit a `block`, and `level` shows the players what level they are on. All of these variables are used in the function `DrawHUD()`.

What Is SeedRnd?

You might wonder why I always use the command `SeedRnd Millisecs()` before using the Rand function. The fact is no computer is random. Because it was created to do certain tasks correctly each time, it cannot truly create random numbers. Because of this fact, using `Rand` by itself in a program would cause the same number to be generated over and over. The program uses `SeedRnd` to change the starting point of the random generator each time, so it does not generate the same numbers over and over. `MilliSecs()` is a good function to use to seed the generator because `MilliSecs()` is never the same twice.

The command

```
Dim blocks(BLOCKROWS, BLOCKCOLUMNS)
```

creates a multidimensional array called `blocks`. If you recall, a multidimensional array is just like a regular array but it has rows as well as columns. This fits in easily with the block setup.

Refer to Figure 3.33 to see the block rows and columns, complete with subscripts. You can see that the columns extend from the top to the bottom, and the rows extend from the left to the right.

The next two variables created are `ball` and `player`. These two variables create the ball and player from the ball and paddle types.

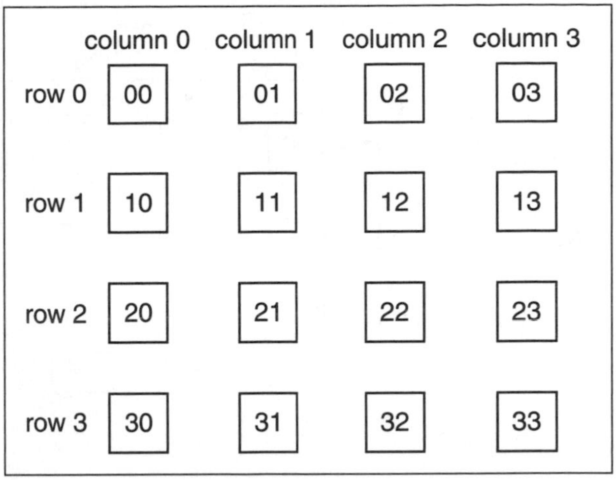

Finally, you initialize the level by calling `NewLevel()`. This user-defined function creates all of the blocks and sets up the ball and paddle. The function is defined as:

```
Function NewLevel()
For rows=0 To BLOCKROWS - 1
       For cols=0 To BLOCKCOLUMNS - 1
            blocks(rows,cols) = 1
       Next
Next
ResetLevel()
End Function
```

	column 0	column 1	column 2	column 3
row 0	00	01	02	03
row 1	10	11	12	13
row 2	20	21	22	23
row 3	30	31	32	33

Figure 3.33 Rows and columns.

The first `for` loop counts each of the rows and the second `for` loop counts each of the columns. Notice that I make the `for` loops count to the number of rows and columns minus 1. This subtraction offsets the fact that the starting number in an array is 0. Referring to Figure 3.34, you can see that this counter goes through each of the columns in the first row before moving to the next row and starting again. Whenever you see dual `for` loops to count through the blocks, all of the columns in the first row are counted before moving to the next row. Each of the blocks is set to one, which means they will be drawn (if they are destroyed, the blocks are set to zero).

The next line calls the function `ResetLevel()`. `ResetLevel()` is defined as this:

```
Function ResetLevel()
ball\x = 320
ball\y = 150
ball\directiony = 12
ball\directionx = Rand(-5,5)
player\x = STARTX
player\y = STARTY
Delay 500

End Function
```

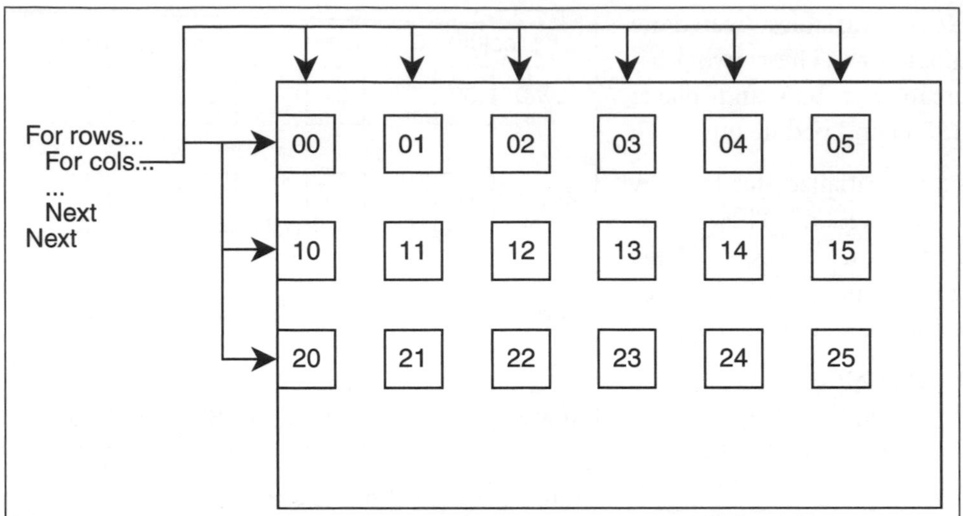

Figure 3.34 The for loops.

This function sets up the starting variables for the player and ball. The ball appears at the top-center corner of the screen and the player appears at the constant starting position. The ball is set to move toward the paddle at 12 pixels a frame and left or right randomly. The randomness of the ball's movement can sometimes cause a problem, however. There is always a chance that `directionx` will be equal to 0, and the ball will move straight up and down, without moving left or right at all. I left this problem in the program to illustrate a problem with random functions, and to give you an exercise. Try to fix this problem so a `directionx` of 0 can never occur!

Well, that was initialization. Next up, the game loop:

```
While Not KeyDown(1)
    Cls

    DrawHUD()
    TestInput()
    DrawBlocks()
    DrawPaddle()
    CheckBall()


    Flip
Wend
```

As you can see, the loop does almost nothing other than calling other functions. If you look at Figure 3.35, you will see the function layout for this program—which functions call which other functions, and so on.

note

You might wonder what the `Flip` command does. This command switches the background buffer with the foreground buffer. Don't worry what this means—it is explained in Chapter 5.

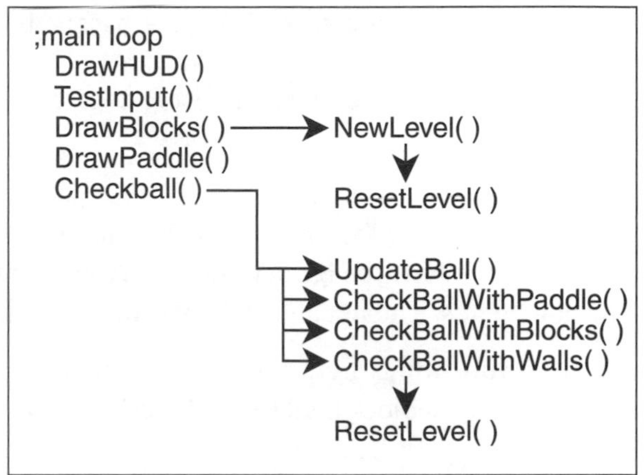

Figure 3.35 Textanoid!'s function outline.

The first call the loop makes is to `DrawHUD()`. Referring to Figure 3.36, you can see that `DrawHUD()` simply shows the players what level they are on, what their score is, and how many blocks they have hit.

```
Function DrawHUD()
Text 0,440, "Level: " + level ;write the level
Text 0,450, "Score: " + score ;write the score
Text 0,460, "Block Hits: " + blockhits ;write the block hits
End Function
```

Not too bad, huh? The only thing you might want to notice are the coordinates. The x coordinate is 0, which means it is on the left side of the screen, and the y coordinate is 440, 450, and 460, which is pretty close to the bottom (the total height of this window is 480, as seen in the `Graphics` call at the beginning of the program).

The next call from the loop is to `TestInput()`. `TestInput()` determines if the player moves her paddle or quits the game.

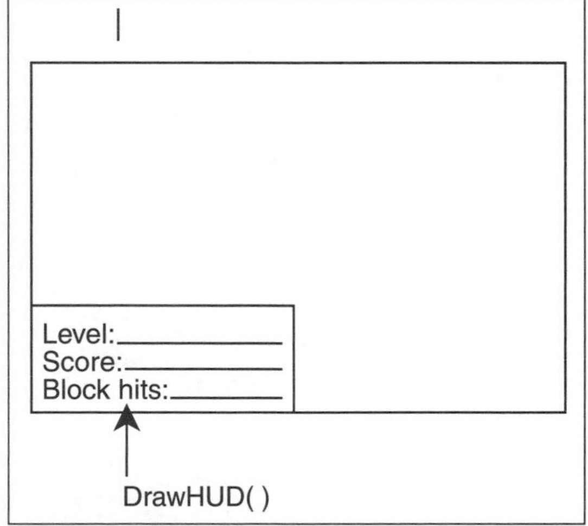

Figure 3.36 The `DrawHud()` function.

```
Function TestInput()
If KeyDown(ESCKEY) ;hit Esc
        End ;quit the game
ElseIf KeyDown(LEFTKEY) ;hit left arrow
        player\x = player\x - 10 ;move paddle left
ElseIf KeyDown(RIGHTKEY) ;hit right arrow
        player\x = player\x + 10 ;move paddle right
EndIf
End Function
```

Just for review, the `KeyDown(`*`scancode`*`)` function determines if the selected key was pressed. This function tests the Esc key, the left arrow, and the right arrow. If the player pressed Esc, the game ends. The left and right arrows move the paddle around the board.

The next function is `DrawBlocks()`. This function loops through each block and draws it if it is equal to 1. If a block is set to 0 (a block is set to 0 when it is hit by the ball), it is not drawn.

```
Function DrawBlocks()

      x = BLOCKXORIGIN
      y = BLOCKYORIGIN
;This variable creates a new level if there are no blocks
      newlevel = 0

;For all the rows
      For rows = 0 To BLOCKROWS - 1
;reset rows position
           x = BLOCKXORIGIN

           For cols = 0 To BLOCKCOLUMNS - 1

                ;If the block exists, draw it onscreen
                If (blocks(rows,cols) = 1) Then
                     Text x,y, BLOCKSTRING$
                     newlevel = newlevel + 1
                EndIf
           ;Move over to the next block
           x = x + BLOCKXGAP

           Next
           ;Move to the next column
           y = y + BLOCKYGAP
      Next
      If newlevel = 0
```

```
        level = level + 1
        NewLevel()
    EndIf

End Function
```

This might be tough to understand, but I'm here to help! The function starts with setting x and y to `BLOCKXORIGIN` and `BLOCKYORIGIN`. Refer to Figure 3.37 to see how the origin variables define how far from the top-left corner the first block is.

The `newlevel` variable determines if there are any blocks left. Every time a block is found, `newlevel` is incremented. At the end of the function, if `newlevel` equals 0, a `new level` is created.

The function now creates two `for` loops to iterate through the rows and columns of blocks (just like in `NewLevel()`). The only line between the two `for` loops is

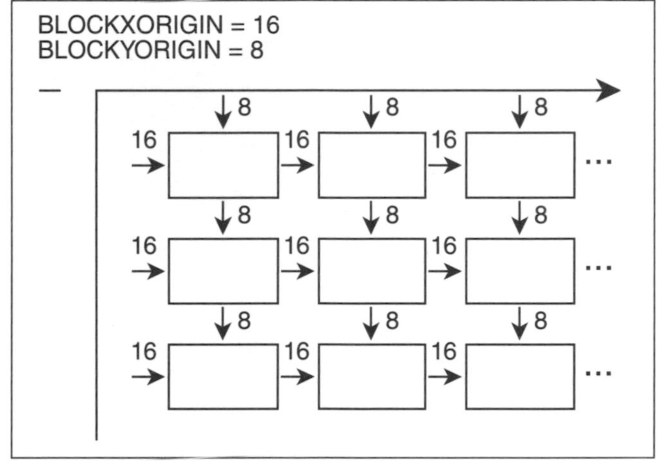

Figure 3.37 The X and Y origins.

```
x = BLOCKXORIGIN
```

This line resets the `x` value to `BLOCKXORIGIN` after all of the columns in one row have been tested. This line is necessary; if it were not included, the program would believe that the second row started offscreen. This is shown in Figure 3.38.

The next few lines test each block:

```
If (blocks(rows,cols) = 1) Then;If the block exists
      Text x,y, BLOCKSTRING$
      newlevel = newlevel + 1
EndIf
```

Figure 3.39 shows how each block is tested. If the current block is equal to 1, the block is drawn; if not, it is not drawn. At least one block must be drawn to continue the level; if no blocks are drawn, the `newlevel` variable never increases and stays at zero.

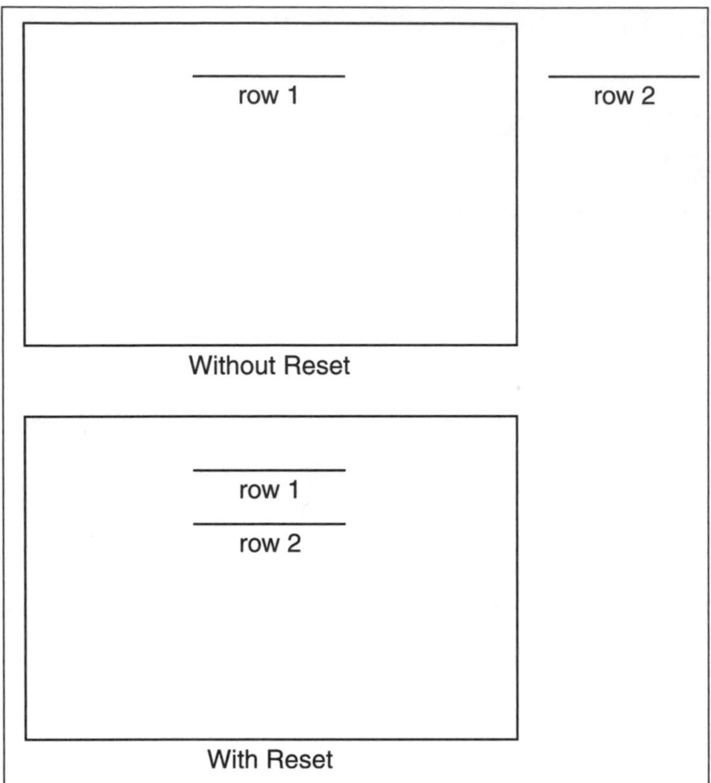

Figure 3.38 `DrawBlocks()` with and without resetting the x value.

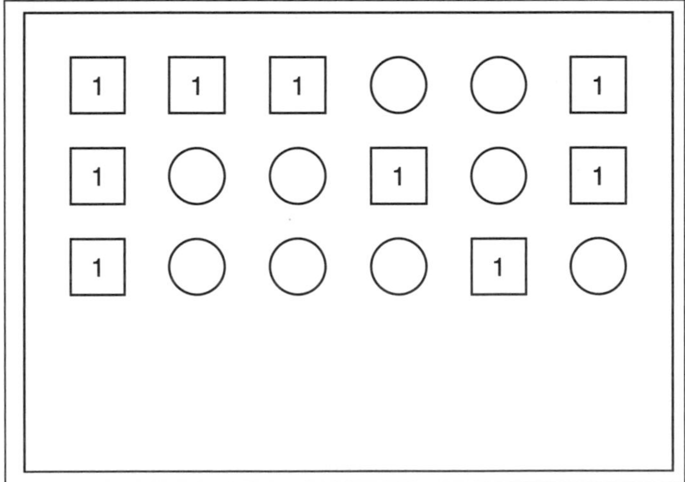

Figure 3.39 The block test.

The final line before the column loop's `Next` command is

```
x = x + BLOCKXGAP
```

This line advances the `x` variable to the next block. The `BLOCKXGAP` constant contains the number of pixels between each block in a single row (otherwise known as every column).

After all the columns in the first row have been tested, the loop moves to the next row. This is achieved by adding a gap to the y variable:

```
y = y + BLOCKYGAP
```

Just like `BLOCKXGAP`, `BLOCKYGAP` is the amount of pixels between each row. After all the boxes in one row are tested, the `y` value moves down a few pixels to begin drawing a new row.

The final lines of the function test the `newlevel` variable to determine if any blocks were hit. If none were (and `newlevel` equals 0), the level is increased and `NewLevel()` is called. This call begins the next level and redraws all the blocks.

Back to the game loop, the next function called is `DrawPaddle()`. `DrawPaddle()` is very simple.

```
Function DrawPaddle()

Text player\x,player\y,PADDLESTRING$

End Function
```

The only action this function performs is drawing the players at their x and y positions.

Finally, the game loop makes its final call—`CheckBall()`.

```
Function CheckBall()

UpdateBall() ;Move and draw ball
CheckBallWithPaddle()
CheckBallWithBlocks()
CheckBallWithWalls()
End Function
```

This function is the biggest one in the program. First off, it updates the position of the ball.

```
Function UpdateBall()
ball\x = ball\x + ball\directionx ;Move the ball to the left or right
ball\y = ball\y + ball\directiony ;Move the ball up or down
Text ball\x, ball\y, BALLSTRING$  ;Draw the ball
End Function
```

This function begins by moving the ball based on its `directionx` and `directiony` variables. Then it draws the ball on the screen.

Next, the `CheckBall()` function calls `CheckBallWithPaddle()`.

```
Function CheckBallWithPaddle()
If ball\x >= player\x And ball\x <= player\x + PADDLEWIDTH
And ball\y + BALLHEIGHT>= player\y
And ball\y + BALLHEIGHT <= player\y + PADDLEHEIGHT
ball\directiony = -ball\directiony + Rand(-3,3)
EndIf
End Function
```

This function is pretty simple. The `If` statement determines if the ball hit the paddle. You might have trouble understanding the `If` test, so I'll explain it to you.

See Figure 3.40 to understand how the test works. The line tests the ball and determines whether its x value falls between the left side of the paddle and the right side and whether its y value falls between the top and the bottom of the paddle.

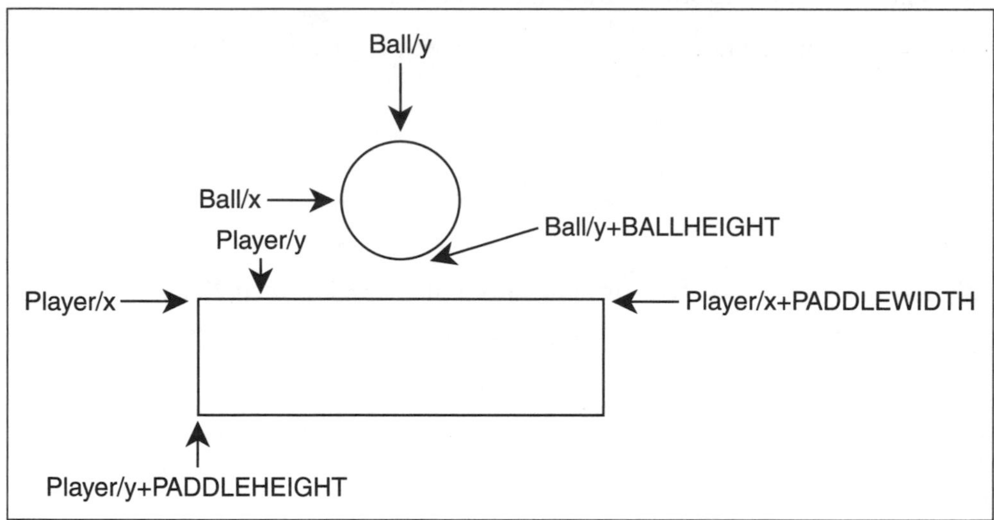

Figure 3.40 The ball-paddle collision.

If the ball has collided with the paddle, the `directiony` variable is flipped. This makes the direction move upward instead of downward. Also, if it hits the paddle, the speed of the ball increases by a value between −3 and 3 (if it increases by a negative value, the ball slows down).

Next, the `CheckBall()` function calls `CheckBallWithBlocks()`. This function tests the ball to determine if it has hit any blocks.

```
Function CheckBallWithBlocks()
;y is the first row
```

```
y = BLOCKYORIGIN

For rows=0 To BLOCKROWS - 1

   ;Reset x to first block of column
   x = BLOCKXORIGIN

   For every column of blocks
   For cols = 0 To BLOCKCOLUMNS - 1;

          ;If it exists
          If blocks(rows,cols)

               ;If the ball hit the block, delete the block
               If ball\x >= x And ball\x <=  x + BLOCKWIDTH
And ball\y >= y And ball\y <= y + BLOCKHEIGHT

                     blocks(rows,cols) = 0  ;Delete block

                     ball\directiony = -ball\directiony + Rand(-2,2)
                      ;Reverse its direction and add randomizer

                     score = score + 75

                     blockhits = blockhits + 1

                     ;It can't hit more than one block, so leave function
                     Return
               EndIf
          EndIf

          ;move to next column
          x = x + BLOCKXGAP
   Next

   ;move to next row
   y = y + BLOCKYGAP
Next

End Function
```

This function might seem tough, but it is a lot like `DrawBlocks()`. The first thing the function does is set up the origins. Then it begins the rows loop and resets the `x` value, just as in `DrawBlocks()`. Now, in the column loop, the block is tested to see if it exists. If it does, the ball is tested with the block. If the ball does hit the block, the block is deleted (by setting it to 0) and the direction is reversed along with a random speed increase. Finally, the score is updated, the `blockhits` variable is increased, and the function returns (because the ball can't hit two blocks in one frame).

The last action the `CheckBall()` function performs is to check the ball with the walls.

```
Function CheckBallWithWalls()
;If ball hits the left wall, reverse its direction and add randomizer
If ball\x <= 0
        ball\directionx = -ball\directionx + Rand(-2,2)

;If ball hits top wall, reverse its direction and add randomizer
ElseIf ball\y <= 0
        ball\directiony = -ball\directiony + Rand(-2,2)

; If it hits right wall, reverse its direction and add randomizer
ElseIf ball\x >= 640 - BALLWIDTH
        ball\directionx = -ball\directionx + Rand(-2,2) ;

;If ball hits lower wall, dock points for missing ball
ElseIf ball\y >= 480
        score = score - 200

        ;Reset the level
        ResetLevel()
EndIf
End Function
```

If the ball hits the top, left, or right wall, it is reversed. If it hits the bottom wall (if the paddle fails to hit it), 200 points are subtracted from the score, and the level is reset.

Hey, take a look at Figure 3.41. It's the final version of Textanoid!

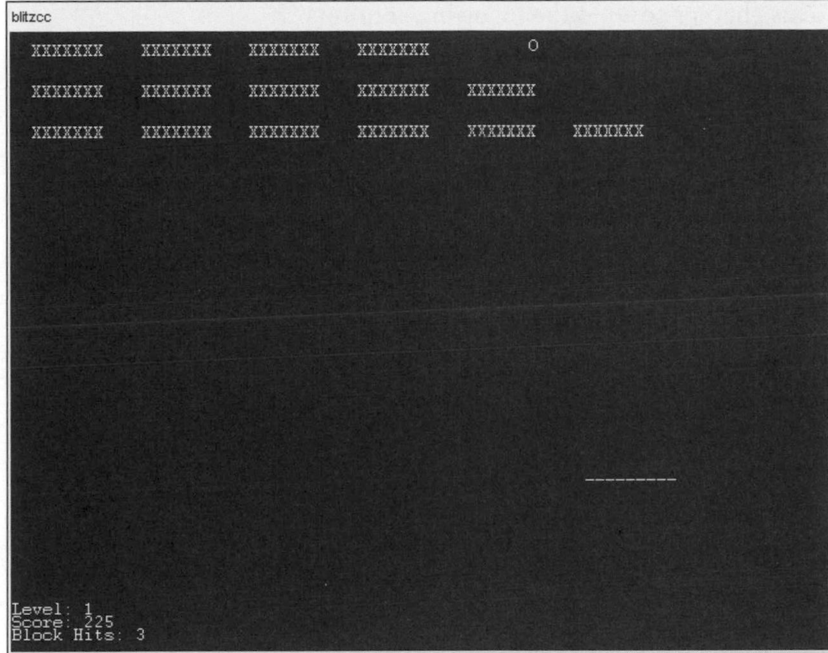

Figure 3.41 Textanoid!

Summary

Well, this has been one heck of a chapter. We learned about loops, functions, arrays, and types, and created our first animated game! This chapter is probably one of the most important in the book. You learned the basics of any Blitz Basic program, and you are now able to write any text-based program you can think of. I suggest you take a break now, and try to digest and understand what you have read. You might want to reread the parts you don't understand, and go through the listings again. Also, read and try to understand the full game from Chapter 1. It uses everything you have learned here with a small bit of graphics code added. Again, you can ask help online at www.maneeshsethi.com or by e-mailing me at maneesh@maneeshsethi.com if you have any questions.

I have an exercise for you, if you feel like expanding on your learning. When you play the final game from this chapter, you might notice that every once in a while, the ball moves only straight up and down, or slows to a complete stop. Try to fix this issue so the ball cannot slow down too much or stop moving left and right. (Hint: try randomizing `directionx` to make sure it does not move straight up and down.)

This chapter covered the following concepts:

- Loops
- Functions
- Arrays
- Types
- Creating Textanoid!

Okay, this chapter is now officially over. Get some rest and have some fun, or whatever. I'll be waiting for you whenever you feel like learning some more.

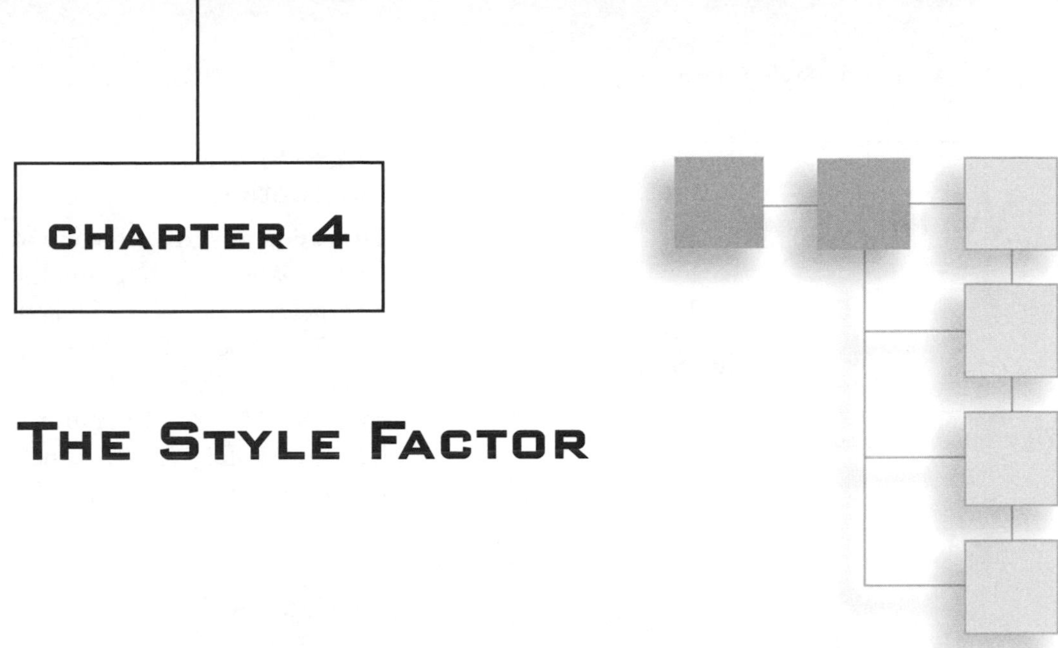

Chapter 4

The Style Factor

I intend to make this chapter short and sweet, so that we can get on to the graphics stuff as soon as possible. A question you may be asking yourself right now is "What is style?" Well, my computer dictionary says that style is "Distinctive and stylish elegance."

In my eyes, style is not just how something looks. Style is how something *feels.* I have looked at one piece of code with contempt and another with understanding, simply because of the way it feels. But, of course, to achieve the feeling, you have to create the look.

Style in computer programming is creating code that is understandable and readable. It is code that you can see day after day and not detest. Style is one of the most overlooked and underappreciated parts of computer programming. This chapter quickly introduces you to the foundations of style, and leads you to create your own.

Another thing to note is that a lot of times, ugly code is also poorly written. It is illogical and tough to understand, and that usually leads to unnecessary bad coding. Try to keep the code neat and your programs will be better.

Developing Style

Everyone has his or her own style of coding; it's an inevitable fact. No two people enjoy their code the same way. Basically, to create a style for yourself, you just have to discover what is right for you and stick with it. Lesson one in the style primer: *Be Consistent.*

Let's start out with the most basic form of style: white space. Examples of white space are tabs, spaces, and new lines. Under most circumstances, you can add as much white space as you like to the beginning and end of most lines. White space can also be included between test commands (such as < and >) and what is being tested, as in Figure 4.1.

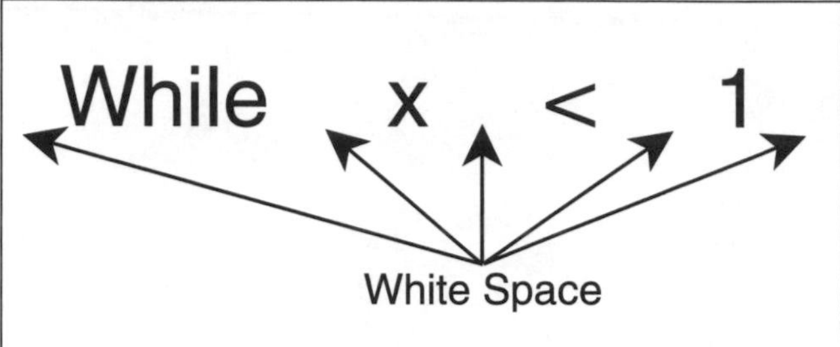

Figure 4.1 White space.

White Space and Indentation

The easiest way to see the use of white space is with examples. The first code snippet I will show you is a block of code using white space. This is what your code should look like. You can ignore what the program actually does and just see how it looks.

```
For x = 0 To 10
        If x > 5
                Print "x is greater than 50; it's equal to " + x + "."

If x > 7
                        Print "Wow, x is really high, it's " + x  + " ."
                EndIf

        Else
                Print "Too bad, x is less or equal to 50."
        EndIf
Next
```

Not a bad looking format, eh? It's pretty easy to figure out which `If` statement goes with which `EndIf` statement, right? Well, the next example is the same code with absolutely no white space. Try understanding it now!

```
For x = 0 To 10
If x > 5
Print "x is greater than 50; it's equal to " + x + "."
If x > 7
Print "Wow, x is really high, it's " + x + " ."
EndIf
Else
Print "Too bad, x is less or equal to 50."
EndIf
Next
```

This code is much harder to understand. If you wanted to actually comprehend its meaning, you would have to look closely and try to follow through the `If` commands. Now, imagine this code block was 10 or 15 times the length of the one I just showed you (programs can commonly grow that large in big games). It would be terribly difficult and a waste of time trying to understand all that code!

One thing you should know: adding white space does not affect the output of the program at all. There will be neither extra spaces nor new lines anywhere in the output of your program. See Figures 4.2 and 4.3 to see the outputs of both programs: white space and no white space.

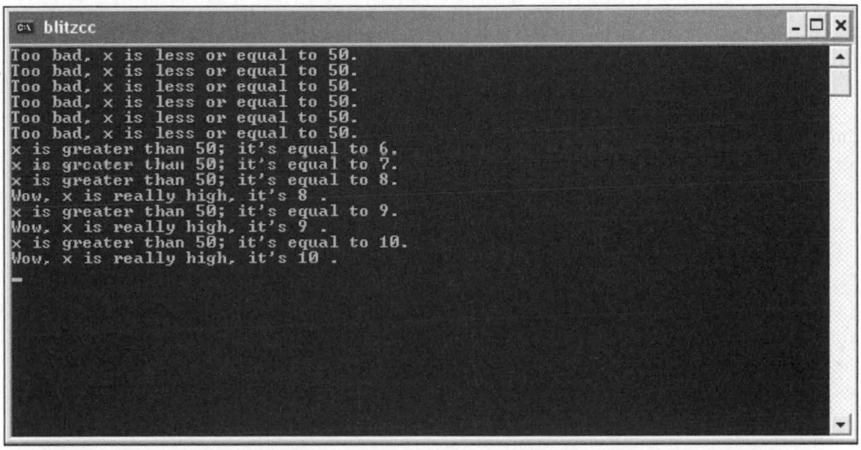

```
blitzcc
Too bad, x is less or equal to 50.
Too bad, x is less or equal to 50.
Too bad, x is less or equal to 50.
Too bad, x is less or equal to 50.
Too bad, x is less or equal to 50.
Too bad, x is less or equal to 50.
x is greater than 50; it's equal to 6.
x is greater than 50; it's equal to 7.
x is greater than 50; it's equal to 8.
Wow, x is really high, it's 8 .
x is greater than 50; it's equal to 9.
Wow, x is really high, it's 9 .
x is greater than 50; it's equal to 10.
Wow, x is really high, it's 10 .
```

Figure 4.2 and Figure 4.3 Output of programs with white space (above) and without white space (below).

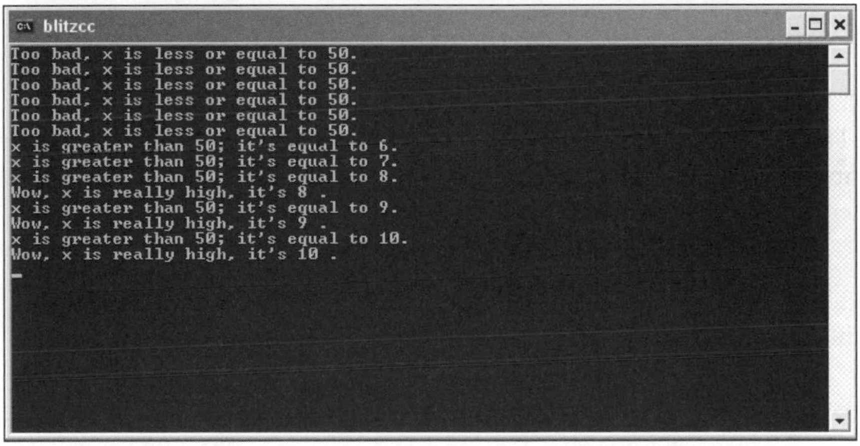

```
blitzcc
Too bad, x is less or equal to 50.
Too bad, x is less or equal to 50.
Too bad, x is less or equal to 50.
Too bad, x is less or equal to 50.
Too bad, x is less or equal to 50.
Too bad, x is less or equal to 50.
x is greater than 50; it's equal to 6.
x is greater than 50; it's equal to 7.
x is greater than 50; it's equal to 8.
Wow, x is really high, it's 8 .
x is greater than 50; it's equal to 9.
Wow, x is really high, it's 9 .
x is greater than 50; it's equal to 10.
Wow, x is really high, it's 10 .
```

Comments

I may have talked a little about comments previously, but I am going to explain them in depth now. Comments, as you know, are simply statements you write within your program to explain what you are doing. In a program, comments look like this:

```
Print "This is a statement." ;this is a comment
```

Make sure you notice the semicolon before the comment. The semicolon is required for every comment; in fact, it is how a comment is identified to the compiler. Comments are used to explain how a part of a program works: it may define what a single statement does, or it may tell what a whole block of statements does. I use almost one comment every other line in my programs; it helps because I often forget what I was trying to do after I finish a program. When I come back a few days or weeks later, the comments are still there to help guide me through my code.

Comments aren't only used to offer help for a single statement. I usually create a block of comments at the beginning of my programs to tell me what the program does. I often use a large box to draw my eyes toward it like this (the full listing for this program is named demo04-01.bb on the CD):

```
;;;;;;;;;;;;;;;;;;;;;;;;;;;;;;;;;;;;;;;;;;;;;;;;;;;;;
; HelloWorld.bb;;;;;;;;;;;;;;;;;;;;;;;;;;;;;;;;;;;;;;
; By Maneesh Sethi;; ;;;;;;;;;;;;;;;;;;;;;;;;;;;;;;;;
; This program prints "Hello World to the screen.;;;;;
; There are no input variables required;;;;;;;;;;;;;
;;;;;;;;;;;;;;;;;;;;;;;;;;;;;;;;;;;;;;;;;;;;;;;;;;;;;
```

As you can see, this box of comments is the intro to a HelloWorld program. I put a box like this at the top of most programs. It tells the reader four things: what the filename is, who the author is, what the purpose of the program is, and any extra info the user needs to use it.

There are some extra rows of information that you can add to the box. Maybe you want to tell the reader what version of the program this is, and you might want to reference others who helped you with it. Perhaps you have some special restrictions on the program ("this program does not run on Windows XP"), or something of that nature.

The next part of the program is that actual code. With comments, it might look something like this:

note

This program is way more complex than it needs to be. There isn't much sense in using functions and variables in a simple Hello World program. The only reason I used functions and variables in this program is to demonstrate the use of comments.

```
;VARIABLES
;The hello string to be printed on the screen
hellostr$ = "Hello World!";END VARIABLES

;MAIN PROGRAM
;Pass "hellostr$" to PrintString function
```

```
PrintString(hellostr$)

;Wait for five seconds before closing
Delay 5000
;END MAIN PROGRAM

;FUNCTIONS
;;;;;;;;;;;;;;;;;;;;;;;;;;;;;;;;;;;;;;;
;Function PrintString(strng$);;;;;;;;;;;
;This function prints the variable strng$
;Parameters: strng$ - the string to be printed
;;;;;;;;;;;;;;;;;;;;;;;;;;;;;;;;;;;;;;;
Function PrintString(strng$)
;Print str$ on screen
Print strng$
End Function
;END FUNCTIONS
```

And there you have it! A fully commented version of Hello World, as in Figure 4.4. Let's take a look at some of these comments.

Pre-Program Comments

Before the actual main program, I create a few commented sections that I call the pre-program comments. This usually includes local variables, global variables, constants, array dimensions, and anything else that you declare before the program starts. For each section, I write a line of code that explains what is following. For example, in demo04-01.bb, I created a section for variables. At the end of the declarations, I add a line of code that tells the reader that it is the end of the section (`END VARIABLES` in the Hello World example).

Figure 4.4 Hello World!

I also comment each variable individually to explain what they do specifically. Adding these simple lines of code makes it much easier to find out what a variable is named and what its value is simply by searching the top of a program.

Main Program Comments

I add some simple comments to the beginning of and inside the actual main program. At the beginning, I add a comment detailing the starting point of the actual program. I also add comments after statements, just as in the rest of the program.

Main program comments also tell where the main game loop begins and ends. I add those comments at the top and bottom of the `While…Wend` loop. Comments are usually included near function calls, such as the call to `PrintScreen(strng$)` in demo04-01.bb. The comments detail which function it calls and what the function does.

Function Comments

The function comments are written at the beginning of each and every function. I usually begin the function definitions after the end of the main program; consequently, I comment the `;FUNCTION` header directly after `;END OF MAIN PROGRAM`.

Refresher: The Difference between a Declaration and a Definition

I use the terms definition and declaration a lot in this chapter, and now is as good a time as any to go over the difference again. A declaration simply refers to or states a function or variable, and a definition actually defines it. For example, the declaration of `PrintString` is `PrintString(strng$)`. The actual definition, however, is

```
Function PrintString(str$)
Print str$ ;Print str$ on screen
End Function
```

In summary, when I refer to the declaration of a function, I am talking about the call to it in code or the title of the function. When I refer to the definition of a function, I am talking about the actual code inside the function.

Before I define any functions, I always create a box that explains the function. On demo04-01.bb the `PrintString(strng$)` function is commented like this:

```
;;;;;;;;;;;;;;;;;;;;;;;;;;;;;;;;;;;;;;;;
;Function PrintString(strng$);;;;;;;;;;;
;This function prints the variable strng$
;Parameters: strng$ - the string to be printed
;;;;;;;;;;;;;;;;;;;;;;;;;;;;;;;;;;;;;;;;
```

As you can see, this block states the name of the function, its purpose, and its parameters. Make sure you add a block like this to the beginning of every function—it makes understanding them a heck of a lot easier.

Function and Variable Names

Naming your variables correctly can help solve a lot of problems in programs. Every once in a while you might come across the problem of not knowing what a variable does. You will have to backtrack and follow your program from the beginning. A way to solve this problem, however, is to name your variables a very easy-to-understand name. This can help reduce, if not eliminate, later forgetfulness.

Names

When declaring and defining variables, make sure you come up with a name that easily describes what the variable does. For example, when writing the Hello World program, I could have easily named the variable anything. I could have chosen names like

```
i$
row$
howareyou$
_123$
hellostr$
```

but there is a reason I didn't. For most of them, they don't make sense. For example, what does `howareyou` have to do with a string? (Unless of course, I am asking how the user is feeling.) You may be wondering, though, why I didn't pick `hellostr$`. In this program, it would have been fine; however, in most programs, the contents of a variable changes. Because they usually do change, creating a variable that tells exactly what is inside the variable rather than what kind of data it contains can create the exact same problem it is supposed to fix. If you changed the program so that `hellostr$` was equivalent to `"Today is my birthday,"` the `hellostr$` no longer makes sense in the context, and you might have to change all of the variable names in the program.

Naming Format

The format of your variable names is largely up to you. There are no rules set in stone as to how to name your functions and variables. The only thing that is required is that your format stays consistent throughout the program.

Here are some different ways to format the same variable.

```
hellostr$
Hello_Str$
helloStr$
HelloStr$
Hellostr$
```

As you can see, these variables are all the same. However, each name is slightly changed.

The first variable is my choice for regular variables. I keep it simple: both words are in lowercase. Some people use two words separated by an underscore (an underscore is a key achieved by pressing Shift+Dash). Others use the two words in different capitalization patterns.

Functions can also be named in similar ways. For example:

```
PrintString
printstring
Print_String
printString
PrintString
Printstring
```

I usually choose the first method for functions: two joined words that are both capitalized. Once again, feel free to pick whichever you like, but make sure you stick with it.

Some other naming formats you might like to vary are constants, global variables, and array names.

I usually keep all the letters in a constant uppercase, like this:

```
Const CONSTANT = 1
```

My global variables are usually the same as regular variables, like this:

```
globalvar = 10
```

A lot of people prefer to add a `g_` to the beginning of global variables. I choose not to, but feel free to try it.

For arrays, I keep it simple. I use one word if possible, and I keep it lowercase.

```
Dim array(numofelements)
```

Summary

Well, I hope you enjoyed this chapter. I tried to give the best explanation of style that I could, and hopefully I did a good job. I wrote this chapter because I believe style and clarity are important to every program, and also because it is tough to find any style primers out there.

Once again, nothing in the chapter must be followed *exactly*. Style is an individual thing; what may appeal to one person may not appeal to the next. Try out all of the given styles and see which one fits you. The only thing I request of you is that you make your program simple and easy to understand. There is no need to use complex commands if you can get away with using a simpler block of code, even if it is a bit longer.

Try to get your programs to read like an essay—keep it organized and straightforward. Make sure you have your pre-program section listed, and try to comment any line of code that requires it. Make sure your style is consistent; if one function has an underscore between two words, make sure the next one does, too. Other than that, keep experimenting, and eventually you will develop your own style.

This chapter covered the following concepts:

- Developing style
- Comments
- Function and variable names

Hey, we just finished Part One. Take a break if you feel like it, or jump straight into Part Two. We are finally getting into graphics; I guarantee it'll be more fun than you've ever had.

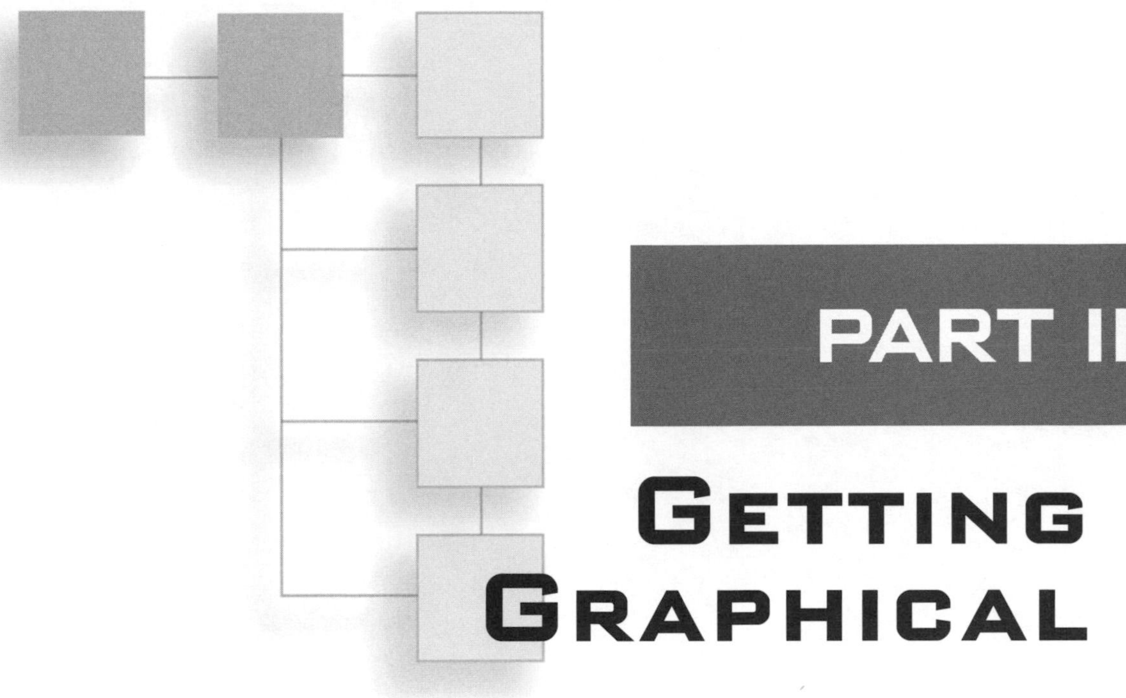

PART II

Getting Graphical

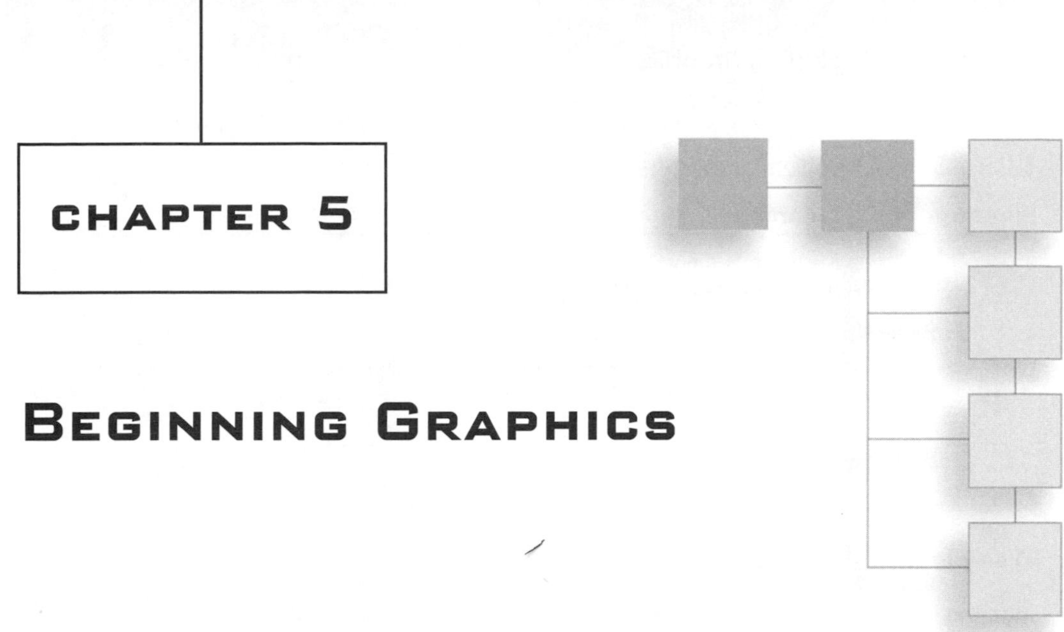

CHAPTER 5

Beginning Graphics

Hey, welcome back! Today, we're gonna start using graphics in our program. This chapter will be a huge jump for you; it teaches you how to initialize the graphical window and how to perform image loads. It also shows you how to display and move your images on the screen.

Anyway, get ready. This chapter is simple, but it's packed with some serious stuff.

Creating the Graphics Window

A graphics window is a little bit different from the text windows we have been using thus far. Unlike the programs we have been running to this point, which could only display text, graphical windows can also display graphics, such as images and pictures. They can also change colors of text.

Every BlitzPlus graphical program contains a line of code that initializes the window. This process basically sets up the window for later use. To set up a graphical window, call the function `Graphics`. `Graphics` is declared as follows:

```
Graphics width, height, color depth, [mode]
```

Table 5.1 details each parameter.

Table 5.1 Graphics Parameters

Parameter	Meaning
`width`	The width of the window in pixels
`height`	The height of the window in pixels
`color depth`	The colors per pixel (in bits)
`[mode]`	The mode of the window: 0 = auto, 1 = full-screen mode, 2 = windowed mode, 3 = scaled-window mode

What Is Initialization?

I use the term *initialization* a lot in this chapter, and you might wonder what it means. To initialize a window is to set the window up, so, when you initialize the graphics in BlitzPlus, you are setting it up. After initialization, you will be able to use graphics in the program.

Width and Height

Let's discuss each parameter in depth. Take a look at `width` and `height`—they affect your program in a huge way, but only a few modes are commonly used. These modes are shown in the following list. You might be wondering why we only use these modes, and there certainly is a reason.

- 640×480
- 800×600
- 1024×768
- 1280×1024
- 1600×1200

If you were to take a ruler to your computer monitor and measure the height and width, you would always come out with a bigger width than height. But the cool part is, the numbers you come up with are always proportional to one another. For example, my monitor is 14.66 inches wide and 11 inches tall. If you divide 14.66 by 11, you get 1.33. This means that my computer monitor's width is 1.33 times its height. This proportion works for all monitors and most televisions as well. Try it out!

Because the monitor's width is longer than its height, all of the pixel values on the monitor must change. If you were to draw a box that was an exact square, it would end up looking like a rectangle on the monitor (its width would be longer than its height). To combat this problem, resolutions make the height pixels larger than the width pixels. The pixels are stretched out a bit, and the square actually looks like a square. Refer to Figure 5.1 to see the monitor's proportion.

Color Depth

note

Take note that setting the color depth only makes a difference in full-screen mode. In windowed mode, the color depth of your game is limited to the color depth of the player's desktop; in full-screen mode, the color depth can be set to any one of the color depths from Table 5.2. To see your desktop's color depth, right-click on your desktop and select Properties. Then find the Settings tab. Your color depth is under Color Quality.

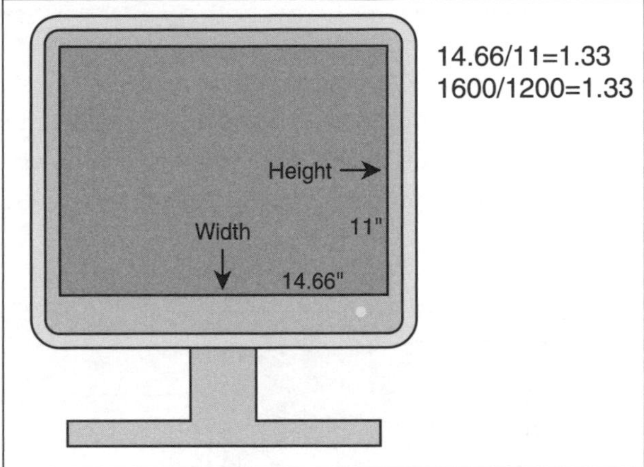

Figure 5.1 The monitor's proportion.

The next variable is color depth. The color depth is actually the number of colors that each pixel can be, and is numbered in bits. See Table 5.2 for the common color depths and their respective color counts.

Table 5.2 Color Depth

Color Depth (Bits)	Colors
8	256
16	65536
24	16,777,216
32	4,294,967,296

note

To determine how many colors each color depth provides, simply raise 2 to the power of the color depth. For example, if you want to find out how many colors a color depth of 8 gives, multiply 2 by itself 8 times (2 × 2 × 2 × 2 × 2 × 2 × 2 × 2) or find 2 to the 8th power (2^8).

note

Although these are the only color depths used commonly today, other depths have been used in the past. For example, some very old games might have run in a color depth mode of 1, which provides only two colors—black and white.

caution

Make sure you know which bit depth you should be using before you select it. If you use a color depth of 8, for example, but the colors in your game need at least a color depth of 16, the colors in your game won't show up.

If you aren't quite sure which color depth to select, BlitzPlus can automatically select the best color depth for you. To have Blitz do this, just omit the color depth or set it to 0. Basically, what this means is, if you know what color depth you need, pick it yourself; if not, let BlitzPlus pick for you.

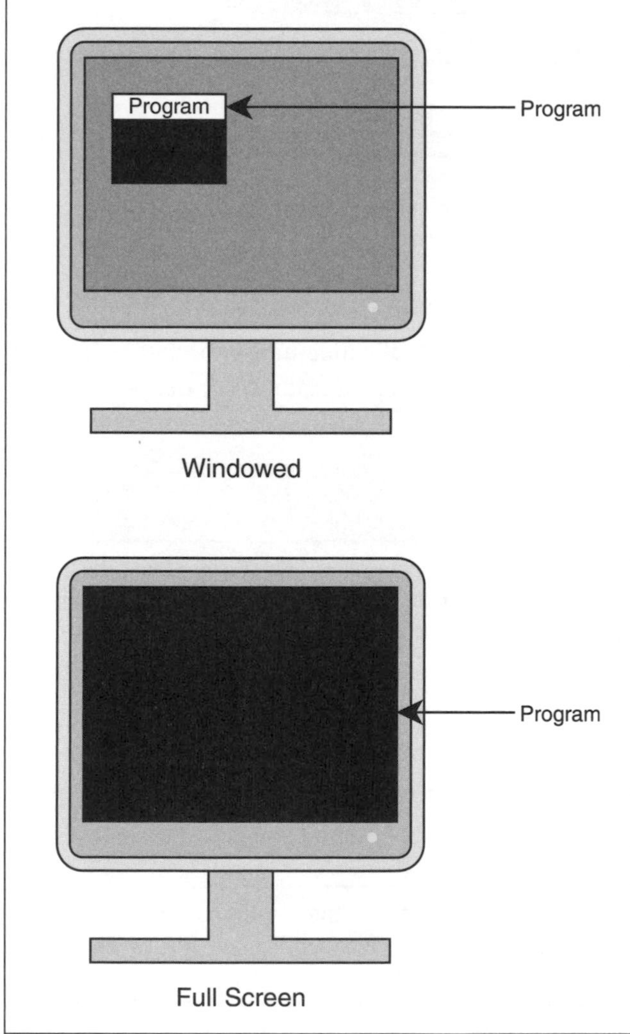

Figure 5.2 Full-screen and windowed modes.

[Mode]

The final variable in the `Graphics` function is the `[mode]` variable. `[Mode]` can be one of four choices—0, 1, 2, or 3. The `[mode]` variable determines how the program window behaves.

0 is `[mode]`'s default value; if you leave `[mode]` blank, it is automatically set to 0. When your program runs in auto mode, it runs windowed in debug mode and full screen otherwise. Figure 5.2 shows the difference in full-screen and windowed modes.

What Is Debug Mode?

I refer to debug mode a lot, and you might want to know what it means. When writing a game, you often come across hidden bugs that are extremely hard to find. Debugging allows you to step through a program line-by-line to discover where your program goes wrong. Debugging offers another reason for using functions—discovering bugs in a program where most of the code is located in functions separate from the main code is much easier than finding bugs in a program where all the code is thrown together in the main function.

When you are planning on debugging a game, you work in debug mode. This allows you to see the line you are debugging and find out what value each variable contains. When you have finished your game, you turn debug off and distribute the actual game. To turn debug mode on and off, check or uncheck Program>Debug Enabled. See Figure 5.3 to see how to enable Debug Mode.

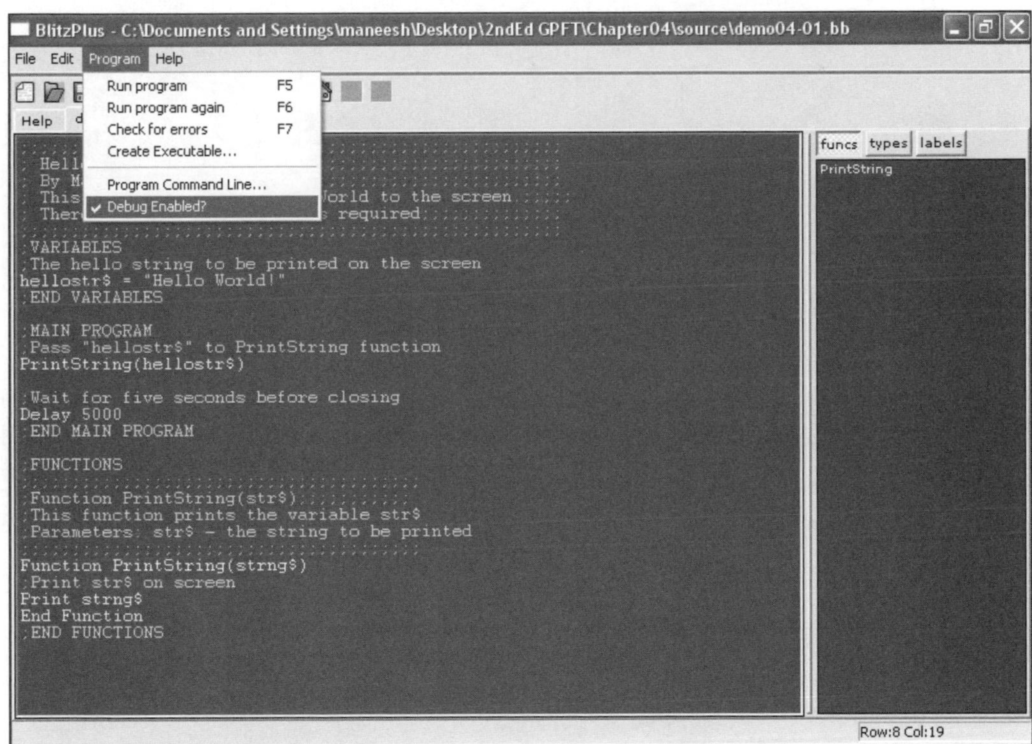

Figure 5.3 Debug mode.

Table 5.3 details each of `[mode]`'s possible values. Selecting 1 for the `[mode]` variable causes your game to run full screen. A game in full-screen mode takes up the entire screen; there are no other windows or programs on the screen. Of course, the other programs are running, they are just hidden under the game. Full-screen mode tends to make the game run faster, but it takes over most of the player's computer screen. Figure 5.4 is a screenshot of a full-screen game.

Table 5.3 [mode]'s Values

Value	Mode Name	Meaning
0	auto	Runs in windowed mode when in debug mode and full screen when not.
1	full screen	Game takes up the full screen—no other programs can be seen.
2	windowed	Game runs as a regular windows program.
3	scaled windowed	Game runs as a regular windows program but also allows resizing, minimizing, and so on.

Figure 5.4 KONG in full-screen mode.

Setting [mode] to 2 forces your game to run like a normal windows program. This means that your program has a toolbar and can be moved around just like a normal program, as in Figure 5.5. However, you cannot resize your window.

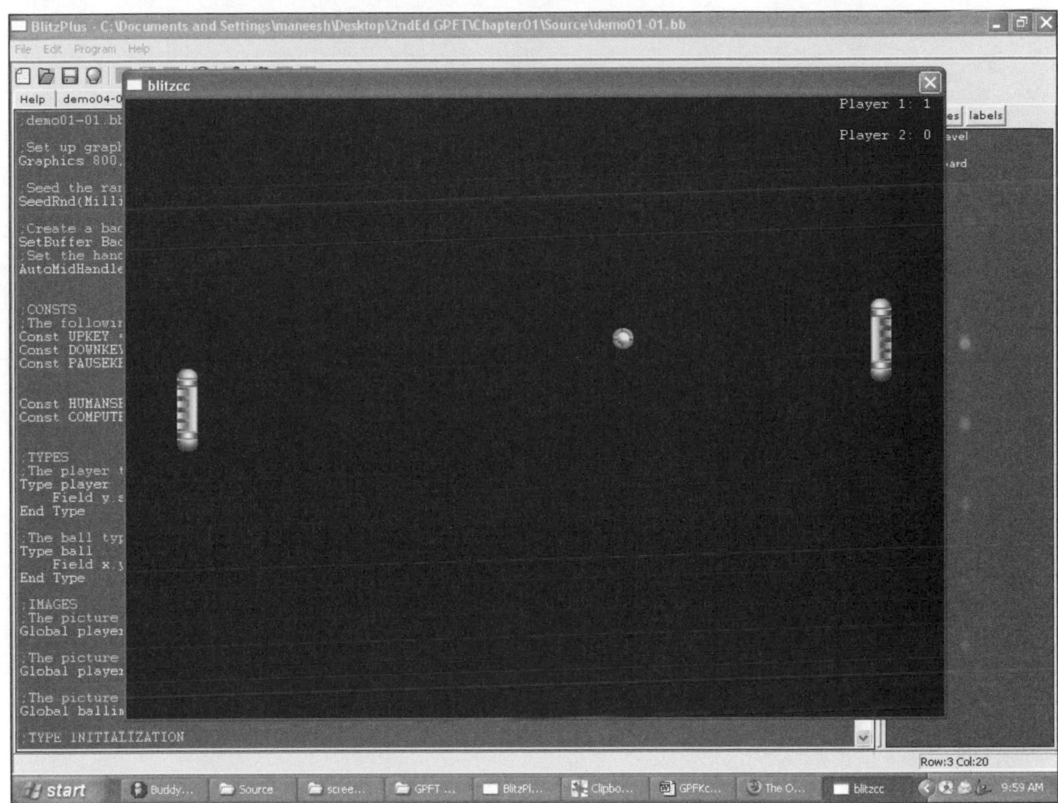

Figure 5.5 KONG in windowed mode.

If [mode] is set to 3, your program acts just like it would if it were set to 2, but you are able to resize, minimize, and maximize the window to your liking. However, this advantage comes at a price—a drastic decrease in speed often occurs as a result of scaled window mode. See Figure 5.6 for an example of what a scaled window could look like.

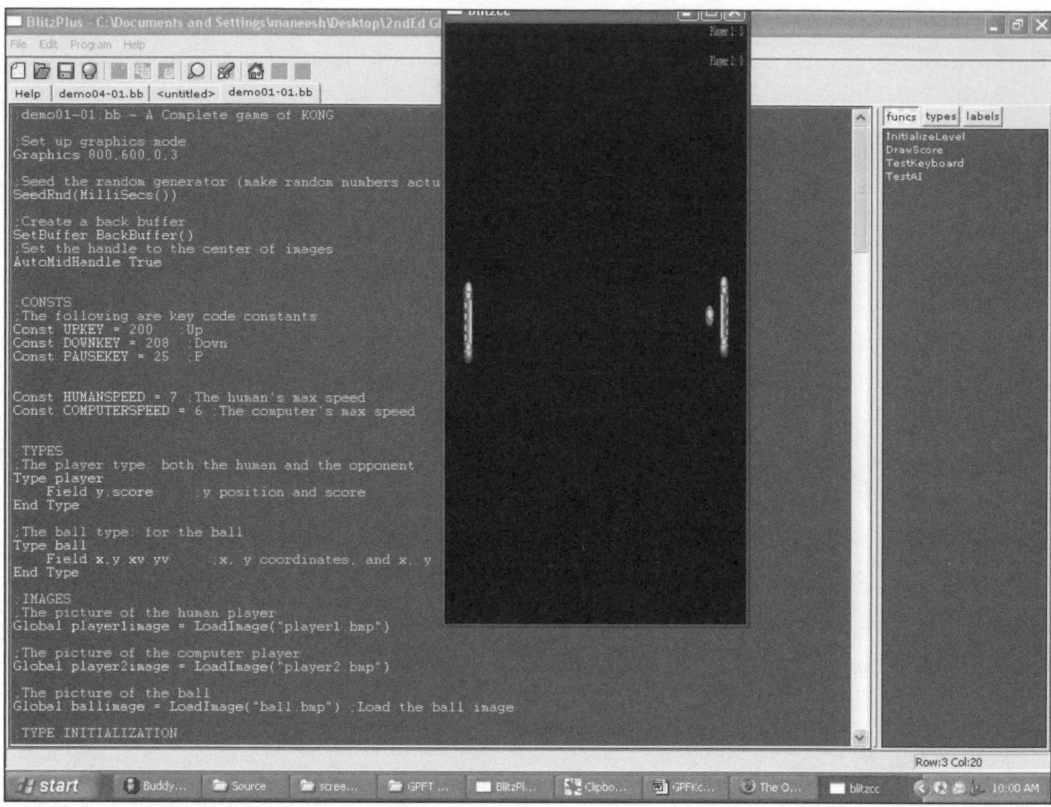

Figure 5.6 KONG in scaled windowed mode.

Images

Whew, that was one big graphics call! Let's get into more specialized graphics stuff. This section explains how to load an image, how to draw it onscreen, and the like. Are you ready?

LoadImage

The first call we will be using is `LoadImage`. This function loads the image of your choice into your program's memory. You must load an image before you can display it or manipulate it in your program. `LoadImage` is defined as this:

```
LoadImage(filename$)
```

Table 5.4 examines each parameter. To load an image, just substitute the file name of the image for `filename$` (make sure the file name is in quotes), and assign it to a variable, like this:

```
Global playerimage = LoadImage("playerimage.bmp")
```

Table 5.4 LoadImage's Parameter

Parameter	Description
`filename$`	The path of the image

Why .bmp?

Unfortunately, the demo version of BlitzPlus only allows you to use bitmap files for image processing. This means that you can't just open some image off your computer and use it, unless it has a .bmp extension. However, there is a simple way around this problem. Just take the jpeg, gif, or png file, and open it in Microsoft Paint or in Paint Shop Pro (which is included on the CD). Then choose Save As and convert the image to a bitmap!

note

Check out what I set the file name variable to. Making the file name just the name of the file (without adding any path info) works only if the image is in the same directory as the game. If not, you might need to include your drive information. It might look something like this:

```
Playerimage = LoadImage("c:\windows\desktop\playerimage.bmp")
```

Even so, I suggest you keep all of your images in the same folder as the game because if you ever decide to distribute your game, the game won't work on other computers unless the user puts the images in the exact same folder as yours.

I usually name my image variables in such a way that I can easily see that they are images. This means I begin my image names with its actual job (*player* in playerimage.bmp) and suffix it with image.

The name that you assign to the loaded image is called a *handle*. Basically, a handle is just an identifier that refers to an image in memory, like in Figure 5.7.

`LoadImage()`, by default, searches directly in the same folder as the location of the BlitzBasic file. If you want to load an image from another directory, you must provide the full path to the image.

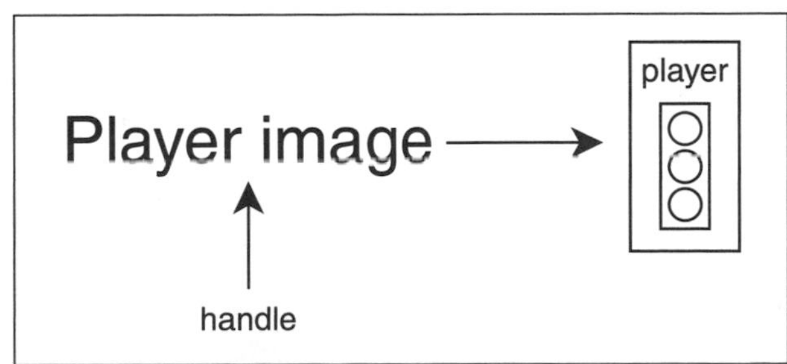

Figure 5.7 A handle to an image in memory.

Okay, now that we've got this `LoadImage` stuff down, its time to actually draw it!

DrawImage

It is pretty easy to guess what this function does: it draws images! Table 5.5 examines each parameter. Let's start with the declaration.

```
DrawImage handle,x,y,[frame]
```

`DrawImage` has a couple of parameters, so let's move on to a discussion of the handle variables.

Table 5.5 DrawImage's Parameters

Name	Description
`handle`	The variable that holds the image
`x`	The drawn image's x coordinate
`y`	The drawn image's y coordinate
`[frame]`	Advanced, leave as 0

Handle

This is a pretty easy-to-understand parameter. Remember when you loaded an image like this?

```
playerimage = LoadImage("player.bmp")
```

Well, the handle is `playerimage`. So, when you're sending parameters to `DrawImage`, use the same image handle that you loaded earlier as the `DrawImage` handle parameter.

X and Y

The x and y parameters work just like most x and y coordinates in BlitzPlus. Using `DrawImage`, your selected image is drawn at the x and y coordinates, as shown in Figure 5.8. Its top-left corner is located at the given x and y values. However, there is a way to center the image so that the image's center is located at x,y.

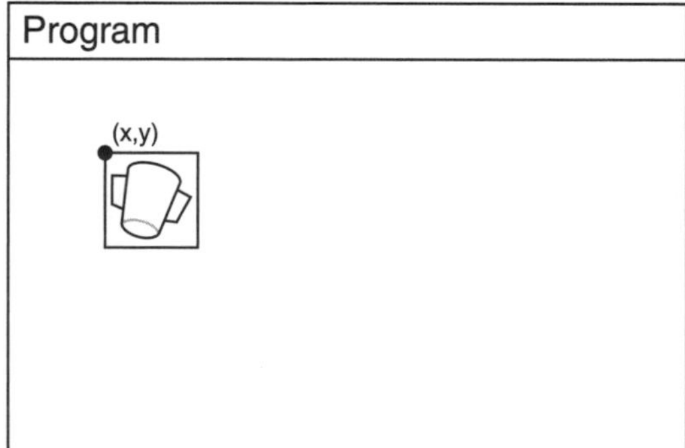

Figure 5.8 The image at x,y.

Very often, you will want to center the image. This is most useful when rotating images because rotating images around the top-left corner looks bad (not to mention trippy) due to the fact that you would expect images to rotate around their centers. Check out demo05-01.bb to see how an image looks when it is rotated around the top-left corner.

Although actual rotation is a more advanced technique and is explained in a later chapter, I am using it to illustrate the use of placing the x and y values in the center of the image. The actual function is called `AutoMidHandle` and is declared like this:

```
AutoMidHandle true|false
```

note

What does "|" mean? | means or. When I say `AutoMidHandle true|false`, I mean `AutoMidHandle` can use either `true` *or* `false`.

To use this function and place the x and y values in the center of the image, call `AutoMidHandle` with the parameter `true`, like this:

```
AutoMidHandle true
```

Easy, huh? And to set the x and y location back to the top left, just call `AutoMidHandle`, like this:

```
AutoMidHandle false
```

It is a good idea to use `AutoMidHandle` because it helps you understand exactly where the images are located. Because your access point is directly in the center of the image, you won't need to worry about the image's width and height as much as if the access point was in the top left.

Table 5.6 details the parameters, and Figure 5.9 shows how demo05-02.bb, which uses `AutoMidHandle true`, works. Look at the difference in Figures 5.8 and 5.9. In Figure 5.8, you can see how the x and y coordinates are located at the top-left corner of the image. In Figure 5.9, the x and y coordinates are in the center of the image. Try running demo05-02.bb and watch how it rotates from the center instead of from the left corner, as in demo05-01.bb.

Table 5.6 AutoMidHandle's Parameters

Name	Description
`true`	Places the x and y coordinates in the center of the image.
`false`	Places the coordinates at the top left of the image.

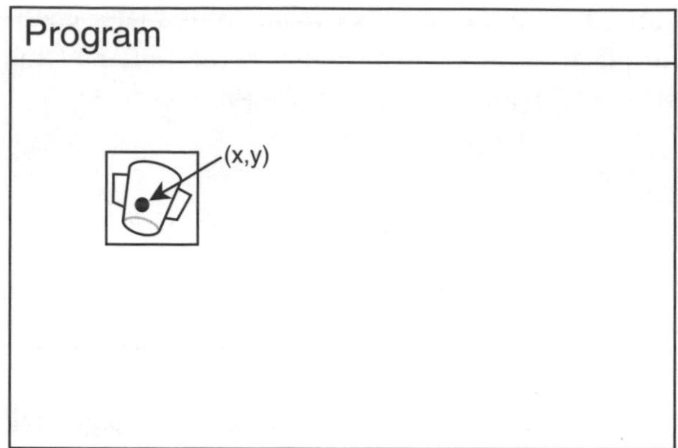

Figure 5.9 The image at x,y with AutoMidHandle set to true.

Make absolutely sure that you place `AutoMidHandle True` before you load the image, otherwise the function won't work.

By the way, there is another function called `MidHandle` that is a lot like `AutoMidHandle`, except that it doesn't set the x and y coordinates to the center of all of the images. It only sets the x and y coordinates to the center of an image you choose. It is declared like this:

```
MidHandle image
```

The image handle you pass it will be reset to the center of the image. Use this if you only want one image handle to be in the center of the image, rather than all of them.

[Frame]

Okay, this command is very advanced. `[Frame]` allows you to draw images that are animated. It is too advanced right now, but we will be going over using animated images very soon!

CreateImage

This function is pretty cool. It allows you to create an image that looks like whatever you want, and use it just like a loaded image. For example, say you wanted to create an image with 100 dots on it. First, call the `CreateImage` function, which has a declaration like this:

```
CreateImage(width, height, [frames])
```

`Width` and `height` explain how big the image is; `[frame]` is used with animated images and should be set to 0 for now. To create the image, call `CreateImage` like this:

```
dotfieldimage = CreateImage(100,100,0)
```

Okay, you now have the handle to the image. Now, you have to populate the field with dots. The following is the full source for the program, which can also be found on the CD as demo05-03.bb:

```
;;;;;;;;;;;;;;;;;;;;;;;;;;;;;;;;;;;
; demo05-03.bb;;;;;;;;;;;;;;;;;;;;;
; By Maneesh Sethi;;;;;;;;;;;;;;;;;
; Creates an image and displays it!
; No input parameters required;;;;;
;;;;;;;;;;;;;;;;;;;;;;;;;;;;;;;;;;;
;INITIALIZATION

;Set up the graphics
Graphics 800,600



;Seed the Random Generator
SeedRnd MilliSecs()

;CONSTANTS
;The length of each block
Const LENGTH = 100

;The height of each block
Const HEIGHT = 100

;The amount of dots in each block
Const DOTS = 100
;END CONSTANTS




;IMAGES
;Create the dotfield image
dotfieldimage = CreateImage(LENGTH,HEIGHT)
;END IMAGES

;For each dot, draw a random dot at a random location
For loop = 0 To DOTS ;For every star
;draw only on created image
SetBuffer ImageBuffer(dotfieldimage)

;Plot the dot
Plot Rnd(LENGTH), Rnd(HEIGHT)

Next
```

```
;Set buffer back to normal
SetBuffer BackBuffer()
;END INITIALIZATION

;MAIN LOOP

;Tile the image until the user quits (presses ESC)

Cls
TileImage dotfieldimage
Flip

WaitKey


;END MAIN LOOP
```

Figure 5.10 shows the dot field.

Figure 5.10 The dot field.

There are a few new functions introduced in this program, and I'll go over them now. The first new function is `ImageBuffer()`.

`ImageBuffer()` acts a lot like `BackBuffer()`. You will learn how `BackBuffer()` allows you to draw on the back buffer instead of the front buffer, so that you can flip the buffers and create animation. Well, `ImageBuffer()` is just like `BackBuffer()`, but instead of drawing on a buffer, you are drawing on an image. `ImageBuffer()` is declared as this:

```
ImageBuffer(handle, [frame])
```

where `handle` is the handle of the selected image and `[frame]` is the chosen frame to draw on (leave as 0 for now). Drawing on an image buffer is a lot like Figure 5.11. As you can see, calling `SetBuffer ImageBuffer(dotfieldimage)` allows you to extract the image from the program and only draw on that. Then, when you finish, you call the `SetBuffer` function again. In this program, I used `SetBuffer FrontBuffer()`, only because there is no page flipping; however, in most games use `SetBuffer BackBuffer()`. Table 5.7 details `ImageBuffer's` parameters.

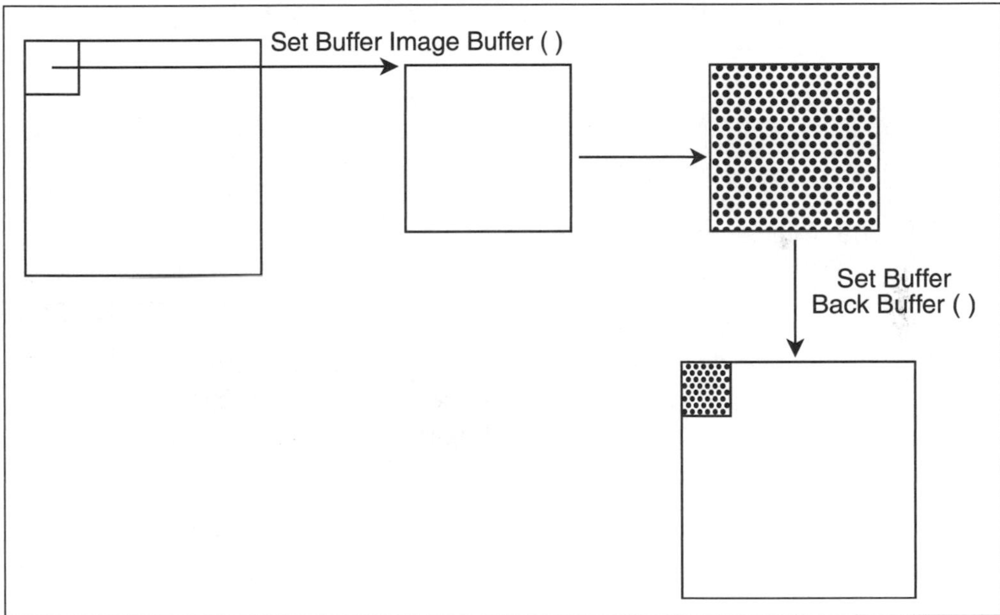

Figure 5.11 `SetBuffer ImageBuffer()`.

Table 5.7 ImageBuffer's Parameters

Name	Description
`handle`	The handle of the selected image
`[frame]`	The chosen frame to draw on; leave as 0 for now

The next function introduced is `TileImage()`. `TileImage()` is declared like this:

```
TileImage handle, [x], [y], [frame]
```

`TileImage` works like this: it takes an image you give it and it places copies of it all across the programming board. Think of it like a chess board—there are only two images on a chessboard, black and white. But these two images are tiled over and over until the entire board is filled with black and white tiles. See Figure 5.12 for a visual aid to tiling, and Table 5.8 for a list of each parameter.

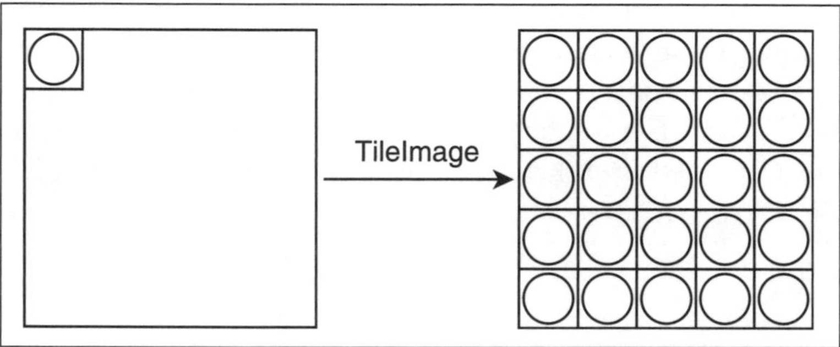

Figure 5.12 The `TileImage` function.

Table 5.8 TileImage's Parameters

Name	Description
`handle`	The image you wish to tile
`[x]`	The starting x coordinate of the tiled image; 0 by default
`[y]`	The starting y coordinate of the tiled image; 0 by default
`[frame]`	The chosen frame to tile; 0 by default

To tile an image, call `TileImage` with the handle of an image you wish to tile. BlitzPlus will take care of the rest. By the way, in later chapters, you will learn how to move the tiled field up and down to simulate movement.

The last part of the program calls the function `WaitKey`. This function simply pauses the program until a key is pressed.

MaskImage

All right, the next function I want to go over is called `MaskImage()`. `MaskImage()` is defined like this.

```
MaskImage handle, red, green, blue
```

`MaskImage()` allows you to define a color of your image as transparent. What does that mean? Let me show you.

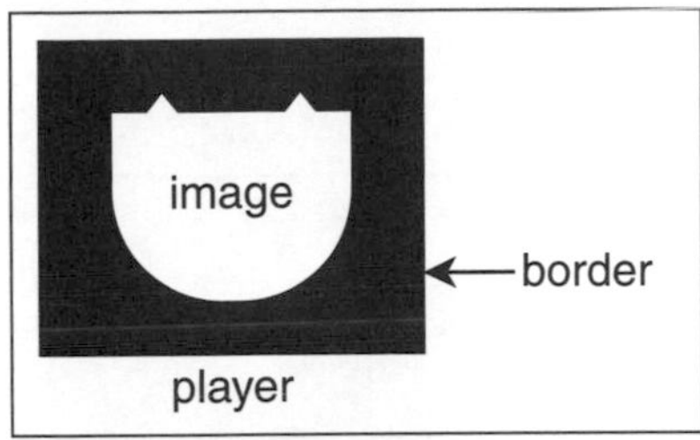

Figure 5.13 An unmasked image.

When you draw or create an image, you always have a border that is not part of the image. See Figure 5.13 for a description of the border. As you can see, the outer part of the image is not used, and should be discarded. You don't want the border to be shown, like in Figure 5.14, do you?

Figure 5.14 A drawn image with a border.

note

Because black is automatically masked by default, the image in Figure 5.14 does not have a purely black border. I added a tiny amount of blue to the image so that the background wouldn't be masked. The RGB value of this image's background is 0,0,10.

Calling `MaskImage()` can get rid of that border for you. Table 5.9 explains each parameter. Because the RGB value of this background is 0,0,10, call the `MaskImage()` function with the correct parameters.

Table 5.9 MaskImage Parameters

Name	Description
`handle`	The image you wish to mask
`red`	The red value of the mask
`green`	The green value of the mask
`blue`	The blue value of the mask

The full program is detailed next:

```
;;;;;;;;;;;;;;;;;;;;;;;
;demo05-05.bb
;By Maneesh Sethi
;Demonstrates the use of masking
;No Input Parameters required
;;;;;;;;;;;;;;;;;;;;;;;
;Initialize graphics
Graphics 640,480


 ;Load Background
lilliesimage = LoadImage("lillies.bmp")
;Draw background
DrawImage lilliesimage,0,0


;Load the frog
frogimage = LoadImage("frog.bmp")
;Center the frog
MidHandle frogimage
;Mask the Frog Image
MaskImage frogimage,0,0,10
;Draw it in the center
DrawImage frogimage,320,240

Flip
;Wait for user to press a button
WaitKey
```

Figure 5.15 is a picture of this program. Beautiful, isn't it? It looks as if the frog is actually part of the image! On the CD, demo05-04.bb is a program without masking, and demo05-05.bb is the same program with masking.

Figure 5.15 An image drawn with a mask.

One thing to note: an RGB value of 0,0,0 is the default. 0,0,0 is the color of black. This means that if your image is drawn with a black border, it will automatically be masked. In other words, try to make all your images have a black background so you don't need to worry about masking images.

You might have noticed the command `Flip` at the end of the program. By default, BlitzPlus draws its information on the back buffer. By using `Flip`, you move the information from the buffer to the screen. We will learn more about this in later chapters.

Colors

Before I end this chapter, I want to teach you how to work with color. Of course, color is an integral part of any program. When using page flipping (which is explained in the next chapter), color takes on an even greater importance.

You need to know some functions before you move on to the next chapter. These functions are `Color`, `Cls`, and `ClsColor`. You also need to understand RGB values.

RGB

When working with color, you will often encounter RGB (red, green, blue) values. These numbers allow you to pick any one of 16 million different colors. That's a lot, huh?

> **Why 16 Million?**
>
> When you are using RGB values, you usually pick a number between 0 and 255 for each color. What does this have to do with the amount of colors? Well, if you multiply 256 by itself three times because there are three colors ($256 \times 256 \times 256$), you get 16.7 million. This means that you have all 16.7 million values to choose from.

When color is used in functions, there are usually three fields for you to enter your choices—red, green, and blue. For each field, you can pick a number between 0 and 255 (256 choices total). The higher the number, the more of that color there will be. For example, if you set the red value to 255 and the green and blue values to zero (255,0,0), you will have a perfectly red color. 0,0,0 is black, and 255,255,255 is white.

Now, you may be wondering how you are supposed to find the exact values for the color you want. Well, there are two ways. You can use guess and check (by putting in guesses for the red, green, and blue fields) or you can use a program, such as Microsoft Paint.

Open Microsoft Paint by going to Start Menu>All Programs>Accessories>Paint. See Figure 5.16 for a visual image of Microsoft Paint and how to open it (the background is Paint, the foreground is the Start menu [your menu will probably be a little different]). Now choose Colors>Edit Colors. A window will pop up. Click where it says Define Custom Colors. Figure 5.17 shows you the custom colors box.

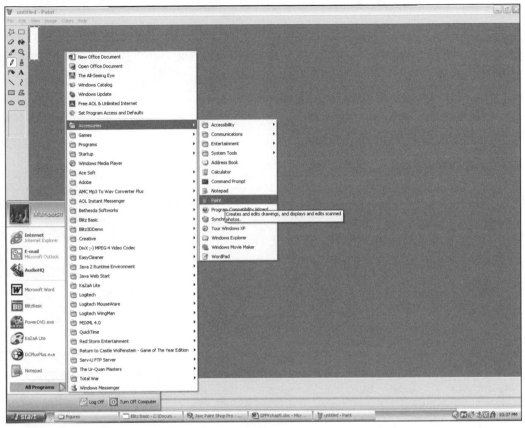

Figure 5.16 Opening Microsoft Paint.

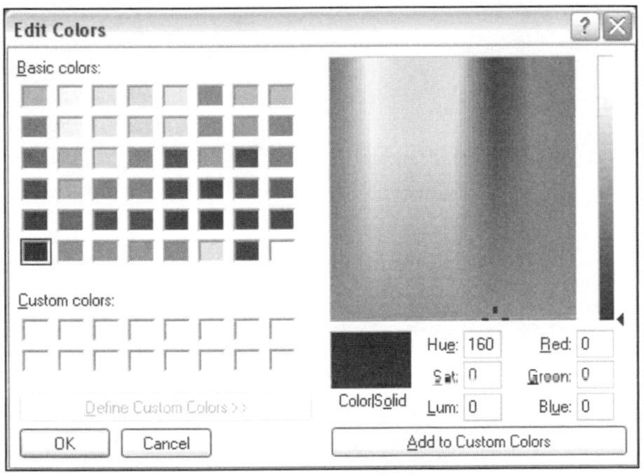

Figure 5.17 Defining custom colors.

Now choose your color, and it should tell you the RGB value on the bottom. If it doesn't work at first, move the scrollbar on the far right, and then proceed to pick your color.

That's pretty much all there is to RGB. You're ready to use color in your programs now.

Color

Color is kind of a fun function. It defines what the default color of the program is. When you draw something, be it lines, shapes, or text (not images), it will be drawn with the defined color.

What can you do with Color? If you want to make the text anything other than white, just use this. Or maybe you want to draw a green triangle. Just set the color to green and draw it! You can change the color at any time.

note

> The default color of any BlitzPlus program (before you call Color) is white (RGB 255,255,255).

You can start with the function declaration.

```
Color red, green, blue
```

See Table 5.10 for the parameters. You will most likely just put in the red, green, and blue values to get your color.

Table 5.10 Color's Parameters

Name	Description
red	The color's red value
green	The color's green value
blue	The color's blue value

Now let's write a program that uses this function. This program will draw a bunch of ellipses with random sizes and colors.

```
;;;;;;;;;;;;;;;;;;;;;;
;demo05-06.bb
;By Maneesh Sethi
;Demonstrates the Color function, draws ellipses
;No Input Parameters required
;;;;;;;;;;;;;;;;;;;;;;
Graphics 800,600

;Seed random generator
SeedRnd (MilliSecs())


;Max width of ellipse
Const MAXWIDTH = 200
 ;Max Height of ellipse
```

```
Const MAXHEIGHT = 200

;Main Loop
While Not KeyDown(1)

;Clear the screen
Cls

;Set the color to a random value
Color Rand(0,255), Rand(0,255), Rand(0,255)


;Draw a random oval
Oval Rand(0,800),Rand(0,600),Rand(0,MAXWIDTH),Rand(0,MAXHEIGHT), Rand(0,1)

;Slow down!
Delay 50
Flip
Wend
```

Pretty cool, huh? Figure 5.18 shows a screenshot from the program. Let's look a little closer. The program first sets the graphics mode and seeds the random generator. Then it defines the maximum width and height of each ellipse. Feel free to change the values.

Next, the game enters the main loop. It first sets the color to a random value, using the line

```
Color Rand(0,255), Rand(0,255), Rand(0,255)
```

This allows the next line to draw an ellipse with the random color. The ellipse function (notice that it is actually called `Oval`—I just like the word ellipse) is defined like this:

```
Oval x,y,width,height[,solid]
```

Take a look at Table 5.11 for each parameter.

Table 5.11 Oval's Parameters

Parameter	Description
`x`	The x coordinate of the ellipse
`y`	The y coordinate of the ellipse
`width`	The width in pixels of the ellipse
`height`	The height in pixels of the ellipse
`[solid]`	Default value is 0; set to 1 if you prefer the ellipse to be filled. Otherwise, the inner region will be transparent.

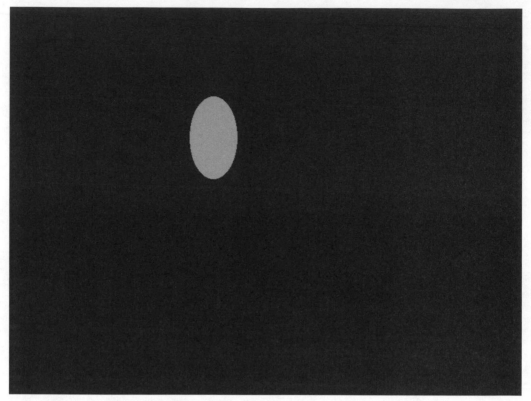

Figure 5.18 The demo05-06.bb program.

Well, that's pretty much it for the `Color` function. Next up—the `Cls` and the `ClsColor` functions.

Cls and ClsColor

We are almost done with this chapter! Before I send you packing, though, I want you to have a bit of basis for the next chapter.

The function `Cls`'s action is pretty simple. All it does is clear the screen. The next chapter goes over it in more depth. The `ClsColor` function works with `Cls` to allow you to change the background of your program.

`ClsColor` is defined like this:

```
ClsColor red,green,blue
```

See Table 5.12 for a description of each parameter.

Table 5.12 ClsColor's Parameters

Name	Description
`red`	The color's red value
`green`	The color's green value
`blue`	The color's blue value

`ClsColor`'s job is to change the background color. This means that you can leave the default black behind and make the background anything you want it to be. To use this function, call `ClsColor` with the red, green, and blue values you want, and then call Cls to actually clear the screen with the background color.

Let's try a program. Demo05-07.bb makes a bunch of colors appear on the screen (along with some advice you should follow). Try it out!

Summary

Okay, you now have a working knowledge of graphics in video games. In this chapter, we learned about a lot of functions: `Graphics`, `LoadImage()`, `DrawImage()`, `CreateImage()`, `ImageBuffer()`, and `MaskImage()`. Believe me, you will find many uses for all of these functions in your games.

This chapter studied the topics of:

- Creating a graphics window
- Loading, drawing, and using images
- Using colors

Next up, we learn about page flipping and basic input. The following chapter is important because you learn about basic animation.

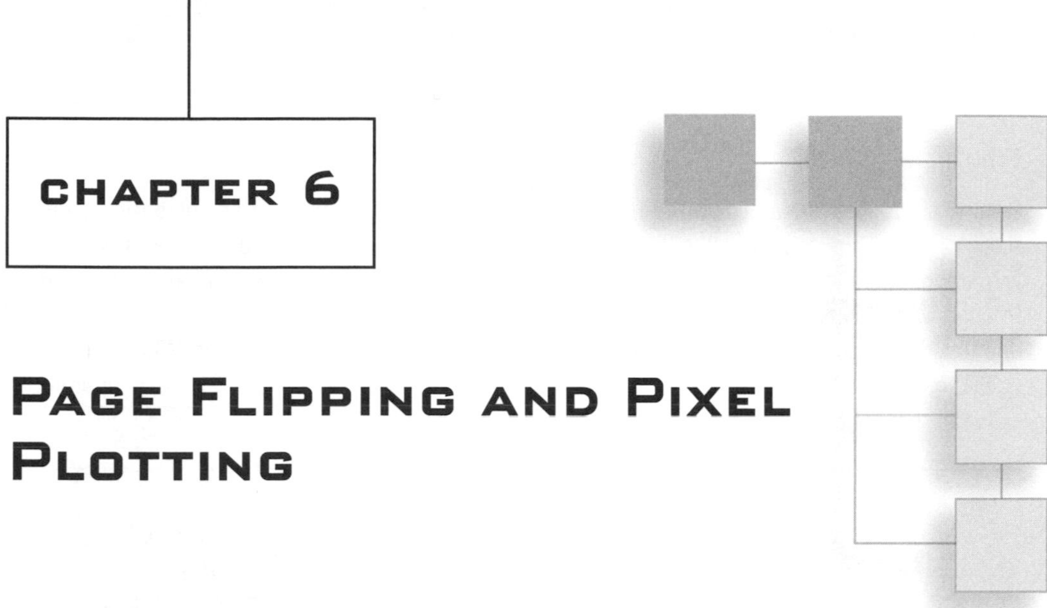

Chapter 6

Page Flipping and Pixel Plotting

This chapter explains animation and pixel plotting. Animation is created through a process called *page flipping*, and it takes each frame of your game and seamlessly ties them together. *Pixel plotting* allows you to draw pixels, which are small dots, directly to the screen.

You have already been introduced to page flipping. Page flipping was discussed briefly in some of the earlier chapters. Page flipping is integral to most high-end games; it is the process that actually produces animation. So, why wait? Let's get started!

Page Flipping

Page flipping is named for its similarities to a flipbook. Remember those? They were the small books that, when flipped through quickly, seemed to make an image move. In a video game, a similar process is used. A picture is drawn on an off-screen image called a buffer. The buffer is the page after the one you are currently looking at in the flipbook. When the pages are flipped, the off-screen image is flipped with the front screen image. It looks like Figure 6.1.

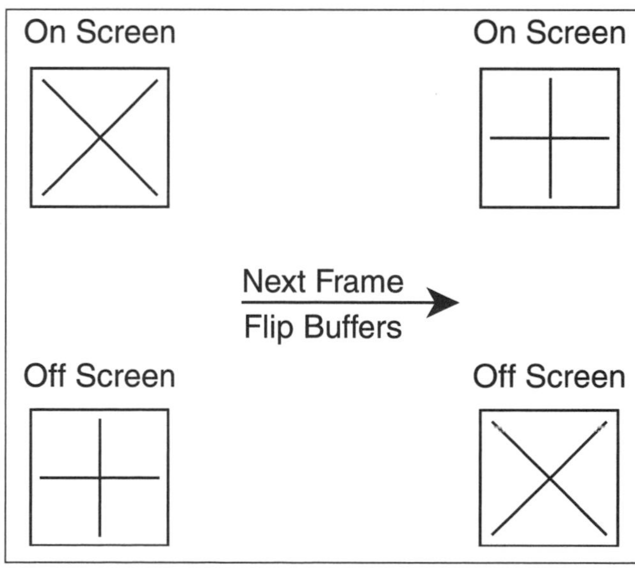

Figure 6.1 Page flipping.

What Is a Frame?

From what you have learned so far in this book, you should know that a frame is basically one scene of animation that is tied with other scenes so quickly that it creates an illusion of smooth animation. Essentially, a frame is a single iteration of the main loop. (In case you forgot, to iterate through a loop is to go through it once—in other words, to perform the instructions of the loop one time.) In a game, you iterate through the loop until the user quits the game. When a frame goes through the loop once, the game has achieved one frame of animation. This loop continues to iterate until the game is over.

Now, you might wonder how this would create animation. Well, this process happens at least 30 times a second. That means that in one second, at least 30 different frames are drawn on the screen. In a flipbook, a single page is the equivalent of a frame. It is impossible to see each individual page when the book is flipped, and the page-flipping procedure is no different. The frames flip quickly so to create smooth animation: it is impossible to tell the difference between the individual frames.

Page flipping has been used in a lot of games in this book so far, but I really haven't explained how it works. Let's start with a sample of what a game looks like without page flipping. This file can be run from the CD; it is called demo06-01.bb:

```
;demo06-01.bb - A not-so-greatly animated ship
;Initialize the Graphics
Graphics 800,600

;load the ship image
shipimage = LoadImage("ship.bmp")

;Seed the random generator
SeedRnd(MilliSecs())

;create a ship type
Type ship
       Field x,y   ;the x and y coords
End Type

;create the ship
ship.ship = New ship

;position the ship randomly
ship\x = Rand(0,800)
```

```
ship\y = Rand(0,600)

While Not KeyDown(1)
	;Clear the screen
	Cls
	;move ship left and right
	ship\x = ship\x + Rand(-8,8)
	;Move ship up And down
	ship\y = ship\y + Rand(-8,8)

	;If ship goes offscreen, move it back on
	If ship\x < 0
		ship\x = 15
	ElseIf ship\x > 800
		ship\x = 790
	ElseIf ship\y < 0
		ship\y = 10
	ElseIf ship\y >600
		ship\y = 590
	EndIf

	;Draw the ship
	DrawImage(shipimage,ship\x,ship\y)
Wend
```

Figure 6.2 shows three frames from demo06-01.bb. Do you see how the ship flashes on and off as it moves? This is because there is no page flipping involved, hence, no animation.

When you run this program, you will probably see nothing on the screen. Try clicking another program and clicking back on the game, and you will start to see the ship. I will explain why this occurs later in the chapter.

By the way, clicking a different program is called *changing the focus* of your computer.

Figure 6.2 A game without page flipping.

Page flipping works because the next frame is drawn onto a back buffer so that the back buffer is flipped with the front buffer quickly and seamlessly. In this example, however, there is no back buffer, so the frame is drawn as the ship is moved. There is no way the computer can draw the image fast enough to provide smooth animation.

Let's get started!

Buffers

I know I've probably gone over this a hundred times, but I think it might be easier to create a section that explains what a general buffer is for future reference. Maybe it will also help you understand the idea.

A buffer is an image. Each frame of your game is drawn onto a buffer; hence, each frame of your game is an image (frame = buffer, buffer = image, frame = image). Now, to create smooth animation (in other words, to make the game actually run), you usually need at least two buffers, although three buffers are used in many modern games.

The two buffers are known as the *front buffer* and the *back buffer*. The difference is that the front buffer is displayed on the screen, and the back buffer is drawn offscreen. Think of it like this: the front buffer is drawn on the top of a pad of paper, and the back buffer is drawn a sheet below, like in Figure 6.3.

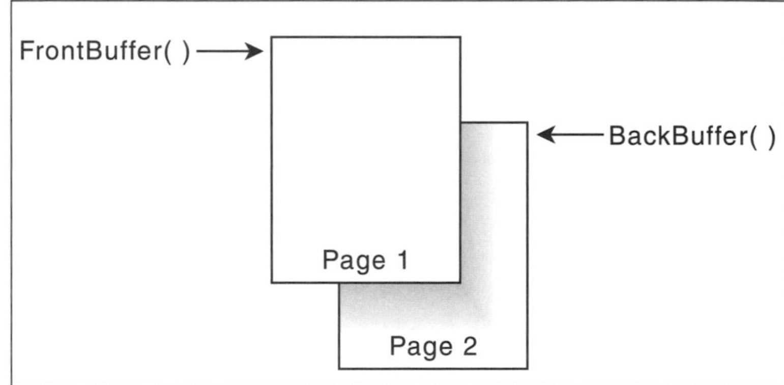

Figure 6.3 A buffer as a pad of paper.

By the way, there is another type of buffer called an *image buffer*. An image buffer is just like any other buffer, but it usually holds an image that you want to draw to manually. So, for example, assume you wanted to have a buffer where you want to draw two rectangles. Well, you can use the image buffer to create two drawn rectangles, and then move the image buffer into the actual game at anytime. The cool thing about image buffers is that they can be any size, whereas the front and back buffers must be as large as the screen.

Buffers are commonly used in page flipping. Because I have already explained the process, I'll go over it very quickly with respect to buffers. Basically, you have two buffers, buffer A and buffer B. Buffer A is the front buffer and buffer B is the back buffer. While you are in the game, the image is drawn to buffer B. At the end of the frame, buffer A is swapped with buffer B, so the old frame, A, is now being drawn in the offscreen. Buffer B is now being displayed. See Figure 6.4 for a visual aid. Notice that the back buffer and front buffer never actually change locations.

This example brings up an interesting point: If the buffers are swapped each frame, shouldn't you have to alternate between drawing on the front buffer and drawing on the back buffer? The answer is no. Only the data is swapped between the two buffers, not the actual buffers themselves. This means that you only draw on the back buffer when producing animation.

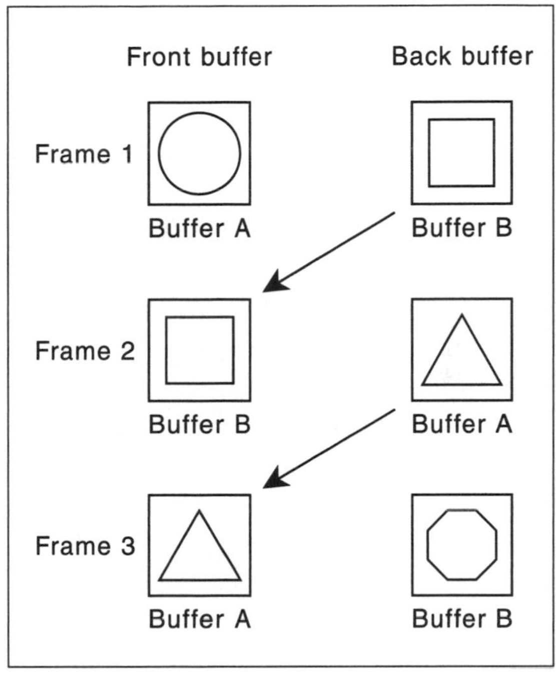

Figure 6.4 Buffers A and B.

SetBuffer

This function is very important, and it is integral to a page-flipping application. Usually, the `SetBuffer` function appears just after the `Graphics` call in any game. The `SetBuffer` command is defined like this:

```
SetBuffer buffer
```

See Table 6.1 for a description of SetBuffer's parameter.

Table 6.1 SetBuffer's Parameter

Parameter	Meaning
`buffer`	Used to designate which surface will be drawn on: can be `FrontBuffer()`, `BackBuffer()`, or `ImageBuffer()`. Default is `BackBuffer()`.

Basically, if you plan to use page flipping, you will probably draw to the `BackBuffer()`. After you initialize the graphics, you will not need to set up the `BackBuffer()` because it is automatically set, but you can explicitly set it like this:

```
SetBuffer BackBuffer()
```

Pretty simple, huh? Well, before we go any further, you need to know more about the three types of buffers:

- `FrontBuffer()`
- `BackBuffer()`
- `ImageBuffer()`

FrontBuffer()

`FrontBuffer()` and `BackBuffer()` are pretty self-explanatory, but it is still imperative that we go over them. As stated before, when drawing on the screen, you draw to a buffer. In most gaming situations, you usually draw to the `BackBuffer()`. The reason is speed: when drawing the `FrontBuffer()`, your game can slow down tremendously.

This `FrontBuffer()` slowdown problem occurred a lot in the old version of BlitzPlus (called Blitz Basic), so as a remedy, they removed the capability of drawing directly to the front buffer. Now, setting the `FrontBuffer()` doesn't do anything because `FrontBuffer()` is just a name for BlitzPlus's `BackBuffer()`.

The reason for the slowdown is easily defined. Think of a cat walking by a bush. Every time the cat moves a little (every frame), the background must be erased, and redrawn with different parts of the bush covered by the cat. This breaks down animation. Using `BackBuffer()`, the bush and cat are drawn hidden from the player, and simply displayed on the screen. You may be wondering why you would ever want to draw to the `FrontBuffer()`, and the reason is that sometimes you just want to draw straight to the screen. In the old Blitz Basic, you would just draw directly to the `FrontBuffer()` because you don't really care about double buffering; you just want straight-up drawing. This is useful when writing a program like demo06-02.bb. However, in BlitzPlus, you must use double buffering, so this program won't work correctly. When you run this program, you draw directly on the `BackBuffer()`, so changes don't show to the screen unless you change the focus of the screen to another program and then change it back again. This program draws a bunch of lines to the screen.

```
;demo06-02.bb - Draws a bunch of random lines to screen.

;Initialize Graphics
Graphics 800,600,0,2

;Draw only to the front buffer
SeedRnd(MilliSecs())

While (Not KeyDown(1))
        ;Set a random color
        Color Rand(0,255),Rand(0,255),Rand(0,255)
```

```
    ;Draw a random line
    Line Rand(0,800), Rand(0,600), Rand(0,800), Rand(0,600)

    ;Slow it down
    Delay(25)
Wend
```

Figure 6.5 shows the output of this program after switching the focus.

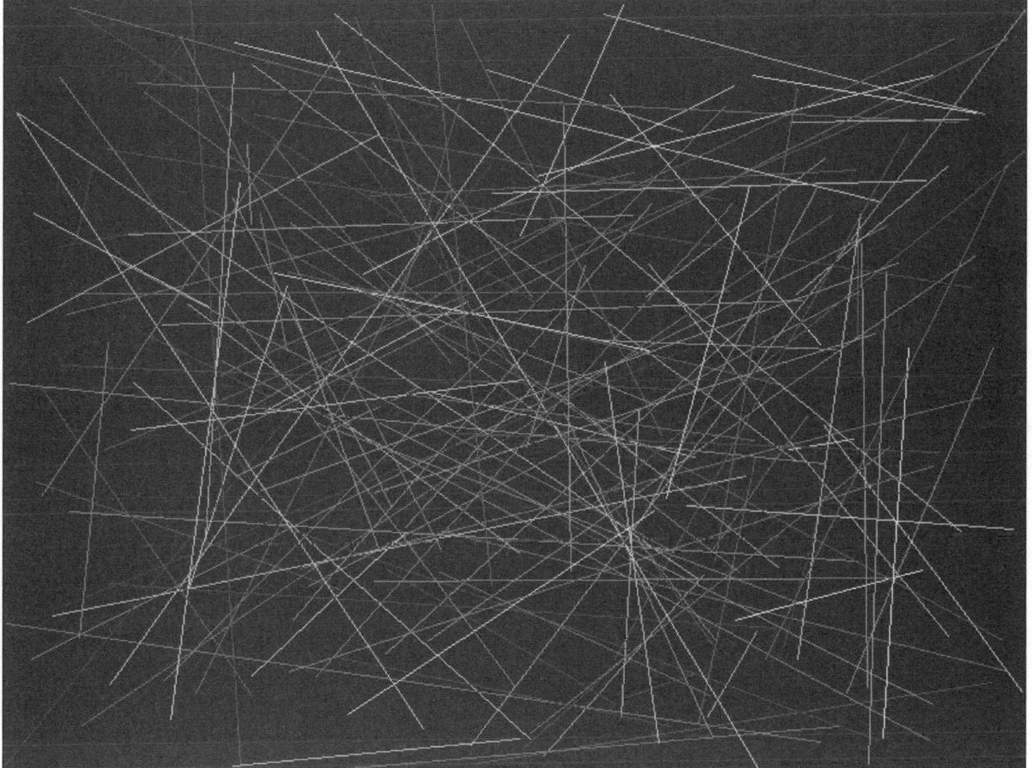

Figure 6.5 The demo06-02.bb program.

note

Because `BackBuffer()` is default, omitting the line

```
SetBuffer BackBuffer()
```

changes nothing—the program still draws on the back buffer.

BackBuffer()

Using `BackBuffer()` is a little different. When you have `SetBuffer` set to `BackBuffer()`, everything you draw is offscreen. This means that whatever you just drew (in this example, the random line) will be invisible. This is the basis of page flipping; now, all you have to do is get that buffer to flip with the front buffer. To do this, use the `Flip` command. `Flip` looks like this: `Flip`. This statement is very powerful—it exchanges all the data in the back buffer with all of the data in the front buffer.

caution

> Be careful where you place the `Flip` command. `Flip` should always be placed near the end of the main loop of your program. In the following example, you can see that `Flip` is located just after the `DrawImage` function. The reason for this is that if you add the `Flip` statement before drawing the image, your program will always flip the blank animation onto the screen. Because `Cls` is used at the beginning of every loop, your frame will delete the spaceship image from the previous frame and have nothing in the back buffer when the next `Flip` command arises. Of course, you can easily solve this problem by placing the `DrawImage` command near the top of your loop.

Now, let's go back to demo06-01.bb in this chapter—the program with the badly animated ship. This program runs poorly because there is no page flipping; hence, no smooth animation. To fix this problem, we will first put in the `Flip` command near the bottom of the loop. The new, fixed version of the game is named demo06-03.bb, and it is located on the CD. Following is the game loop from the game.

```
While Not KeyDown(1)
	;Clear the screen
	Cls

	;move ship left and right
	ship\x = ship\x + Rand(-8,8)

	;Move ship up And down
	ship\y = ship\y + Rand(-8,8)

	;If ship goes offscreen, move it back on
	If ship\x < 0
		ship\x = 15
	ElseIf ship\x > 800
		ship\x = 790
	ElseIf ship\y < 0
		ship\y = 10
	ElseIf ship\y >600
		ship\y = 590
```

```
    EndIf

    ;Draw the ship
    DrawImage(shipimage,ship\x,ship\y)
    Flip

Wend
```

Wow, looks pretty cool, huh? Figure 6.6 shows a screenshot from the program. Let's go through the loop and see how everything works.

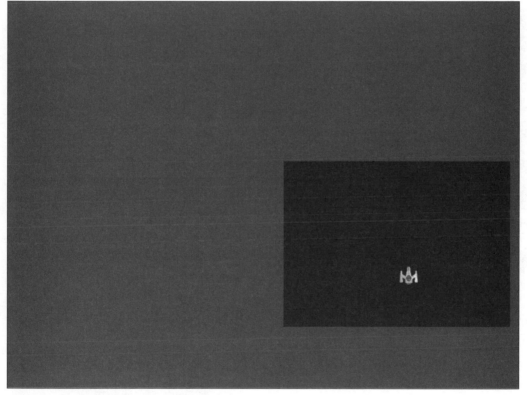

Figure 6.6 The demo06-03.bb program.

The first line after the opening test is:

```
Cls ;Clear the screen
```

This is a very important part of a page-flipping program. Basically, it just clears the screen of anything that was drawn on it in previous frames. It might seem unnecessary, but if you don't include it, the game will look like Figure 6.7.

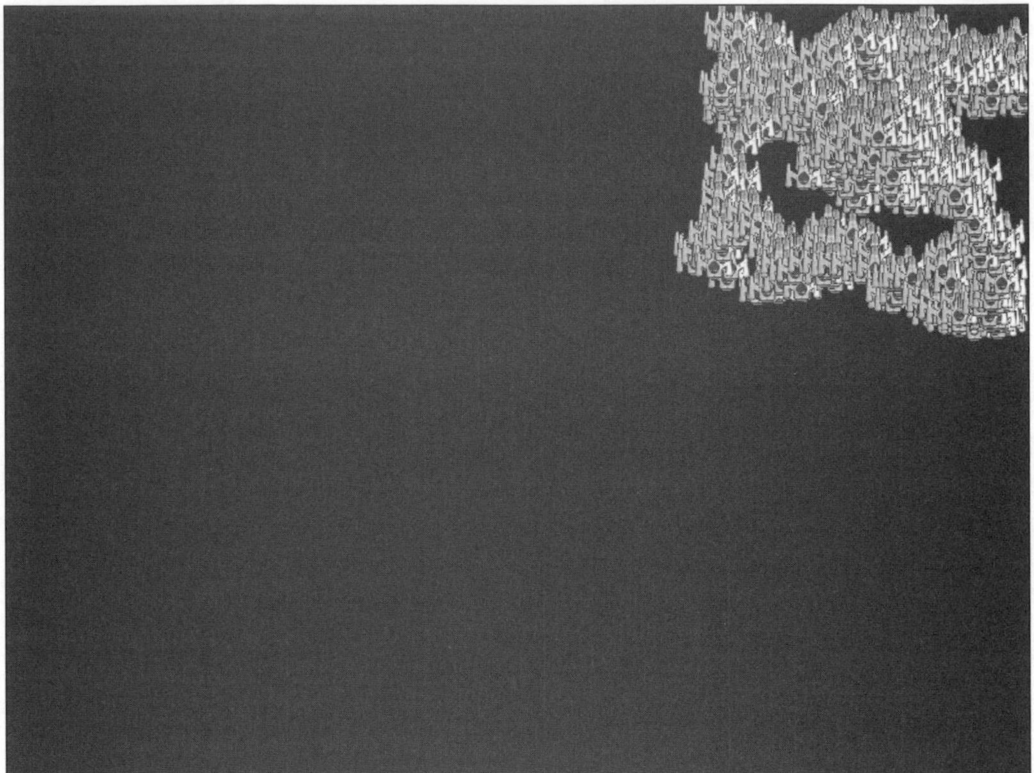

Figure 6.7 Demo06-03.bb without Cls.

As you can see, without `Cls`, trails of the spaceship are very obvious. The `Cls` forces all of these trails to be deleted at the beginning of every frame, so it looks like the spaceship is actually moving. Figure 6.7 shows how the previous program would look without `Cls`.

Just for kicks, you might want to change the color of the background. You can do that using the command `ClsColor`, from the previous chapter.

So, that's a basic overview of page flipping. Now, let's move onto working with image buffers.

Image Buffers

Image buffers are really cool to use, but kind of hard to understand. Say that you have a painting somewhere in your game and you want your player to be able to paint on the painting. Well, using image buffers, you can simply have the player draw on the painting, and the image will show up! Because the painting needs no flipping, the image buffer is just drawn on top of the entire image. It's kind of like a separate layer—the front buffer is drawn underneath it. See Figure 6.8 for an example.

You might also use an image buffer in a space simulator. On many space simulators, you have a mini map in the HUD. A *mini map* is just a small version of the entire playing field that shows where the enemies and power-ups are. Using an image buffer is a good way to draw the mini map and plaster it on top of the HUD display.

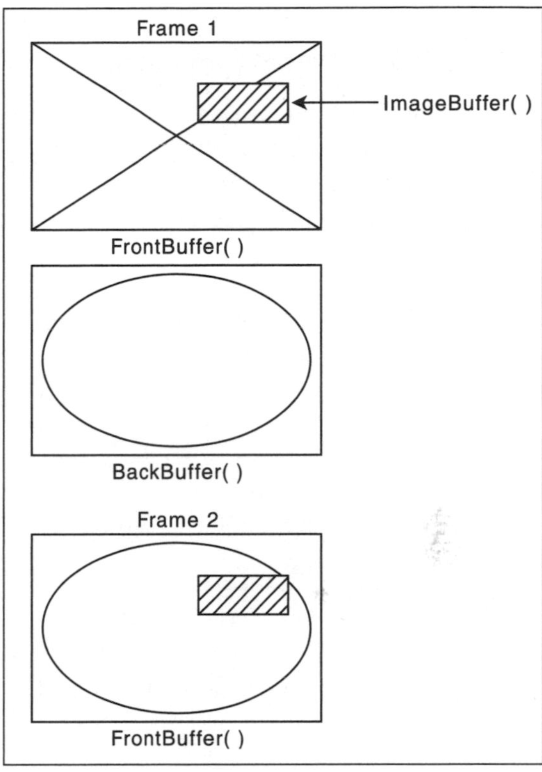

Figure 6.8 Image buffers as layers.

There are two ways to use an image buffer. The first way is to take an image you already have and load it into the image buffer using `LoadImage()`. This allows you to draw on top of a pre-made image. The other way to do this is to create a blank image. Let's start with that.

CreateImage

When you create an image, you are just making a blank image. The created image can be any size; it is not constrained to the size of the back buffer.

The declaration of `CreateImage` is:

```
CreateImage(width,height,[frames])
```

Why Do We Use Parentheses?

You might have noticed that some functions use parentheses and others don't. There is a pretty simple reason for this. Parentheses are required when the function returns a value. When the function does not return a value, the parentheses are optional. For example, `LoadImage()` requires parentheses because it returns the address of the loaded image like this:

```
image = LoadImage("image.bmp")
```

whereas Text doesn't require parentheses at all:

```
Text 0,0, "No parentheses!"
```

When you write functions, it is always good practice to include parentheses, even if they aren't required.

> **Refresher: Optional Parameters**
>
> Recall that an optional parameter is surrounded by brackets in the function definition and is not required. This means that you do not need to include any values with it in your program—it already has a default value. For example, in `CreateImage()`, the default value for `[frames]` is 0. You can change it if you want, but you aren't required to do so.

See Table 6.2 for an explanation of the parameters. The `CreateImage()` function returns the created image, so it must be set equal to an image handle. It might look something like this:

```
wallimg = CreateImage(200,200)
```

Table 6.2 CreateImage()'s Parameters

Parameter	Description
`width`	The width in pixels of the created image
`height`	The height in pixels of the created image
`[frames]`	Optional; the number of frames in the created image; leave this blank for now

Okay, you now have a blank image. Right now, it is just pure black. So, let's put something in it.

The first thing we have to do is switch the buffer to the image buffer. How do we do this? Simple! Just use `SetBuffer`.

```
SetBuffer ImageBuffer(wallimg)
```

We have now selected the image. Let's draw a white square in it (RGB 255,255,255).

```
Color 255,255,255
Rect 0,0,200,200,1
```

Look closely at the call to `Rect`. `Rect`, if you recall, draws a rectangle using the coordinates you feed it. The top-left corner of the rectangle is located at the coordinate position given by the first two parameters, and the bottom-right corner of the rectangle is located at the coordinate position given by the third and fourth parameters. The final parameters define whether the rectangle is solid or unfilled. Because the call in the previous snippet draws a rectangle from (0,0) to (200,200), you probably expect it to draw a white box from the top left of the program to (200,200), that is, the top-left corner of the screen. However, the image buffer is selected into memory because of the preceding call to `SetBuffer ImageBuffer()` instead of the front buffer. What actually happens is that the image buffer, instead of the front buffer, is drawn on. Therefore, the rectangle is drawn onto the image buffer, which is offscreen. The size of the image buffer is 200 pixels × 200 pixels. (We chose this size when we called `CreateImage()`.) Because it is 200×200, the entire square will be filled. If you don't quite understand what is going on, take a look at Figure 6.9.

If you remember from the previous section, to draw in a different color, you must first use the `Color` function. Here, the `Color` function sets the default color to white and the `Rect` function draws in that color.

Next, we must set the program's selected buffer back to the main buffer (the back buffer). This is easily accomplished using `SetBuffer`.

```
SetBuffer BackBuffer()
Flip
```

Remember, the three choices for `SetBuffer` are `FrontBuffer()`, `BackBuffer()`, and `ImageBuffer()`. Also remember that setting the buffer to `FrontBuffer()` does nothing—in most cases, just leave it as the default and do not change the buffer. The `Flip` command flips the image onscreen.

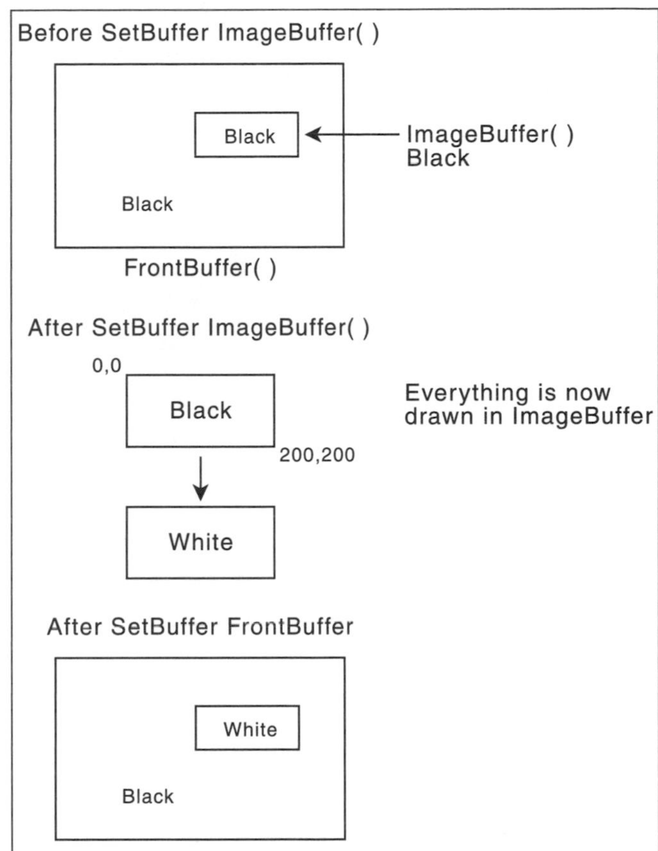

Figure 6.9 Image buffers in memory.

note

> You might be wondering why we switched back to the back buffer. The fact is that if we didn't switch back, we would continue drawing on the image buffer. Any new text or shapes are confined to the small 200×200 pixel box allocated for the image buffer. And guess what happens when we try to draw an image buffer on to itself? You guessed it—absolutely nothing!

All right, now we are back into the front buffer. To finish the program, we have to draw the image buffer onto the main program. For this, we use the function `DrawImage`. If you remember, `DrawImage` is defined like this:

```
DrawImage handle,x,y,[frame]
```

See Table 5.5 from the preceding chapter for a description of the parameters. Here, all you have to do is plug in the handle (`wallimg`) and the x and y values. It looks like this:

```
DrawImage wallimg, 400,300
```

Pretty simple, huh? Take a look at the entire program (with comments). It's also on the CD as demo06-04.bb:

```
;;;;;;;;;;;;;;;;;;
;demo06-04.bb
;By Maneesh Sethi
;Demonstrates CreateImage
;No Input Parameters Required
;;;;;;;;;;;;;;;;;;

;Set up graphics mode
Graphics 800,600

;Set automidhandle to true
AutoMidHandle True

;create the blank image
wallimg = CreateImage(200,200)

;set the buffer to the image
SetBuffer ImageBuffer(wallimg)

;make the color white
Color 255,255,255

;draw a rectangle from topleft to bottomright of buffer
Rect 0,0,200,200

;switch back to back buffer
SetBuffer BackBuffer()

;Flip the image onscreen
Flip
```

```
;draw the image buffer
DrawImage wallimg,400,300


;wait for user To press a key Before exiting
WaitKey
```

tip

Remember to comment your code often. It really helps you and others understand what you are trying to do. When you forget to comment your code, you will often forget what you were writing about. Refer back to Chapter 4, "The Style Factor," for more tips on comments and style.

Looks pretty cool, huh? Figure 6.10 is a screenshot from the program. Let's go over a few things. First start with the graphics initialization. Next, you call `AutoMidHandle` with the parameter `true`. If you remember, `AutoMidHandle` moves the image's handle to the center of the image, so you don't have to do it manually. Think about it—if it weren't for `AutoMidHandle`, you would have to manually find the centering points! For a good exercise, try to find an equation that will help you find those centering points.

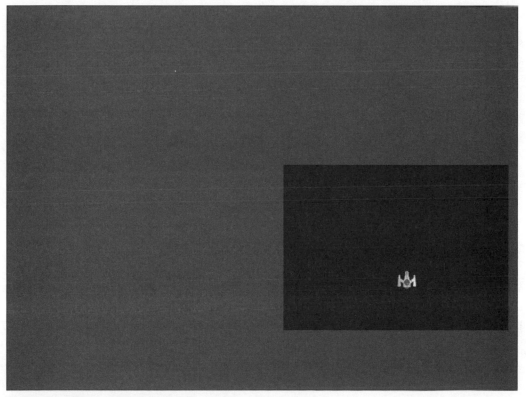

Figure 6.10 The demo06-04.bb program.

Next up, we call `SetBuffer` and start drawing on the image buffer. We set the color to white and draw a rectangle. Then we switch back to the front buffer. Finally, we draw the image on the back buffer so everyone can see it. To show the image, we flip it on the screen. `WaitKey` waits for the users to press a button so they can see the beauty that is a white box before the program closes.

Some of this stuff might be getting tough to understand. See Figure 6.11 for a visual picture. As you can see, there are three checkpoints—before the first `SetBuffer`, before the second `SetBuffer`, and at the end of the program. At the first point, the back buffer is selected and the blank image buffer is not visible. At the second point, the image buffer is selected and filled with the white rectangle and the back buffer is deselected. At the final checkpoint, the image buffer has been drawn onto the selected back buffer and flipped onscreen.

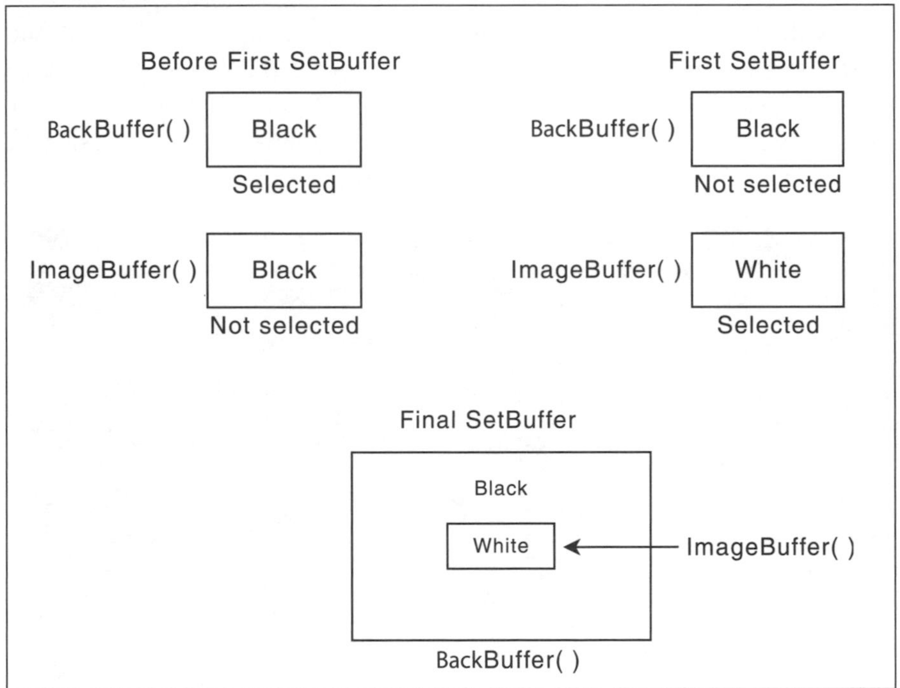

Figure 6.11 A diagram of demo06-04.bb.

Whew, that was a big section on image buffers, and we ain't done yet. The next chapter teaches you how to use image buffers in an even cooler fashion. (I'll give you a hint: it shows you *parallaxing*. When a word sounds like that, it must be cool.)

Before you move on, let's do some other stuff with these buffers.

SaveBuffer

Ever heard of screenshots? Well, screenshots are snapshots taken of a game during runtime. In other words, you are able to save a photo of what the game is displaying. `SaveBuffer()` was made for this—call it and it takes and saves a photo of whatever is going on onscreen.

The definition of `SaveBuffer()` is pretty much what you would expect:

```
SaveBuffer (buffer,filename$)
```

Table 6.3 has a description of each of the parameters. Basically, `buffer` is the buffer that you want saved and `filename$` is the file name of the saved image. `Filename$` is usually a .bmp file.

Table 6.3 SaveBuffer()'s Parameters

Parameter	Description
`buffer`	The buffer you want saved to the hard drive
`filename$`	The file name of the bitmap file

Your choice of inputs for buffer are limited—you can only select `FrontBuffer()`, `BackBuffer()`, or `ImageBuffer(buffer, [frame])`. This allows you to pick which image you want saved, so, if you had an image buffer as a painting on a wall, the player can save just the painting rather than the whole wall. Cool, huh? For example, try this: Add the line

```
SaveBuffer (FrontBuffer(), "screenshot1.bmp")
```

before the `DrawImage` command and the line

```
SaveBuffer (FrontBuffer(), "screenshot2.bmp")
```

after the `DrawImage` command in demo06-04.bb. See Figures 6.12 and 6.13. Notice the difference? Because the buffer is still blank before `DrawImage`, screenshot1.bmp is just blank. However, in the second screenshot, the white box has been drawn. Therefore, you see the white box inside the black background.

note

Note that I am using `FrontBuffer()` instead of `BackBuffer()` here. Actually, the word `FrontBuffer()` is just an alias for the `BackBuffer()`, so they actually mean the same thing. However, using FrontBuffer() here helps emphasize that you are saving what is on the screen, so it helps understanding.

Figure 6.12 `SaveBuffer()` **before** `DrawImage`.

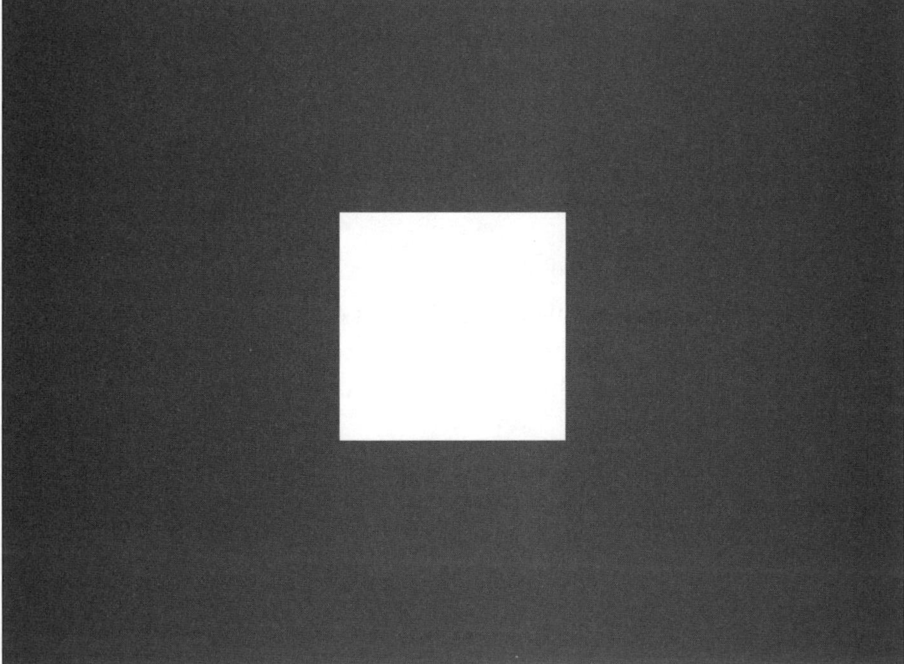

Figure 6.13 `SaveBuffer()` **after** `DrawImage`.

Try messing around with the parameters of `SaveBuffer()` to see how the buffers look at different points in the program.

Okay, so let's use this function in a program. This is on the CD as demo06-05.bb. Let's take a program that draws random squares on the page. Pressing the F10 button will take a screenshot. Ready?

```
;demo06-05.bb - Demonstrates the usage of SaveBuffer()
Graphics 800,600

;Seed the Random Generator
SeedRnd (MilliSecs())

;68 is keycode for f10
Const f10key = 68

;Screenshot number, begin at one (it is an integer)
snnum = "1"

While Not KeyDown(1)

	;Set up random color
	Color Rand(0,255),Rand(0,255),Rand(0,255)

	;Draw a random rectangle
	Rect Rand(0,800),Rand(0,600),Rand(0,200),Rand(0,200),Rand(0,1)

	;Wait a little while
	Delay 45

	;If user presses f10, take a screenshot
	If KeyHit(f10key)
		SaveBuffer(FrontBuffer(), "screenshot" + snnum + ".bmp")

		snnum = snnum + 1 ;Add 1 to the end of the filename
	EndIf

Wend
```

caution

If you try to run this program off the CD, you will get an error when you take a screenshot. This is because it is impossible to write to a CD, so you can't save a screenshot to it. If you want to try out this program, make sure you save it to your hard drive first. If you need to, you can download the source at www.maneeshsethi.com.

Figure 6.14 is a screenshot from the program. Let's quickly review it.

Figure 6.14 The demo06-05.bb program.

We first start with an initialization. The constant `f10key` is set to the key code for the F10 key. We then set the variable `snnum` to 1 to symbolize the screenshot.

Inside the loop, we call `Color` and `Rect` to draw a random rectangle with a random color. The screenshot code appears next, following the `If` statement. The `If` statement determines whether the F10 key has been pressed. If so, it takes a screenshot.

The first line in the `If` control loop is `SaveImage()`. As you can see, this line takes a screenshot of the front buffer. The `string` command works easily also: it creates the file name `screenshotnumber.bmp`, where *number* is the only part that changes. The next line adds on 1 to the end of the string, `snnum$`.

Well, there you have it! Screenshots are really fun to use, and they are good tools for debugging. Say you are not sure what one of your image buffers looks like at one point in your program. Using `SaveBuffer()`, you can easily save the image and see what it looks like at that specific point in time!

Now we are going to move on to the exact opposite of `SaveBuffer()`—`LoadBuffer()`.

LoadBuffer()

LoadBuffer() has a multitude of uses. With LoadBuffer(), you can load a previously saved image back onto your program. Of course, the image can be anything; it doesn't have to have been saved by the same program.

`LoadBuffer()` is a lot like `LoadImage()`, except for one difference. With `LoadImage`, you load the image into a handle that you can assign around in the program, but with `LoadBuffer()`, you load the image directly onto a buffer. Because of this fact, `LoadBuffer()` is normally used to load a title screen. However, you can also use it to make a slideshow projector, or something like that.

LoadBuffer() is defined like this:

```
LoadBuffer (buffer, filename$)
```

Where `buffer` is the buffer you want the image loaded upon and `filename$` is the name of the file you want opened. Table 6.4 also has a handy quick reference of the parameters.

Table 6.4 LoadBuffer's Parameters

Parameter	Description
`buffer`	The buffer on to which you will load the image
`filename$`	The name of the file that will be loaded

Let's write a program that opens all the screenshots provided by the previous listing (the `SaveBuffer()` example with the random rectangles), given that the files are in the same directory.

Start with the initialization section from demo06-06.bb on the CD.

note

While running this program, you might notice that the files load a bit slowly. This is because it has to read the image buffers off the disk. A good exercise is to read these buffers off the disk before beginning the slideshow in order to reduce time between slides. Try it!

```
;demo06-06.bb - A slideshow of images
;Set up graphics
Graphics 800,600

;Set up counter for loading images
snnum = 1

;Grab images from center
AutoMidHandle True
```

This just creates the variable `snnum` with `1` and sets up initialization mode. It also sets `AutoMidHandle` to be true.

Next, we enter the main loop. This part gets kind of tough, so let's take it slow.

```
;As long as another image exists, load it and display it
;Since we are loading it to the front buffer, it will be automatically displayed
While (LoadBuffer(FrontBuffer(),"screenshot" + snnum + ".bmp") <>0)

        ;Write out the name of it
        Text 400,300,"Image screenshot" + snnum + ".bmp"

        ;Move to next image
        snnum = snnum + 1
        WaitKey

      ;Flip image onscreen
      Flip
Wend
```

The test may look weird, but it's not that difficult. Remember that `LoadBuffer()` (and most other image functions) returns 0 if the image is illegal, and returns 1 if the image is legal. So, in this line, we are testing to see whether this `LoadBuffer()` statement is legal. The first time through, it tries to load screenshot1.bmp to the screen. If that works, the loop does not equal zero and continues through the loop so it can be displayed on the screen. If screenshot1.bmp is illegal, the program skips the loop and runs the ending procedure.

The rest of the loop is pretty standard. It first displays some text stating the name of the image, and then the file name is updated. Finally, `WaitKey` is called so the user can choose when to switch to the next slide.

We have one last function to go over. Here we go!

FreeImage

FreeImage releases any image from memory. Simply put, whenever you load an image into your program, you are removing its value as a variable name. For example, you may load an image called skeletonimage. Well, say the game uses levels, and after you get to the second level, the skeletons look different. You can free skeletonimage and use that variable name for the new skeletons.

The declaration of FreeImage is:

```
FreeImage handle
```

See Table 6.5 for a description of its parameter. `FreeImage` releases the memory that is used for the image. This can add speed and memory to your game.

Table 6.5 FreeImage's Parameter

Parameter	Description
`handle`	The variable name of the image you want to free

Using `FreeImage` is very easy; just call it after you are done with an image. I'll show you the basics of it next.

Say you have a bunch of images loaded, like this.

```
image1 = LoadImage ("image1.bmp")
image2 = LoadImage ("image2.bmp")
image3 = LoadImage ("image3.bmp)
```

Well, when you finish with them, throw them away. So, say `image1` is a title screen. You might do something like this:

```
;Display  Title screen
DrawImage 0,0,image1
FreeImage image1
```

Seems easy. Now if `image2` and `image3` are used until the end of the program, don't forget to free them.

```
While Not KeyDown(1)
...
Wend
FreeImage image3
FreeImage image2
```

So, even though it is the end of the program, I still release the final two images. Notice that I released them in the reverse order that I loaded them. This is just a personal taste on my part; it doesn't really make a difference what order you release images.

By the way, you should probably note that it isn't always necessary to use this function. If you never need to use the variable name, and you aren't worried too much about the speed and memory of your game, you might not need to use it. However, using it is very good style, and it is always good to brush up on your housekeeping skills. You never know when this function might keep your program running!

Locking and Unlocking Buffers

This chapter is going to exhaust all the possibilities of what we can do with buffers. We've pretty much gotten to it all, except for locking and unlocking buffers. Locking a buffer refers to a function that makes the buffer unavailable for use to other parts of a program. It might seem bad to restrict access to a buffer, but locking has a big benefit—it allows you to use the following special functions:

- `ReadPixel()`
- `WritePixel`
- `ReadPixelFast()`
- `WritePixelFast`
- `CopyPixelFast`
- `CopyPixel`

Using these functions, you can edit and copy any pixels in your buffers. So, let's get started.

Lock/Unlock

`Lock` and `Unlock` are declared like this:

```
LockBuffer buffer
UnlockBuffer buffer
```

Both `Lock` and `Unlock's` parameters are summarized in Table 6.6.

Table 6.6 Lock/Unlock's Parameter

Parameter	Description
`buffer`	The name of the buffer you want to lock or unlock in order to perform high-speed pixel operations

Well, using these functions makes the buffers unavailable for most uses. The operations it opens up, though, are high-speed pixel operations that allow copying and editing of pixels throughout your buffers. Using `LockBuffer` and `UnlockBuffer` often looks like this.

```
;Time to Lock buffer
LockBuffer BackBuffer()

;Perform Pixel operations

UnlockBuffer BackBuffer()
```

note

> Did you notice that I used `BackBuffer()` for the locked buffer? You might wonder why I chose to lock the back buffer instead of the front buffer. If I were to choose the front buffer, there would be a huge slowdown while producing the pixel effects (not that there were any in the previous example). Also, actually including `BackBuffer()` is not really necessary. If you omit the buffer variable, the locked buffer is set to the default buffer, designated by the `SetBuffer` command (not shown, but assumed to be `SetBuffer BackBuffer()`).

Okay, that's pretty much it on how to lock and unlock buffers. Let's move in to the actual commands.

ReadPixel()/ReadPixelFast()

`ReadPixel()` and `ReadPixelFast()` are the first functions that you need to know to work with pixel editing. These functions read in the color values for individual pixels. Usually, you will use an array to keep track of these values.

Refresher: Arrays

Remember arrays? Arrays allow you to hold massive amounts of similar data in only one variable. Single-dimensional arrays can be declared like this:

```
Dim sdarray(100) ;Create an array with 100 values
```

Or, multidimensional arrays can be declared like this:

```
Dim mdarray(100,3) ;Create an array with 100 rows, 3 columns
```

Figures 6.15 and 6.16 show the difference between the two. One other point—while in a `For...Next` loop, you can easily loop through a multidimensional array like this:

```
For columns = 0 To 3
For rows = 0 To 100
mdarray(rows, columns) = 314 ;set it to whatever you want
Next
Next
```

When you take a look at Figures 6.15 and 6.16, notice how the array index has nothing to do with the value of the array. The index on Figure 6.16 is on the right of the array, and is the row and column value put together (in such a way that row 2 column 3 is index (2,3)). The value inside the array is `x`, which literally means that it can be *any* value, any number, or even a string.

Array	Index
x	0
x	1
x	2
x	3
...	...
x	100

Figure 6.15 A single-dimensional array.

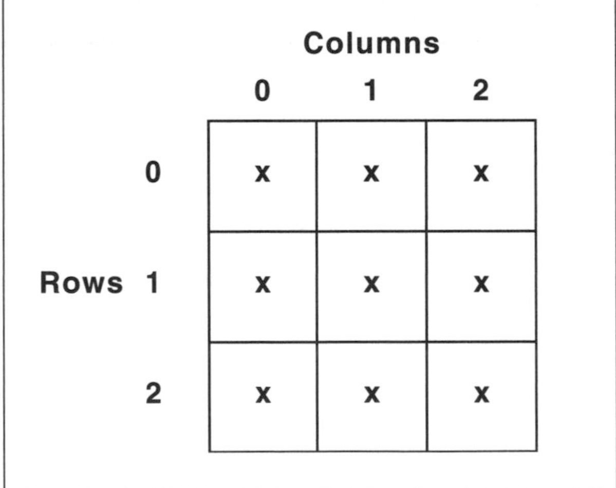

Figure 6.16 A multidimensional array.

note

Yeah, these two functions sound very similar, don't they? Well, there is a small and subtle difference between them. For one, the `ReadPixelFast()`function is faster than the `ReadPixel()` function. Why? Because "fast" is appended to it? That may be a reason, but another is that `ReadPixel()` doesn't truly require the buffers to be locked to perform actions; however, `ReadPixelFast()` does. This allows it to be more tuned toward locked buffers, and therefore, a bit faster. In other words, it is usually a good idea to lock your buffer and use `ReadPixelFast()` rather than leave it unlocked and use `ReadPixel`. This goes for all the other `Pixel` and `PixelFast` functions also.

caution

Watch out! If you decide to use one of the `PixelWrite` functions without locking the buffer, you are making a huge mistake. This command will only work on a locked buffer. If the buffer is not locked, your computer might crash while running this program. Also, watch for the coordinates of the read in pixels. If they are located offscreen, you will only get garbage values.

`ReadPixel()` and `ReadPixelFast()` are defined like this:

```
ReadPixel (x,y,[buffer])
ReadPixelFast (x,y,[buffer])
```

caution

Make sure you include the parentheses when you use this command. Recall that when you set a variable to the return value of a function, you must include parentheses around the parameters.

See Table 6.7 for an explanation of the parameters.

Table 6.7 ReadPixel() and ReadPixelFast()'s Parameters

Parameter	Description
x	The x coordinate of the read-in pixel
y	The y coordinate of the read-in pixel
[buffer]	The buffer you want to read in from (BackBuffer(), FrontBuffer(), or ImageBuffer())

Well, we really can't do anything so far, so I'll show you quickly how to use it. This code sample assumes that you are reading the pixels from a bitmap in the top-left corner.

```
Dim pixelarray(GraphicsWidth(),GraphicsHeight())

LockBuffer BackBuffer() ;Buffer MUST BE LOCKED
For cols = 0 To GraphicsHeight()
	For rows= 0 To GraphicsWidth()
		pixelarray(rows,cols) = ReadPixelFast (rows,cols)
	Next
Next
```

GraphicsWidth() and GraphicsHeight()

Did you notice the two new functions, `GraphicsHeight()` and `GraphicsWidth()`? These two functions are very useful and pretty simple: they return the height and width of the screen. So, for example, if you initialize the graphics at the beginning of your program like this:

```
Graphics 800,600
```

then

```
x = GraphicsWidth()
```

will set `x` to 800 and

```
y = GraphicsHeight()
```

will set y to 600. You might wonder why you should use `GraphicsHeight()`and `GraphicsWidth()` instead of plugging in the numbers 800 and 600. The reason for this is that you might change the resolution while you're testing your program. If you change the resolution without changing the 800 and 600, your program will become corrupt and could easily crash your computer! Just remember, it's better to make your code as general and portable as possible.

Pretty cool, huh? This code saves the pixels of the entire screen into `pixelarray`. The `for` loops work so that each pixel of one column is read before the next line is read. Figure 6.17 shows a visual example of this. Well, using only `ReadPixel()/ReadPixelFast()`, you can't really do much with it yet, so let's go on to `WritePixel/WritePixelFast`!

WritePixel/ WritePixelFast

`WritePixel` and `WritePixelFast` are just the opposite of `ReadPixel()/ReadPixelFast()`. Both of these functions are normally used together to copy and paste pixels from the screen.

`WritePixel` and `WritePixelFast` are defined like this:

```
WritePixel x,y,rgb,[buffer]
WritePixelFast x,y,rgb,[buffer]
```

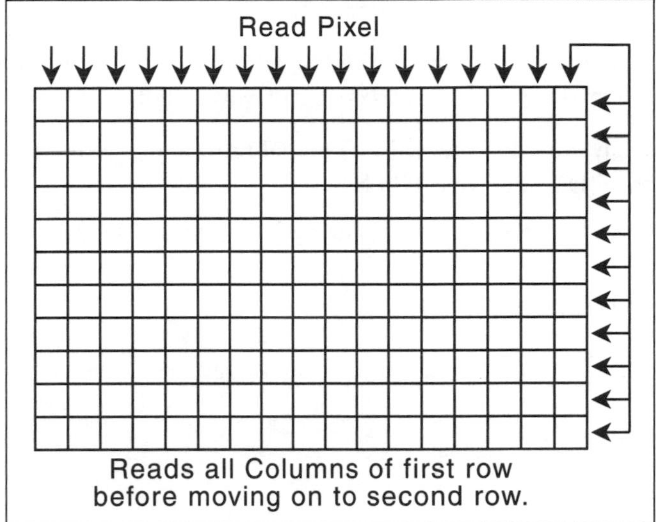
Read Pixel
Reads all Columns of first row
before moving on to second row.

Figure 6.17 The reading process of the for loops.

note

You will notice that you never retrieve the return value of the `WritePixel` functions, unlike the `ReadPixel()` functions which do have variables that retain those variables. For this reason, parentheses are not necessary around the parameters of `WritePixel/WritePixelFast` when they are called, although they are allowed.

See Table 6.8 for a description of each parameter. The only parameter I want to examine is `rgb`. As you know, when you used `ReadPixel()/ReadPixelFast()`, we stored all of the pixels in an array. The array index of the individual pixel you want to draw should be input for this parameter. In other words, use the `pixelarray` array for the `rgb` parameter.

Table 6.8 WritePixel/WritePixelFast's Parameters

Parameter	Description
x	The x coordinate of the plotted pixel
y	The y coordinate of the plotted pixel
rgb	The color of the plotted pixel (often stored in an array)
[buffer]	The optional buffer you want to plot to

Using `WritePixel/WritePixelFast` is very simple. You just include the parameters! Here is an example:

```
WritePixelFast 0,0,pixelarray(0,0)
```

This line will draw, at the top-left corner of the screen, the pixel that was stored at 0,0 when `ReadPixel()/ReadPixelFast()` was called.

Okay, now let's get into an actual sample program. This program is fully commented on the CD as demo06-07.bb:

```
; demo06-07.bb - A ReadPixelFast/WritePixelFast Example

Graphics 350,350,0,2

Text 0,0, "Press any key to use ReadPixel"

;Flip text onscreen
Flip

;wait for user to do something
WaitKey

;load rectangle image
image =LoadImage("rectangle.bmp")

;Draw the intro screen
DrawImage image,0,0
DrawImage image,100,100

;Flip image on screen
Flip

;Hold up  a second
Delay (1000)

;Create a pixel array that will hold the entire screen
Dim pixelarray(GraphicsWidth(),GraphicsHeight())


;lock the buffer REQUIRED
LockBuffer

;Copy all of the pixels of the screen to the array
For rows=0 To GraphicsWidth()
```

```
    For cols=0 To GraphicsHeight()

        ;Copy the current pixel
        pixelarray(rows,cols)=ReadPixelFast(rows,cols)
    Next
Next

;Unlock the buffer
UnlockBuffer

Cls

Text 0,0, "Press another key to copy pixels backwards"

;Flip text onscreen
Flip


;Wait for key press
WaitKey

;Lock the buffer to allow WritePixelFast
LockBuffer

;Use WritePixelFast to redraw the screen
;using the color information we got earlier
For rows=0 To GraphicsWidth()
    For cols=0 To GraphicsHeight()
        ;Draw the current pixels
        WritePixelFast rows,cols,pixelarray(GraphicsWidth()-rows,cols)
    Next
Next

;Flip image onscreen
Flip

; Unlock buffer after using WritePixelFast
UnlockBuffer

Text 0,0, "Press a key to exit"

;Flip text on screen
```

```
Flip
WaitKey
```

Figure 6.18 shows a screenshot taken from the program.

Figure 6.18 The demo06-07.bb program.

This program is probably pretty tough to understand, so let's go over it. The program begins by initializing the graphics and loading the images. After it loads the images, it delays the program so that the user can see what will be copied. After this, it calls `LockBuffer` and uses `ReadPixel()`/`ReadPixelFast()`, like this:

```
LockBuffer
For rows=0 To GraphicsWidth()
        For cols=0 To GraphicsHeight()
                pixelarray(rows,cols)=ReadPixelFast(rows,cols)
        Next
Next
UnlockBuffer
```

Remember, `LockBuffer` *must be called* before using `ReadPixelFast()`. Just like all of the other pixel-plotting functions, `ReadPixelFast()` requires a locked buffer; otherwise, the program will not act correctly and might crash. `ReadPixelFast()` works in the same way as the example a few sections ago: it copies all of the pixels in a row before moving to the next row. Each of these pixel values is stored in an array. Now, because you are finished with `ReadPixelFast()`, you must call `UnlockBuffer` so that you can use other functions.

Now you are finally to the `WritePixelFast` section.

```
LockBuffer
For rows=0 To GraphicsWidth()
	For cols=0 To GraphicsHeight()
		WritePixelFast rows,cols,pixelarray(GraphicsWidth()-rows,cols)
	Next
Next
UnlockBuffer
```

This snippet of code works just like `ReadPixelFast()`. It first locks the buffer, and then it begins a couple of `for` loops that count from each column in a row before moving to the next one. The `WritePixelFast` command is where the cool part of the program is, though.

```
WritePixelFast rows,cols,pixelarray(GraphicsWidth()-rows,cols)
```

I did something very wrong in this function call. Can you guess what it is? The problem is, I used the `rows` and `cols` variable in the x and y coordinate parameters. This is a bad idea, but I wanted to make a point. In this case, it works, but this is a rare case. Usually, you won't be copying the entire screen, but only a small part of it. You need to use another `for` loop to get the correct x and y values, or you can increment the x and y values inside the existing `for` loops.

The first few parameters of this function are simple: it draws the pixel at the given x,y position. (The x,y position is held in `rows,cols` and is determined by the `For...Next` loop.) The parameters in the array are not as simple, however. This program draws the pixels in the array backwards on the left side, so you use the `array` value

```
pixelarray(GraphicsWidth()-rows,cols)
```

to draw each pixel backwards flipped from the left to the right but still the same from top to bottom. If you wanted to make the image flip vertically, you would call `WritePixelFast` with this `pixelarray`:

```
pixelarray(rows, GraphicsHeight()-cols)
```

Pretty cool, huh! You are now done with the `WritePixel/WritePixelFast` and `ReadPixel/ReadPixelFast` functions, although there is another if you would like to research it. It is called `CopyPixel/CopyPixelFast` and is defined like this:

```
CopyPixel src_x,src_y,src_buffer,dest_x,dest_y,[dest_buffer]
CopyPixelFast src_x,src_y,src_buffer,dest_x,dest_y,[dest_buffer]
```

If you want to use this function, try to use this definition and make a few sample programs!

Using Buffers: A Paint Program

You have learned a lot about buffers in this chapter. You'll now put all of your knowledge together and write a full program. The program that is demonstrated is a paint program. It allows the player to draw content in the main part of the screen, and the picture can be saved. This program is on the CD—demo06-08.bb. I recommend that you have this program open on your computer while reading this section, because it will be much easier to understand if you have the full source directly in front of you.

Let's brainstorm for a bit on what we will need in this program. In this case, let's think about how we will accomplish our goal—to create a program that allows the user to draw. First, for this program, I gave the user the option to draw in five colors: green, red, blue, black, and white. The user can change the selected color by clicking each color's corresponding number. The color choice menu will look something like Figure 6.19.

```
Choose your Color
1 Green
2 Red
3 Blue
4 Black
5 White
```

Figure 6.19 A prospective color menu.

> **Why Do We Draw Outlines?**
>
> You have probably noticed that the last figure was a drawing instead of a screenshot. I am trying to simulate the actual creation process of a program or game. Before writing the first line of code, you should know exactly what you are writing. A good way to do this is to draw an outline of your program. Pictures are best, but words are good also. Try to illustrate what will happen when the user performs an action. Also, show how the characters or images in the game will look.

We will definitely need to add some text that tells the user what he chose as his selected color. Also, just for kicks, we will add a position indicator that informs the users where the mouse is located.

note

Mouse? What the heck is that? The mouse (most likely) is the thing in your right hand that you are using to pinpoint objects on the screen. For this program, I was forced to use a mouse to make it user-friendly. Because you do not know how to use the mouse in programs, don't worry about it. You will be educated on using input via the mouse in a later chapter.

Let's put the position and selection indicator next to the color choice menu. This will be our HUD, which stands for heads-up display. The outline for the full HUD is shown in Figure 6.20.

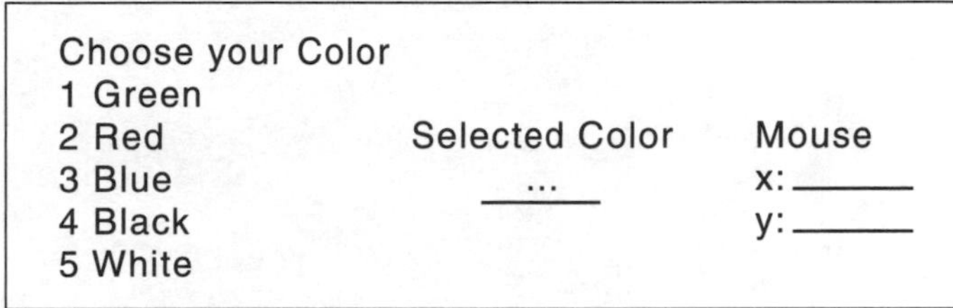

Figure 6.20 A full HUD outline.

What Is a HUD?

A HUD, otherwise known as a heads-up display (a phrase taken from the cockpits of fighter jets), is the control panel for most programs. The word "HUD" is normally used in the context of video games, but it carries over to other programs, such as this one. The lower-left corner of Figure 6.21 shows an example HUD, which tells the user's statistics. In essence, the HUD is the section of the screen that is devoted to information, rather than game play.

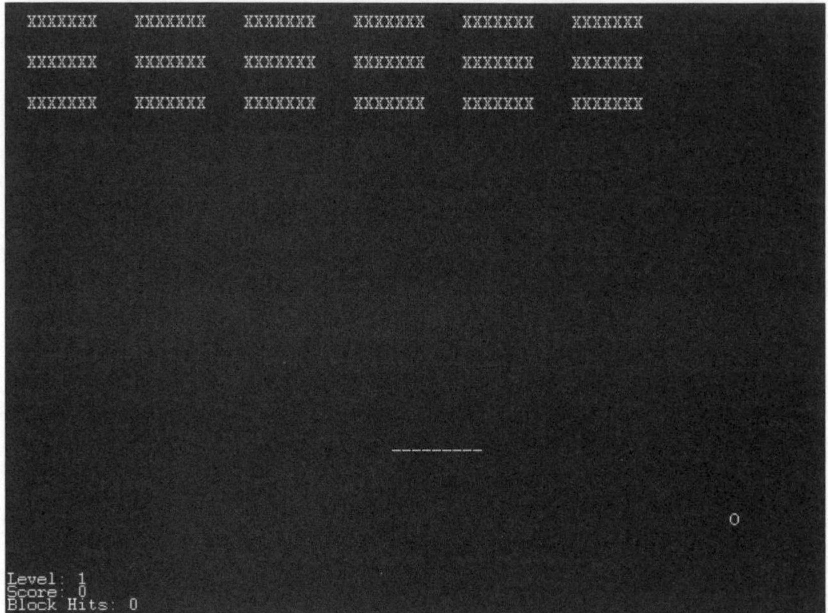

Figure 6.20 A full HUD outline.

Well, because the top part of the window is reserved for the HUD, let's have the rest of the window reserved for painting. Now we need to get into actually writing the program.

Initialization

As always, we begin with a properly marked initialization section. The initialization section begins with the `Graphics` call.

```
;Set up Windowed Graphics Mode
Graphics 640,480,0,2
```

You might have forgotten what all four parameters mean. The first two refer to the width and height of the program, respectively; the third parameter deals with the amount of colors in the program; and the fourth parameter selects the mode. In this program, the window is created with a 640×480 resolution, with the default amount of colors, and it is set up as windowed mode (`2` indicates windowed mode).

After the `Graphics` call, set up the back buffer. Next, we define the constants:

```
;Backbuffer
SetBuffer BackBuffer()


;Constant the keyboard keys
```

```
Const ESCKEY = 1, ONEKEY = 2,TWOKEY = 3,
THREEKEY = 4, FOURKEY = 5, FIVEKEY = 6, F10KEY = 68

;Tweak these numbers
Const BUFFERHEIGHT = 480, BUFFERWIDTH = 640
```

You can change the height and width of the buffer if you want. Tweaking these values will change the amount of space you have to draw on (Note: the drawing space cannot be more that 640×480).

Next, we must load all the images that will be in our program. In this case, the user can choose between five colors: green, red, blue, black, and white. Thus, we will need to load five images of those colors. When the users decide to draw one of the colors, they will in actuality be drawing an image of the color on the screen.

```
;Global Images
Global greenimage = LoadImage("greencolor.bmp")
Global redimage = LoadImage("redcolor.bmp")
Global blueimage = LoadImage("bluecolor.bmp")
Global blackimage = LoadImage("blackcolor.bmp")
Global whiteimage = LoadImage("whitecolor.bmp")
```

Figure 6.22 shows how big each color image is (8 pixels by 8 pixels).

Figure 6.22
A single color image.

We also need to load the mouse cursor image. This image will show the user where his mouse is located (as opposed to the mouse x and y indicator, which *tells* the user where the mouse is).

```
Global mouseimage = LoadImage("mousearrow.bmp")
```

The final image is the most important. This image is the canvas on which the actual drawing takes place—I call it a picture buffer. The picture buffer is not loaded; instead, it is created. It is produced in this call:

```
; Create a blank image that will be used to draw on
Global picturebuffer = CreateImage(BUFFERWIDTH,BUFFERHEIGHT)
```

Now that the picture buffer is loaded, all we need is a call to `ImageBuffer` with `picturebuffer` as a parameter to make the screen capable of drawing to. This call will occur in a later function.

We now move to the variables section of our code. There is only one defined variable: `selectedcolor`.

This line of code automatically makes green the default color.

```
;Automatically select green as the color
Global selectedcolor = 1
```

The five color choices are

1. Green
2. Red
3. Blue
4. Black
5. White

The final section of the initialization part of the code is a section called *masks*. If you remember, a mask allows the program to change the color that is made transparent on the images. In this program, there are two masks.

```
MaskImage mouseimage,255,255,255 ;Mask the white around icon
MaskImage blackimage,255,255,255 ;change mask so black is visible
```

The first mask is in the mouse image. The background of the mouse image is white, so we need to mask it to get rid of the white block that normally would exist behind the cursor. See Figure 6.23; it shows the mouse cursor and the mask. The second mask is a little bit different. Because the black image is pure black, and the default mask color is black, I changed the mask so none of it would be deemed invisible. If I had left this off, drawing with black would have made no difference.

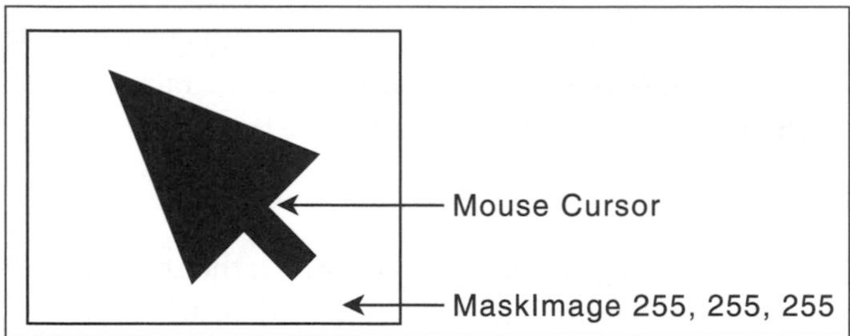

Figure 6.23 The masked mouse cursor.

Well, that's the end of the initialization section. Next, we are in the main loop.

Main Loop

Usually I try to make the main loop as short as possible; this program is no exception. The main loop only makes a few calls to other functions. It also draws the picture buffer on the screen. See Figure 6.24 for an outline.

```
;MAIN LOOP
While Not KeyDown(ESCKEY)

;Clears the screen
Cls
;Draws everything text
related
DrawAllText()

;Draws the mouse cursor
DrawMouse()

;Test what keyboard buttons
were pressed
TestKeyboardInput()

;Test to see if user pressed any mouse buttons
TestMouseInput()

;draw the picture
DrawImage picturebuffer,0,100

;flip the buffers
Flip
Wend
;END MAIN LOOP
```

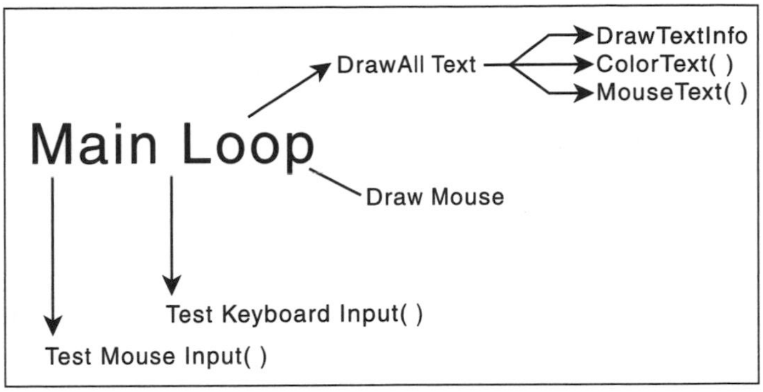

Figure 6.24 The main loop.

As you can see, the main loop itself does almost nothing; rather, the radiating functions do the work. Table 6.9 details all of the functions and what they do.

Table 6.9 Demo06-08.bb's Function List

Function	Description
DrawAllText()	This function calls all of the functions that relate to the text panel. This is the same as drawing the HUD.
DrawMouse()	This function draws the mouse cursor wherever the user positions the mouse.
TestKeyboardInput()	This function tests all of the keyboard input. It is normally used when the user wants to take a screenshot or change the selected color.
TestMouseInput()	This function tests where the users move the mouse and if they press the left mouse button (in order to draw).

Along with the function list, this main loop also includes some of the intrinsic calls to most video game programs. `Cls` clears the screen and `Flip` flips the front and back buffers. The program also draws the picture buffer on the screen:

```
;draw the picture
DrawImage picturebuffer,0,100
```

The picture is drawn at 0,100, so that it doesn't mess with the HUD.

Well, that is the end of the main loop! The final part of the program is the function list.

Functions

Functions, functions, functions. There are a lot of them.

The first called function is named `DrawAllText()`. This function calls the other functions that draw the HUD. `DrawAllText()` is defined as this:

```
;;;;;;;;;;;;;;;;;;
;Function DrawAllText()
;Calls functions that draw HUD of program
;No Parameters
;;;;;;;;;;;;;;;;;;

Function DrawAllText()

;Draws the color choices
DrawTextInfo()
;Draws the selected color
ColorText()

;Draws the location of the text
MouseText()
End Function
```

Of course, this doesn't make any sense without seeing `DrawTextInfo()`, `ColorText()`, and `MouseText()`. `DrawTextInfo()` looks like this:

```
;;;;;;;;;;;;;;;;;;
;Function DrawTextInfo()
;Displays the user's color choices
;No Parameters
;;;;;;;;;;;;;;;;;;
Function DrawTextInfo()
;Display color choice
Text 0,0, "Press the number of the color you wish to draw"
```

```
Text 0,12, "Colors:"
Text 0,24, "1. Green"
Text 0,36,"2. Red"
Text 0,48,"3. Blue"
Text 0,60,"4. Black"
Text 0,72,"5. White"
Text 0,84,"Press F10 to save image (text WILL NOT be saved)"
End Function
;END FUNCTIONS
```

`ColorText()` is defined like this:

```
;;;;;;;;;;;;;;;;;
;Function ColorText()
;Chooses the selected color and writes it on the scren
;No Parameters
;;;;;;;;;;;;;;;;;
Function ColorText()

;Assign the name of the color to selectedcolortext$
Select (selectedcolor)
        Case 1
                        selectedcolortext$ = "Green"
        Case 2
                        selectedcolortext$ = "Red"
        Case 3
                        selectedcolortext$ = "Blue"
        Case 4
                        selectedcolortext$ = "Black"
        Case 5
                        selectedcolortext$ = "White"
End Select

;Write out the selected color
Text 240, 20, "Selected Color: " + selectedcolortext$
End Function
```

And last, `MouseText()` looks like this:

```
;;;;;;;;;;;;;;;;;
;Function MouseText()
;Writes the mouse's location on the screen
;No Parameters
;;;;;;;;;;;;;;;;;
```

```
Function MouseText()
mousextext$ = "Mouse X: " + MouseX()
mouseytext$ = "Mouse Y: " + MouseY()
Text 540,20,mousextext$
Text 540,40,mouseytext$
End Function
```

These functions look long, right? Actually, they ain't too difficult. Let's get into each one.

First off, we have `DrawTextInfo()`. This function tells the user what his color choices are. It also explains how to save the picture. Figure 6.25 is the output of the `DrawTextInfo()` function.

```
Press the number of the color you wish to draw
Colors:
1. Green
2. Red
3. Blue
4. Black
5. White
Press F10 to save image (text WILL NOT be saved)
```

Figure 6.25 Output of `DrawTextInfo()`.

note

Compare Figure 6.25 with Figure 6.19, the outline that we made earlier. Notice that both are very similar, but there are a few minor changes. This is important: although an outline should always be drawn, they are rarely definite. You can always change it a little, but try to keep the infrastructure intact.

The writing is in 12 point font (the default in BlitzPlus), so each item is 12 pixels down from the one above it.

The next function is `ColorText()`. This function draws the selected color on the screen. As you know, the user changes the selected color by pressing 1, 2, 3, 4, or 5. Because you want to indicate which color the user picked, rather than just report a number, we use a `switch` statement. This statement assigns a variable, `selectedcolortext$`, to the selected color based on what the selection number is. After the `select` statement, the chosen color is drawn on the screen.

The final function is `MouseText()`. You don't know anything about mice yet, so in essence, this function finds the mouse's x and y values and writes them to the screen. Figure 6.26 shows the entire HUD. Compare it with Figure 6.20 and see how it has changed.

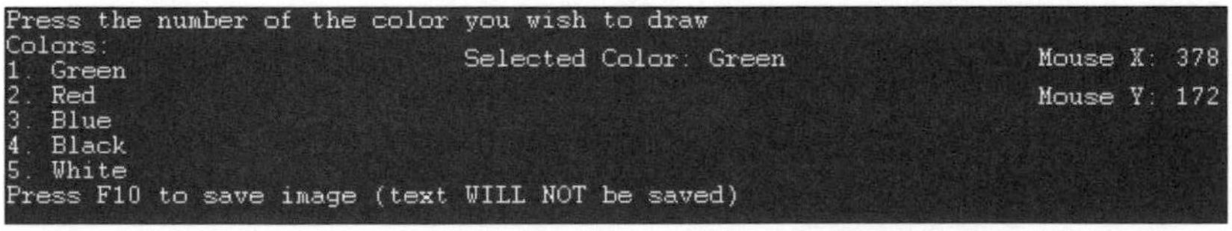

```
Press the number of the color you wish to draw
Colors:                        Selected Color: Green             Mouse X: 378
1. Green                                                         Mouse Y: 172
2. Red
3. Blue
4. Black
5. White
Press F10 to save image (text WILL NOT be saved)
```

Figure 6.26 The complete HUD.

All right, one function down, and just a few more to go. The next function we will look at is `TestKeyboardInput()`. This function reads in whatever the users press and reacts accordingly.

note

You might have noticed that I skipped a function, `DrawMouse()`. I decided not to include an explanation for it because we haven't learned mouse input yet. However, it is pretty simple to understand, so if you want to read it, just boot up the CD and open demo06-08.bb.

This program has only a few input possibilities: a color change or a screenshot. There are five color changes, so we need to test for those.

```
;;;;;;;;;;;;;;;;;;
;Function TestKeyboardInput()
;Tests if the keyboard wants to change the selected color or take a screenshot
;No Parameters
;;;;;;;;;;;;;;;;;;


Function TestKeyboardInput()

;If user presses a number, select the corresponding color
If KeyDown(ONEKEY)
	selectedcolor = 1
ElseIf KeyDown(TWOKEY)
	selectedcolor = 2
ElseIf KeyDown(THREEKEY)
	selectedcolor = 3
ElseIf KeyDown(FOURKEY)
	selectedcolor = 4
ElseIf KeyDown(FIVEKEY)
	selectedcolor = 5
EndIf


;If user presses F10, take a screenshot
If KeyDown(F10KEY)
	;Save the picture buffer as screenshot.bmp
	SaveBuffer ImageBuffer(picturebuffer), "screenshot.bmp"
EndIf

End Function
```

note

If you try to name ONEKEY "1key," the program will not work. Why is that? When defining variables, you must begin the name with a character or an underscore "_". You cannot begin with a number or a symbol (#,$, and so on).

This block of code tests each of the color selection keys to determine whether they were pressed. ONEKEY, TWOKEY, THREEKEY, FOURKEY, and FIVEKEY are all defined in the constant section of the initialization of the code. Each key name corresponds to same key number. (ONEKEY is the same as "1", TWOKEY is the same as "2", and so on.)

The final line of this function takes a screenshot of the drawn picture.

```
;If user presses F10, take a screenshot
If KeyDown(F10KEY)
	;Save the picture buffer as screenshot.bmp
	SaveBuffer ImageBuffer(picturebuffer), "screenshot.bmp"
EndIf
```

First off, this block of code tests the F10 key (located at the top of your keyboard). F10KEY is the key code for F10, and it is defined in the constant section. When the user presses F10, this action is performed:

```
SaveBuffer ImageBuffer(picturebuffer), "screenshot.bmp"
```

If you remember, SaveBuffer() saves a buffer (the first parameter) to a specified filename (the second parameter). Because we specified ImageBuffer(picturebuffer) to be saved, the text of the image will not be included in the saved file. See Figure 6.27 for an illustration of what is happening.

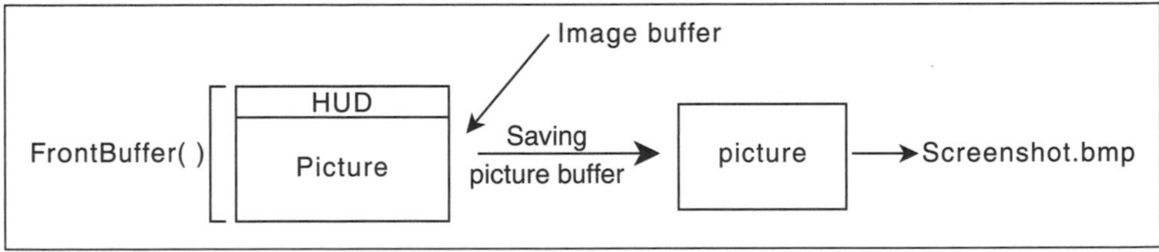

Figure 6.27 Using SaveBuffer.

caution

Do not try to save the image if you are running this program off the CD. Because the current directory is on the CD, and the CD cannot be written to, the saving operation will fail. To fix this problem, simply copy the program off the CD and onto your computer.

After the picture is readied, the image buffer is saved to screenshot.bmp. You can find this saved file in the same directory as the sample program. Make sure that if you run this program, you copy it off the CD onto your computer. The operation will fail if you try to save the buffer while the executable is still on the CD.

The last function remaining in the program is `TestMouseInput()`. This function determines whether the user has pressed any mouse buttons. If the user has pressed a mouse button, the program draws the selected color.

`TestMouseInput()` looks like this:

```
;;;;;;;;;;;;;;;;;;
;Function TestMouseInput()
;If player presses on mouse, draw the color
;No Parameters
;;;;;;;;;;;;;;;;;;
Function TestMouseInput()


;If player presses the left mouse button, draw the selected color
If MouseDown(1)


        ;Begin drawing only on image
        SetBuffer(ImageBuffer(picturebuffer))

        ; draw the selected color at the mouse location
        Select (selectedcolor)
        Case 1
                DrawImage(greenimage,MouseX(),MouseY()-100)
        Case 2
                DrawImage(redimage,MouseX(),MouseY()-100)
        Case 3
                DrawImage(blueimage,MouseX(),MouseY()-100)

        Case 4
                DrawImage(blackimage,MouseX(),MouseY()-100)

        Case 5
                DrawImage(whiteimage,MouseX(),MouseY()-100)

End Select
End If
```

```
;reset the buffer back to the back buffer
SetBuffer BackBuffer()

End Function
```

The first action this function performs is a test to determine whether the left mouse key was pressed. If so, the program sets the default buffer to `ImageBuffer(picturebuffer)`. Thus, the player can draw only on the image surface, and not the rest of the program. The `Select` block determines the default color, and depending on what that color is, a certain block of color is drawn. The `DrawImage` command:

```
DrawImage(*image,MouseX(),MouseY()-100)
```

draws the specific image at the x and y position, although the y position is set to be 100 pixels higher because the image buffer is drawn 100 pixels below the top of the screen. Take out the "-100" and see what happens!

note

In the example of `DrawImage`, I made the image handle "`*image.`" In this case, the "`*`" symbol can mean one of five things: green, red, blue, black, or white.

Well, that's it for the sample program. Figure 6.28 shows a sample image in the program, and Figure 6.29 shows how the saved image looks. Notice that the title bar is gone. Once again, the reason for this is that only the `ImageBuffer(picturebuffer)` is saved.

Here is an idea for a good exercise: change the program so that a different screenshot is created each time. This way, the user can save more than one image. Also, try to change the program so the users can determine where the file is saved.

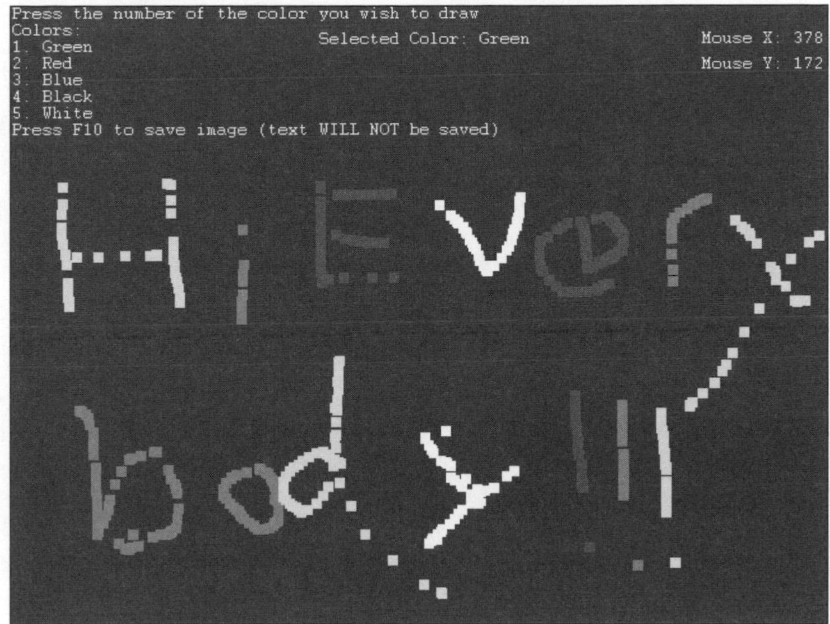

Figure 6.28 The full demo06-08.bb program.

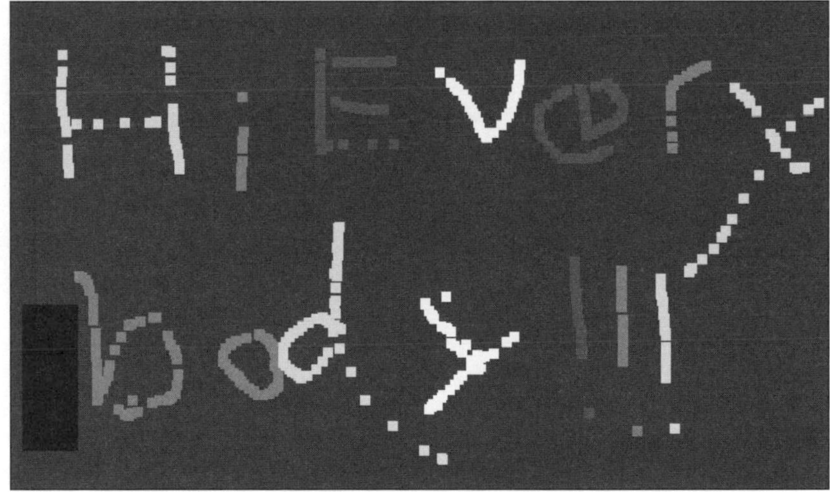

Figure 6.29 The saved picture from demo06-08.bb.

Summary

Whew, that was one long chapter. Hopefully, you've grasped all the topics we have covered so far. In this chapter, we learned:

- The different types of buffers
- How buffers are used in page flipping
- How to load and save buffers
- How to unlock and lock buffers
- How to quickly write and read pixel information
- How to write a full program based on buffers

I hope all of this information makes sense to you. This is an important chapter to understand, so if you don't "get" something, make sure you reread the section before progressing to the next chapter.

Now, strap on your seatbelt because the next chapter moves ahead to the crazy world of image programming!

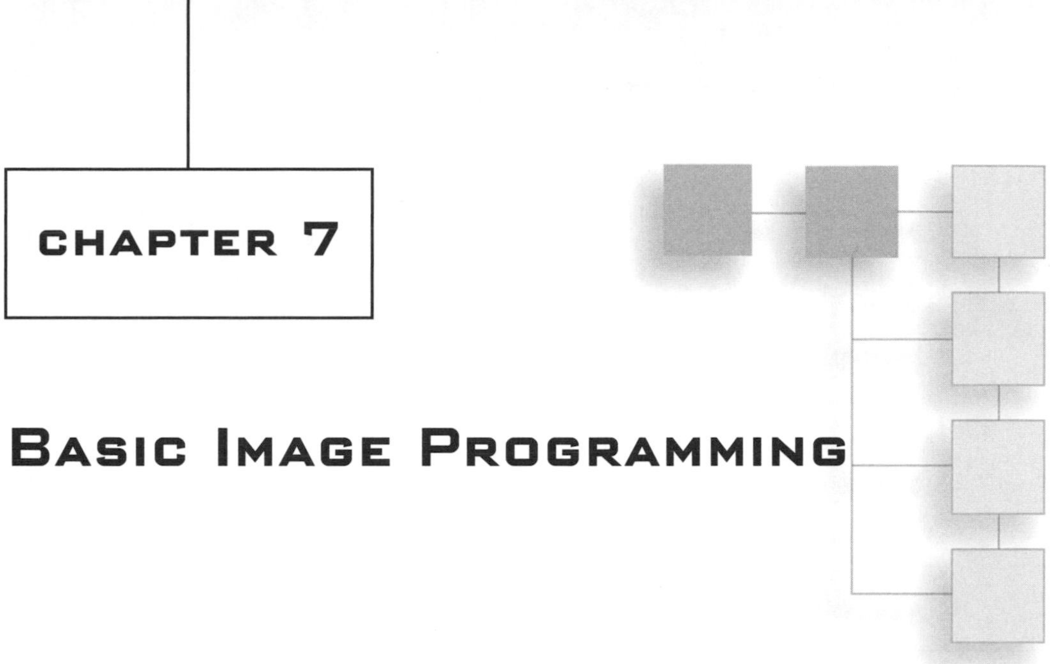

Chapter 7

Basic Image Programming

Welcome to Chapter 7! In this chapter, you learn how to use special effects on your images. These include rotation, scaling, and translations. You also learn the art of image tiling and parallaxing (which are both really cool). You probably don't understand what I'm talking about right now, but don't worry, these terms are explained thoroughly in the chapter.

Anyway, get ready, because here we go!

Transformations

Transformations are very important in game programming. They are used everywhere that you have movement; they change an image's position or direction. There are three types of transformations: translating, scaling, and rotating. Let's begin with translating.

Translating

When you hear the word translation, you probably think of languages. Well, translating images is completely different! When using translations in game programming, you take an image at its current position and then "translate" it to another position, so translate is just a fancy way of saying move!

Translation is moving an image from one coordinate to another. When complete, translation looks something like Figure 7.1.

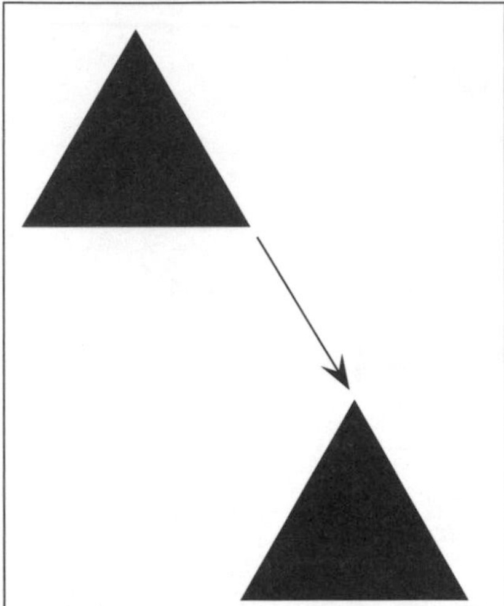

Figure 7.1 Translations.

Translation is really simple. You are basically drawing an image at a different position. For example, say you have an enemy ship that moves from the top-left corner of the screen to the bottom-right corner of the screen, and you want the ship to move at five pixels a second. You might have an initialization section that looks like this:

```
shipx = 0
shipy = 0
```

Refresher: Coordinate Position

Everybody forgets things after a while, huh? You might have forgotten how coordinate positions work, and because they are extremely important in this chapter, it might be a good idea to go over them.

The coordinate system has two axes: the x-axis and the y-axis. An axis is a named number line. The two axes on a computer screen look like Figure 7.2. (As you probably noticed, there are dash marks with numbers next to them. Of course, these dashes are not visible on the computer screen.) As you can see, the 0 point of both the x- and the y-axes is in the top-left point of the screen. If you travel farther across or down the monitor, the x- and y-axes are incremented. If you increment both, you can put the point anywhere you want on the screen. Figure 7.3 demonstrates a point that is 10 pixels to the right (on the x-axis) and 16 places down (on the y-axis).

Obviously, there must be a better way to explain this point than "10 pixels to the right (on the x-axis) and 16 pixels down (on the y-axis)." This way is inside parentheses; put the x coordinate first, and then a comma, and then the y coordinate. Thus, the point in Figure 7.3 is 10,16. The "10" means 10 pixels on the x-axis, and the "16" means 16 pixels on the y-axis.

This just places the position of the ship at the top-left corner of the screen. You now begin the game loop. Because we are moving the ship diagonally down at five pixels a second, we will have to update the ship with some code like this:

```
While Not KeyDown(1)
Cls
DrawImage shipimage, shipx, shipy
shipx = shipx + 7
shipy = shipy + 5
Flip
Wend
```

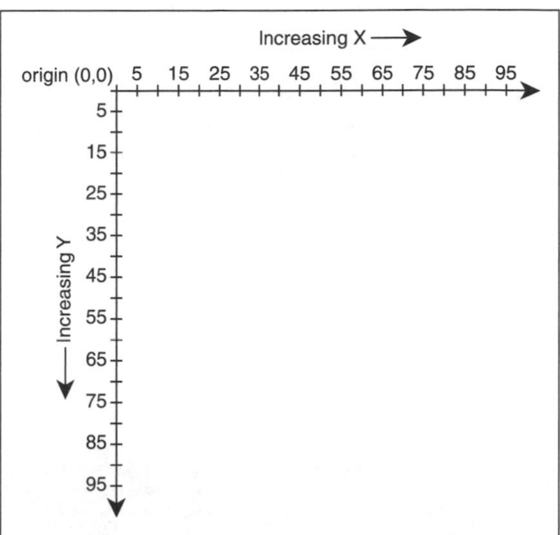

Figure 7.2 The coordinate system.

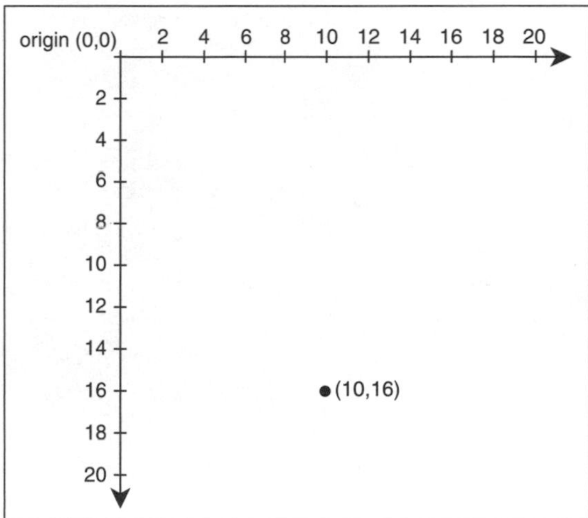

Figure 7.3 A point on the coordinate system.

Let's go through this. We start off with a loop, just like any other game. We first clear the screen, so that we can use page flipping. Then, we draw the ship image. Note that you have a choice where to put your `DrawImage` command. I chose to put it at the beginning of the loop so that you can see the ship image at 0,0, but you can put it at the end of the loop. The `DrawImage` command draws the ship image at the set x and y coordinates. When the loop runs through the first time, the `ship x` and `ship y` are both set equal to 0, but this changes with the next line of code. This line adds 7 to `shipx` and 5 to `shipy`. Because the additions occur each frame, the ship moves seven pixels to the right and five pixels down each frame. Figure 7.4 might help clear up the coordinate positions for you—it is a table of the values and the frame number. The equation, written next to the table in the figure, allows you to determine the position of x and y by plugging in a frame number. Of course, once the x and y values are off the screen, the image can't be seen anymore, but the image's coordinates are still updated.

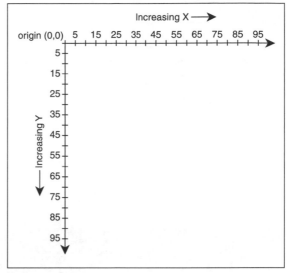

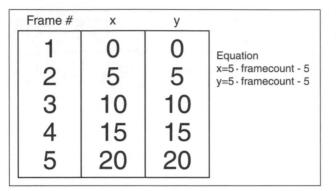

Frame #	x	y
1	0	0
2	5	5
3	10	10
4	15	15
5	20	20

Equation
x=5 · framecount - 5
y=5 · framecount - 5

Figure 7.4 A table of coordinate values.

The rest of the main loop is a `Flip` command that works with page flipping. Please see Chapter 6 for a review if you don't understand what `Flip` does. By the way, the full program is available on the CD as demo07-01.bb. Figure 7.5 is a screenshot of the program.

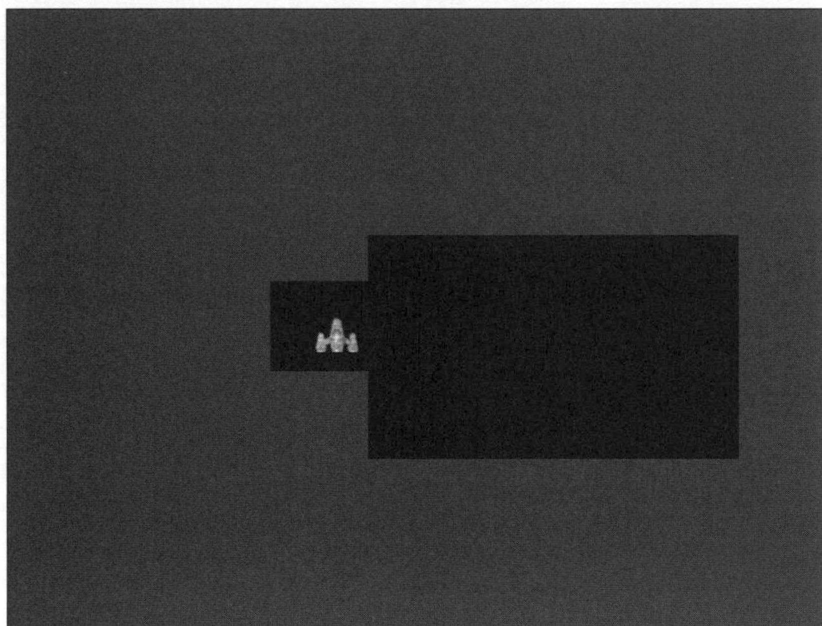

Figure 7.5 The demo07-01.bb program.

Let's quickly come up with an equation for translation. This formula is very simple, but hey, so is translation!

```
x[1] = x + dx
y[1] = y + dy
```

note

The d in dx and dy is there for a reason; it isn't just a random letter. In Greek, the letter delta, which is symbolized as a triangle (Δ) means "change in". If you "read" the variable, you can see that dx and dy mean, "the change in x" and "the change in y."

What does this mean? Well, if you input the proper coordinates (in this case, the x and/or y values) and add a number you would like to translate by (this number, dx or dy, can be negative or positive), you will get the new coordinate position for the variable. For example, in the lines of code:

```
shipx = shipx + 7
shipy = shipy + 5
```

shipx and shipy are x[1] and y[1], respectively. Shipx and shipy are x and y, and 7 is dx and 5 is dy. All of these variables are taking the place of the constants in the previous equation. Note that the x[1] and y[1] variables are the same as the x and y variables. This doesn't matter because you are updating them in order to move the image.

Are you ready to write a Translate function? Translate() translates any point you send it. Let's begin with a function declaration.

We are going to need an input coordinate and a transformation ("d") variable. So, the function might look something like this.

```
Function Translate(x,dx)
```

Easy, eh? And of course, the body of the function will be just as simple:

```
Return x + dx
```

Cool, huh? Table 7.1 describes each of the parameters for this function.

Table 7.1 Translate()'s Parameters

Parameter	Description
x	The coordinate you want to translate
dx	The factor by which the x variable is translated

Let's rewrite the main loop with the new function.

```
While Not KeyDown(1)
Cls
DrawImage shipimage,shipx,shipy
shipx = Translate(shipx,7)
```

```
shipy = Translate(shipy,5)
Flip
Wend

Function Translate(x,dx)
Return x+dx
End Function
```

And there we are! We now have a working translation function. Although it might seem trivial, it is probably a lot easier to understand the line

```
shipx = Translate(shipx,5)
```

rather than

```
shipx = shipx + 5
```

Don't you agree? Notice that the `Translate()` function does not use global variables, which makes this function extremely portable, because it can now be used in any other program. Copy the code and you can use `Translate()` as much as you want. By the way, the program using the `Translate()` function, is available on the CD as demo07-02.bb. If you need help understanding the main loop, see Figure 7.6.

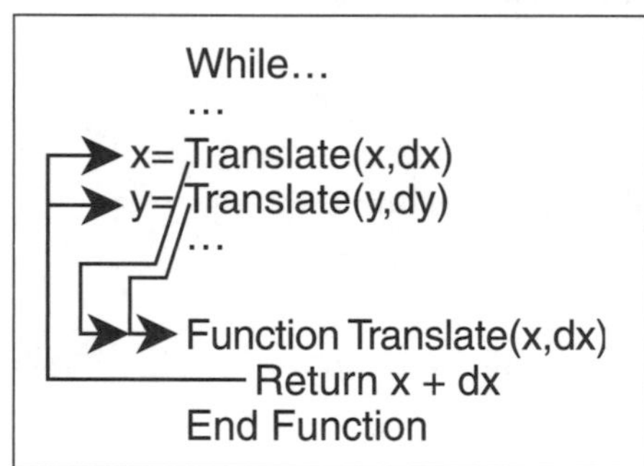

Figure 7.6 The main loop.

Okay, now that we've learned about translation, let's pump it up: next, we do scaling.

Scaling

When you scale an object, you make the object bigger or smaller (or the same size, if you really want to). Scaling means making something a smaller or larger size but usually keeping the same proportions. Proportionality, though, is not required. Unlike translation, you cannot scale a point. This is because a point is a point is a point—you cannot make a point a different size.

Let's start off by learning what a proportion is and how it is used.

Proportion? What the Heck Is That?

A proportion is a ratio or a fraction. For example, the ratio of an object to another object that is two times bigger is 1:2 or 1/2. If the other object were three times as big, the ratio would be 1:3 (and the fraction would be 1/3). If you take a look at the fraction, you will notice that 1/3 is the same as 1 divided by 3. This is sort of interesting: the smaller object (the "1" in 1:3) is exactly 1/3 the size of the bigger object. If you flip the top and bottom on the fraction, you get 3/1, which is the size of the larger object compared to the smaller object (the bigger object is three times the size of the smaller one). Take a look at Figure 7.7. In this figure, you can see the picture of a regular sized man on the left. The picture on the right is the same man, but he is scaled. He is 1/5 the size of the original man (the big man to small man ratio is 5:1).

You can also use ratios and fractions when an object becomes smaller. Say you have object A and object B. Object B is five times smaller than object A. The ratio in this example is 5:1, and the fraction is 5/1 (or just 5: any number divided by 1 is that number). As you can see, object A, which is the "5" in 5:1, is five times bigger than object B. If you flip the fraction 5/1, you get 1/5, which is the size of object B in comparison to object A.

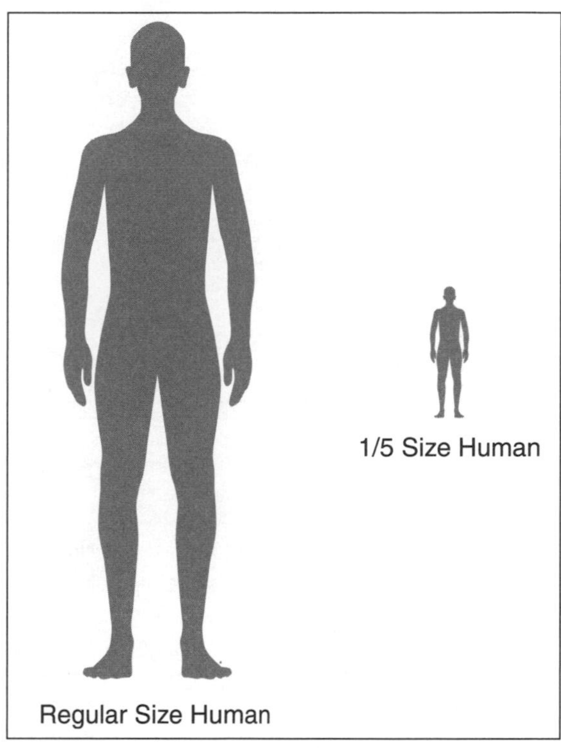

Figure 7.7 A man and his 1/5 scaled counterpart.

A proportion can be thought of as a ratio or a fraction. You can also use percentages. When using BlitzPlus, you typically use percentages. In other words, when you want to scale the size of an object, you multiply by a percentage number. For example, say you want to make something four times as large as it is. Just multiply each coordinate by 4. Referring to Figure 7.8, you can see a box with coordinates 0,0, 0,5, 5,0, and 5,5. By multiplying each coordinate by 4 such that 0,0 remains 0,0; 0,5 becomes 0,20; 5,0 becomes 20,0; and 5,5 becomes 20,20, the box becomes four times as large. However, what if you want to make the object something like 5/8 as large? All you have to do is bust out a calculator and divide 5 by 8. Because 5/8 = .625, the multiplication factor will be .625.

So, now we have a basic outline for our scaling equation. The scaled equation looks a lot like the translation equation:

```
x[1] = x * sx
y[1] = y * sy
```

Notice the differences between translations and scaling. When translating, you add the `d` variable to the current x; however, when scaling, you multiply the `s` variable by the current x to scale it.

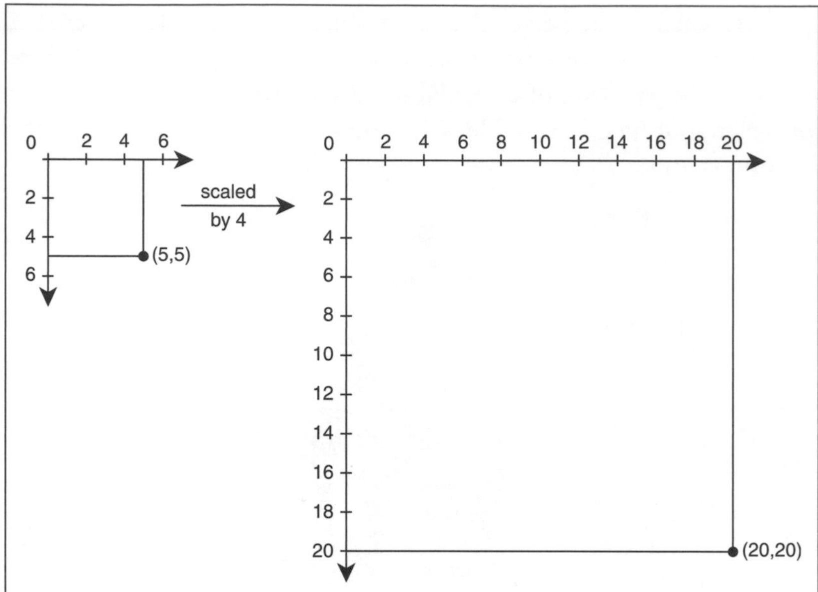

Figure 7.8 A scaled rectangle.

tip

When scaling an object, you must use decimal percentages. If you want to make one object scaled to 50% of the previous one, don't multiply by 50. Your new object will be 50 times as large as the older one! Instead, think of it as a fraction. You want to make the new object 1/2 as large as the previous one. If you divide 1 by 2, you get .5. Multiply the object by .5 and your object is scaled to 50%.

Scaling Shapes

Shape scaling is relatively simple. Just multiply the ending coordinate by the scaling factor, and you're done! The next step is to scale different kinds of shapes, such as rectangles and triangles. Ready to move?

Scaling Rectangles

Let's write a few programs that utilize scaling within shapes. The first draws a rectangle, waits for the user to choose a ratio, and draws a new rectangle with a new size. On the CD, this file is named demo07-03.bb.

We begin with a graphics call. After that, we initialize the variables:

```
;demo 07-03.bb - Demonstrates Scaling

Graphics 800,600,0,2
```

```
;VARIABLES
;Create the variables that define the rectangle
rectbeginx = 25 ;The x coordinate of the top-left corner
rectbeginy = 25 ;The y coordinate of the top-left corner
rectwidth  = 256 ;The x coordinate of the bottom-right coordinate
rectheight = 256 ;The y coordinate of the bottom-right coordinate
```

All that has happened so far is the creation of a few variables. I offset the box from 0,0 so that you can see the scaling more clearly. If you feel like it, change any of these variables.

Next, we move to the main section of the code. The first part deals with the first rectangle.

```
;MAIN SECTION
;Make sure the text goes near the bottom of the screen
Text 0,700, "This is our first rectangle."

;Draw the first rectangle, and make it not filled
Rect rectbeginx,rectbeginy,rectwidth,rectheight,0

;Show old rectangle
Flip
```

We first start off with a call to `Text`. This forces the text, "`This is our first rectangle`" to appear near the bottom of the screen, so it doesn't interfere with the rectangles. Next, we call the `Rect` function. This function, which is compiler defined, draws a rectangle from the starting coordinates (`rectbeginx` and `rectbeginy`) to the ending coordinates (`rectwidth` and `rectheight`). See Table 7.2 to see the `Rect`'s parameters. The 0 at the end leaves the rectangle unfilled (you can set it equal to 1 if you want the rectangle filled, but it looks kind of ugly if you do so).

Table 7.2 Rect's Parameters

Parameter	Description
`x`	The x coordinate of the top left of the rectangle
`y`	The y coordinate of the top left of the rectangle
`width`	The width in pixels of the rectangle
`height`	The height in pixels of the rectangle
solid	If set to 0, the rectangle is not filled; if it is set to 1, the rectangle is filled

So, why did I put a `Flip` command in there? Remember, in BlitzPlus, everything is drawn on the `BackBuffer()`. Because we want to be able to see the rectangle that we just drew, we must use the `Flip` command to show it on screen.

Next up: finding the scaling factor.

```
;Ask the user what the scaling factor is
sxy# = Input ("What would you like the scaling factor to be? (Ex: 50% = .5)? ==> ")
```

This statement asks the users what they would like to scale the x and y coordinates by. For this program, both x and y are scaled by the same amount. If you feel like it, rewrite this program so the users can scale both x and y by different amounts.

note

When using the `Input()` function, a window will pop up asking for information. It does not ask for the information directly on the screen, but rather in an external window. Because of this, when using the `Input()` function, you should not use a maximized window. Use a small, desktop-sized window instead.

note

We haven't touched on variable types for a long time. In case you have forgotten, when `#` is appended to the end of a variable name, the variable is a floating-point variable. If a variable is floating point, it can hold decimal places. In other words, `xyx` can be 314, whereas `xyx#` can be 314.13. If you try to make a non-floating-point variable (an integer) include a decimal, the decimal portion will be truncated (removed). For example, the number 1.9 will become 1 because the .9 has been truncated or deleted. Be careful when doing this because if you truncate decimal numbers, you will lose information. And unless you intended to do this, it could be really bad. For example, if you were computing tax with the number 0.08 and got rid of the decimal part, you would end up with a tax rate of 0! In this program, the user can multiply the variable by any number, such as 1.5, .3, and so on. It would not be very good if the decimal was truncated, because the new variable would (most likely) end up being either 1 or 0. What a boring program it would be if the new rectangle was either deleted or kept the same size!

The scaling factor is stored in the variable `sxy#`. This variable is used in the next section of code.

```
;Multiply the width and height by the scaling factor
rectwidth = rectwidth  * sxy#
rectheight = rectheight * sxy#

;Show new input
Flip
```

To scale the new object, you must multiply each coordinate by the scaling factor. The scaling factor was determined, via user input, in the previous section of code. Here, both the x and y values are multiplied by the scaling factor to make the rectangle as big as the user wants it to be.

The final section of the code draws the second rectangle and exits the program.

```
;Draw the new rectangle
Rect rectbeginx,rectbeginy,rectwidth,rectheight,0

Print "Press any key to exit."

;Wait for the user to press a key before exiting.
WaitKey
```

Note that the `WaitKey` function will work only when the actual rectangle drawing program has focus, not when the input window has focus.

The first line here draws a new rectangle with the scaled coordinates. Because the beginning x and y values remain the same, the rectangle is drawn over the old one.

The final two lines ask the user to press any key. Once the user presses a key, the program is over. Figure 7.9 shows a screenshot from the program.

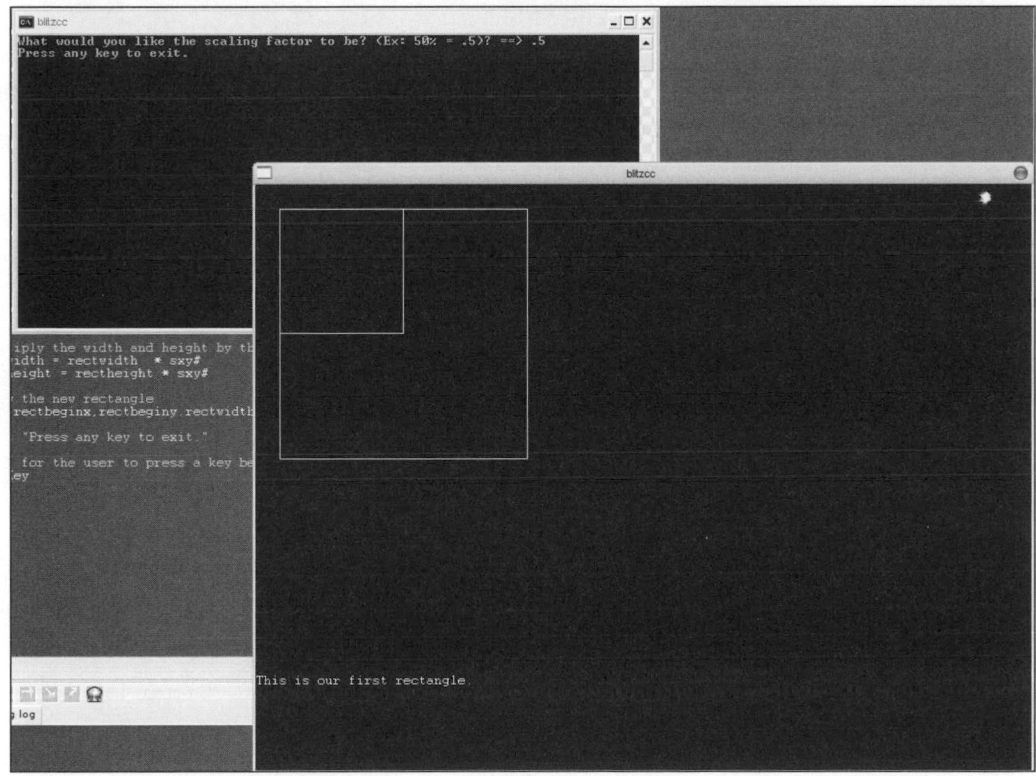

Figure 7.9 The demo07-03.bb program.

This program teaches a lot of important ideas. Try this out: change the code to work with ellipses (using the `Oval` function).

You might have noticed something strange when using a scaling factor. When scaled by 2, as in Figure 7.10, the original rectangle is only 1/4 of the size of the new rectangle, even though you might expect it to be 1/2. The reason is that each coordinate is scaled by 2, not the rectangle as a whole. Therefore, the new rectangle is actually four times the size of the original rectangle.

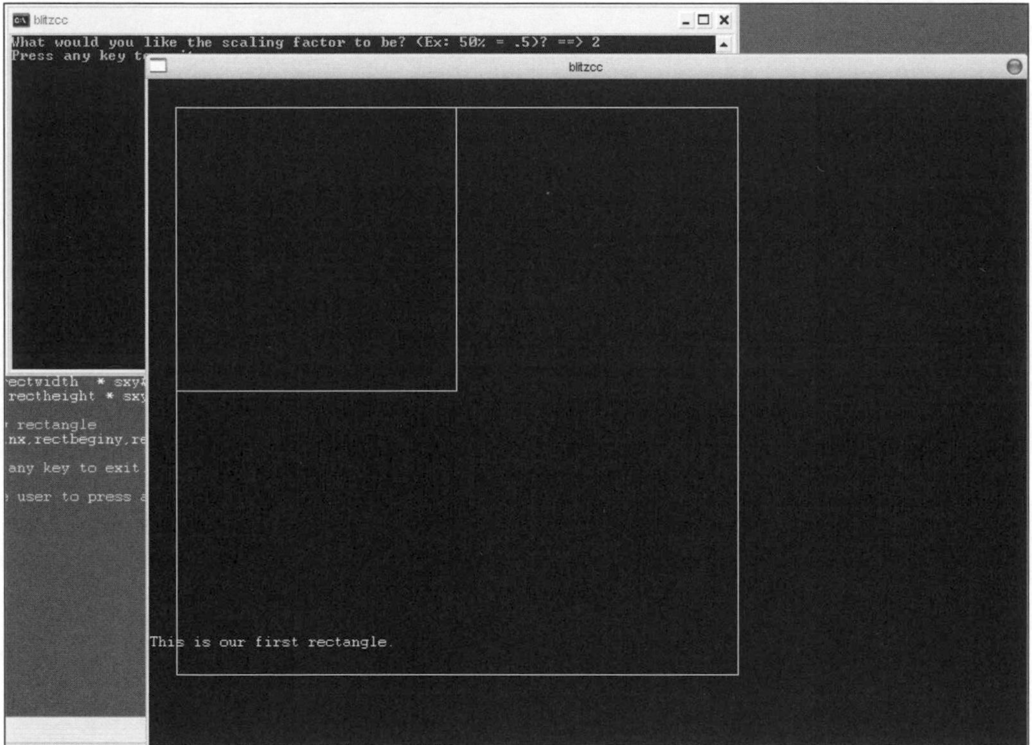

Figure 7.10 Demo07-03.bb with a scaling factor of 2.

Scaling Triangles

We can now move on to something a bit more challenging: scaling a triangle. Unlike the rectangle, triangles don't have a function. We have to draw each line manually.

Before we can begin discussing how to scale a triangle, we need to understand the difference between local and global coordinates.

There is a huge difference between global and local coordinates. A local coordinate, much like a local variable, is only visible from the object that is being drawn. Global coordinates, on the other hand, are the same for all objects.

Maybe an analogy will help to understand the difference. Take a human; for instance, let's take you. You are a person. There are many people. But you are the center of everything that you can see. To you, everything revolves around you. Therefore, your local coordinates stem from the top of you to the bottom of you. However, remember that this holds true for everyone else as well. Each person has his or her own local coordinates.

Now, imagine a spaceship watching Earth from the sky. To the aliens, people are everywhere. Each person is not central to the spaceship; instead, the Earth as a whole is. So, to the aliens, the Earth is a coordinate plane (it isn't actually a plane, but never mind that). Where you are now is located at some coordinate position (maybe 13,14), but that will change when you take a step to another area. Latitude and longitude perform the same actions as global coordinates—you can pinpoint a certain position anywhere in the world by indicating the latitude and longitude coordinates.

Look at Figure 7.11, which shows a map of the world with two people, Person A and Person B. Person A and Person B each believe they are the center of the world; that is, they think of themselves as located at 0,0. However, the spaceship that is watching them (you are the spaceship for now) sees them in two very different coordinate positions, shown by their latitude and longitude values.

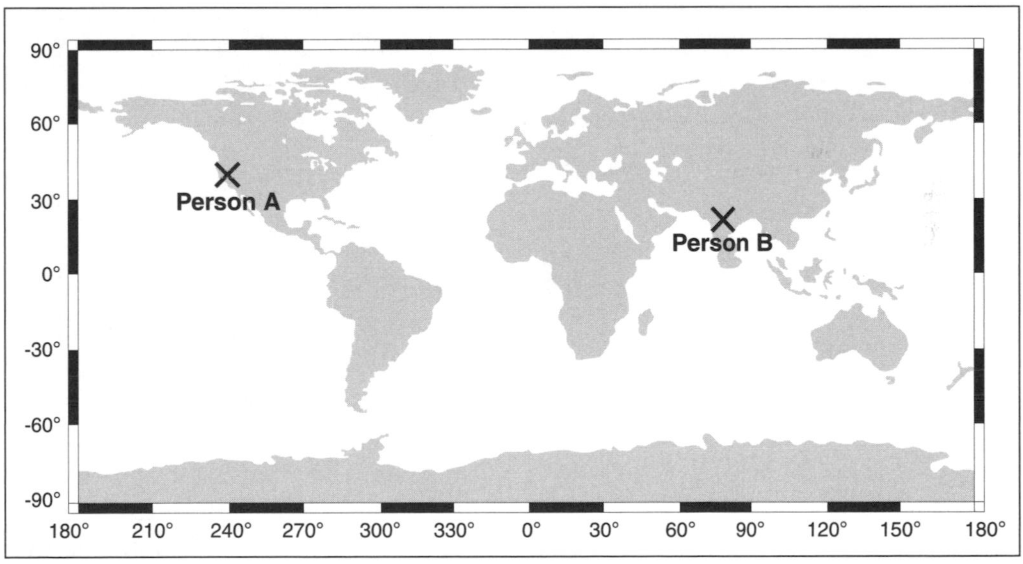

Figure 7.11 The spaceship and the world.

When you move around, your global coordinates change. However, your local coordinates remain the same. Your viewpoint does not change, and therefore, your local coordinates stay with you no matter where you go.

With objects in BlitzPlus, this analogy works extremely well. To the triangle we are using in the following program, the center begins at coordinates 0,0. The object's global coordinates begin wherever it is displayed on the screen. Referring to Figure 7.12, you can see that the local coordinates of an object begin at the top-left corner and end at the bottom-right corner.

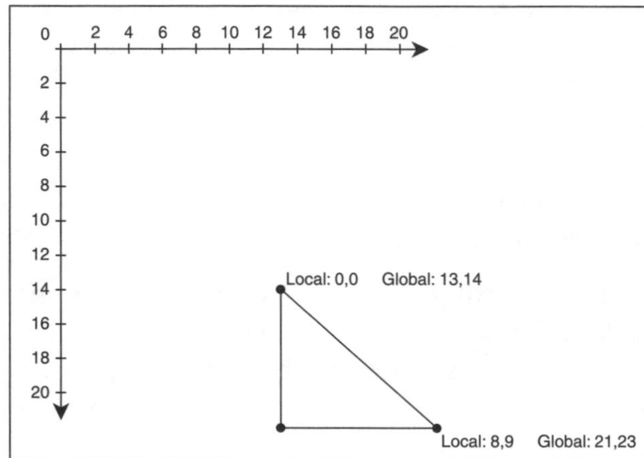

Figure 7.12 Global and local coordinates.

Now that we understand local and global coordinates, let's get into this program. We first set up the graphics mode.

```
Graphics 800,600,0,2
```

Now we are going to create a type called `point`. `Point` will contain two fields: its x and y coordinates.

```
Type point
	Field x,y
End Type
```

We need to have three points for this triangle: one for each vertex. A vertex (plural *vertices*) is a point where a line changes direction—in the case of a triangle, there are three vertices, one at each corner.

```
point1.point = New point
point2.point = New point
point3.point = New point
```

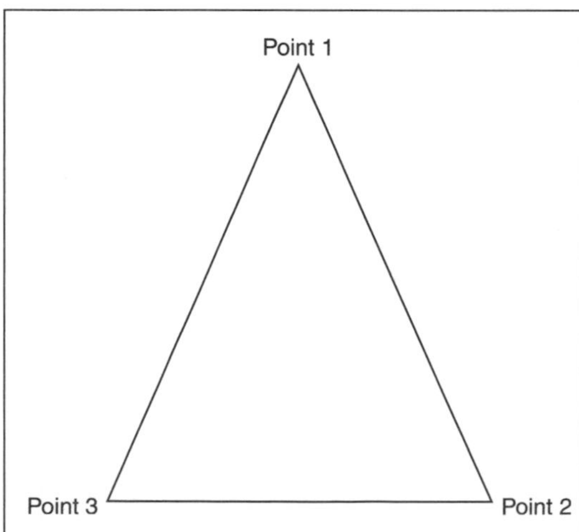

Figure 7.13 `point1`, `point2`, and `point3`.

`point1`, `point2`, and `point3` are the three different vertices on the triangle. Referring to Figure 7.13, you can see that `point1` begins at the apex, or top, of the triangle, and `point2` and `point3` follow in a clockwise manner. The line that begins at point1 extends to `point2`, the line from `point2` extends to `point3`, and the line from `point3` extends to `point1`.

Next, we have to define the local coordinates for our first triangle. In demo07-04.bb, the vertices are defined like this:

```
;These variables define each vertex and are in local coordinates
point1\x= 0
point1\y= -100
point2\x= 100
point2\y= 100
point3\x= -100
point3\y = 100
```

These points are centered around 0,0. Note that all of these coordinates are local: obviously, you can never have negative values for global coordinates. Figure 7.14 shows the coordinates of each point on the triangle. As you can see, the origin point, 0,0, is in the exact center of the triangle.

As stated earlier, to obtain global coordinates, we will add a constant value to each local coordinate of the triangle. The constant section of this program has two variables.

```
;CONSTANTS
;The global indicators that are added
to each local coordinate
;to place it on screen
Const xs = 400
Const ys = 300
```

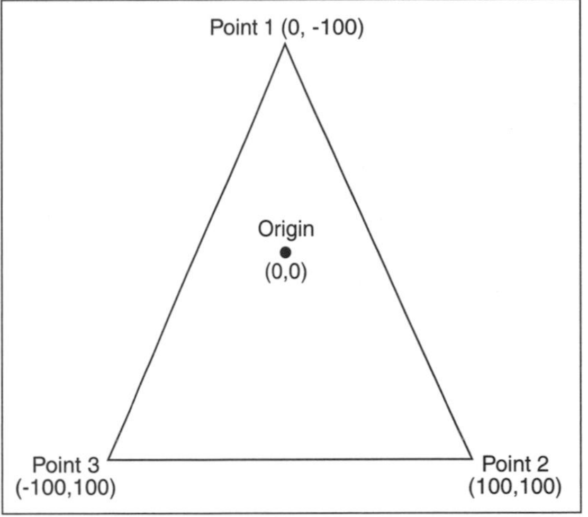

Figure 7.14 Local coordinates.

I chose these two numbers because they center the triangle onscreen. Note that the program is 800 pixels by 600 pixels (these numbers are defined in the `Graphics` call), and 800 / 2 = 400 and 600 / 2 = 300. To achieve the correct global coordinates, the `xs` variable is added to each x coordinate and `ys` is added to each y coordinate.

Now that we have all of our initialization values defined and variables created, let's move on to the actual program. The program begins with these two lines:

```
Locate 0,700
Print "This is our first triangle."
```

As you probably know, the `Locate` command places all of the `Print` commands near the bottom of the screen. The `Print` statement then writes, "This is our first triangle," on the screen.

Next, we draw the first triangle. This is accomplished with the `Line` function, which draws a line from one coordinate position to another. `Line` is declared like this

```
Line x,y,x1,y1
```

Table 7.3 explains each parameter individually.

Table 7.3 Line's Parameters

Parameter	Description
x	The x position of the starting coordinate
y	The y position of the starting coordinate
x1	The x position of the ending coordinate
y1	The y position of the ending coordinate

In essence, the `Line` function draws a straight line from coordinates `x,y` to coordinates `x1, y1`. For this program, there are three `Line` calls for each triangle.

```
;Draw out first triangle
Line point1\x + xs, point1\y + ys, point2\x + xs, point2\y + ys
Line point2\x + xs, point2\y + ys, point3\x + xs, point3\y + ys
Line point3\x + xs, point3\y + ys, point1\x + xs, point1\y + ys
```

As you can see, each `Line` call draws a line from one of the vertices to another of the vertices. If you look closely, you can see that `xs` is added to each x coordinate and `ys` is added to each y coordinate. These numbers are added to the triangle's local coordinates in order to move the triangle onscreen so they can be seen in the program. Figure 7.15 demonstrates the triangles local and global coordinates.

Okay, now that we have drawn the original triangle, let's find out what the user wants the scaling factor to be. This is accomplished with a call to `Input`.

```
Flip
;Find scaling factor from user
sxy# = Input ("What would you like the scaling factor to be? (Ex: 50% = .5)? ==> ")
Flip
```

The user now has a chance to input a scaling factor, which is stored in `sxy#`. Note that this variable is a float, as signified by the `#` symbol.

note

In general, whenever using the `Input()` function, you want to put a `Flip` command before and after the `Input()` call.

After the user has chosen a scaling factor, we scale each point. The following lines perform the scaling actions.

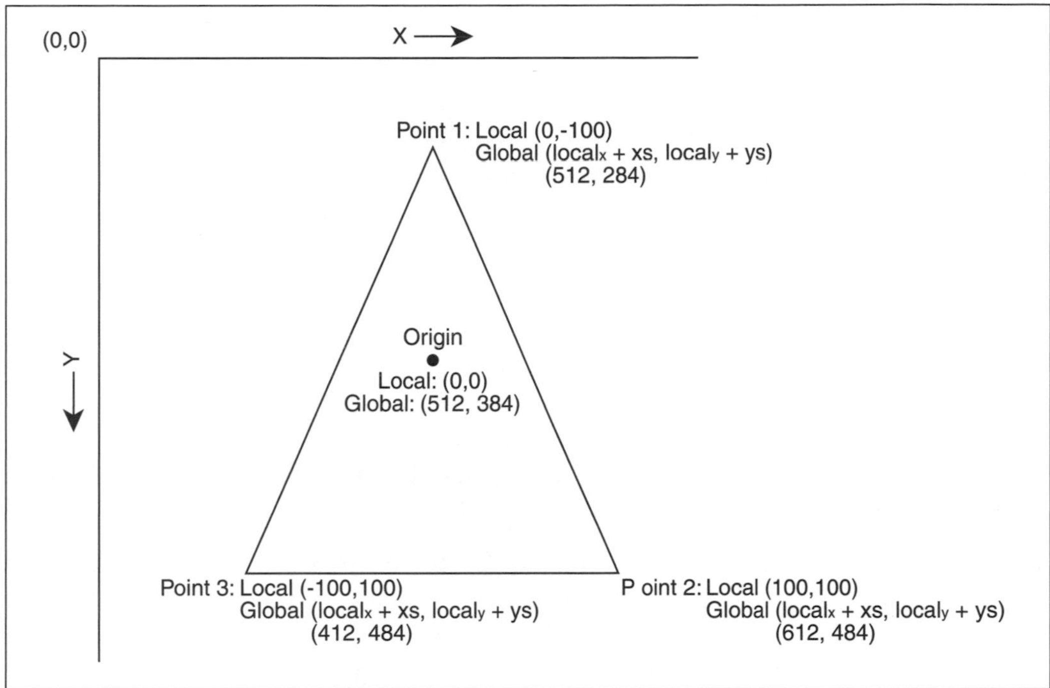

Figure 7.15 Local and global coordinates of the sample triangle.

```
;Multiply all the coordinates by the scaling factor
point1\x = point1\x * sxy#
point1\y = point1\y * sxy#
point2\x = point2\x * sxy#
point2\y = point2\y * sxy#
point3\x = point3\x * sxy#
point3\y = point3\y * sxy#
```

Pretty easy, eh? All this block of code did was multiply each vertex's x and y position by `sxy#`.

Okay, now we must get ready to draw out the new triangle. Since we want the new object to be easily seen, you need to change the color of the lines. This is easily accomplished using the `Color` function.

```
;Change the default color to green
Color 0,255,0
```

This makes all following `Line` commands green.

Now, all we have to do is draw the new triangle. This is accomplished by calling `Line` for each point, as we did for the original triangle.

```
;Draw final triangle (with scaled coordinates) in green
Line point1\x + xs, point1\y + ys, point2\x + xs, point2\y + ys
Line point2\x + xs, point2\y + ys, point3\x + xs, point3\y + ys
Line point3\x + xs, point3\y + ys, point1\x + xs, point1\y + ys
```

Excellent! The program has now printed lines connecting each vertex, and therefore, drawn a new triangle.

Now all we do is finish the program.

```
Print "Press any key to exit."

;Wait for user to press a key before exiting
WaitKey
```

These lines of code tell the user to press any key, and the program then waits for the user to press a key before exiting.

That's the complete program. Figures 7.16 and 7.17 demonstrate the program with scaling factors of 2 and .5. You won't be able to see that the new lines are drawn in green in the figures, but you can look at the program on the CD to see the new triangles drawn in green. If you notice, the new triangle is centered in respect to the original triangle. But, what if you don't want to keep it centered? All you have to do is change the local coordinates.

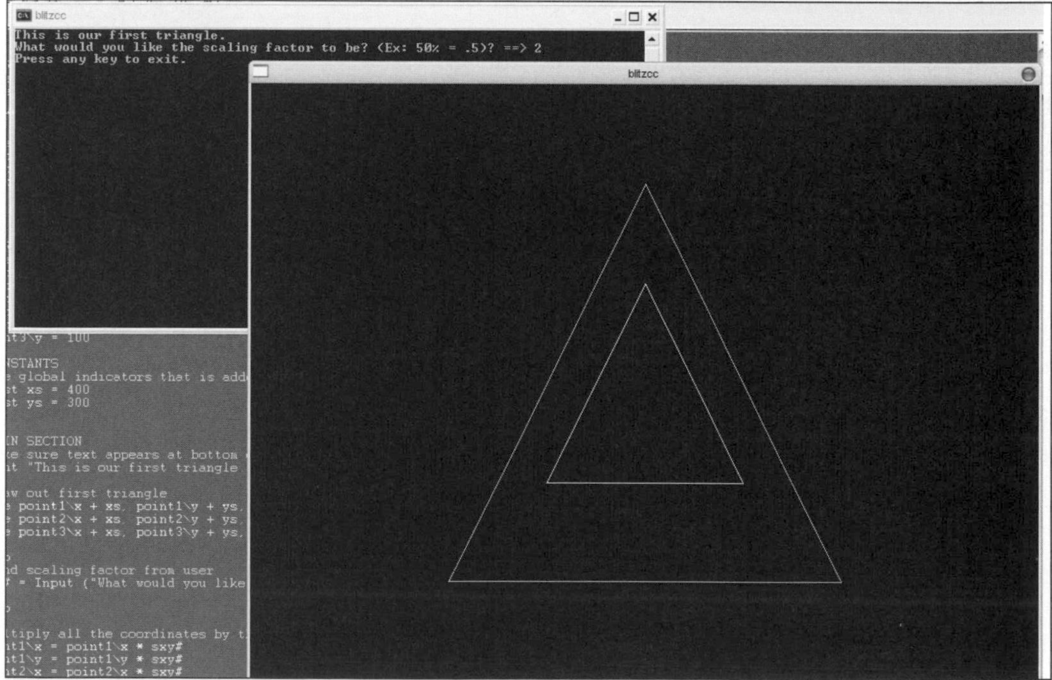

Figure 7.16 Demo07-04.bb with a scaling factor of 2.

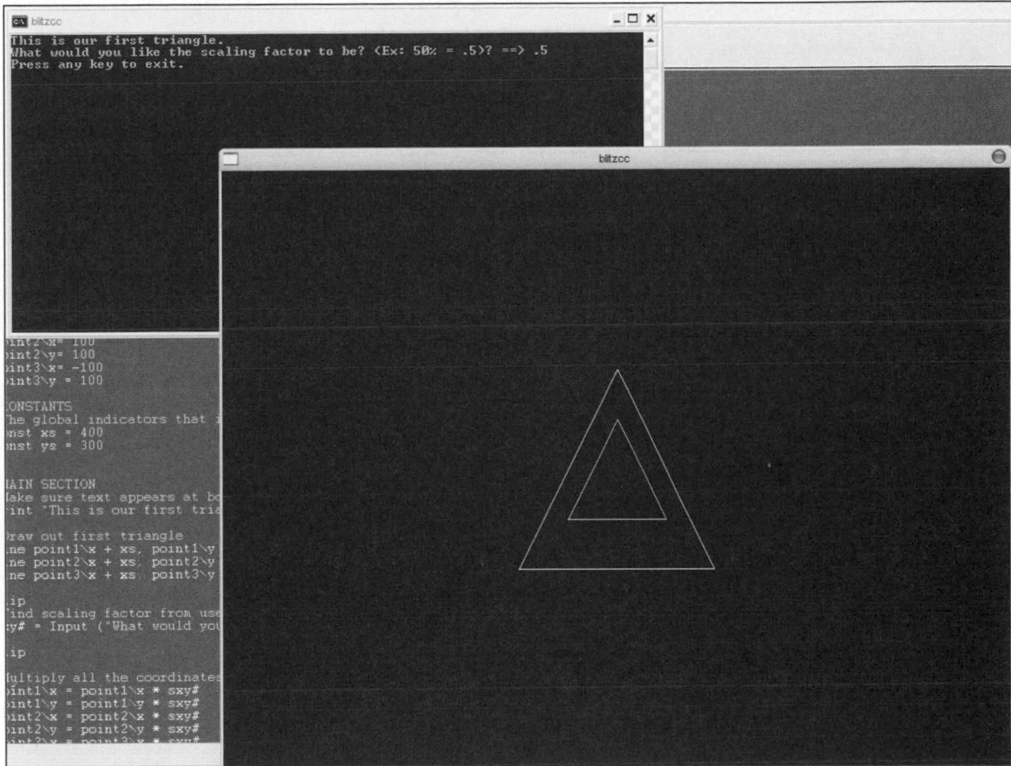

Figure 7.17 Demo07-04.bb with a scaling factor of .5.

tip

Wanna see something cool? When you are asked to input `sxy#`, enter a negative number. The new triangle is flipped. Check out Figure 7.18; it shows the program with an `sxy#` value of −1.

Figure 7.19 shows demo07-05.bb. As you can see, the triangle grows downward, but it does not remain centered. Demo07-05.bb is almost exactly the same as demo07-04.bb, except the beginning variables have been changed. The variables are now initialized with different values.

```
;VARIABLES
;These variables define each vertex and are in local coordinates
point1\x= 0
point1\y= 0
point2\x= 100
point2\y= 100
point3\x= -100
point3\y = 100
```

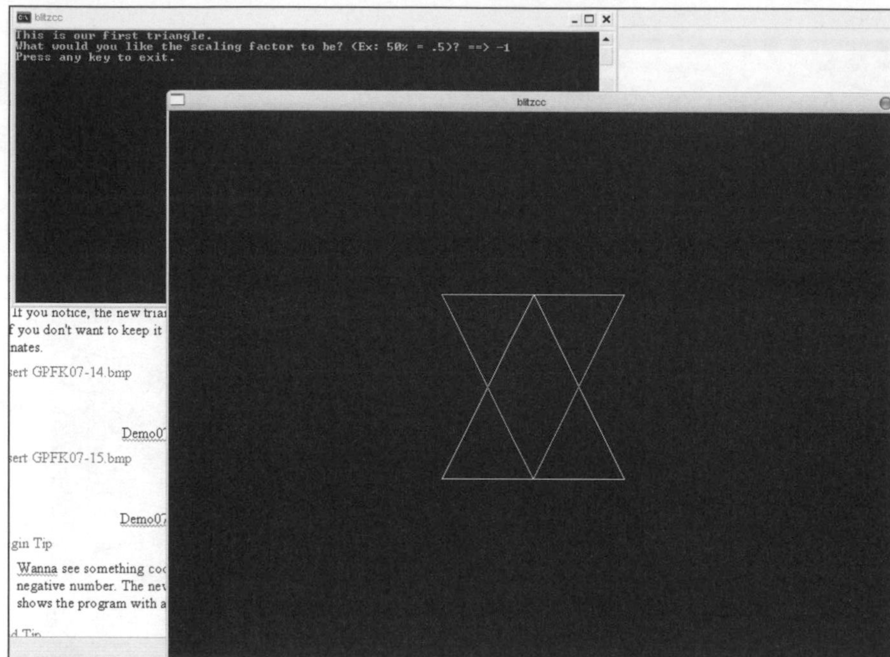

Figure 7.18 Demo07-04.bb with a scaling factor of −1.

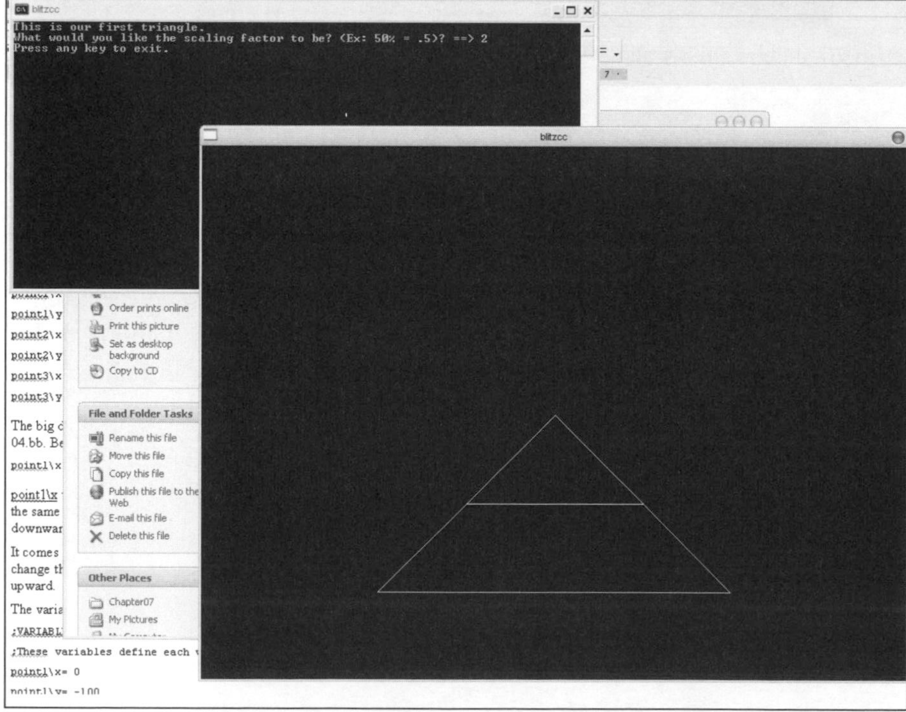

Figure 7.19 The demo07-05.bb program.

The big difference here is that `point1\y` has been changed to 0 from its value in demo07-04.bb. Because any number multiplied by 0 equals 0, when `sxy#` is multiplied in the line:

```
point1\x = point1\x * sxy#
```

`point1\x` will always equal 0. Because the variable does not change, `point1` will remain the same position throughout the program. Thus, the triangle will grow from the top downward.

It comes out pretty nicely, don't you think? By the way, if you want it to grow upward, change the bottom points' y values to 0. Demo07-06.bb shows the triangle growing upward.

The variables have been changed slightly; now they are

```
;VARIABLES
;These variables define each vertex and are in local coordinates
point1\x= 0
point1\y= -100
point2\x= 100
point2\y= 0
point3\x= -100
point3\y = 0
```

As you can see, the two lower points are equivalent to 0. Now, when it is scaled by 2, it grows upward, as in Figure 7.20.

One thing you should know about the previous program: because changing the y values for the bottom two points moves the figure up a little, I changed the `ys` variable a little. The constants section now reads:

```
;CONSTANTS
;The global indicators that is added to each local coordinate
;to place it onscreen
Const xs = 400
Const ys = 400
```

The `ys` variable in demo07-06.bb was changed from 300 to 400 to offset the 100-pixel difference between the original triangle in demo07-04.bb and the new triangle in demo07-06.bb.

Now let's create a scale function.

```
Function Scale(x,sx)
Return x*sx
End Function
```

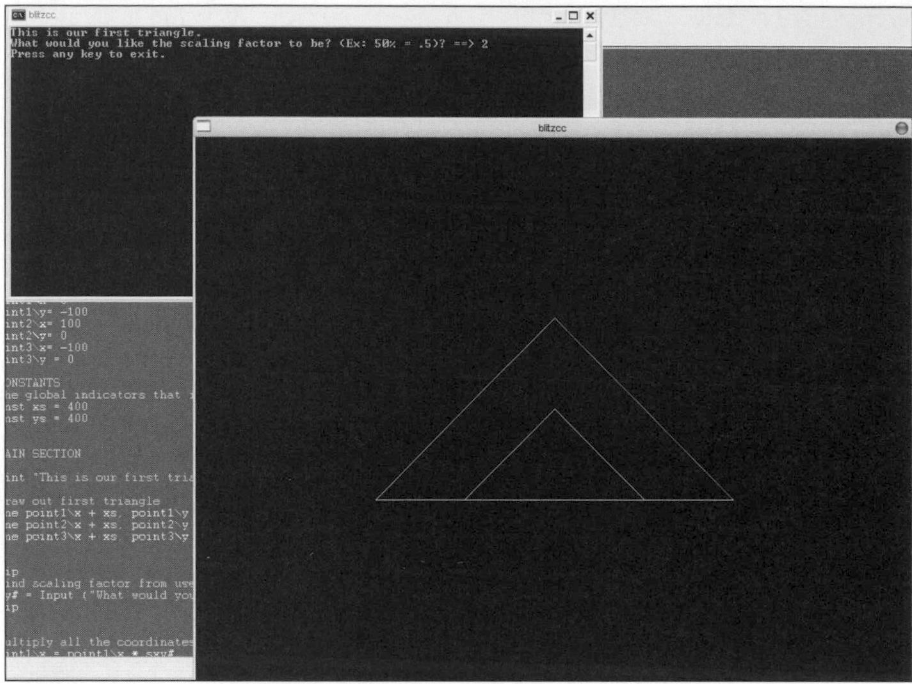

Figure 7.20 The demo07-06.bb program.

Table 7.4 examines each parameter. If you wanted to scale the x coordinate of `point1`, just call it like this:

```
Scale(point1\x,sxy#)
```

assuming that `sxy#` is the scaling factor.

Table 7.4 Scale()'s Parameters

Parameter	Description
x	The value you want to scale
sx	The scaling factor

Scaling Images

BlitzPlus makes scaling images extremely easy by providing the function `ScaleImage`. `ScaleImage` is defined like this:

```
ScaleImage image,xscale#,yscale#
```

Table 7.5 explains each parameter. Basically, just include the image handle and the x and y scaling values in the call to `ScaleImage`.

Table 7.5 ScaleImage's Parameters

Parameter	Description
`image`	The image handle of the image you want to scale
`xscale#`	The amount you want to scale the x-axis by (1.0 = 100%)
`yscale#`	The amount you want to scale the y axis by (1.0 = 100%)

As an example, we will scale an image of a spaceship. The original spaceship looks like Figure 7.21.

Figure 7.21
The original spaceship image.

Demo07-07.bb is pretty short, so I am just going to show the entire program and explain it at the end.

```
;demo07-07.bb - Demonstrates the use of ScaleImage
Graphics 800,600,0,2

;Set automidhandle to true
AutoMidHandle True

;IMAGES
;Load the spaceship that will be drawn onscreen
spaceshipimage = LoadImage("spaceship.bmp")

;Draw the spaceship directly in the center of the screen
DrawImage spaceshipimage, 400,300

Flip
;Find out what the player wants the x and y scaling factors to be
xs# = Input("What would you like the x scaling value to be? ")
ys# = Input("What would you like the y scaling value to be? ")
Flip

;Prepare the screen for the scaled spaceship by clearing it
Cls
;Scale the image
ScaleImage spaceshipimage, xs#,ys#
```

```
;Draw the new scaled spaceship
DrawImage spaceshipimage, 400,300

Print "This is your updated image"
Print "Press any key to exit"

;Wait for user to press a key before exiting
WaitKey
```

Figure 7.22 is a screenshot from the program. The first thing the program does is initialize the graphics and set `AutoMidHandle` to true, so that the images are centered. It then loads the spaceship and draws it onscreen.

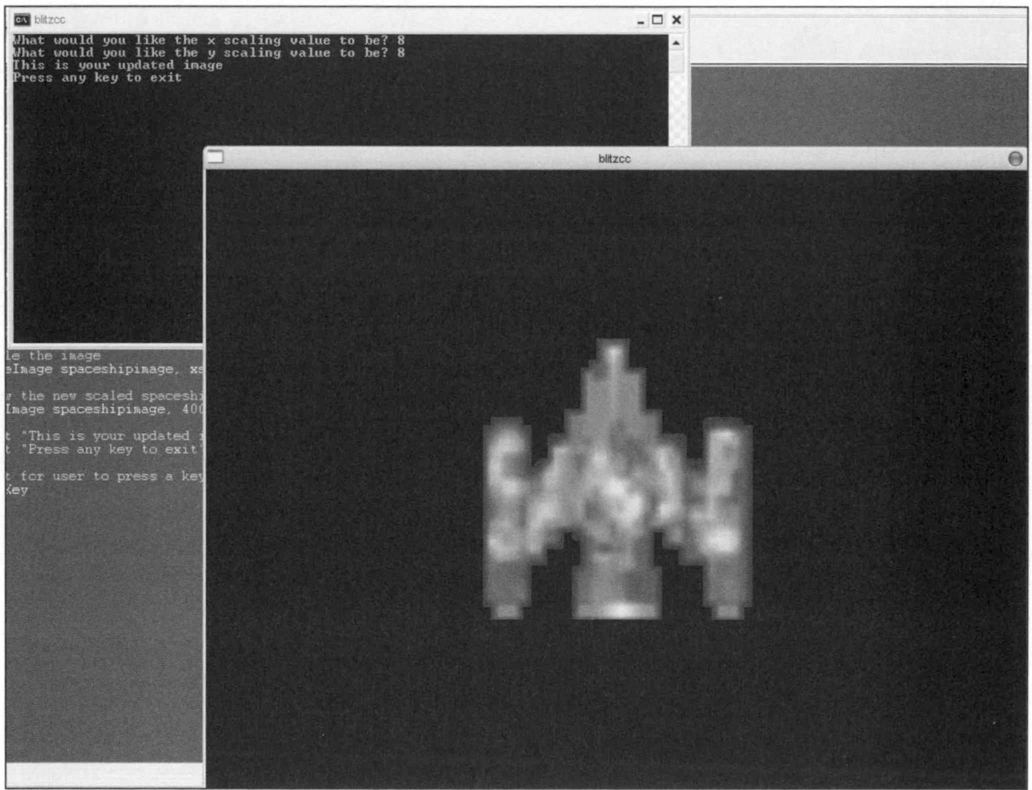

Figure 7.22 The demo07-07.bb program.

Using the `Input` functions, the program finds out what the scaling factors are. It then clears the screen in preparation for the new image.

```
;Scale the image
ScaleImage spaceshipimage, xs#,ys#

;Draw the new scaled spaceship
DrawImage spaceshipimage, 400,300
```

The newly scaled spaceship is drawn directly in the center of the screen, after being scaled by the `ScaleImage` function, which uses the scaling factors provided by the user earlier in the program.

These two lines scale and draw the new image. The program finishes off its tour by asking the users to press a key. Once they do, the program exits.

Note that if you size the image to greater than 100 percent, the image looks a little blurry. The reason is that the scaling function stretches the image and makes each of its pixels a little bit larger.

We can use `ScaleImage` with polygons such as triangles, also. We just need to make a few calls to `CreateImage()` and `ImageBuffer()`. Let's rewrite demo07-04.bb using `ScaleImage`.

Obviously, we first initialize the graphics. We then set `AutoMidHandle` to true so that the images will be centered in the program. We can then initialize the program's variables, such as the starting coordinates and the `point` type. Now is when we change the program a little bit.

We must make a call to `CreateImage()` to get a handle for an image that we can scale. This call should do the trick:

```
image = CreateImage( (point2\x - point3\x),(point2\y-point1\y) )
```

Because we know that `point3` is the farthest vertex to the left, `point2` is the farthest down and right, and `point1` is the highest, we subtract the high and low values to get the width and height of our image.

Now we need to call `SetBuffer` to set the active buffer to the `image` handle so we can draw straight to it.

```
SetBuffer ImageBuffer(image)
```

Now we continue with the `Line` commands. We then must revert back to the `FrontBuffer()` by calling `SetBuffer` again.

```
SetBuffer FrontBuffer()
```

We then use the `DrawImage()` function to display the original triangle.

```
DrawImage image, 400,300
```

Using `Input`, we get the scaling factor, and we call `ScaleImage` like this:

```
ScaleImage image,sxy#,sxy#
```

We then call

```
DrawImage image, 400,300
```

And the program is done! Figure 7.23 shows the demo07-08.bb.

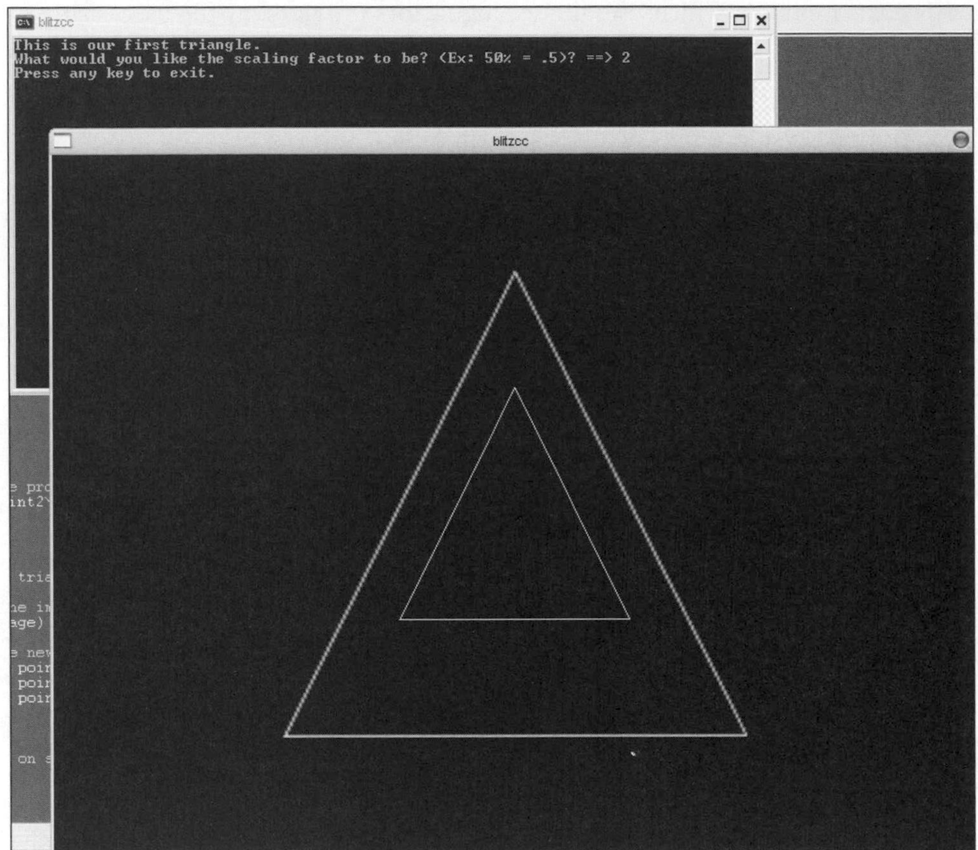

Figure 7.23 The demo07-08.bb program.

Following is the entire source for this program. We will review at the end.

```
;demo07-08.bb - Demonstrates Scaling with ScaleImage
Graphics 800,600,0,2

;Make sure AutoMidHandle is true
AutoMidHandle True
```

```
;STRUCTURES
;The point structure defines one coordinate point
Type point
     Field x,y
End Type

;Create the three vertices
point1.point = New point
point2.point = New point
point3.point = New point




;VARIABLES
;These variables are in local coordinates and define
;the positions of the vertices
point1\x= 100
point1\y= 0
point2\x= 200
point2\y= 200
point3\x= 0
point3\y = 200

;Create a buffer with the proper height and width
image = CreateImage( (point2\x - point3\x) + 1, (point2\y - point1\y) + 1 )


;MAIN SECTION

Print "This is our first triangle."

;Set default buffer to the image we created so that
;we can draw the triangle directly to it
SetBuffer ImageBuffer(image)

;Draw the triangle on the new buffer
Line point1\x, point1\y, point2\x, point2\y
Line point2\x, point2\y, point3\x, point3\y
Line point3\x, point3\y, point1\x, point1\y

SetBuffer BackBuffer()
```

```
;Draw the image centered onscreen
DrawImage image,400,300


Flip
;Find the scaling factor
sxy# = Input ("What would you like the scaling factor to be? (Ex: 50% = .5)? ==> ")
;What is the scaling factor
Flip

;Scale the image by its scaling factors
ScaleImage image,sxy#,sxy#


;Draw the new image
DrawImage image,400,300

Print "Press any key to exit."
;Wait for a key before exiting
WaitKey
```

I want you to notice a few things in this program. First, I removed the `xs` and `ys` constants. Because this triangle is drawn onto an image buffer and the image is drawn in the center, there is no need to convert local to global coordinates.

Second, notice that I added 100 to each of the `point\x` and `point\y` variables. This is necessary to remove the negative coordinates. Negative coordinates will be drawn off the buffer, and we need to move everything on, so we simply get rid of the negative values.

Third, notice that I added 1 to the size of the buffer in the call to `CreateImage()`. This addition was made to allow the entire image to be drawn on the buffer. It is usually a good idea to give a little leeway (here, 1 pixel) to make sure that everything appears on the image.

Last, you will notice that the scaled bitmap is blurry. This happens when bitmaps are scaled, because a bitmap has only a finite amount of information, and when you try to stretch it, the computer has to make up the information to fill in the blanks to make it bigger. The computer does this by averaging pixels in the bitmap and then computing what would be between them. The results of this are blurry images because the computer has to guess what the new and larger image should look like.

Well, that's pretty much it for scaling. We can now move on to a really cool subject: rotation.

Rotation

So far, you have learned two of the three types of transformations. Rotation is the final one that you will learn. Rotation is usually extremely hard to pull off, but BlitzPlus makes it much easier.

Like scaling, BlitzPlus provides a function for rotation—`RotateImage`. `RotateImage` is defined as this:

```
RotateImage image, value#
```

Table 7.6 examines the individual parameters. As you can see, `value#` rotates the given image in a clockwise manner.

Table 7.6 RotateImage's Parameters

Parameter	Description
`image`	The handle of the image you want to rotate
`value#`	The amount of degrees (between 0 and 360) you want to rotate image in a clockwise fashion

Take a look at Figures 7.24 and 7.25. They demonstrate clockwise and counterclockwise directions, respectively. Oh yeah, a clock turns clockwise.

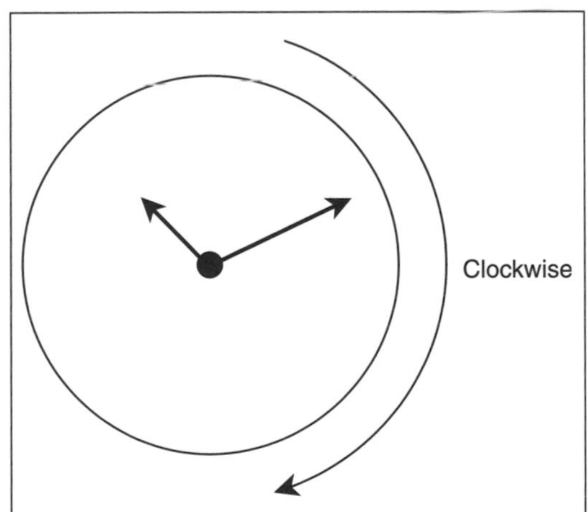

Figure 7.24 Clockwise.

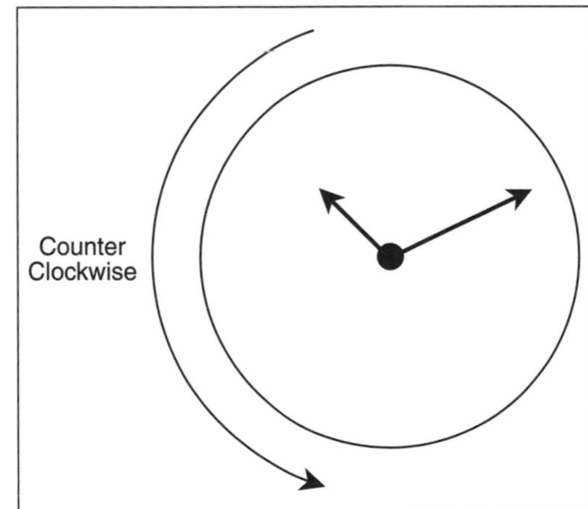

Figure 7.25 Counterclockwise.

`Value#` might be equal to any number between 0 and 360. There are 360 degrees in a circle. Refer to Figure 7.26 to see the degrees in a circle.

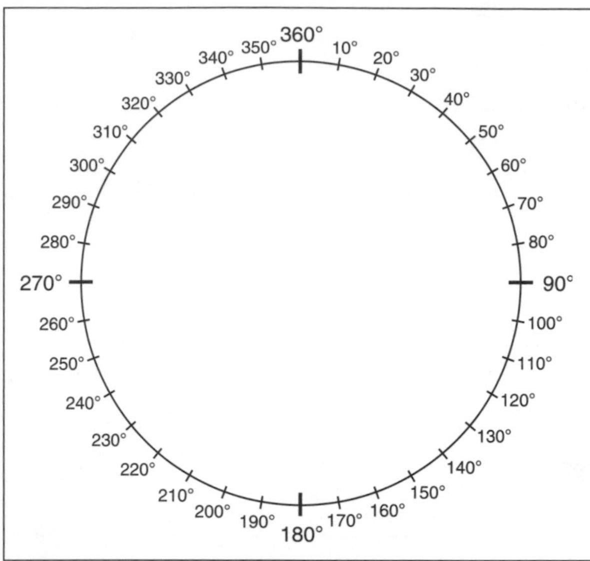

Figure 7.26 Degrees in a circle.

As you can see, rotating an image is pretty simple. Rotating shapes is extremely difficult and requires complex mathematics, so it is often a good idea to use `CreateImage()` and `ImageBuffer()`, as done with scaling in demo07-08.bb. Using `CreateImage()` allows you to turn your shape into an image, which makes rotation algorithms easier to perform.

Let's write a program that rotates a shape. This program loads an image from the hard drive, asks the users how many degrees they want to rotate it, and performs the action.

Following is the rotation section of the code in demo07-09.bb.

```
;Draw the beginning image
DrawImage shipimage,400,300

Flip
;Find out what the rotation value is
rotationvalue# = Input ( "How many degrees would you like to rotate the image? ")
Flip

;Rotate the Image
RotateImage shipimage, rotationvalue#


Print "Your new image is now drawn on the screen"

;Draw the new and rotated image on the screen
DrawImage shipimage, 440,300
```

This section draws the `shipimage` (which was loaded earlier in the program) at the center of the screen. The program then retrieves `rotationvalue#` from the user, and rotates the image using the command

```
RotateImage shipimage, rotationvalue#
```

This line rotates the `shipimage` the amount of degrees entered in `rotationvalue#`. The program then draws the new image to the right of the old image.

That's demo07-09.bb. Figure 7.27 shows a screenshot from the program.

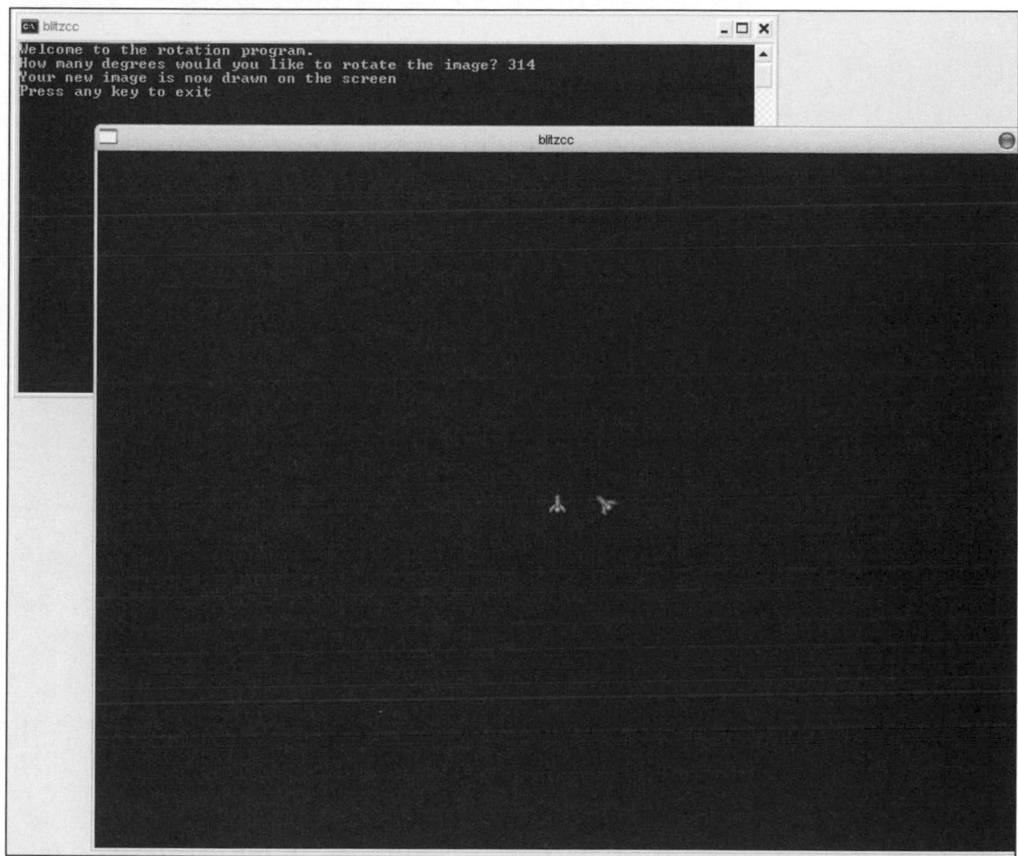

Figure 7.27 The demo07-09.bb program.

Asking a user for a rotation value is nice, but what about real-time rotation? Real-time rotation allows you to rotate an image at the spur of the moment. This effect is used in games such as *Asteroids*, where a spaceship is rotated onscreen.

Real-time rendering is as simple as waiting for the user to press a button and calling `RotateImage`, right? Wrong. If you do this, your program will run extremely slowly. You need to preload your images to allow the program to run at full speed. Before we get into preloading, though, take a look at what a rotation program will look like without it.

Following is the main loop of demo07-10.bb. Read through it and try to understand. An explanation follows.

```
;MAIN LOOP
While Not KeyDown(1)
;Clear the Screen
Cls

;Add Text
Text 10,0, "Press Left to rotate counter-clockwise and right to rotate clockwise,"
Text 10,20,"Press Esc to exit."

;If the player presses left, rotate four degrees left,
;if he presses right, rotate four degrees right
If KeyDown (203)
      RotateImage shipimage, -4
ElseIf KeyDown (205)
      RotateImage shipimage,4
EndIf

;Draw the ship
DrawImage shipimage, 400,300
Flip
Wend
;END OF MAIN LOOP
```

As you can see from the `Flip` and the `Cls` commands, this program uses page flipping. The rest of the program is pretty self-explanatory. If the user presses left (key code 203), the ship is rotated counter-clockwise four degrees. If the user presses right (key code 205), the ship is rotated four degrees clockwise.

This program should work correctly, huh? Unfortunately, it doesn't. Because rotating takes a lot of processor-power, the program runs slowly. To fix this problem, we use a technique called *preloading*,

Preloading is sort of hard to understand, but let me walk you through it. The first thing you want to do is decide how many frames you want. With a lot of frames, you get a little bit better animation. Because the image has a larger number of rotations, there is a smaller difference in degrees of each separate frame. However, with more frames, your program takes up more space in the memory. The program might also run a bit slower.

I usually choose a frame count of 16—it provides decent results but does not take up a lot of memory like higher frame amounts. Figure 7.28 shows each of the 16 rotations of the ship.

What Is Preloading?

Preloading is often a tough concept for beginning programmers to understand. The basic concept behind preloading is that displaying an image that has been changed and saved once in the program is faster than changing the image each time a change is necessary. Preloading does just this: at the beginning of the program, you create the images you will need later in the program and save it to an array that can be called at any time. When you need to display the saved images later, you just draw the necessary image from the array that you created earlier. Think of it like doing your homework. It will make the process a lot easier if you pull out all of your school supplies right when you begin, rather than getting a book only when you need it and getting your pencil when it is necessary. Your homework gets done either way. But it can get done quicker if you have "preloaded" all of your supplies. Of course this analogy works only if you actually do your homework. (Learn more about how to get away with not doing your homework in my other book, *How To Succeed As A Lazy Student*. Check it out at www.maneeshsethi.com.)

In the following rotation program, I rotate the image as many times as I want frames. When the user presses left or right, the next frame is displayed. By the way, when I use frame in this section, I am referring to frames of an image—not iterations of the main loop.

Anyway, let's get to the preloading. The first thing we do is create a constant that will hold the amount of rotations (frames) we want to have for our image. It might look something like this.

```
Const rotations = 16
```

Next, we create an array that holds all of our frames.

```
Dim imagearray(rotations)
```

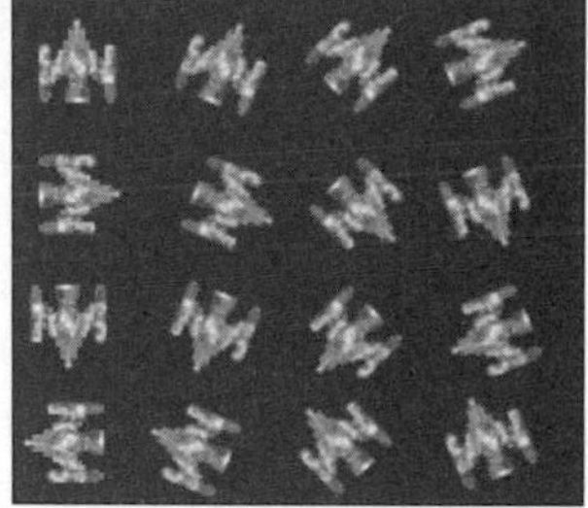

Figure 7.28
The ship's 16 rotations.

As you can see, this array will hold 16 images: one for each rotation. (It will actually hold 17, but we give it one extra space for a buffer). Don't forget that each array begins with 0, so 16 frames will have rotations from 0 to 15.

Now comes the semi-hard part. We have to load the frames into the array. This can be accomplished through a `For…Next` loop.

```
For frame = 0 To rotations - 1
       imagearray(frame) = CopyImage (shipImage)
       RotateImage imagearray(frame), frame*360/rotations
Next
```

What? Let's go through this loop line by line. This particular loop runs 16 times. It begins with 0 and counts to `rotations - 1`. Here, `rotations - 1` is equal to 15 (16-1 = 15). Now we get into the actual copying. Each frame of the array has `shipimage`, the image of the actual image, copied into it. This is accomplished by `CopyImage()`. The following line does the rotating of each frame, and it looks like this:

```
RotateImage imagearray(frame), frame*360/rotations
```

If you remember, `RotateImage`'s first parameter explains what will be rotated and the second parameter determines how much it should be rotated. Here, `imagearray(frame)` is rotated. This frame is the one that was just copied into the array. The rotation amount is a bit harder to understand. The frame number is multiplied by the amount of degrees in a circle (360) and then divided by the total number of rotations. Table 7.7 shows values for an image with 16 rotations.

Table 7.7 Rotation Angle in Degrees with 16 Rotations for a Full Circle

Frame	Subscript Number	Degrees Rotated
1	0	0
2	1	22.5
3	2	45
4	3	67.5
5	4	90
6	5	112.5
7	6	135
8	7	157.5
9	8	180
10	9	202.5
11	10	225
12	11	247.5
13	12	270
14	13	292.5
15	14	315
16	15	337.5

note

Notice that the image is never rotated 360 degrees. Rotating an image 360 degrees is the same as rotating it 0 degrees (the rotations come to a full circle). Therefore, the final frame rotates the image a tiny bit less than a full 360 degrees.

Let me display the full source for the rotation program now. We will go over the main loop right after.

```
;demo07-11.bb - Demonstrates preloading and real-time rotation

Graphics 800,600
;Set up AutoMidHandle and BackBuffer()
AutoMidHandle True
SetBuffer BackBuffer()

;IMAGES
;Load the spaceship image that will be rotated
shipimage = LoadImage ("spaceship.bmp")

;CONSTANTS
;How many rotations do you want total?
Const rotations = 16

;Create the rotation array
Dim imagearray(rotations)

;For all of the rotations you want, copy the spaceship image
;and rotate it the correct amount of degrees
For frame = 0 To rotations - 1
       imagearray(frame) = CopyImage (shipimage)
       RotateImage imagearray(frame), frame*360/rotations
Next


;Begin at frame 0 (facing upwards)
frame = 0

;MAIN LOOP
While Not KeyDown(1)

;Clear the screen
Cls

;Add Text
Print "Press Left to rotate counter-clockwise and right to rotate clockwise."
Print "Press Esc to exit."

;Rotate the ship left if user presses left
If KeyDown (203)
```

```
;Decrement frame by 1 (thus rotating it left)
       frame = frame - 1

;If the frame count is less than 0, put it back at the max value of the array
       If frame <= 0
              frame = rotations - 1
       EndIf
;Rotate the ship right if user presses right
ElseIf KeyDown (205)

;Increment frame by 1 (thus rotating it right)
       frame = frame + 1

;If frame gets too big, set it to the first frame (0)
       If frame >= rotations
              frame = 0
       EndIf

EndIf



;Draw the current frame
DrawImage imagearray(frame), 400,300


Flip

;Wait for a while
Delay 50
Wend
```

A beauty, huh? Figure 7.29 is a screenshot from the program. As usual, the beginning of the program sets up the graphics and initializes the rotation array. It then prints the introductory text to the user and resets `frame` to 0 (so that the ship faces upward).

The main loop tests for two keys—left and right. If the user presses the left key, the frame amount decreases by one, and if the right key is pressed, the frame amount increases by one. If `frame` is 0 and the left key is pressed, `frame` becomes `rotations- 1`, and if `frame` is the max number of rotations and the right key is pressed, `frame` becomes 0.

Figure 7.29 The demo07-11.bb program.

Make sure you understand rotations and preloading by now. If you're still a bit uneasy with the material, please read through the section again. The chapter is now moving onto the subject of parallaxing. Think about it, with a word as cool as parallaxing, how can it not be fun?

Parallaxing

Parallaxing is a very interesting topic, and we are going to jump right into it. Using parallaxing, you can create the effect of movement through 3D space from a fixed viewpoint. You could think of parallaxing as scrolling, if you want; in essence, you are scrolling two or more backgrounds at the same time to simulate movement.

What Is Parallaxing?

Remember the last time you were in a car on the freeway? When you looked outside (assuming you weren't playing a videogame), did you notice that the objects that were closer to you moved faster than the objects that were farther away? The road markers that lined the road shot by you while the trees on the mountains far away moved much slower. Parallaxing creates this effect in games: one part of the background moves faster than the other part, based on distance from the player's viewpoint.

Before we can actually begin parallaxing, we need to go over two BlitzPlus commands: `TileBlock` and `TileImage`.

TileBlock and TileImage

Because parallaxing effects begin in the background, we must first learn how to create backgrounds. Easier said than done, huh? Fortunately, BlitzPlus provides two functions for tiling backgrounds: `TileBlock` and `TileImage`.

note

You should probably know what tiling is, because both `TileBlock` and `TileImage` do it. Tiling takes a single image and plasters it all over your program's background in a tiled pattern. Just like kitchen tiles: each tile is exactly the same as the next one.

Both `TileBlock` and `TileImage` have the same definition.

```
TileBlock image, [x,y,frames]
TileImage image, [x,y,frames]
```

Table 7.8 lists each parameter. As you can see, the only required parameter is `image` (the image you want to be tiled). `x` and `y` move the starting point of the tiles to a location other than the default 0,0. `Frames` is used with animation, which will be discussed in the next chapter.

Table 7.8 TileBlock and TileImage's Parameters

Parameter	Description
`image`	The handle of the image you want tiled
`[x]`	Optional; the beginning x coordinate of the tiling procedure
`[y]`	Optional; the beginning y coordinate of the tiling procedure
`[frames]`	Optional; allows you to use frames in animation

There is a small difference between `TileBlock` and `TileImage`. When using `TileBlock`, all transparency and masking on your image is ignored. Therefore, you cannot draw overlapping backgrounds using `TileBlock`. Of course, because it ignores transparency, `TileBlock` is a little bit faster. For the most part, however, we will be using `TileImage`.

Using `TileBlock` and `TileImage` is really easy. Call the function you want to use with the image you want to tile. For our next demo program, we will be using the image in Figure 7.30.

Figure 7.30
The tiled image.

The following program is called demo07-12.bb. It only has four calls—one that initializes the graphics, one that loads the background image, and one that tiles the image using `TileBlock`. The program's last call is to `WaitKey` so that the user can see the program before it closes. Figure 7.31 shows a sample screenshot of the program.

Figure 7.31 The demo07-12.bb program.

The call to `TileBlock` is very simple.

```
;Tile the image
TileBlock backgroundimage
```

As you can probably guess, `backgroundimage` was previously loaded.

Now that you have tiled the image, we need to figure out how to scroll it up and down. Scrolling causes the game to appear in motion; therefore, it will seem like you are actually flying in space. The following program is located on the CD as demo07-13.bb.

The program begins as it usually does, with graphics initialization and whatnot (I don't think I have ever said *whatnot* before, ever). The initialization also creates the variable `scrolly`, which is used in the `TileImage` command. We then load the background, which is the same as the image in Figure 7.27. Now we enter the main loop.

```
;MAIN LOOP
While Not KeyDown(1)

;Tile the background at the y position of scrolly
TileBlock backgroundimage,0,scrolly

;Scroll the background a bit by incrementing scrolly
scrolly=scrolly+1

;If scrolly gets too big, reset it to zero
If scrolly >= ImageHeight(backgroundimage)
       scrolly = 0
EndIf


Flip
Wend
;END OF MAIN LOOP
```

The loop begins as you probably expect. The first line inside the loop is a `TileImage` command. This line tiles the background image, but it includes the optional parameter `scrolly` for `y`. Because `scrolly` is incremented each frame in the next line of code, the image is tiled a little bit higher each frame. This tiling effect creates a scrolling effect. The last important line in the main loop, the `If` statement, resets `scrolly` when the program has scrolled the image one full time. In other words, if `backgroundimage` is 64 pixels high, every 64th frame will be identical.

Just in case you want to know, `ImageHeight` returns the height of the given image in pixels.

note

Notice that there is no `Cls` command in the main loop. Because you are tiling a background, clearing the screen is worthless, because the `TileBlock` command writes over everything under it. If you use `TileImage`, which retains the image's transparency, you will need to use `Cls`.

Figure 7.32 shows three screenshots of demo07-13.bb at three five-frame intervals. As you can see, each one has changed very slightly.

Figure 7.32 The background at five-frame intervals.

The last thing we have to do is scroll two images at once. Two images will create the effect of distance, because some stars will appear closer (by scrolling them faster) and others will appear farther away (by scrolling them slower). In addition, the closer stars are brighter. Figure 7.33 shows both star images.

Following is the full program demo07-14.bb. As you can see, we loaded two images and scrolled them.

Figure 7.33 The closer (left) and distant (right) stars.

```
;demo07-14.bb - A Parallaxing Program
Graphics 800,600

;Set AutoMidhandle to true and draw everything to back buffer
AutoMidHandle True
SetBuffer BackBuffer()

;IMAGES
;The close and quickly scrolled background
backgroundimageclose = LoadImage("stars.bmp")

;The farther and slowly scrolled background
backgroundimagefar = LoadImage("starsfarther.bmp")

;Create scrolling tracker variable
scrolly = 0

;MAIN LOOP
While Not KeyDown(1)

;Clear the screen
Cls

;Tile both backgrounds at proper speed
TileImage backgroundimagefar,0,scrolly
TileImage backgroundimageclose,0,scrolly*2
```

```
;Increment scrolly
scrolly=scrolly+1

;Reset tracker variable if it gets too large
If scrolly >= ImageHeight(backgroundimageclose)
       scrolly = 0
EndIf



Flip
Wend
;END OF MAIN LOOP
```

The major difference when comparing this program to the previous one is the loading and tiling. Instead of loading one image, this program loads two: `backgroundimageclose` and `backgroundimagefar`. The `TileImage` command tiles both images, but the second image is set to scroll twice as fast. Therefore, it gives the impression of being farther away. Figure 7.34 shows a screenshot of this program.

Figure 7.34 The demo07-14.bb program.

note

Notice that I drew the closer stars after drawing the distant stars. This is kind of important—if I drew the closer ones first, they would appear to be under the distant ones. This would ruin the effect of parallaxing.

Well, that's it for image parallaxing. If you want to have some fun, try adding another image to the mix. Can you do it?

For the final program of the chapter, demo07-15.bb, I simply took the KONG program from Chapter 1 and added a parallaxing star field on the background. It's the same as regular KONG, but now it's in space. Figure 7.35 shows the new KONG running.

Figure 7.35 The demo07-15.bb program.

Summary

Whew, we are finally done with image programming. Cool, huh? Here's a list of the main points covered in this chapter:

- Translating
- Scaling
- Proportions
- Scaling images
- Scaling shapes
- Rotation
- Parallaxing

This chapter is a stepping stone to the next chapter: Animation. Get ready, because you are going to learn how to load and display multiple images to animate an object, making it move, walk, run, jump, explode—anything you want!

CHAPTER 8

Animation

Do you remember all those parameters named `[frame]` that we left set to 0? Well, those parameters are very useful once you understand what they are there for, and that is what you will learn from this chapter. You are going to learn the sweet skill of animation.

As you know, each iteration of the main loop produces one image frame of the actual game. When the image frames are drawn in rapid succession, it seems as if the images on screen are moving fluidly. With the type of animation introduced in this chapter, you will learn how to simulate movement onscreen; for example, you will be able to animate a character and make it appear as if it is walking.

Let's get straight into the meat of the chapter. First things first, we need to review bitmaps again. "Again!" you might say, but this time we are using bitmaps in a different way.

Using Bitmaps in Animation

We have used single bitmaps extensively throughout the book so far. A single bitmap contains only one frame of one static image. However, an image that supports frames contains numerous images—images that are usually related to one another.

Take, for example, Figure 8.1. As you can see, this is a single image.

Figure 8.1
A single static image.

Now, let's put this boy into a program.

```
;demo08-01.bb - A moving static image

Graphics 800,600

;Make back buffer default and set automidhandle to true
SetBuffer BackBuffer()
```

```
AutoMidHandle True

;IMAGES
;Load the image that will be drawn on screen
playerimage = LoadImage("staticboy.bmp")

;TYPES
;This type defines the coordinate position of the player
Type player
     Field x,y
End Type

;Create the player
player.player = New player

;Set up beginning values for player
player\x = 400
player\y = 300


;MAIN LOOP
While Not KeyDown(1) ;While user does not press Esc

;Clear the screen
Cls

;Print text
Text 0,0, "X Coordinate: " + player\x
Text 0,12, "Y Coordinate: " + player\y

;If player presses left, move bitmap left
If KeyDown (203)
     player\x = player\x - 5
EndIf

;If player presses left, move bitmap right
If KeyDown(205)
     player\x = player\x + 5
EndIf

;If player presses up, move bitmap up
If KeyDown (200)
```

```
    player\y = player\y -5
EndIf

;If player presses down, move bitmap down
If KeyDown (208)
    player\y = player\y + 5
EndIf

;Draw the player on screen
DrawImage playerimage, player\x,player\y

Flip

;Slow it down a little
Delay 50

Wend
;END OF MAIN LOOP
```

This program loads an image and displays it on the screen. The coordinates are changed based on the key presses of the players: if they press up, down, left, or right, the boy moves accordingly. Figure 8.2 is a screenshot taken from the program.

Even though this program runs smoothly, it's very boring. All that you see is a moving image—the boy doesn't even move his leg. The image almost looks as if it is floating.

To fix this problem, we are going to make the image appear to walk. To do this, we will use an image with eight frames. Figure 8.3 shows the image.

As you can see, each frame is slightly different from the previous frame. When we put these frames together, as we did with the main loop, we will create the effect of animation.

Some important parts of the program must change. First off, we have to load the image. Loading an animated image is not quite the same as loading a static image. The most obvious change is that we use the function `LoadAnimImage()` instead of `LoadImage()`.

`LoadImage()` is defined like this:

```
LoadAnimImage (filename$, width, height, first, count)
```

There are a few more parameters than `LoadImage()`. The first parameter, filename$, acts just as the parameter with the same name in `LoadImage()`. `Filename$` is just the file name of the image you want to load. The next two parameters, `width` and `height`, are the measurements of the width and height of each of the frames. For example, in Figure 8.3, the measurement of each frame is 71×95 pixels.

Figure 8.2 The demo8-01.bb program.

Figure 8.3 The frames of the walking image.

note

Notice that the width and height values of each frame are exactly the same in the previous example. Make sure you remember that all of the frames of an image must be the same; otherwise, your program will not run.

The parameter `first` tells which frame you want to begin loading. You almost always want to begin with the first frame, so you will set this value to 0, because, in computer languages, counting begins with 0. Rarely, you might want to load the images starting with a later frame than the first one. If this is the case, you will use a different value for `first`. The final parameter, `count`, informs `LoadAnimImage()` how many total frames you are loading.

Table 8.1 summarizes each of `LoadAnimImage()`'s parameters. Now, we can load our animated image using the function

```
playerimage = LoadAnimImage("animatedboy.bmp", 95,71,0,8)
```

Table 8.1 LoadAnimImage()'s Parameters

Parameter	Description
`filename$`	The file name of the image you want to load
`width`	The width in pixels of each frame
`height`	The height in pixels of each frame
`first`	The number of the frame that you want to begin with (usually 0)
`count`	The total number of frames you want to load

All right, loading now looks good. In the following program, demo08-02.bb, we will be creating a type with the player's x and y coordinates. We are also going to need to add another variable to the type, `frame`. `Frame` tells the program which frame should be drawn at that specific time. Following is the entire initialization section of the new program, demo08-02.bb.

```
;demo08-02.bb - A moving animated image

Graphics 800,600

;Set up BackBuffer() and AutoMidHandle
SetBuffer BackBuffer()
AutoMidHandle True

;IMAGES
;Load the animated image of the boy
playerimage = LoadAnimImage("animatedboy.bmp",95,71,0,8)

;TYPES
;Load the player type
Type player
        Field x,y      ;The x and y coordinate position
        Field frame   ;The frame that should be drawn
End Type

;Create the player
player.player = New player
```

```
;Give the player its starting values
player\x = 400
player\y = 300
player\frame = 0
```

We have changed the loading call to make it load the animated image. Also, the `player` type now includes a field `frame`, which is initialized to 0.

Now we enter the main loop. In order to make the image move, we must increment the frame whenever a key is pressed. Therefore, we add the line

```
player\frame = player\frame + 1
```

under the key tests that move the player up and right, and we add

```
player\frame = player\frame - 1
```

to the tests that move the player down and left. In other words, whenever the player presses a button, the image moves to the next frame, and in doing so, the boy seems to walk.

Of course, because there are only eight frames, we need to make sure that `player\frame` never goes above 7 (remember that `frame` begins at 0). We also must make sure that if the user goes below frame 0, the frame is reset to 7, so that the animated image resets itself and continues to animate. This is accomplished with this block of code:

```
If player\frame > 7
        player\frame = 0
ElseIf player\frame < 0
        player\frame = 7
EndIf
```

Following is the full source for the main loop.

```
;MAIN LOOP
While Not KeyDown(1)

;Clear the screen
Cls

;Position text at the top left corner of the screen
Text 0,0, "X Coordinate: " + player\x
Text 0,0, "Y Coordinate: " + player\y

;If player presses left, move him left and decrement the frame number
If KeyDown (203)
        player\x = player\x - 5
        player\frame = player\frame - 1
```

```
EndIf

;If player presses right, move him right and increment the frame number
If KeyDown(205)
       player\x = player\x + 5
       player\frame = player\frame + 1
EndIf

;If player presses up, move him up and increment the frame number
If KeyDown (200)
       player\y = player\y -5
       player\frame = player\frame + 1
EndIf

;If player presses down, move him down and decrement the frame number
If KeyDown (208)
       player\y = player\y + 5
       player\frame = player\frame - 1
EndIf

;If the frame gets too high, reset it back to zero.
If player\frame > 7
       player\frame = 0

;If the frame gets too low, reset it to 3
ElseIf player\frame < 0
       player\frame = 7
EndIf

;Draw the player at the correct position and the correct frame
DrawImage playerimage, player\x,player\y, player\frame

;Wait a while
Delay 100
Flip
Wend
;END OF MAIN LOOP
```

And there we have it. Figure 8.4 is a screenshot from this program. There is one thing I want you to notice in the loop. See the `DrawImage` command? There is an extra parameter that we haven't seen before.

Figure 8.4 The demo08-02.bb program.

If you remember from long ago, the declaration of `DrawImage` is as follows:

```
DrawImage handle, x, y, [frame]
```

We have not used the final optional parameter until now. The `[frame]` parameter allows you to change which frame of an animated image is drawn, as we did in the previous program. Cool, huh?

Making Bitmaps

Now that we know how to load bitmaps, you probably want to know how to create them. First off, decide what the animated image will look like. Usually, each frame will look almost the same, with only one or two small changes.

Take a look at Figure 8.5. This image, as you can see, is a rectangle. Say we wanted to animate this rectangle.

Now, we want to animate this image. Let's rotate it 45 degrees ($1/8^{th}$ of a complete turn). It looks like Figure 8.6.

Figure 8.5 A soon-to-be animated rectangle.

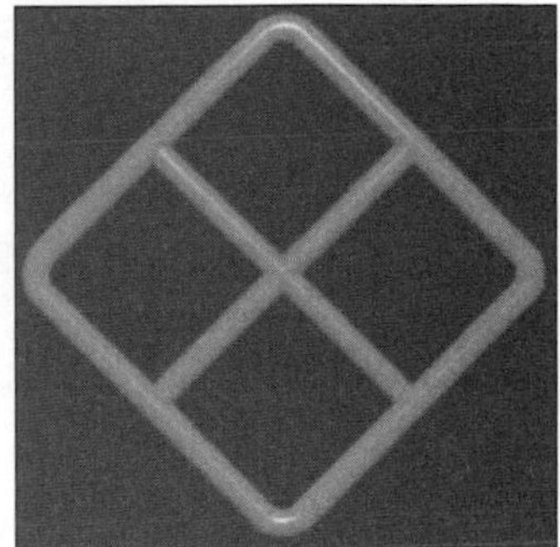
Figure 8.6 The second frame of the animated rectangle.

As you can see, this rectangle has been turned a little sideways. Now, to put these together in a bitmap, we need to use our favorite paint program (I use Paint Shop Pro, which is included on the CD). I created both images, and put them together in one single image. The final image is shown in Figure 8.7.

note

Make sure that you put the frames back to back, with absolutely no space in between. If you happen to add space, the frames will become distorted and you will end up with a Not enough frames in image error. If your frames overlap, the program will display some of frame two in frame one, some of frame three in frame two, and so on.

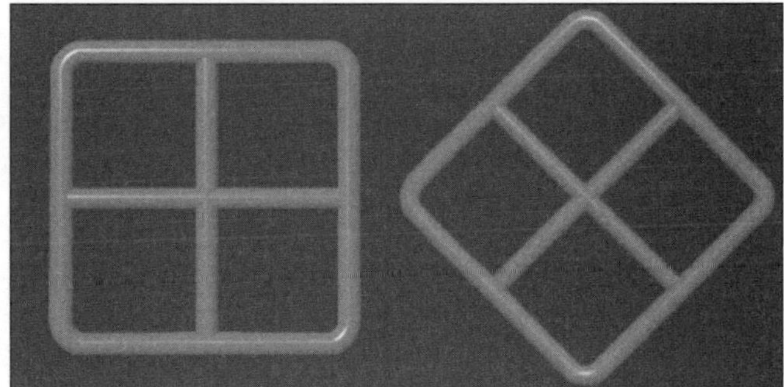
Figure 8.7 The double-framed image.

Now here is the trick: the width and height of *each frame* must be the width and height of the largest frame. In Figure 8.6, each frame is 250 pixels by 250 pixels, but only because the larger frame (frame 2) requires that size. Take a look—see the first frame? There is a lot of black space around it. The first frame is closer to 200×200, but it ends up larger because of the next rotated frame.

Now that we have this image ready to go, we need to write a program around it. The following listing is from demo08-03.bb. Begin with the initialization.

```
;demo08-03.bb - Demonstrates rotation a rectangle
Graphics 800,600
```

```
;Handle images from the center
AutoMidHandle True

;Load the animated rectangles
rectanglesimage = LoadAnimImage("rectangles.bmp",250,250,0,2)

;Create variable that counts how many rotations occurred
rotationcount = 0
```

Obviously, this section just sets up the graphics and loads the image. Make sure you notice that the `LoadAnimImage()` command states that `rectanglesimage` has two frames, each being 250×250 pixels. Also, the variable `rotationcount` is created to count how many times the rotation occurs.

Now move to the important part of this program.

```
;MAIN LOOP
While Not KeyDown(1)
;Clear the screen
Cls

;Print the number of rotations
Text 0,0, "Number of Rotations: " + rotationcount

;Draw the rectangle image with the proper frame
DrawImage rectanglesimage,400,300,rotationcount Mod 2

;Increment the rotation count variable
rotationcount = rotationcount + 1

;Wait a while
Delay 100

Flip

Wend
;END OF MAIN LOOP
```

Figure 8.8 shows a screenshot from the program.

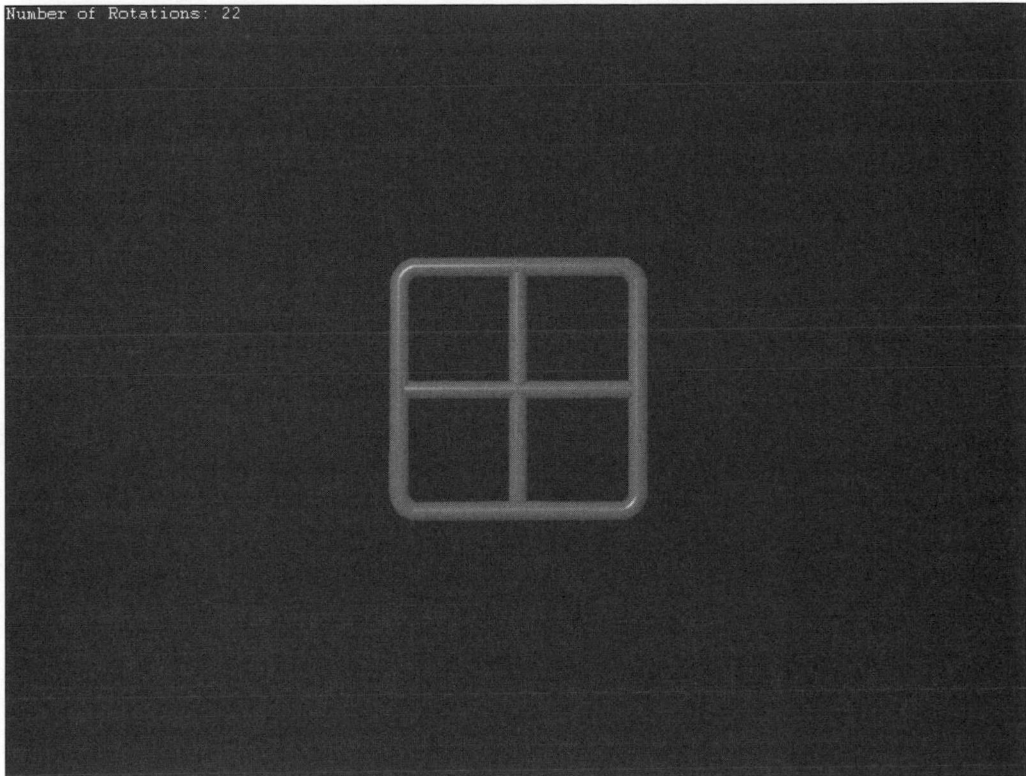

Figure 8.8 The demo08-03.bb program.

Okay, let's start from the top. As usual, the `Cls` clears the screen, so the rotation does not leave streaks. Figure 8.9 shows what the program will look like if you remove the `Cls` command.

The `Text` command displays how many rotations have occurred in the program using the `rotationcount` function.

The program then draws the actual image. The parameters here are pretty clear, except for the final one. As you know, the last frame is the `[frame]` parameter. We want the program to alternate between 1 and 2 for `[frame]`, and to do this, we use the `Mod` operator.

If you remember from long ago, the `Mod` operator returns the remainder of the first operand divided by the second. In other words, 1 `Mod` 2 returns 1, because 1 divided by 2 leaves a remainder of 1, and 2 `Mod` 2 returns 0, because 2 divided by 2 leaves a remainder of 0.

Table 8.2 shows the return value of `Mod` for 1-10 `Moded` by 2.

In other words, depending on the value of `rotationcounter` (if it is even or odd), it will display the first or second frame. If you wanted to expand the image to three frames, you would make the `[frame]` parameter equal to `rotationcount Mod 3`.

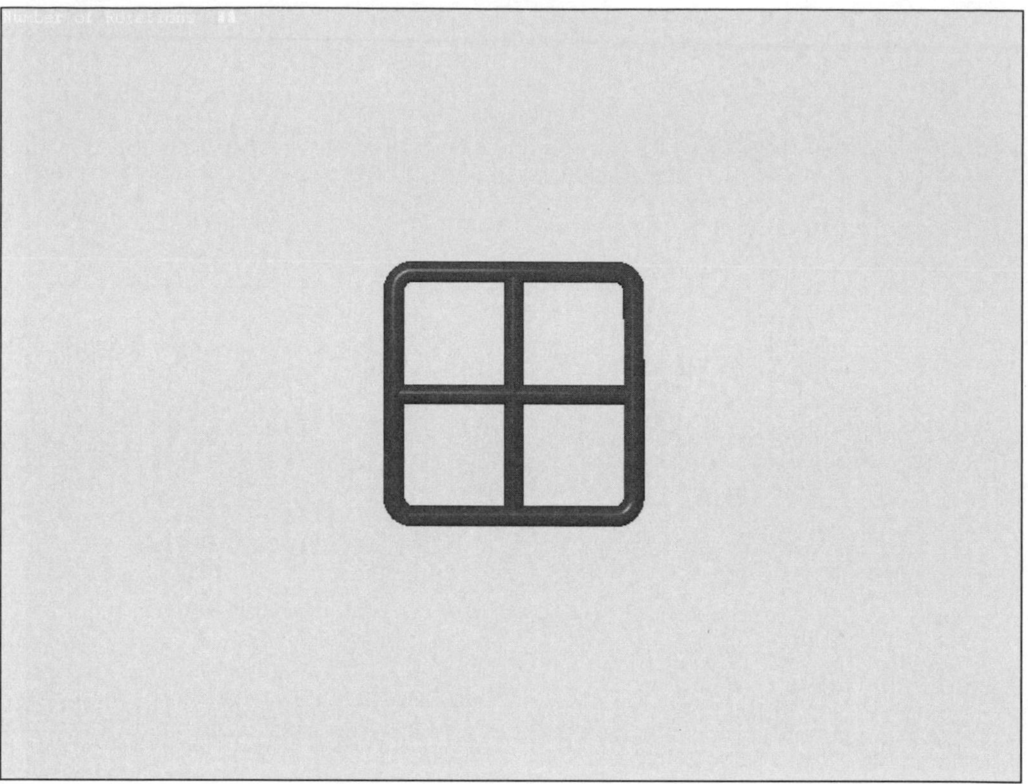

Figure 8.9 Removing `Cls` from demo08-03.bb.

Table 8.2 Results of Mod

First Operand	Second Operand	Result
1	2	1
2	2	0
3	2	1
4	2	0
5	2	1
6	2	0
7	2	1
8	2	0
9	2	1
10	2	0

The next two lines of the code update the value of rotation count and delay the program by 100 milliseconds, respectively. If you remove the `Delay` command, the program runs so fast you can't see the frame changes!

All right, that's how you make a bitmap. Let's go on to something else now—movement.

Displaying Movement

If you remember the previous chapter, you learned how to have Blitz Basic create all of our rotations for us. However, this does not always work. Sometimes, you will decide to put brightness or lighting on one area of the image, but you won't want that lighting rotated. Other times, you might want to have an image walk in numerous directions.

The first thing we need to do is to create the bitmap. This example starts with the image in Figure 8.10.

Okay, now that we have the base, we also need to have the animations. Because this is not going to be rotated, but rather turned around, Blitz Basic cannot do the work for us. Figure 8.11 shows some of the frames of the image.

Figure 8.10 The about-to-be moved image.

Excellent, huh? Now we are going to put the images together into one bitmap that will be used in the program, Figure 8.12. Notice that the bitmap is split into four sections: one section contains the animation for moving left, another for moving up, one more for moving right, and the last for moving down.

Figure 8.11 The frames of movement.

Okay, now that we have the image ready, we need to get into the program. We first begin with the actual coding for demo08-04.bb. As usual, create the back buffer and set the graphics first.

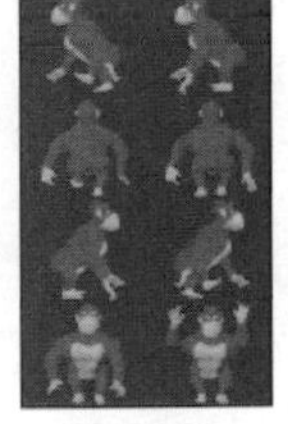

Figure 8.12 The loaded player image.

```
;demo08-04.bb - Demonstrates sprite movement

Graphics 800,600
;Set up backbuffer and automidhandle
SetBuffer BackBuffer()
AutoMidHandle True
```

After this, we write in the constants that will be used in the program.

```
;CONSTANTS
;These constants define the direction that is begin faced
Const DIRECTIONLEFT = 1     ;When direction is left
Const DIRECTIONUP = 2     ;When direction is up
Const DIRECTIONRIGHT = 3     ;When direction is right
```

```
Const DIRECTIONDOWN = 4      ;When direction is down

;These constants define how many pixels are moved per frame
Const MOVEX = 5      ;How many pixels moved left/right per frame?
Const MOVEY = 5      ;How many pixels moved up.down per frame?


;These are key code constants
Const LEFTKEY = 203, UPKEY = 200, RIGHTKEY = 205, DOWNKEY = 208
```

These constants are used throughout the program, and are very useful. Basically, the `DIRECTION*` constants allow the players to have a different direction value based on which direction they are going. For example, if the users are heading up, their direction will be 2, if they are heading right, their direction will be 3.

The `MOVE*` parameters define the number of pixels the player will be moved per frame. Feel free to change them if you want.

Finally, the `*KEY` parameters give the key codes for Left, Up, Right, and Down. Table 8.3 summarizes each of these parameters.

Table 8.3 Demo08-04.bb's Constants

Constant	Value	Description
DIRECTIONLEFT	1	The direction value for the player heading left.
DIRECTIONUP	2	The direction value for the player heading up.
DIRECTIONRIGHT	3	The direction value for the player heading right.
DIRECTIONDOWN	4	The direction value for the player heading down.
MOVEX	5	The number of pixels the player can move left or right per frame.
MOVEY	5	The number of pixels the player can move up or down per frame.
LEFTKEY	203	The key code for Left.
UPKEY	200	The key code for Up.
RIGHTKEY	205	The key code for Right.
DOWNKEY	208	The key code for Down.

Alright, next we move on to the player type.

```
;TYPES
;The player type is used for the character on the screen
Type player
	Field x,y    ;The coordinate position
	Field direction    ;The direction that is being faced (one of the DIRECTIONXXX
constants)
```

```
        Field frame     ;The frame that should be drawn
        Field image     ;The image that should be drawn
End Type
```

x and y indicate the coordinate position of the player, direction identifies which direction the player is facing, and frame chooses which frame of the player image is drawn. Image tells the program which image is loaded and animated.

Table 8.4 explains each parameter.

Table 8.4 Demo08-04.bb's Type Fields

Field	Description
x	The x coordinate of the player.
y	The y coordinate of the player.
direction	The direction the player is facing, based upon the DIRECTION* constants.
frame	The frame of the player image which is to be drawn.
image	The image which will be loaded and animated.

Now we need to set up the player type.

```
;Create the player
player.player = New player

;Give the player starting variables
player\x = 400
player\y = 300
player\direction = DIRECTIONLEFT
player\frame = 0
;Load the player's image
player\image = LoadAnimImage("monkeyanim.bmp",48,40,0,8)
```

As usual, when creating a type, you must create an instance of the type by calling the New command. Here, we create player, based upon the player type. We then get into the actual fields.

The player begins existence directly in the center of the screen (400,300). I then decided to begin the player heading left, so player\direction is set to DIRECTIONLEFT. The frame is then set to 0, so that the player will begin facing the correct direction with the correct starting point.

Note that we set AutoMidHandle to true earlier in the program. This allows the object to be centered and displayed correctly. Notice that I did this right before the following

`LoadAnimImage()` command. `LoadAnimImage()` loads the player picture with the proper parameters: each frame is 48×40, and there are eight frames (beginning with 0 and ending with 7).

Okay, now that that is over with, we move on to the actual loop. At this point, the player is facing left, and is displaying frame 0. In the game loop, we want the player to be able to move the image around.

First off, begin the loop with some setup.

```
;MAIN LOOP
While Not KeyDown(1)

;Clear the screen
Cls

;Print player info
Text 0,0, "Player X: " + player\x
Text 0,12, "Player Y: " + player\y
Text 0,24, "Player Direction: " + player\direction
Text 0,36, "Frame: " + player\frame
```

These lines display the values of all of the fields of the player type (besides `image`, of course).

Now, I want to stop you for a moment. The next part of the code is going to be hard to comprehend, so I'm going to only show you one part of it and explain it to you before showing you the rest.

We now have to allow the player to change the direction of the character on the screen. To do this, we first test to see what has been pressed.

```
If KeyDown(LEFTKEY)
```

Therefore, the following lines of code will occur only when the user presses left. Now you actually need to move the user left, by changing his x coordinate.

```
player\x = player\x - MOVEX
```

As you might expect, this pushes the user a bit left. Next, we change the direction the user is facing.

```
player\direction = DIRECTIONLEFT
```

This just tells the computer that the player is facing left.

The next line is probably the most difficult to understand. It computes the frame that's displayed based on the direction that the player is facing.

```
player\frame = (player\frame + 1 )Mod (2) + (2 * (player\direction)-2)
```

Whew! That's a big math problem. Let me show you what happens.

1. `player\frame` is incremented by 1. In this example, `player\frame`, which began the program as 0, is now equal to 1.
2. `player\frame` is divided by 2, and the remainder is returned using the Mod function. In this example, `player\frame`, which is equal to 1, is divided by 2. Because 1 / 2 leaves a remainder of 1, `(player\frame + 1 )Mod (2)` returns 1.
3. 2 multiplied by the direction of the player, and − 2 is added to the frame value. This expression gives the appropriate value of the frame depending on the direction of the player. In this example, `2 * player\direction` (which is equal to 1) − 2 = 0, which is added to `player\frame` (which, according to step 2, is equal to 1). Thus, `player\frame` is equal to 1.

Hopefully, most of this isn't *that* hard to comprehend, except for the expression `2 * player\direction - 2`. Basically, think of this equation as analogous to global and local coordinates. If you remember, with global and local coordinates, you find the position of something at its own local space and add it to the position of the screen. The same thing is occurring here; you are determining the difference in the frame (either 0 or 1, the local coordinates), and adding it to the `2 * player\direction - 2` (between 0 and 7, the global coordinates). Table 8.5 lists all the possible values for `player\frame`, complete with the value of `2 * player\direction - 2` for that frame.

Table 8.5 Each Frame's Values

Frame Number	Direction	2 * player\direction − 2
0	1	0
1	1	1
2	2	2
3	2	3
4	3	4
5	3	5
6	4	6
7	4	7

note

Make sure you understand that the expression `2 * player\direction - 2` only works because there are two frames for each direction. If there were three frames for each animation (for a total of 12 frames, if there are still only four directions), the equation would be `3 * player\direction - 3`. If there were five frames per direction, the expression would be `5 * player\direction - 5`, and so on.

Now that you (hopefully) understand how we find the frame of the player, at least for when he moves left, let me show you the entire game loop.

```
;MAIN LOOP
While Not KeyDown(1)

;Clear the screen
Cls

;Place the text in top left hand corner
Locate 0,0

;Print player info
Print "Player X: " + player\x
Print "Player Y: " + player\y
Print "Player Direction: " + player\direction
Print "Frame: " + player\frame

;If player hits left, move him left, and find the correct direction and frame
If KeyDown(LEFTKEY)
        player\x = player\x - MOVEX      ;Move him left
        player\direction = DIRECTIONLEFT      ;face him left
        player\frame = (player\frame + 1 )Mod (2) + (2 * (player\direction)-2)
      ;find frame

;If player hits up, move him up, and find the correct direction and frame
ElseIf KeyDown(UPKEY)
        player\y = player\y - MOVEY      ;Move him up
        player\direction = DIRECTIONUP      ;face him up
        player\frame = (player\frame + 1 )Mod (2) + (2 * (player\direction)-2)
;find frame

;If player hits right, move him right, and find the correct direction and frame
ElseIf KeyDown(RIGHTKEY)
        player\x = player\x + MOVEX      ;move him right
        player\direction = DIRECTIONRIGHT      ;face him right
        player\frame = (player\frame + 1 )Mod (2) + (2 * (player\direction)-2)
;find frame

;If player hits down, move him down, and find the correct direction and frame
ElseIf KeyDown(DOWNKEY)
        player\y = player\y + MOVEY      ;Move him down
        player\direction = DIRECTIONDOWN      ;face him down
```

```
        player\frame = (player\frame + 1 )Mod (2) + (2 * (player\direction)-2)
;find frame
EndIf

;Draw the player at correct position and frame
DrawImage player\image,player\x,player\y, player\frame

;wait a (fraction of a) sec
Delay 50

Flip
Wend
;END OF MAIN LOOP
```

Cool, huh? Figure 8.13 shows a screenshot of this program.

Figure 8.13 The demo08-04.bb program.

The final parts of the program react just as you would expect them to. When you press Right, the player moves five pixels to the right, as shown by the following line of code.

```
player\x = player\x + MOVEX
```

The same thing, only with y values, occurs when the user presses Up or Down.

At the end of the program, the image is drawn onscreen with the `DrawImage` command.

```
DrawImage player\image,player\x,player\y, player\frame
```

This draws the selected frame (`player\frame`) of the player's image (`player\image`) and the player's x and y coordinates (`player\x,player\y`).

The program ends by delaying for 50 milliseconds. Without the delay, the animation occurs very quickly—sometimes so quickly, it is almost hard to see the actual movement!

Figure 8.14
The tiled grass.

Well, that's it for demo08-04.bb. Just for fun, I wrote demo08-05.bb. The program is exactly the same as demo08-04.bb, but this time the player is walking on grass instead of nothing. Figure 8.14 shows the grass that is tiled.

Figure 8.15 shows a screenshot from demo08-05.bb.

This chapter is nearly complete, so let's review some of the most important things to remember when creating bitmaps.

- Make sure each frame of your bitmap is the same size.
- Make sure that all of the bitmaps are lined up directly next to one another.

Also, remember that it is easier to understand animations when you make the bitmaps line up. For example, on demo08-04.bb (and also demo08-05.bb), I created four sets of two animations. The same would be done for other rotations. For example, say you were rotating a ship 12 times. Put the first four rotations (from facing up to facing right) in one row, the next four rotations (facing right to facing down) in another row, and so on.

Figure 8.15 The demo08-05.bb program.

Summary

Alright, we did it! That's the end of this chapter. In this chapter, you learned the following concepts.

- Using bitmaps in animation
- Making bitmaps
- Displaying movement

Are you ready for the next chapter? We are moving up to collision detection. Whoopee!

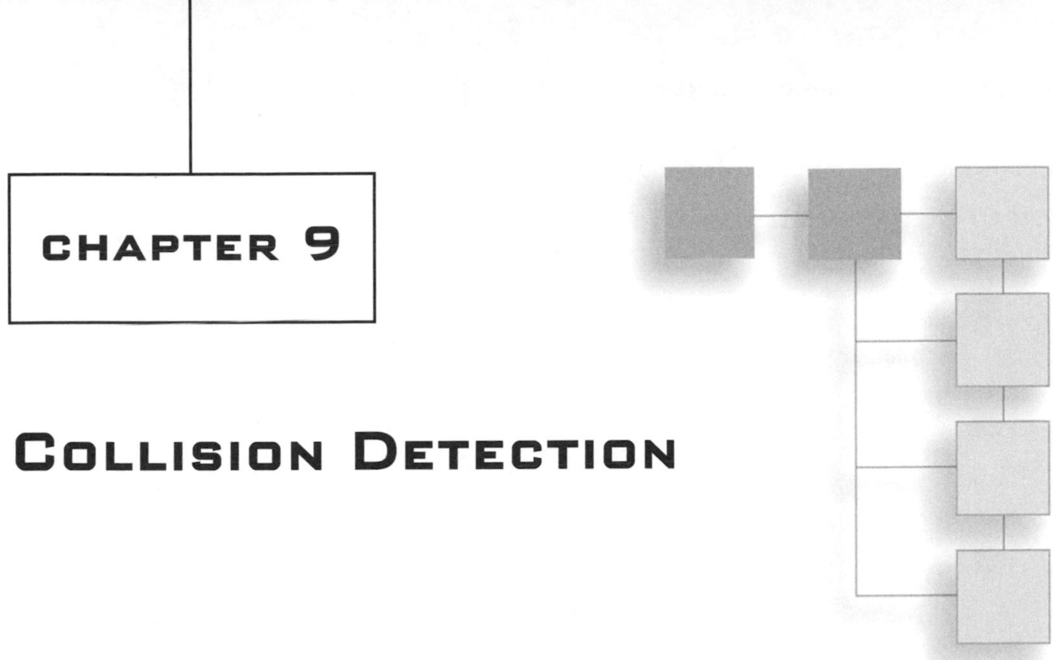

Chapter 9

Collision Detection

You are nearing the end of Part 2. This chapter explains the art of collision detection. Collision detection allows your program to determine whether an object on your screen has been hit by another object, and performs actions based on the check. For example, if you made a space shooter, and you wanted to determine whether a missile hit an enemy ship, you would use collision detection. If the ship had been hit, you might decrease its hit points or destroy it all together.

There are a few ways to check for collision detection, and we are going to go through them now. We can use bounding boxes, both rectangular and circular, and pixel-perfect collisions. Let's start off checking collision with a single pixel.

Basic Collisions

Before we learn how to check for collisions of objects (images, shapes, and so on), let's go over basic pixel collisions. To determine if a pixel collision has occurred, you just check the pixel you are tracking and make sure that its x and y values are not the same as the object you are testing it against. See Figure 9.1 for an example.

For the following program, demo09-01.bb, we will allow the player to control a single pixel that can be moved up, down, left, or right. If the pixel hits a wall (the wall being the edge of the screen), the pixel position will be reset and the collision counter will be updated.

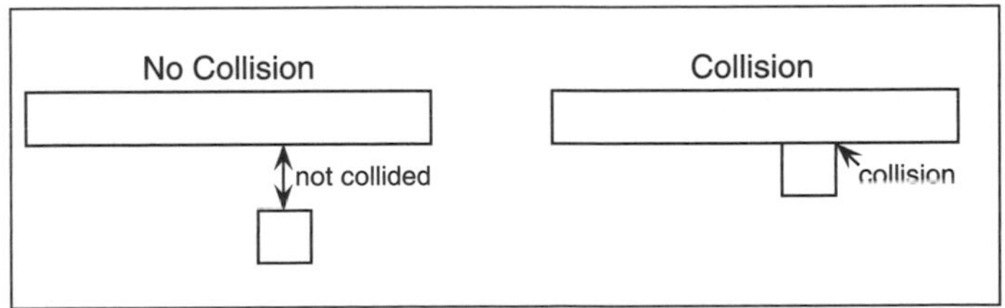

Figure 9.1 Difference between a collision and no collision.

Following is the source for demo09-01.bb:

```
;demo09-01.bb - Demonstrates Pixel Collisions
Graphics 400,300

;create variables that define coordinate position of pixel
Global x = 200
Global y = 150

Cls

;This variable contains the amount of times a collision has occurred
collisions = 0

;CONSTANTS
;These are the key code constants
Const UPKEY = 200, DOWNKEY = 208, LEFTKEY = 203, RIGHTKEY = 205

;MAIN LOOP
While Not KeyDown (1)


;Print intro
Text 0,0, "Press the arrow keys to move the pixel around."

;Print the number of collisions
Text 0,12, "Collisions: " + collisions

;Move player around depending on the key he pressed
If KeyDown(UPKEY)
     y = y - 5
ElseIf KeyDown(DOWNKEY)
     y = y + 5
ElseIf KeyDown(LEFTKEY)
     x = x - 5
ElseIf KeyDown(RIGHTKEY)
     x = x + 5
EndIf

;Call the CheckForCollisions function and determine if a collision occurred
collisions = CheckForCollisions(collisions)

;Draw the pixel on the screen
```

```
Plot x,y

;wait a (fraction of a )sec
;Delay 100

Flip



Wend
;END OF MAIN LOOP



;FUNCTIONS

;Function CheckForCollisions(collisions) - Returns number of total collisions, tests for
new ones
;collisions: the number of collisions at the time of calling the function
Function CheckForCollisions(collisions)

;If the pixel is offscreen, report a collision
If x <= 0 Or x >= 400 Or y <= 0 Or y >= 300
     collisions = collisions + 1     ;increment collisions
     Cls     ;clear the screen
     Text 100,150,"A Collision Has Occurred"
     Flip
     Delay 1000     ;wait a sec
     Cls     ;clear screen again
     Flip
     Cls



     x = 200     ;reset x
     y = 150     ;reset y
EndIf

;return the amount of collisions
Return collisions
Cls
End Function
```

This program works pretty much as you would expect it to. It begins by setting the graphics and creating the variables `x,y`, and `collisions`. It then enters the main loop.

note

Notice that while `x` and `y` are global variables, `collisions` is not. This fact will be important later in the program.

Inside the main loop, the program determines whether any arrow keys have been pressed. If so, it increments the `x` and `y` variables accordingly. The program also displays the number of collisions at the top of the screen.

Near the end of the loop, the program calls the function `CheckForCollisions()`. It includes `collisions` as a parameter. It also sets `collisions` equal to the return value of the function. Table 9.1 details the parameter.

Table 9.1 CheckForCollisions()'s Parameter

Parameter	Description
`collisions`	The number of collisions that have occurred thus far in the program. The number of collisions is also returned by the function.

Consider the `CheckForCollisions()` function further. The first and hardest part of the function to understand is the test. The test looks like this:

```
If x <= 0 Or x >= 400 Or y <= 0 Or y >= 300
```

This test determines if the point has gone offscreen. Referring to Figure 9.2, you see that the x tests pertain to the right and left walls of the screen and the y tests pertain to the upper and lower walls.

Now, if the program finds that the point has hit one of the walls, it begins its reset procedure. First, it adds 1 to `collisions`, which increases the collision counter by 1. It then displays `"A Collision Has Occurred"` on the screen. The x and y coordinates are then reset.

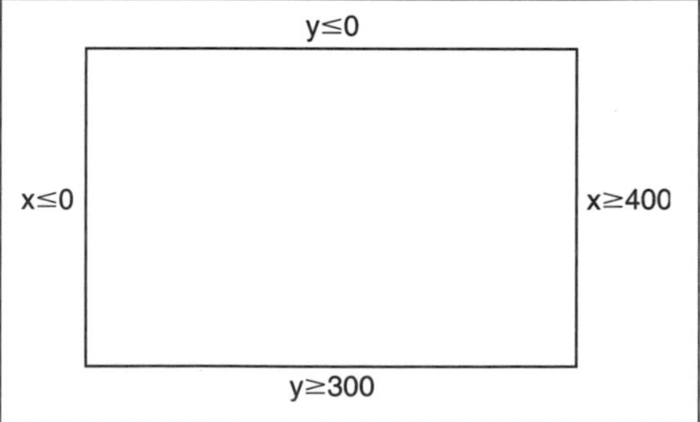

Figure 9.2 The wall tests.

Whether or not a collision occurs, the function returns the value of `collisions` to the main loop. If there was no collision, `collisions` will remain the same; if there was a collision, `collisions` increases by one.

The rest of the main loop draws the pixel on the screen and delays the program for 1/10 of a second.

That's it for demo09-01.bb. Figure 9.3 is a screenshot from the program.

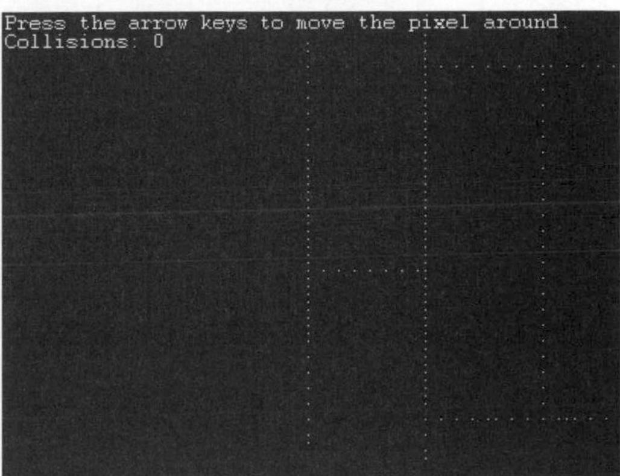

Figure 9.3 The demo09-01.bb program.

Bounding Circles

Now that we know how to check single pixels for collision, we need to learn how to check for collision of objects. Objects are shapes, images, and the like. There are a few ways to check shapes for collisions.

Bounding circles is the first method. Basically, it involves placing invisible circles around the objects we are testing. If the circles overlap, a collision has occurred. See Figure 9.4 for an example.

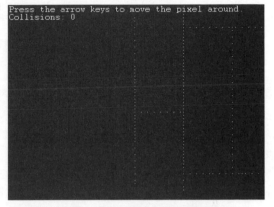

If you look carefully at Figure 9.4, you will notice that the objects didn't actually collide—only their bounding circles did. This usually isn't a big deal; because the objects are so close to one another that it appears as if there was a collision.

Before I can show you how this works, you need to understand two concepts: one about distance between points, and one about the radius of a circle.

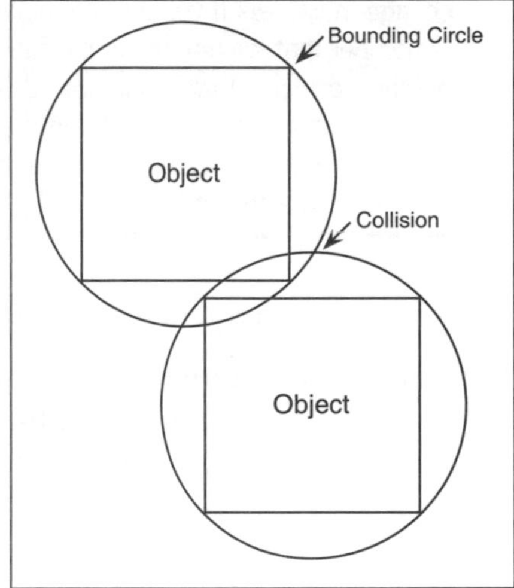

Figure 9.4 Overlapping circles.

Distance between Points

When we use bounding circles, we will have to compare the distances of points. To find the distance of two points, we can use a mathematical equation. Following is the equation.

```
distance = sqrt((x2-x1)^2 + (y2-y1)^2))
```

note

Have you ever seen the ^ symbol? It means "to the power of." In this case, ^2 means you raise the number by a power of two, or you square it. To square a value means to multiply a value by itself. In other words, 10^2 is read as "10 squared," and is equal to 10 × 10, or 100.

How do you read this? To find the distance between two points, you take the second x coordinate minus the first x coordinate and the second y coordinate minus the first y coordinate. You then square (multiply each of the values by itself) each number and add their results together. Finally, you take the square root of the final number. Figure 9.5 shows how you might compare the distance between two different points.

Difficult to understand, huh? Well, don't worry about it. I wrote the following function, `Distance()`, just for you.

```
Function Distance(x1,y1,x2,y2)
        dx = x2 - x1
        dy = y2 - y1
        Return sqr((dx*dx) + (dy*dy))
End Function
```

note

> Remember in Chapter 7, "Basic Image Programming," when we read about the change in values? If you do, you might also remember that we referred to the change in numbers as delta. That is what the "d" in the `dx` and `dy` variables stands for in the `Distance()` function. Delta means "the change in"—here, it is the change in x and y.

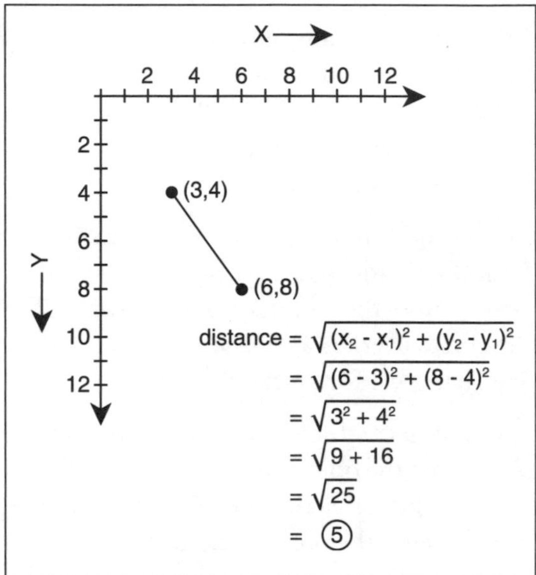

Figure 9.5 Testing distance.

There's a new concept or two introduced here. Let's go over them.

First, notice that I computed what `x2-x1` and `y2-y1` were equal to before actually finding the distance. This makes reading the code much easier. If I had neglected to pre-compute those numbers, the function's return statement would look something like this.

```
Return sqr(((x2-x1)*(x2-x1)) + ((y2-y1)*(y2-y1)))
```

Much uglier, huh? Finding out the values made my code much easier to read and comprehend.

Also, notice the function `sqr()`. This function returns the square root of the number that it is provided. The square root is a number that when multiplied by itself gives the given number. Huh? Basically, if you multiply the square root of a number by itself, you achieve the number. For example, the square root of 4 is 2. You can prove this by multiplying 2 by itself. Because $2 \times 2 = 4$, 2 is the square root of 4 (so is -2, but that is a different matter altogether).

To find the square root by hand is an incredibly complex procedure. That is why BlitzPlus provides the `sqr()` function for you. Following is the declaration for `sqr()`.

```
Sqr (value#)
```

Table 9.2 lists the parameter for `sqr()`.

Table 9.2 Sqr()'s Parameter

Parameter	Description
value#	The value you want to square root.

Well that's just about it for finding the distance between two points. Just for reference, following is the declaration for the `Distance()` function.

```
Distance(x1,y1,x2,y2)
```

Table 9.3 lists each of `Distance()`'s parameters.

Table 9.3 Distance()'s Parameters

Parameter	Description
x1	The x coordinate for the first point you want to compare.
y1	The y coordinate for the first point you want to compare.
x2	The x coordinate for the second point you want to compare.
y2	The y coordinate for the second point you want to compare.

Okay, now we move onto finding the radius of a circle.

Radii

Is your brain hurting from the distance section? Well don't worry, this part is much easier. First off, the radius (plural radii, a very cool word) of a circle is equal to 1/2 of the diameter of the circle.

In a circle, there is one point directly in the center. From here on, I will call this point the "center of the circle." Well, anyway, the diameter of a circle is the distance from any point on a circle to another point on a circle, provided it crosses through the "center of the circle." What do I mean? Check out Figure 9.6.

Notice that the diameter shown in Figure 9.6 is just one of many. In fact, can you guess how many diameters there are in a circle? If you guessed 1, you are wrong. 360? Nope, wrong again. There are actually *infinite* diameters in a circle. That's right; there are an infinite number of diameters in a circle. However, all of them must extend from side to side and through the center of the circle, thus their lengths are all the same.

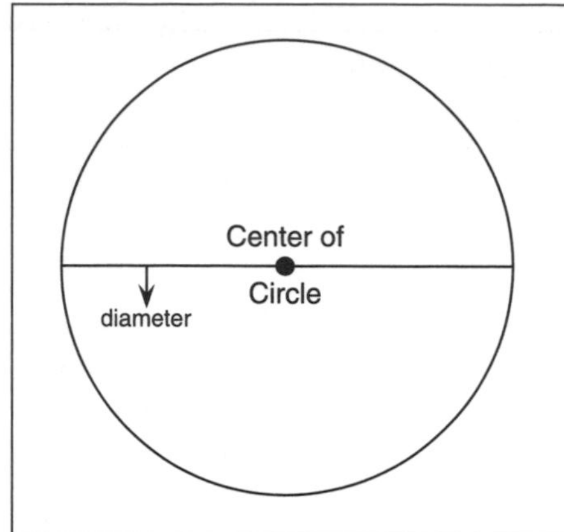

Figure 9.6 The diameter of a circle.

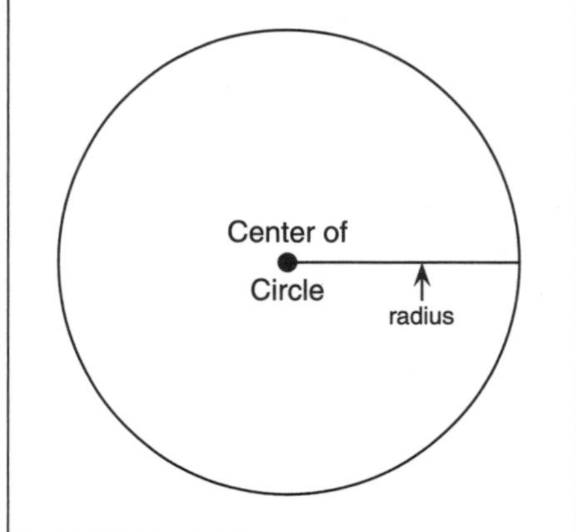

Figure 9.7 The radius of a circle.

Anyway, getting back to radii, the radius of a circle is 1/2 the diameter. You might be thinking, isn't that the same as the distance from the "center of the circle" to the actual circle? You are absolutely correct! Figure 9.7 shows the radius of a circle.

Make sure you understand that any point on the circle is exactly the same distance from the "center of the circle" as any other point on the circle. Ready for another cool word? Each point on the circle is *equidistant* from the "center of the circle."

Okay, we are now good to go. How can we find the radius of an object? It's a big problem, so let's figure out how to do it.

We are going to use code to figure this out. First we load an object—say, an image.

```
imagehandle = LoadImage("image.bmp")
```

Not too terribly difficult, eh? Now we have to find the radius. Before we can do that, we need to go over two very basic functions. These functions are `ImageWidth()` and `ImageHeight()`.

These two functions return the width and height in pixels of the image whose handle you provide. Following are their declarations.

```
ImageWidth(imagehandle)
ImageHeight(imagehandle)
```

Tables 9.4 and 9.5 list their parameters.

Table 9.4 ImageWidth()'s Parameter

Parameter	Description
`imagehandle`	The handle to the image whose width in pixels is returned by the function.

Table 9.5 ImageHeight()'s Parameter

Parameter	Description
`imagehandle`	The handle to the image whose height in pixels is returned by the function.

Anyway, getting back to the actual coding, we now need to find the radius of our image. Let's define the radius of the image as the distance from the center of the image to the outer parts of the image. Make sure you understand that every bitmap is rectangular and not circular in nature. Therefore, the radius collision test will not be perfectly accurate.

You might be thinking that we can just take the result of either `ImageHeight()` or `ImageWidth()` and divide it by two to get a radius. However, this isn't a good idea. Because the images are not square, but rather rectangular, taking only the width or only the height into account can give you an inaccurate radius. What we are going to do is take the average of one-half of the height and width of the image. Let's write such a function, `FindRadius()`.

```
Function FindRadius(imagehandle)
	Return ((ImageWidth(imagehandle)/2) + (ImageHeight(imagehandle)/2) / 2)
End Function
```

This function returns the approximate radius of the image it is given. Table 9.6 lists the parameters.

Table 9.6 FindRadius()'s Parameter

Parameter	Description
`imagehandle`	The handle to the image whose approximate radius is returned by the function.

Okay, now we need to know how to test the image from `FindRadius()` with another object for collision. All that we do is test the point to determine whether its distance from the image is less than the distance of the radius. The following program, demo09-02.bb, demonstrates how to do this. It's a long one, so I don't want to list it all out in the book. Let me show you some cool parts, though.

We haven't read about using the `Each` keyword in `for` loops lately. Let's review how they work.

First of all, we have to create a type. In this program, we used a type for every point. The type is defined like this.

```
;the point type defines each object that can be hit by the ship
Type point
	Field x,y	;the x and y coordinate of the ship
End Type
```

Now, we want to create a lot of these points. This is accomplished through the `For...Each` loop.

```
;Create NUMBEROFOBJECTS new points with random x and y coords
For counter = 0 To NUMBEROFOBJECTS
	point.point = New point
	point\x = Rand (0,800)
	point\y = Rand (0,600)
Next
```

This loop creates `NUMBEROFOBJECTS` points and gives them all random x and y values.

If you are wondering what the constant `NUMBEROFOBJECTS` means, check out Table 9.7.

Table 9.7 demo09-02.bb's Constants

Constant	Value	Description
NUMBEROFOBJECTS	50	The amount of points that can be hit by the player's ship.
LEFTKEY	203	The key code for Left.
UPKEY	200	The key code for Up.
RIGHTKEY	205	The key code for Right.
DOWNKEY	208	The key code for Down.
MOVEX	5	The amount of pixels the player can move left or right per frame.
MOVEY	5	The amount of pixels the player can move up or down per frame.

Sound good? Good. Now that we have created each of the objects, we also need to know how to delete all of the objects. We delete the objects when the level is reset.

```
;Delete every point onscreen
For point.point = Each point
	Delete point
Next
```

This deletes all of the points that have been created previously.

By the way, if you don't remember how the `For...Each` loop works, check out Chapter 3, "Loops, Functions, Arrays, and Types," for a review.

Okay, the next thing I want to go over is `TestCollisions()`. This function tests all of the objects on the screen to determine whether the ship hit them.

```
;FUNCTION TestCollisions() - Tests the objects and the ship for collisions
;No input parameters
;Returns 1 if there was a collision, 0 if there was none
Function TestCollisions()

;Check every object to see if it is within
     player's radius. If it is, return that
     there was a collision.
For point.point = Each point
       If Distance(player\x,player\y,point\x,point\y) < player\radius
              Return 1
       EndIf
Next

;If there was no collision, return 0
Return 0 ;There was no collision

End Function
```

Not too bad, huh? It checks each point to determine whether the point is within the radius of the ship. If so, 1 is returned. In the main loop, if there was a collision, the level is reset and the amount of collisions is incremented by one.

There are quite a few functions defined in this program, so Table 9.8 lists them all.

Table 9.8 demo09-02.bb's Functions

Function	Description
`ResetLevel()`	Deletes and renews all the objects; resets the player's starting coordinates.
`TestCollisions()`	Tests all objects to see whether they have collided with the spaceship, and returns 1 if a collision took place.
`TestKeys()`	Tests the keyboard to see whether any keys have been pressed.
`Distance()`	Finds the distance between two points.
`FindRadius()`	Finds the radius of an image.

All right, that's just about it for this section of the code. Next, we move on to bounding boxes. By the way, Figure 9.8 shows a screenshot from the program.

Figure 9.8 The demo09-02.bb program.

Bounding Boxes

Okay, now that we have learned how to use bounding circles, let's learn how to use bounding boxes. Bounding boxes are just like bounding circles, except that instead of comparing overlapping circles, it compares overlapping rectangles. Check out Figure 9.9 for an example of a bounding rectangle.

If you check out Figure 9.10, you will notice that a collision does not always occur even though a collision is reported. This is usually not a big deal, though, because the collision is pretty close.

Unlike using bounding circles, BlitzPlus provides a way to test for collisions using bounding boxes. You'll read about this in a minute, after I show you how to do it manually.

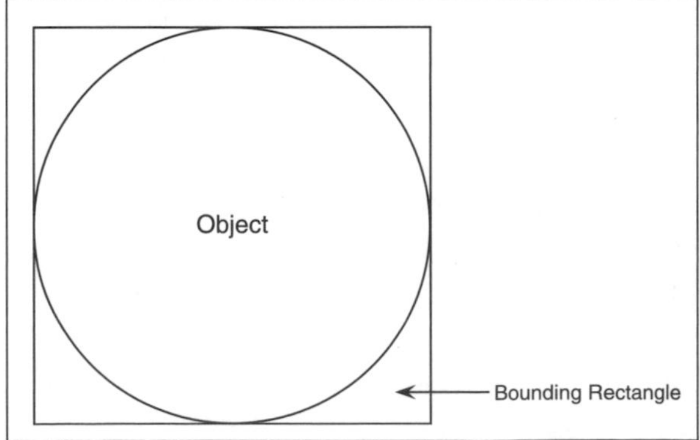

Figure 9.9 A bounding rectangle.

We have to use `ImageHeight()` and `ImageWidth()` again, but this time in a different way. The bounding box for the rectangle is going to be the outer edge of the image. See Figure 9.11 for an example.

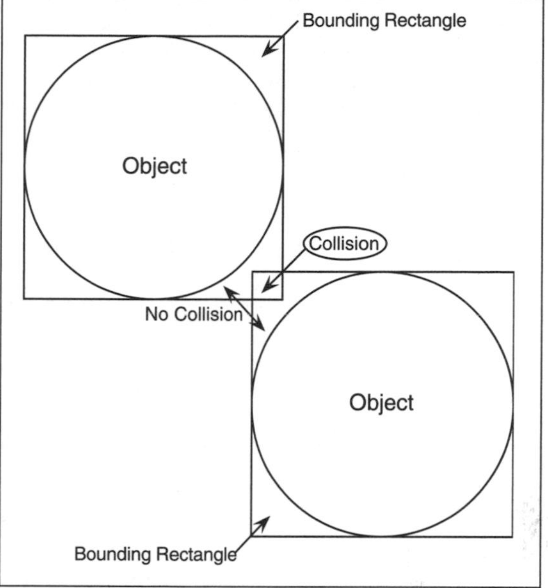

Figure 9.10 An imperfect collision.

Now, how are we going to go about finding this bounding box? First of all, remember that when we use images, the handling point is directly in the center of the image. This is defined by `AutoMidHandle`. Because it is in the center, we need to determine the upper-left and lower-right corners to find the bounding box.

If the mid handle had been set to the top-left corner of the image, this would be an easy problem to fix. We would begin with the mid handle for the upper corner. The mid handle's x coordinate plus `ImageWidth()` would be the lower-right corner's x coordinate, and the lower-right corner's y coordinate would be the mid handle's y coordinate plus `ImageHeight()`. Check out Figure 9.12 for an example of how this works with an image that is 32 pixels wide by 32 pixels high.

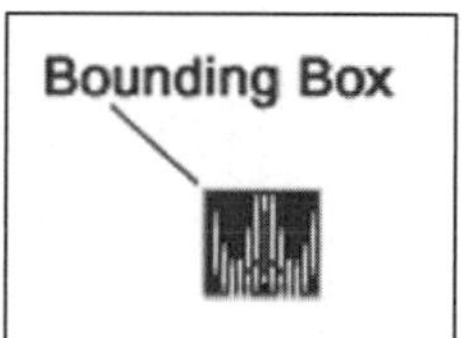

Figure 9.11
A bounding box.

Well, now, here's the thing. Because the mid handle isn't at the top-left corner, we need to use another formula. Basically, the bounding box will have an upper-left corner of:

−1/2 * `ImageWidth()`, −1/2 * `ImageHeight()`

And a lower-right corner of:

1/2 * `ImageWidth()`, 1/2 * `ImageHeight()`.

Figure 9.13 illustrates this.

How does this work? Well, `AutoMidHandle` sets up the handling point directly in the center of the image rectangle. We need to move the handling point to the top-left corner of the image so that we can draw a rectangle around the bitmap. Because the handling point is directly in the center, we need to move the handling point 1/2 of the height of the rectangle up, and 1/2 of the width of the rectangle left. This allows you to grab the rectangle by the top-left corner.

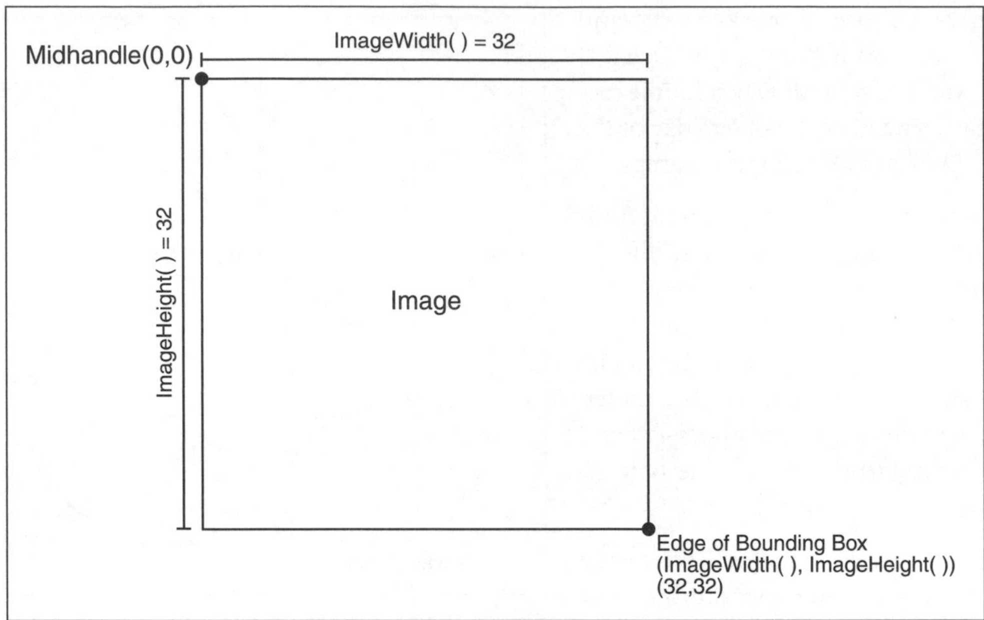

Figure 9.12 A bounding box with the mid handle at the upper-left corner.

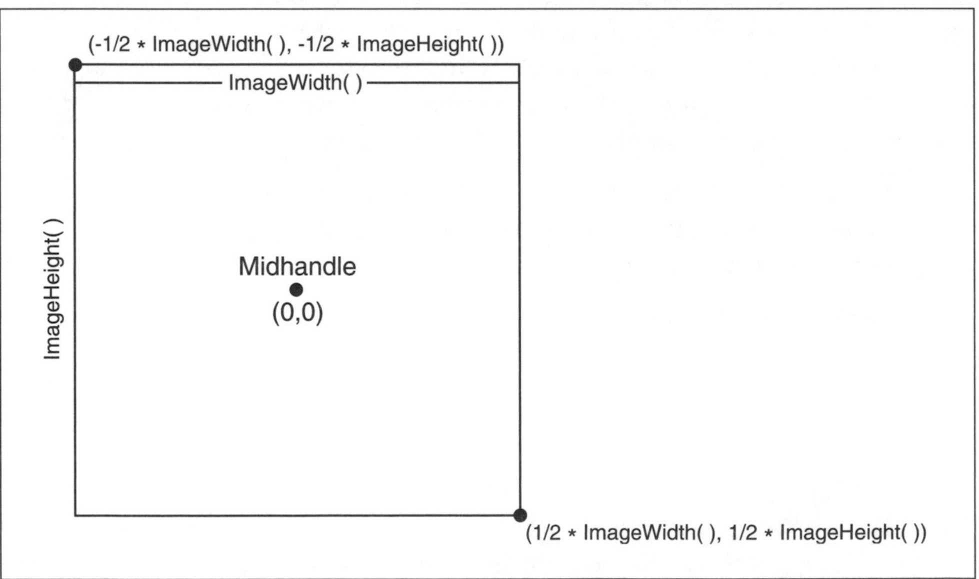

Figure 9.13 A bounding box with mid handle at the center.

Okay, now, before we write our collision detection program, let's write a program that demonstrates the bounding box technique. The following program, demo09-03.bb, draws a rectangle around the bounding box of a spaceship.

```
;demo09-03.bb - Draws a bounding box

Graphics 800,600

;Set default backbuffer and automidhandle to true
SetBuffer BackBuffer()
AutoMidHandle True

;IMAGES
;Load the ship image
Global shipimage = LoadImage("ship.bmp")

;Give the ship default parameters
Global x = 400
Global y = 300



;CONSTANTS
;The key code constants
Const UPKEY = 200, DOWNKEY = 208, LEFTKEY = 203, RIGHTKEY = 205

;These constants define how many pixels are moved per frame
Const MOVEX = 5
Const MOVEY = 5

;MAIN LOOP
While Not KeyDown(1)
;Clear the screen
Cls

;Find out if any important keys on the keyboard have been pressed
TestKeys()

;Draw the bounding box around the player
DrawPlayerRect()

;Draw the image of the ship
DrawImage shipimage,x,y
```

```
Flip

;Slow it down
Delay 20

Wend
;END OF MAIN LOOP


;FUNCTION DrawPlayerRect() - Draws a bounding rectangle
Function DrawPlayerRect()

;find the width of the image
iw = ImageWidth(shipimage)

;Find the upper-left coordinates
x1# = ((-ImageWidth(shipimage)/2) +x)
y1# = ((-ImageHeight(shipimage)/2) + y)

;Draw the entire bounding box
Rect x1#,y1#,ImageWidth(shipimage),ImageHeight(shipimage), 0

End Function


;FUNCTION TestKeys() - Tests all of the keys to see if they were hit
Function TestKeys()

;If up is hit, move player up
If KeyDown(UPKEY)
      y = y - MOVEY
EndIf

;If down is hit, move player down
If KeyDown(DOWNKEY) ;If down was hit
      y = y + MOVEY
EndIf

;If left is hit, move player left
If KeyDown(LEFTKEY)
      x = x - MOVEX
EndIf
```

```
;If right is hit, move player right
If KeyDown(RIGHTKEY)
        x = x + MOVEX
EndIf

End Function
```

To me, the most difficult thing to understand is the function `DrawPlayerRect()`.

`DrawPlayerRect()` draws the bounding box around the player's image. If you remember correctly, I said that the bounding box extends from −1/2 * `ImageWidth()`,−1/2 * `ImageHeight()` to 1/2 * `ImageWidth()`, 1/2 * `ImageHeight()`. However, the `DrawPlayerRect()` function seems to make the bounding box look a lot different.

```
;FUNCTION DrawPlayerRect() - Draws a bounding rectangle
Function DrawPlayerRect()

;find the width of the image
iw = ImageWidth(shipimage)

;Find the upper-left coordinates
x1# = ((-ImageWidth(shipimage)/2) +x)
y1# = ((-ImageHeight(shipimage)/2) + y)

;Draw the entire bounding box
Rect x1#,y1#,ImageWidth(shipimage),ImageHeight(shipimage), 0

End Function
```

First of all, take the variable `x1#`. As you can see, instead of being set to `1/2 * ImageWidth()`, it is set to `ImageWidth()/2`. However, `1/2 * ImageWidth()` and `ImageWidth()/2` are equivalent. Multiplying something by 1/2 is the same as dividing something by 2. Therefore, `1/2 * ImageWidth()` is the same as `ImageWidth()/2`.

Also, notice that I added the x coordinate to the rectangle when finding `x1#`.This places the bounding box into the actual player space—if I forgot to add it, the rectangle would begin at the top-left corner of the screen. This is the same as global and local coordinates. Finding the bounding box is finding the local coordinates, but by adding the proper x value, you move it to the correct global coordinates. We do the same thing with the `y1#` variable.

Last, the `Rect` call might be a little confusing. Let me help you understand it by detailing the declaration of `Rect`.

```
Rect x, y, width, height, solid
```

Remember that? Anyway, as you know, the rectangle begins at `x,y`. We already figured out what x and y are in the previous two variables, `x1#` and `y1#`. We then need to determine the width and height of the rectangle. The rectangle's width and height are the width and height of the image. This is achieved by using `ImageWidth()` and `ImageHeight()`.

Of course, we don't want the rectangle to be filled—it'll make the ship look ugly! So we set solid to 0, which leaves it unfilled. Figure 9.14 shows a screenshot from the program.

Figure 9.14 The demo09-03.bb program.

By the way, there is a much easier way to grab the image by the top-left corner than using ImageHeight() and ImageWidth(). BlitzPlus provides a function named HandleImage that lets you choose where on the image you want your handle (grabbing point) to be located. HandleImage is declared like this.

```
HandleImage image, x, y
```

To set the grabbing point to the top-left corner, you would just call `HandleImage` as follows.

```
HandleImage shipimage, 0, 0.
```

All right, we are now ready to determine if an object has collided with the spaceship using bounding boxes. This program, demo09-04.bb, is the same as the one in demo09-02.bb, except it does not use bounding circles.

Let's go over the changes in the program. First of all, the player type has changed from this:

```
;The player type is the spaceship on the screen
Type player

        Field x,y     ;the x and y coordinate of the player
        Field collisions     ;the number of collisions that have occurred
        Field radius      ;the radius of the player image
        Field image     ;the actual image of the player

End Type
```

to this:

```
;This type contains the player
Type player
        Field x,y    ;the x and y coordinate of the player
        Field collisions    ;the number of collisions that have occurred
        Field image     ;the actual image of the player
End Type
```

Yeah, that's right. We got rid of the `radius` field! Anyway, getting back to the program, we changed the `TestCollisions` function quite a bit.

```
;FUNCTION TestCollisions() - Tests the objects and the ship for collisions
;No input parameters
;Returns 1 if there was a collision, 0 if there was none
Function TestCollisions()

;Test each point to see if it is within the player's radius
For point.point = Each point

;Find player's bounding box
x1 = -ImageWidth(player\image)/2 + player\x
x2 = ImageWidth(player\image)/2 + player\x
y1 = -ImageHeight(player\image)/2 + player\y
y2 = ImageHeight(player\image)/2 + player\y

;If the point is within collision radius, return 1
       If (point\x > x1) And (point\x < x2) And (point\y > y1) And (point\y < y2)
              Return 1
```

```
        EndIf
Next    ;Move on to next point

;There were no collisions if the function makes it here, so return 0
Return 0
End Function
;END TestCollisions()
```

As you can see, the function begins by finding the size of the rectangle. Recall that the bounding rectangle extends from `-ImageWidth()/2 + x`, `-ImageHeight()/2 + y` to `ImageWidth()/2 + x`, `ImageHeight()/2`. The `If` statement determines whether any of the points are within the bounding box, and if so, a collision is reported.

Also, one last major change. The `FindRadius()` and the `Distance()` function have been changed to this:

Yep! Those functions are no longer necessary, so they have been deleted.

Pixel-Imperfect Collisions

One thing you might have noticed is that these programs test the ship only against single pixels. What if we want to test an image against another image? Say, a bullet against a ship, or a missile crash? BlitzPlus provides an excellent way to do this.

note

> Notice that this section is called "Pixel-Imperfect Collisions". In other words, there might not be a perfect collision, because it is imperfect. The next section covers pixel-perfect collisions.

There is a function provided by BlitzPlus called `ImagesOverlap()`. It is defined like this:

```
ImagesOverlap (image1,x1,y1,image2,x2,y2)
```

Table 9.9 explains all the parameters.

Table 9.9 ImagesOverlap()'s Parameters

Parameter	Description
`image1`	The handle to the first image you want to test for collision.
`x1`	The x coordinate of the first image.
`y1`	The y coordinate of the first image.
`image2`	The handle to the second image you want to test for collision.
`x2`	The x coordinate of the second image.
`y2`	The y coordinate of the second image.

Now, let's write a program that uses this function. The following, demo09-05.bb, allows you to control a ship. If you hit the randomly moving ship that is also onscreen, a collision occurs.

The program is pretty easy to follow, so I am just going to list some important parts. Following are the types from the program, and the initial values for these types.

```
;TYPES
;The enemy ship is a randomly moving object on the screen
Type enemyship
        Field x,y     ;the x and y coordinates
        Field xv,yv     ;The velocity
        Field image    ;the image
End Type

;The playership type defines the player
Type playership
        Field x,y    ;The x and y coordinate position
        Field collisions     ;How many collisions have occurred
        Field image     ;The player's image
End Type


;Create the enemy and assign it default variables
Global enemy.enemyship = New enemyship
enemy\x = 400
enemy\y = 200
enemy\xv = Rand(-5,5)
enemy\yv = Rand(-5,5)
enemy\image = LoadImage("enemyship.bmp")
```

```
;Create player and assign it default and random variables
Global player.playership = New playership
player\x = 400
player\y = 400
player\collisions = 0
player\image = LoadImage("ship.bmp")
```

The only major difference between the player and the enemy is that the player has velocity fields, xv and yv. These velocity values are added to the x and y coordinates of the enemy each frame and serve as movement values.

Following is the main loop. Notice how little it actually does.

```
;MAIN LOOP
While Not KeyDown(1)
;Clear the screen
Cls

;Make sure all text appears in top-left corner
Text 0,0, "Collisions: " + player\collisions

;Find out if enemy hit a wall
TestEnemyCollisions()

;Test keyboard
TestKeys()

;If player and enemy overlap, increment collisions and reset player and enemy
If (ImagesOverlap(player\image,player\x,player\y,enemy\image,enemy\x,enemy\y))
        player\collisions = player\collisions + 1
        player\x = 400
        player\y = 400
        enemy\x = 400
        enemy\y = 200
      enemy\xv = Rand(-5,5)
enemy\yv = Rand(-5,5)
EndIf

;Move the enemy
enemy\x = enemy\x + enemy\xv
enemy\y = enemy\y + enemy\yv

;Draw the player and the enemy
DrawImage enemy\image,enemy\x,enemy\y
```

```
DrawImage player\image,player\x,player\y

Flip

;Slow it down
Delay 20

Wend
;END OF MAIN LOOP
```

The main loop does this: it prints out how many collisions have occurred, it calls `TestEnemyKeys()` and `TestKeys()`, it determines whether any collisions have occurred, it moves the enemy, and it draws the two ships. The only major line of interest is the test.

```
If (ImagesOverlap(player\image,player\x,player\y,enemy\image,enemy\x,enemy\y))
```

This determines whether the player's image and the enemy's image have overlapped. Figure 9.15 shows a screenshot from the program.

Figure 9.15 The demo09-05.bb program.

That's just about it for pixel-imperfect collisions. Next, you'll learn how to find out if collisions have actually occurred using pixel-perfect collisions.

Pixel-Perfect Collisions

So far, we have been doing all of our collision tests with pixel-imperfect calculations. Do you understand the difference between pixel-imperfect collisions and pixel-perfect collisions? Let me help you understand.

When using pixel-imperfect collisions, every collision that occurs is approximate. This means that while the collision might not actually occur, usually it is so close that it seems like it did. This creates a problem, sometimes, when the collision obviously should not have happened. Referring to Figure 9.16, you can see how a bounding box collision can be extremely incorrect. In this figure, the bounding boxes have slightly overlapped, yet the actual objects are still very far apart from one another.

However, BlitzPlus provides a very easy way to fix this problem. Simply use the function `ImagesCollide()` instead of `ImagesOverlap()`.

`ImagesCollide()` is declared like this:

```
ImagesCollide (image1,x1,y1,frame1,image2,x2,y2,frame2)
```

Table 9.10 summarizes ImagesCollide's parameters.

`ImagesCollide()` checks every nontransparent pixel of the first image to determine whether it is overlapping with a nontransparent pixel of the second pixel. If so, a collision is reported. However, this checking means that your program will run a bit slower when using `ImagesCollide()` than when using `ImagesOverlap()`.

When using `ImagesCollide()`, collisions will look more like those in Figure 9.17.

Table 9.10 ImagesCollide()'s Parameters

Parameter	Description
`image1`	The handle to the first image you want to test for collision.
`x1`	The x coordinate of the first image.
`y1`	The y coordinate of the first image.
`frame1`	The frame of the first image you want to check—unless you are using animation, set this to 0.
`image2`	The handle to the second image you want to test for collision.
`x2`	The x coordinate of the second image.
`y2`	The y coordinate of the second image.
`image2`	The frame of the second image you want to check—unless you are using animation, set this to 0.

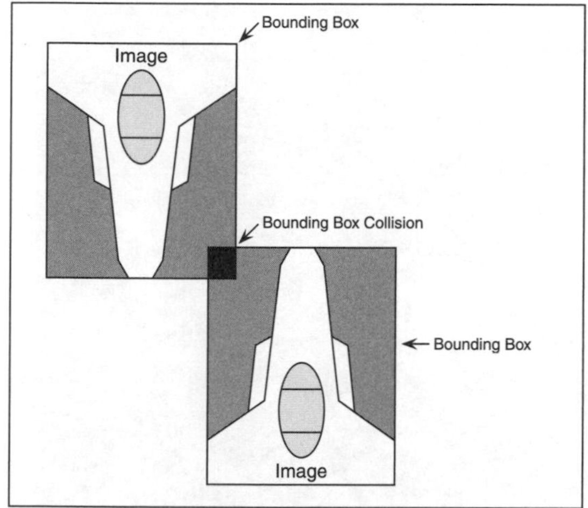

Figure 9.16 The problems with pixel-imperfect collisions.

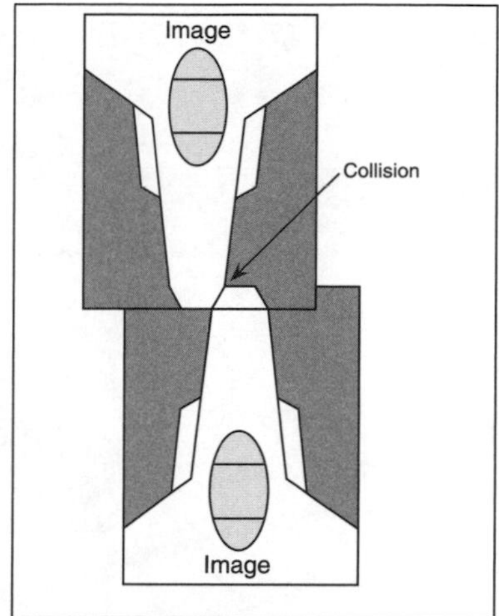

Figure 9.17 Using `ImagesCollide()`.

I rewrote demo09-05.bb to make demo09-06.bb. The only change I made was in the main loop. I changed

```
;If player and enemy overlap, increment collisions and reset player and enemy
If (ImagesOverlap(player\image,player\x,player\y,enemy\image,enemy\x,enemy\y))
        player\collisions = player\collisions + 1
        player\x = 400
        player\y = 400
        enemy\x = 400
        enemy\y = 200
EndIf
```

to

```
;If player and enemy collide, increment collisions and reset player and enemy
If (ImagesCollide(player\image,player\x,player\y,enemy\image,enemy\x,enemy\y))
        player\collisions = player\collisions + 1
        player\x = 400
        player\y = 400
        enemy\x = 400
        enemy\y = 200
EndIf
```

Play through and see if you notice the differences. Figure 9.18 shows a screenshot from the program.

Before we finish this chapter, I just want to warn you about overusing `ImagesCollide()`. When using `ImagesCollide()` a lot, your program can experience a drastic slowdown. Unless you are sure it is necessary, a lot of times it is better to stick with `ImagesOverlap()`.

Figure 9.18 The demo09-06.bb program.

Summary

Whoohoo! We have now reached the end of Chapter 9, and also, the end of Part Two. In this chapter, you learned how to use several types of collision-detection methods. Don't forget them, because they will be useful in your programs!

In this chapter we covered these concepts:

- Basic collisions
- Bounding circles
- Distance between points
- Bounding boxes
- Pixel-imperfect collisions
- Pixel-perfect collisions

Starting with the next chapter, we are going to learn more topics of BlitzPlus, and we will progress toward our own final game. Cool, huh?

PART III

Completing the Puzzle

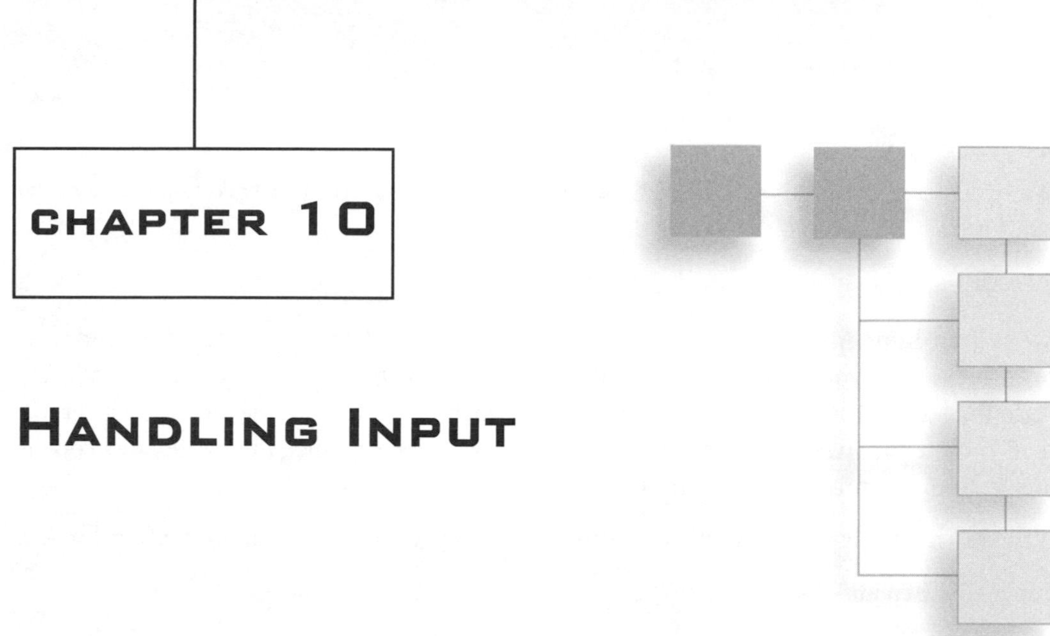

Handling Input

We are finally on the last part of the book! When you're finished with this part, you will know everything you need in order to make games. So, let's get started with making decisions based on user input. Of course, every game requires handling of input. Otherwise, it isn't a game; instead, it's a movie. Sometimes you might want to include movies and other sections of game that don't accept user input in your game—*cinematics*, for instance, are bits of a game that explain the storyline without any actual game play. The main part of your game, however, will rely on input from the user.

Although there are a number of ways that the player can interact with the game (using game pads, racing wheels, and so on), BlitzPlus simplifies all of the choices to three input sources: the mouse, the keyboard, and the joystick. This chapter covers the first two and introduces the third. First up: the keyboard!

Handling the Keyboard

You use the keyboard every time you use your computer; heck, I am using it to type these words right now. So, of course, the keyboard is probably going to be a common source of input for most games you make. We better get crackin' if we want to figure out what the player wants to do.

We have read about the keyboard's role in a very limited way thus far: basically, you know how to determine whether the users have pressed the Esc key and a few select other keys. The following sections review what we know and then teach you a bit more. So, let's begin by reviewing the functions `KeyDown()` and `KeyHit()`.

KeyDown()

We have been using this function throughout the book, so you most likely already know what it does. First off, let's go over the declaration of `KeyDown()`.

```
KeyDown (scancode)
```

Memories, huh? Anyway, `KeyDown()` tests the keyboard to determine if the scan code has been pressed. If you don't remember, let me redefine *scan code* for you. A scan code is a code that represents a certain key. Each key on your keyboard is represented by a certain scan code. By the way, I might use the word "key code" every once in a while. Key code is just a synonym for scan code—they mean exactly the same thing.

If the key has been pressed, `KeyDown()` returns 1. If a key was not pressed, `KeyDown()` returns 0.

Table 10.1 explains the parameters of `KeyDown()`.

Table 10.1 KeyDown()'s Parameters

Parameter	Description
`scancode`	Tests if the key represented by scan code has been pressed.

There are numerous scan codes that are built into BlitzPlus, and all of them are listed in Appendix A. However, I decided to list a few of them right here, in Table 10.2.

Table 10.2 Relevant Scan Codes

Key	Scan Code
`Esc`	1
`#'s 1-9`	2-10
`# 0`	11
`Enter`	28
`Left Control`	29
`Left Shift`	42
`Spacebar`	57
`F10`	68
`Up`	200
`Left`	203
`Right`	205
`Down`	208

As you probably noticed, the letters on the keyboard were not mentioned in the table. Unfortunately, BlitzPlus has the scan codes for the letters a bit scattered around, and because there are 26 letters, the table might get a bit too long. Anyway, just flip to Appendix A, and you will find a list of all the scan codes you could ever use.

So how do we use this information? Well, usually we test `KeyDown()` with an `If` statement. For example, if we wanted to determine whether the user pressed the spacebar, we would write something like this.

```
If KeyDown(28)
        ;Do Something
Endif
```

Let's go through this code in depth. As you know, the `If` statement performs the following actions if what it tests amounts to true. If you remember, in computer speak, 1 is equal to true, and 0 is equal to false. `KeyDown()` returns 1 if the key specified by its scan code is pressed on the keyboard. Therefore, the statements inside the `If...Endif` block are executed if and only if the user pressed the spacebar.

Let's write a program around this. The following program, demo10-01.bb, moves an outer space background when the user presses the up, down, left, and right keys.

```
;demo10-01.bb - Demonstrates usage of KeyDown()

;Initialize Graphics
Graphics 800,600

;Load the background image
backgroundimage = LoadImage("stars.bmp")

;CONSTANTS
;The following constants are used for testing key presses
Const ESCKEY = 1, UPKEY = 200, LEFTKEY = 203, RIGHTKEY = 205, DOWNKEY = 208

;scrollx and scrolly define how much the image should be moved
scrollx = 0
scrolly = 0


;MAIN LOOP
While Not KeyDown(ESCKEY)

;If the player hits up, we will scroll the background up
If KeyDown(UPKEY)
	scrolly = scrolly - 5 ;scroll background 5 pixels up
EndIf ;End of UPKEY test

;If the player hits left, we will scroll the background left
If KeyDown(LEFTKEY)
	scrollx = scrollx - 5 ;scroll background 5 pixels left
EndIf ;End LEFTKEY test

;If player hits right, we will scroll the background right
If KeyDown(RIGHTKEY)
	scrollx = scrollx + 5 ;scroll background 5 pixels right
EndIf ;End RIGHTKEY test
```

```
;If player hits down, we will scroll the background down
If KeyDown(DOWNKEY)
      scrolly = scrolly + 5 ;Scroll background 5 pixels down
EndIf ;End of DOWNKEY test

;Tile the background image on the screen so it looks like actual outer space
TileBlock backgroundimage,scrollx,scrolly

;Wait a fraction of a second.
Delay 35
Flip

Wend ;END OF MAIN LOOP
```

This program demonstrates the concepts of `KeyDown()` quite well. Let's begin at the top. I created a section of constants that define the keys that will be used throughout the program. Constants, as you probably remember, are variables whose values cannot be changed; thus, they are perfectly suited to hold the scan code numbers. Because the scan codes of each key never change, you should always create constants for your keys. Believe me; they will help you in many ways. For one, you will know, just by looking at your constants section, which keys are used throughout your program. For two, the following code:

```
If KeyDown(DOWNKEY)
      ;Move Player Down
Endif
```

is a lot easier to understand than this

```
If KeyDown(208)
      ;Move Player Down
Endif
```

Also, you won't have to memorize the scan codes for each key used in your program. Listen carefully: a good statement to live by is that if there is a way to make something easier, do it. Work is hard, and memorization is work. Using constants allows you to forget about the individual code and just remember the key that you are testing.

Anyway, back to the code. We move on to the main loop. As you can see, the main loop only functions as long as the Esc key is not pressed, as seen by this line of code.

```
While Not KeyDown(ESCKEY)
```

Like the `If` statement, `While` only functions as long as the following statements are true, or equal to 1. Because `KeyDown()` returns 0 unless the key is pressed, and `Not` flips 0 into 1 and 1 into 0, `Not KeyDown(ESCKEY)` is 1 (true) as long as the key is not being pressed. Therefore, the main loop executes only as long as the Esc key is not pressed.

The program then moves into the actual key tests. Following is the test for the up key.

```
;If the player hits up, we will scroll the background up
If KeyDown(UPKEY)
      scrolly = scrolly - 5 ;scroll background 5 pixels up
EndIf ;End of UPKEY test
```

Here, the statements execute as long as `UPKEY` is pressed. The statements change the value of the `scrolly` variable, and the background scrolls up a little.

The previous test is repeated three more times to test all four arrow keys: up, down, left, and right. Figure 10.1 is a screenshot taken from the program.

Figure 10.1 The demo10-01.bb program.

Notice that when the map scrolls left, it seems like you are moving right, and vice versa. The same happens when you scroll up. It's a cool effect, don't you think?

Okay, I think you get the gist of that. However, I want to go over one problem with using `KeyDown()`. Sometimes when you type something on your keyboard, `KeyDown()` believes that you held the key down for longer than one frame. This happens because the game loop iterates extremely fast, and you might be holding the key down for more than one frame at a time. Of course, this is what you want to happen on some games, especially with movement. When you are performing an action like moving a spaceship around the screen, you want the player to be able to simply hold down the key to move the character around. However, every once in a while, you will have a case where you don't want the users to be able to hold down the keys for more than one frame.

Take this, for example: when you are creating a game, you usually want the player to be able to quit the game by pressing Esc. Now, maybe you want to show something on the screen before the game actually closes, so you print "Press any key to exit" on the screen. The program then waits for a keypress by using the function `WaitKey`, which pauses the program until a key is pressed. `WaitKey` has no parameters; it just stops a program's execution. Here is the problem, though: when the player presses Esc, the key is carried over to the `WaitKey` statement and the program exits immediately.

You have to find a way to halt the program from retrieving the key immediately. There is one easy way to do this.

What we need to do is clear the computer's memory of what keys have been pressed. This will cause the computer to forget about any previously held down keys. To perform this action, we use the function `FlushKeys`. `FlushKeys`'s declaration is extremely simple:

```
FlushKeys
```

There are no parameters—just call the function by itself. Anyway, by calling `FlushKeys`, you clear the key input memory. Thus, any key that was held down previously is deleted.

Let's see the difference in a sample program. The following demo, demo10-02.bb, demonstrates what will happen when you don't use `FlushKeys`.

```
;demo10-02.bb - Demonstrates problem with not using FlushKeys

Graphics 800,600

;Create the background image that will be scrolled
backgroundimage = LoadImage ("stars.bmp")

;Create variable that determines how much background has scrolled
scrolly = 0

;MAIN LOOP
While Not KeyDown(1)

;Scroll background a bit by incrementing scrolly
scrolly = scrolly + 1
```

```
;Tile the background
TileBlock backgroundimage,0,scrolly

;Reset scrolly if the number grows too large
If scrolly > ImageHeight(backgroundimage)
       scrolly = 0
EndIf

;Print necessary text
Locate 0,0 ;Locate text to top left corner of the screen
Print "When you want to quit, press Esc."
Print "Hopefully, a message stating 'Quitting' will appear after you hit Esc."

;Delay the program for a fraction of a second
Delay 25
Flip

Wend ;END OF MAIN LOOP


Text 0,24,"Quitting..."
Flip
Delay 1000
Flip
```

Figure 10.2 is a screenshot taken from the program.

note

If you decide to open the program code in your BlitzPlus compiler and go to Program>Run Program, you will notice something weird. Unlike what we have been talking about here, the statement "Press any key to exit" will be shown onscreen. This only happens because of the dialog box that pops up when you run the program out of your compiler. If you want to see what would happen if you compiled the program using the full version of BlitzPlus, add the command `End` directly after `WaitKey`.

Looks good, huh? However, try running the executable file, demo10-02.exe, from the CD.

Demo10-03.bb is the same program with a ship drawn in the center of the screen. You can't move the ship, but it sure looks nice! Figure 10.3 shows a screenshot.

Let's move on to the next keyboard input function: `KeyHit()`.

Figure 10.2 The demo10-02.bb program.

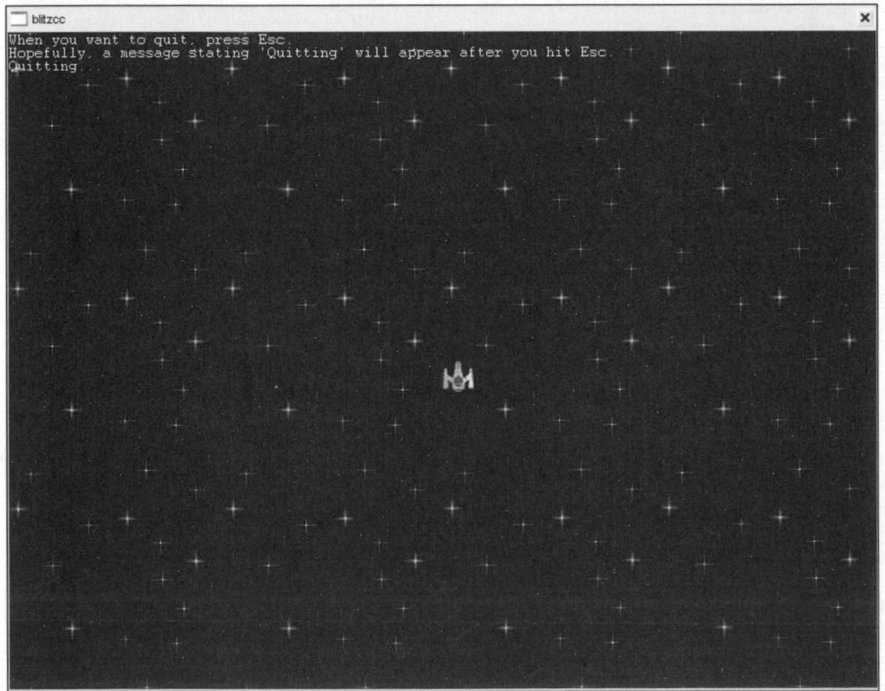

Figure 10.3 The demo10-03.bb program.

KeyHit()

This is the last function that we will be going over for keyboard input. `KeyHit()` acts an awful lot like `KeyDown()`, except for a small but important difference. Whereas `KeyDown()` allows the player to hold down a key, `KeyHit()` only lets the player press the keyboard once. Thus, you can only read which key the player pressed one time. Take, for example, demo10-04.bb. This program draws a spaceship on a tiled space background. It allows the player to move the spaceship using `KeyHit()`. Figure 10.4 is a screenshot taken from this program.

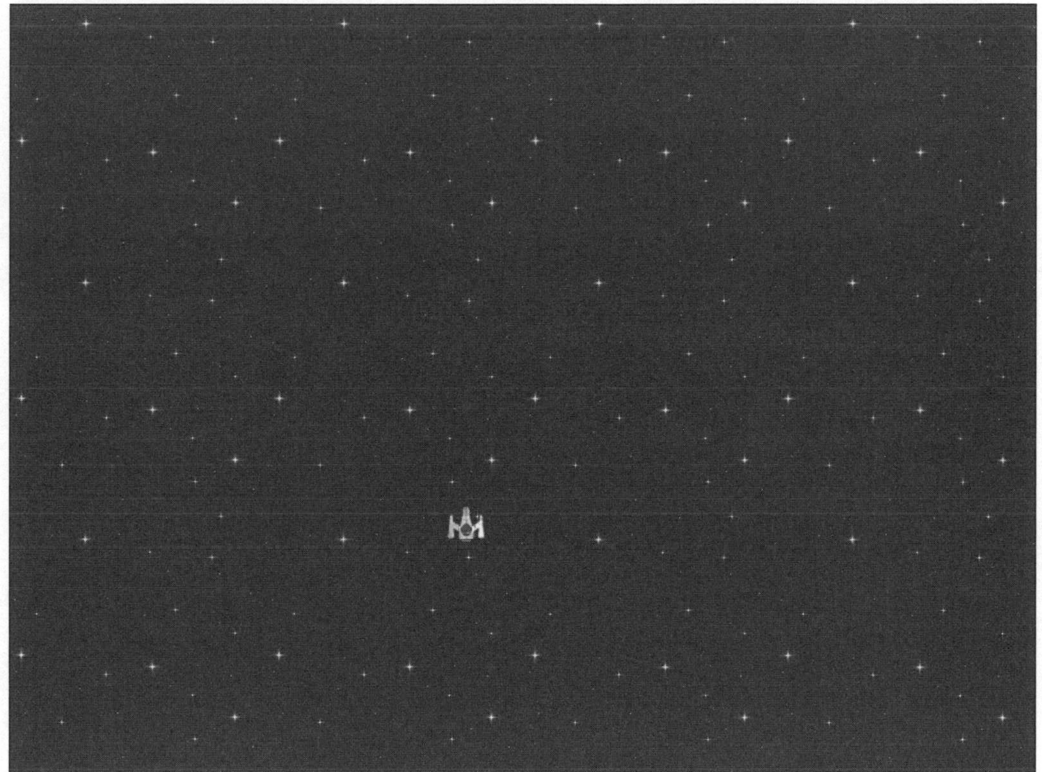

Figure 10.4 The demo10-04.bb program.

In demo10-04.bb, you will find the `KeyHit()` command nested in `If` statements. Following is the source from the program that uses `KeyHit()`.

```
;If the player hits up, move player up
If KeyHit(UPKEY)
        y = y - 5    ;move player 5 pixels up
EndIf

;If the player hits left, move player left
```

```
If KeyHit(LEFTKEY)
       x = x - 5   ;move player 5 pixels left
EndIf

;If player hits right, move player right
If KeyHit(RIGHTKEY)
       x = x + 5   ;move player 5 pixels right
EndIf

;If player hits down, move player down
If KeyHit(DOWNKEY)
       y = y + 5   ;move player 5 pixels down
EndIf
```

By the way, `KeyHit()`'s declaration is exactly the same as `KeyDown`'s declaration.

```
KeyHit (scancode)
```

Table 10.3 examines the parameter.

Table 10.3 KeyHit()'s Parameters

Parameter	Description
`scancode`	The scan code of the key you want to test for input.

If you run the program, you will notice that you can only move the player by pressing the arrow keys multiple times. Usually, you would rather allow the player to move around by holding down the arrow keys, but sometimes you might prefer to only let the player do something by pressing the key over and over again.

Let's take a space-simulation game, for example. We want to allow the player to be able to move around the screen and fire bullets. To do this, we will allow the players to hold down the arrow keys for movement, but they have to press the spacebar to produce a bullet.

Following is the initialization section from demo10-05.bb.

```
;demo10-05.bb - A Space Simulation with KeyHit()

Graphics 800,600

;Set automidhandle to true
AutoMidHandle True
;Set up Backbuffer
SetBuffer BackBuffer()
```

```
;TYPES

;Bullet type = hold the information for each bullet
Type bullet
	Field x,y   ;the coordinates of the bullet
End Type


;Player type - holds the actual player
Type player
	Field x,y   ;the coordinates of the player
End Type

;Create player and initialize field
Global player.player = New player
player\x = 400
player\y = 500


;CONSTANTS
;The following constants are used for testing key presses
Const ESCKEY = 1, UPKEY = 200, LEFTKEY = 203, RIGHTKEY = 205, DOWNKEY = 208, SPACEBAR =
57



;IMAGES
playerimage = LoadImage("ship.bmp")
Global bulletimage = LoadImage("bullet.bmp")
backgroundimage = LoadImage("stars.bmp")

;Create a scrolling indicator variable
scrolly = 0
```

The initialization section acts pretty much how you would expect it to. It begins by setting the graphics mode and setting `AutoMidHandle` to true. After that, it sets the starting buffer to be the back buffer. Next, it creates the types that are used in the program.

The first type is the bullet type. Every bullet that is to be created uses this type. The next type is the player type. Both `bullet` and `player` have the same fields: x and y. As you probably have guessed, x and y define the coordinates for the bullet and player's positions.

After creating the types, the program initializes the player type. Of course, there is only one player, so a single player is created. The player's beginning x and y coordinates are defined at 400,500, which starts the player roughly in the middle of the screen near the bottom.

The next two sections define the constants and the images. The constants are the scan codes for each of the keys that are used in the game. The program loads three images: `playerimage`, `bulletimage`, and `backgroundimage`. Notice that `bulletimage` is global, implying that it is used in other functions, not just the main function.

The final section of the initialization creates `scrolly`. This indicator variable defines how far the background should scroll at any instant.

Next up, consider the main loop.

```
;MAIN LOOP
While Not KeyDown(ESCKEY)

;Increment scrolling variable
scrolly = scrolly + 1

;Tile the background
TileBlock backgroundimage,0,scrolly

;Reset the scrolling variable when it grows too large
If scrolly > ImageHeight(backgroundimage)
       scrolly = 0
EndIf

;Test input keys
TestKeys()

;Update (move) each bullet
UpdateBullets()

;Draw the player
DrawImage playerimage,  player\x, player\y


;Flip the front and back buffers
Flip

Wend   ;END OF MAIN LOOP
```

The main loop begins by tiling the background. It increments the indicator variable, `scrolly`, and then tiles the background. When `scrolly` grows too large, its value is reset to

0. Following that, the program calls two user-defined functions: `TestKeys()` and `UpdateBullets()`. The first function tests the keyboard to determine if any input has occurred, and the second function moves and updates each bullet on the screen.

The main loop ends by drawing the player's ship and his or her current position. It then flips the front and back buffers using the command `Flip`.

The rest of the program lists the two user-defined functions: `TestKeys()` and `UpdateBullets()`. Following is the source for `TestKeys()`.

```
;FUNCTIONS
;Function TestKeys() - Tests which buttons have been pressed by player
Function TestKeys()

;If the player hits up, we move him 5 pixels up
If KeyDown(UPKEY)
	player\y = player\y - 5 ;move player 5 pixels up
EndIf

;If the player hits left, we move him 5 pixels left
If KeyDown(LEFTKEY)
	player\x = player\x - 5 ;move player 5 pixels left
EndIf

;If player hits right, we move him 5 pixels right
If KcyDown(RIGHTKEY)
	player\x = player\x + 5 ;move player 5 pixels right
EndIf

;If player hits down, we move him 5 pixels down
If KeyDown(DOWNKEY)
	player\y = player\y + 5 ;move player 5 pixels down
EndIf

;If player presses the spacebar, we will create a
;new bullet at the player's current position
If KeyHit(SPACEBAR)
	bullet.bullet = New bullet
	bullet\x = player\x
	bullet\y = player\y
EndIf

End Function
```

The `TestKeys()` function, although not short, is pretty easy to comprehend. The function tests each key to determine if it has been pressed, and if so, it changes something in the program. Table 10.4 explains what each key does when pressed.

Table 10.4 Demo10-05.bb's Keys

Key	Function
Up arrow	Moves the player five pixels up.
Left arrow	Moves the player five pixels left.
Right arrow	Moves the player five pixels right.
Down arrow	Moves the player five pixels down.
Spacebar	Creates a new bullet to be drawn onscreen.

As you can see, the arrow keys do pretty much what you expect them to do. The only new key is the spacebar.

When the player presses the spacebar, a new bullet is created. The code that performs this action follows.

```
If KeyHit(SPACEBAR)
      bullet.bullet = New bullet
```

Notice that the function uses `KeyHit()` instead of `KeyDown()` for the creation of new bullets. This prevents the player from holding down the spacebar and creating hundreds of bullets quickly. Figure 10.5 shows what happens if you exchange `KeyDown()` with `KeyHit()`.

By creating a new bullet, the program adds a new bullet to the bullet type. If you remember, when creating multiple members of the same type, the most recent one becomes active. Thus, the following lines

```
bullet\x = player\x
bullet\y = player\y
```

only relate to the most recent bullet (the one that was just created a few milliseconds earlier). The new bullet is created at the player's current position.

Okay, the next and final function updates each bullet. Following is the source for `UpdateBullets()`.

```
;Function UpdateBullets() - Moves each bullet onscreen
Function UpdateBullets()

;For every bullet, move it up 5 pixels.
;If it goes offscreen, delete it, otherwise, draw it
```

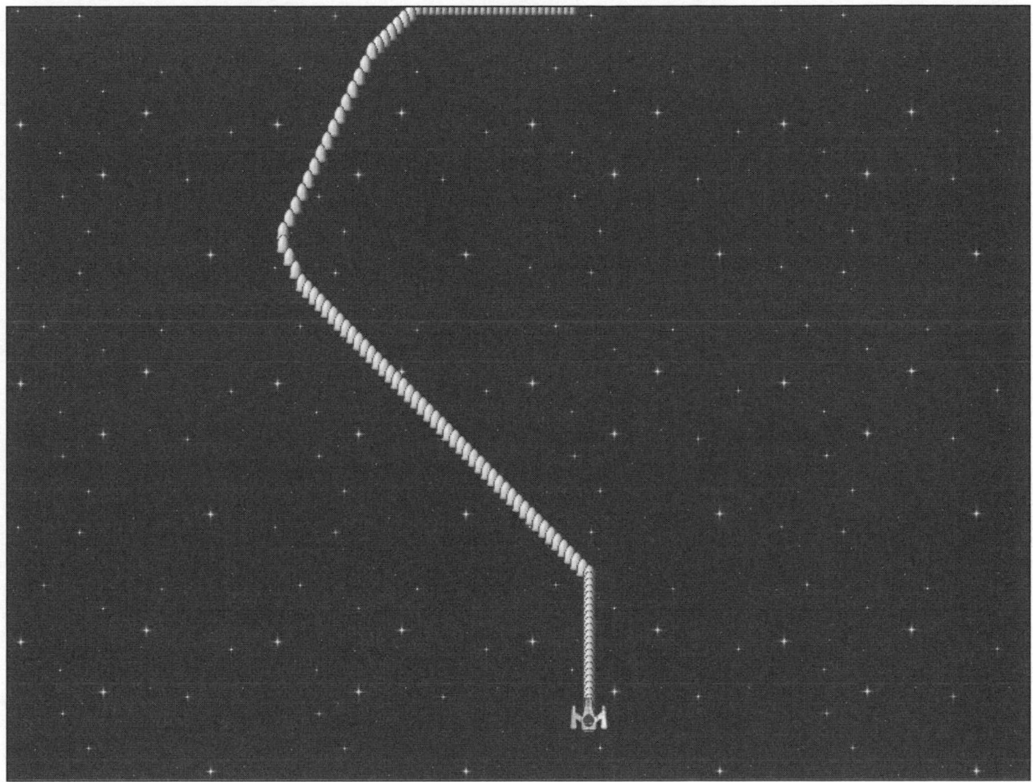

Figure 10.5 Exchanging `KeyDown()` with `KeyHit()`.

```
For bullet.bullet = Each bullet
	bullet\y = bullet\y - 5   ;Move bullet up

	;If bullet moves offscreen, delete it, otherwise, draw it onscreen
	If bullet\y < 0
		Delete bullet
	Else
		DrawImage bulletimage, bullet\x, bullet\y    ;Draw the bullet
	EndIf

Next  ;move to next bullet

End Function
```

The function begins with a `For…Each` loop that tests every created bullet. The function moves each existing bullet five pixels up. The program then determines if the bullet is offscreen. If so, the bullet is deleted. If not, the bullet is drawn onscreen.

The function ends by moving on to the next bullet, and returning to the main function after every bullet has been processed.

Well, that is it for demo10-05.bb. The following screenshot, Figure 10.6, was taken from that program.

Figure 10.6 The demo10-05.bb program.

By the way, try changing `KeyHit()` into `KeyDown()` on the `TestKeys()` function. Seriously, it can provide hours of fun—especially for those who like shiny and fast moving objects (like me!).

Before you move on to mouse input, I want to explain one thing about `KeyHit()`. `KeyHit()` does provide a return value. The function returns the number of times the user pressed a key since the previous `KeyHit()` call (or since the beginning of the program if there are no earlier `KeyHit()` calls). The following demo, demo10-06.bb, demonstrates what it can do.

```
;demo10-06.bb - Demonstrates the return value of KeyHit()

;Set up graphics so that you can read all of the text, make it windowed
```

```
Graphics 800,600,0,2

;Begin introductory text
Text 0,0, "You know what's cool? Game Programming."
Text 0,12,"Although Maneesh ain't that uncool, either."

Flip

;Continue text
Text 0,36, "Anyway, press Esc as many times as you can in the Next 5 seconds."
Text 0,48, "At the end of the program, the number of times will be printed."

Flip

numberofhits=0

;Allow the player 5 seconds to hit esc as many times as possible
timerbegin=MilliSecs()

While timerbegin>MilliSecs()-5000
     If KeyHit(1)
          numberofhits = numberofhits + 1
     EndIf
Wend

;Print the number of times Esc was hit
Text 0,60, "Esc was hit " + numberofhits + " times."
Text 0,72, "You gotta love KeyHit(), huh?"

Flip

;Hold on a sec so the player can see the final text
Delay 5000
```

The main part of the program sets `numberofhits` to `KeyHit(1) and adds the value of the function to numberofhits`—it adds one to `numberofhits` everytime the user pressed Esc since the beginning of the program. Figure 10.7 is a screenshot taken from demo10-06.bb.

Well, that is all for keyboard input. Now we move on to mouse input.

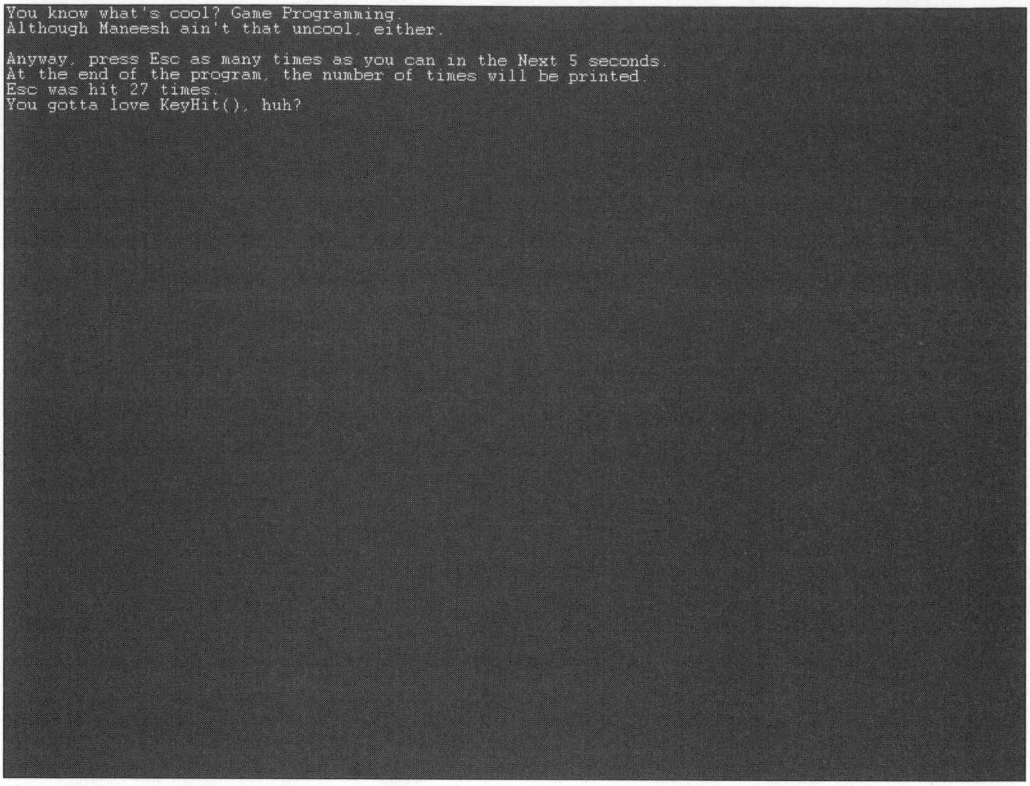

```
You know what's cool? Game Programming.
Although Maneesh ain't that uncool, either.

Anyway, press Esc as many times as you can in the Next 5 seconds.
At the end of the program, the number of times will be printed.
Esc was hit 27 times.
You gotta love KeyHit(), huh?
```

Figure 10.7 The demo10-06.bb program.

Mapping the Mouse to the Screen

Handling the mouse is a lot easier than handling the keyboard. Just look at them: compared to the 105 keys on your keyboard, there are only two or three buttons on your mouse (well, maybe more, depending on the make). Thus, you only have to test the input of three keys maximum. However, when using the mouse, you also have to test the coordinate position on the screen.

Unlike a keyboard, which is ever-present, the mouse only exists onscreen at a certain location. By moving the mouse, you move the mouse cursor on your screen (usually designated by an arrow), and you change where your mouse points. This pointer technology allows you to select or choose anything onscreen by moving your mouse to the location and clicking.

Unfortunately, BlitzPlus does not provide a mouse cursor that allows you to see where your mouse is at the current time. There is an easy way to circumvent this problem, and we take it head-on in the next section.

Displaying the Mouse Cursor

Most of the time, while on your computer, you use the mouse to perform whatever actions you want... err... performed. The following figure, Figure 10.8, shows an example of a standard mouse cursor.

BlitzPlus does not have support for displaying mouse cursors. Obviously, we do need a mouse cursor to function; otherwise, any program that utilizes the mouse will act something like the program from demo10-07.bb. Figure 10.9 shows a screenshot from that program.

Figure 10.8
A mouse cursor.

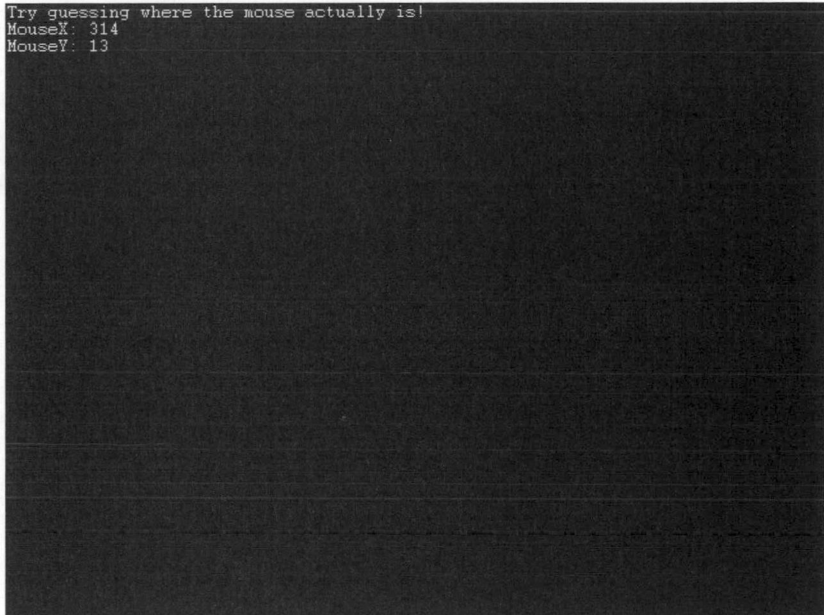

Figure 10.9 The demo10-07.bb program.

note

> If you happen to run your program in windowed mode (by calling `Graphics xxx,yyy,zzz,2`), the default mouse cursor, the one you see when using your computer, will appear.

Pretty stupid, huh? You have no idea where the mouse is, so the program is pretty much worthless. What we need to do is figure out a way to draw the mouse cursor.

What we are going to do is draw an image containing the mouse cursor image at the mouse's x and y coordinates. How do we begin this? First off, we make an image that we want to be used for the mouse cursor. This example uses the cursor shown in Figure 10.10.

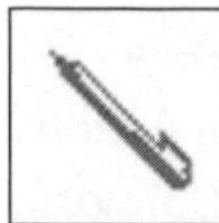

Figure 10.10 The example mouse cursor.

I made the cursor white so that it can be seen against the black backgrounds often used in games. I made the cursor white inside Paint Shop Pro, which you can find on the CD.

Now that we have a mouse image, all we need to do is draw the image at the mouse's position. Before we can do that, we need to know how to find the mouse's current position. But before we can do that, we need to know one thing.

When using mouse images, it is important that you never set the mid handle to the center; instead, the handle should be at the top-left corner of the image. This is because you want the user to select something from the tip of the mouse cursor, not the center. Keeping the handle might be difficult when using the function `AutoMidHandle`, as it sets every handle to the center automatically. The trick here is to use the function `HandleImage` and give it the coordinates 0,0. For example, if you have a mouse image named `mouseimage`, you would call `HandleImage` like this.

```
HandleImage mouseimage,0,0
```

By the way, in case you didn't know, `HandleImage` sets the handle of the image to the position you give it via x and y coordinates.

Okay, now that we have that down, we need to determine the mouse's coordinate position. Fortunately, BlitzPlus provides two functions for this purpose.

These two functions are called `MouseX()` and `MouseY()`. Their declarations follow.

```
MouseX()
MouseY()
```

What could possibly be easier? Anyway, each function returns the position of the mouse's coordinate position: `MouseX()` returns the mouse's x coordinate, and `MouseY()` returns the mouse's y coordinate.

Okay, now let's put all of this into a program. Following is the listing for demo10-08.bb. In addition to checking the mouse, I added a scrolling background, because scrolling backgrounds are cool.

```
;demo10-08.bb - Demonstrates drawing a mouse cursor
Graphics 640,480
;Set default drawing surface to back buffer
SetBuffer BackBuffer()

;IMAGES
;Load the background and the mouse cursor
backgroundimage = LoadImage("stars.bmp")
```

```
mouseimage = LoadImage("mouseimage.bmp")

;Set handle to top left for mouseimage
HandleImage mouseimage,0,0

;Create an indicator variable for scrolling background
scrolly = 0

;MAIN LOOP
While Not KeyDown(1)

;Scroll background a bit by incrementing scrolly
scrolly = scrolly + 1

;Tile the background
TileBlock backgroundimage,0,scrolly

;Reset scrolly if the number grows too large
If scrolly > ImageHeight(backgroundimage)
       scrolly = 0
EndIf

;Print out text
Text 0,0,"Mouse is easier to find now, huh"

;Print X and Y coordinates
Text 0,12, "MouseX: " + MouseX()
Text 0,24, "MouseY: " + MouseY()

;Draw the mouse image
DrawImage mouseimage,MouseX(),MouseY()

;Slow it down
Delay 20

;Flip front and back buffers
Flip

Wend ;End of Main loop
```

Not too terribly difficult, eh? The `DrawImage` line of code draws the mouse at the mouse's current position, which is given by `MouseX()` and `MouseY()`. Figure 10.11 is a screenshot taken from the program.

Figure 10.11 The demo10-08.bb program.

We are making excellent progress! Now we know how to track and draw an object to represent the position of the mouse cursor. The two important functions to determine the position of the mouse were `MouseX()` and `MouseY()`. We also learned how to change the mouse image with `HandleImage`. Next up, we're going to learn how to detect mouse key presses.

What Was That? Handling Mouse Key Presses

Like a keyboard, a mouse also has keys that you can click on the screen. You might use the mouse for many actions throughout your games. For example, say you have a side-scroller game, like *Super Mario Brothers.* You might allow the user to move onscreen by clicking with the left mouse button, and allow the player to jump by using the right mouse button.

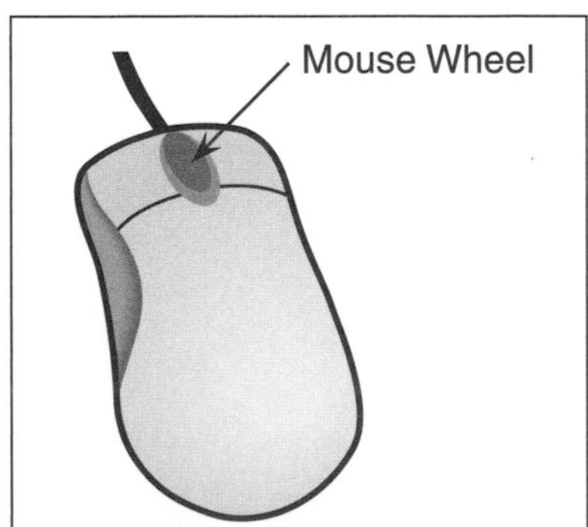

Figure 10.12 A common mouse.

Figure 10.12 shows an average mouse. Notice that it has a mouse wheel. Many mice have mouse wheels, and we will learn how to use the mouse wheel as well as the other two mouse buttons.

Anyway, on to the functions.

MouseDown()

BlitzPlus offers mouse-input functions that are similar to the keyboard-input functions. The function that we will learn about in this section, `MouseDown()`, acts just like its keyboard counterpart `KeyDown()`.

`MouseDown()` has the declaration as follows.

```
MouseDown (button)
```

`Button` is the button that you are checking for: the left mouse button, the right mouse button, or the middle mouse button. Table 10.5 lists all the possibilities for `button`.

Table 10.5 MouseDown()'s Button Possibilities

Button	Key Code
Left mouse button	1
Right mouse button	2
Middle mouse button	3

Easy, huh? How can we use `MouseDown()`? Well, for example, to determine if the user clicked the left mouse button, you would do something like this.

```
If MouseDown(1)
        ;perform actions
Endif
```

Whatever you want to happen when the left mouse button is clicked is placed between the `If` and the `Endif` statements.

`MouseDown()` returns true (1) if the mouse key was clicked, and false (0) if it was not clicked.

I'm neglecting to write a sample program for `MouseDown()` right now; instead, I will use it in a sample program with the next function: `MouseHit()`.

MouseHit()

I bet you can guess the difference between this function and `MouseDown()`, huh? Whereas you can hold down `MouseDown()`, you must click the mouse button over and over when using `MouseHit()` to initiate the action.

This difference is the same as is in `KeyDown()` versus `KeyHit()`, the keyboard-input functions. Just like `KeyHit()`, `MouseHit()` also records the number of times you click the button.

`MouseHit()` is declared like this:

```
MouseHit (button)
```

Button can be any of those listed in Table 10.5.

Anyway, let's rewrite demo10-05.bb to use mouse input. Instead of using keys to move the player's ship, the ship is located at the coordinates of the mouse. For this program, we do not need a mouse cursor, because the ship serves as a sign of the mouse's position.

Also, the mouse buttons have been changed. Although pressing the left mouse button still creates a bullet, holding down the right mouse button creates a laser. Let's try it.

Most of the program has changed, so I am going to copy the source section by section. It begins with the initialization section of demo10-09.bb.

```
;demo10-09.bb - A Space Simulation with MouseDown() and KeyDown()

Graphics 800,600

;Set automidhandle to true
AutoMidHandle True
;Set up Backbuffer
SetBuffer BackBuffer()

;TYPES

;Bullet type = hold the information for each bullet
Type bullet
	Field x,y   ;the coordinates of the bullet
	Field bullettype ;LASER or NORMALBULLET (see constants)
End Type


;Player type - holds the actual player
Type player
	Field x,y   ;the coordinates of the player
End Type

;Create player and initialize field
Global player.player = New player
player\x = 400
player\y = 500


;CONSTANTS
;The following constants are used for testing key presses (mouse and keyboard)
Const ESCKEY = 1, LEFTMOUSEBUTTON = 1, RIGHTMOUSEBUTTON = 2
;The following constants are used for the bullets,
;BULLET is a regular bullet, LASER is a laser
Const NORMALBULLET = 1, LASER = 2
```

```
;IMAGES
playerimage = LoadImage("ship.bmp")
Global bulletimage = LoadImage("bullet.bmp")
Global laserimage = LoadImage("laser.bmp")
backgroundimage = LoadImage("stars.bmp")

HandleImage laserimage, ImageWidth(laserimage)/2, ImageHeight(laserimage)


;VARIABLES
;Create a scrolling indicator variable
scrolly = 0

;Number of times left and mouse buttons were hit
Global leftmouseclicks = 0
Global rightmouseclicks = 0
```

Okay, let's go through this section. The program begins just as it did in demo10-09.bb with the setting of the graphics mode, the creation of the back buffer, and setting `AutoMidHandle` to true. In the next part, the types have changed a bit.

The bullet type looked like this in demo10-05.bb:

```
Type bullet
       Field x,y   ;the coordinates of the bullet
End Type
```

Notice the new field: `bullettype`. This type defines whether the bullet is a normal bullet or laser. We assign this field at the time of the bullet's creation, depending on whether the player clicks the left mouse button or the right mouse button.

The next major change in the program takes place in the constants section. As you can see, we have deleted all of the key code constants besides Esc. Esc remains because we use it to determine if the program should exit in the main loop.

In the key codes place, we created a set of new constants. The first two new constants are `LEFTMOUSEBUTTON` and `RIGHTMOUSEBUTTON`. These two constants are used in the `MouseHit()` and `MouseDown()` tests later in the program—they tell the program which mouse buttons were clicked. The other two constants, `NORMALBULLET` and `LASER`, are used in the `bullettype` field of the bullet type. If `bullettype` is equal to `NORMALBULLET`, the bullets are regular run-of-the-mill bullets. If bullettype is `LASER`, the bullet is a laser.

We loaded a new image, `laserimage`, which is the image of each laser bullet shot by clicking the right mouse button. Figure 10.13 shows what the laser looks like. It is the straight line down the middle.

The laser is very long because it extends from one side of the screen to the other. Thus, the height of the laser is the height of the screen.

We then set the handle to the bottom-center of the image with the line

```
HandleImage laserimage, ImageWidth(laserimage)/2, ImageHeight(laserimage)
```

This line might be a little difficult to understand, so let's go over it. First off, we have to know what `HandleImage` does.

`HandleImage` allows you to choose where the handling point of an image is. `AutoMidHandle` automatically assigns the handling point of any image to the direct center. What does the handling point do? Well, when you move the image around, it moves by its handling point. Imagine picking up a playing card. If you pick it up in the exact center, you will notice that the card extends in all directions from your finger. This is what `AutoMidHandle` does. See Figure 10.14 for an example.

As you can see in Figure 10.14, the handling point, which is where your finger is, is directly in the center of the card. The card's points extend in all directions from the center point. When you move your hand around, the card is still grasped from the center, and thus, the edges of the card always extend from 0,0.

When using the laser image, however, we want the image to be grasped from the bottom. We will be making the laser extend from the front of the player's spaceship to the upper wall of the screen, and because it must begin right on the player, we have to set the handle to the bottom edge of the laser. Figure 10.15 shows what it would look like to set the handle to the bottom of the playing card.

`HandleImage` allows you to set the handle of the laser image to the coordinates you want. In the line

```
HandleImage laserimage, ImageWidth(laserimage)/2, ImageHeight(laserimage)
```

Figure 10.13
The laser image.

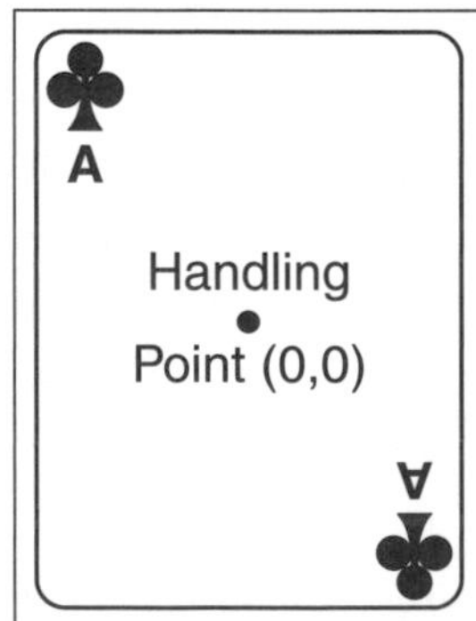

Figure 10.14
AutoMidHandle on a playing card.

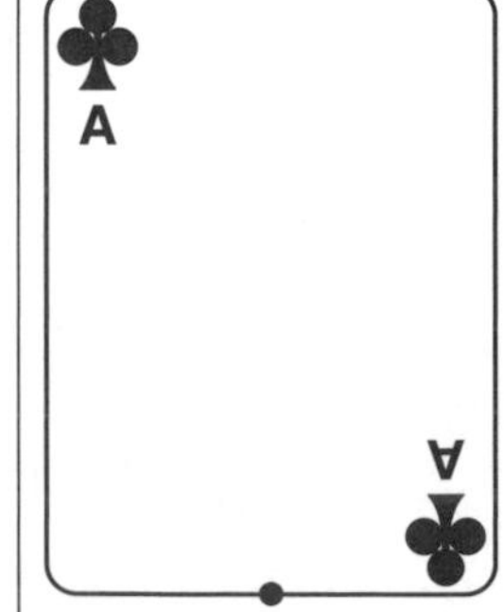

Figure 10.15
The lower handle on a playing card.

the handle is set to `ImageWidth(laserimage)/2, ImageHeight(laserimage)`. What does this mean? The x coordinate of the handle is located at `ImageWidth(laserimage)/2`. This is half of the width of the image, which is in the center of the image. The y coordinate, `ImageHeight(laserimage)`, puts the handle at the bottom of the image. See Figure 10.16 for help.

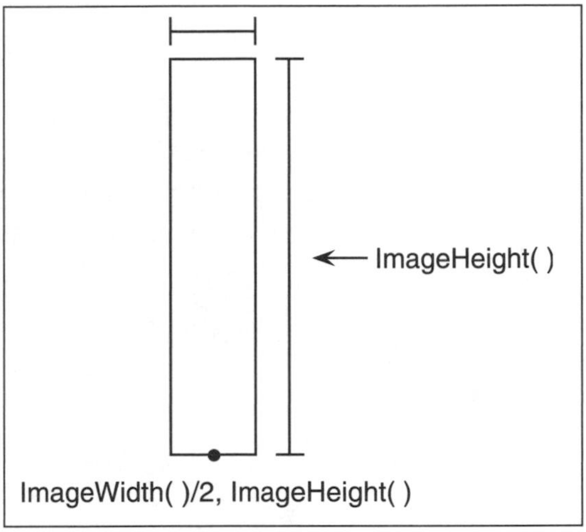

Okay, hopefully we understand the laser image's handle now. Moving on in the initialization section of the program, we get to two new variables, `leftmouseclicks` and `rightmouseclicks`. These two variables record how many times each of their respective buttons were clicked.

Figure 10.16 The handle on the laser image.

Next up is the main loop. Check it out.

```
;MAIN LOOP
While Not KeyDown(ESCKEY)

;Increment scrolling variable
scrolly = scrolly + 1

;Tile the background
TileBlock backgroundimage,0,scrolly

;Set up text
Text 0,0, "Player X: " + MouseX()
Text 0,12, "Player Y: " + MouseY()
Text 0,24, "Number of times left mouse button was hit: " + leftmouseclicks
Text 0,36 "Number of times right mouse button was hit: " + rightmouseclicks


;Reset the scrolling variable when it grows too large
If scrolly > ImageHeight(backgroundimage)
       scrolly = 0
EndIf

;Test mouse buttons
TestMouse()

;Update (move) each bullet
UpdateBullets()

;Draw the player
```

```
DrawImage playerimage,  player\x, player\y


;Flip the front and back buffers
Flip

Wend   ;END OF MAIN LOOP
```

This loop is almost exactly the same as the one in demo10-05.bb, except for two changes. We added some text to the screen that tells the users their position and how many times they have clicked the left and right mouse buttons. The second change is a change in name: `TestKeys()` has been changed to `TestMouse()`, which is the function we examine next.

```
;FUNCTIONS
;Function TestMouse() - Tests which mouse buttons have been pressed and where
 player is located
Function TestMouse()

;Set the player at the position of the mouse
player\x = MouseX()
player\y = MouseY()

;If the player hits left mouse button, create a bullet
If MouseHit(LEFTMOUSEBUTTON)
       bullet.bullet = New bullet    ;create bullet
       bullet\x = player\x    ;place bullet at player's x coordinate
       bullet\y = player\y    ;place bullet at player's y coordinate
       bullet\bullettype = NORMALBULLET    ;make it a normal bullet

       ;increment left mouse clicks
       leftmouseclicks = leftmouseclicks + 1
EndIf

;If the player hits left, we will scroll the background left
If MouseDown(RIGHTMOUSEBUTTON)
       bullet.bullet = New bullet    ;create bullet
       bullet\x = player\x    ;place bullet at player's x coordinate
       bullet\y = player\y    ;place bullet at player's y coordinate
       bullet\bullettype = LASER    ;make it a laser

       ;add amount of right mouse clicks since last frame
       rightmouseclicks = rightmouseclicks + MouseHit(RIGHTMOUSEBUTTON)
EndIf
End Function
```

Whew, big difference, huh? This function had a massive overhaul, because you are no longer using the keyboard. The function begins by assigning the coordinates of the ship to the coordinates of the mouse using the functions `MouseX()` and `MouseY()`. If you remember, `MouseX()` and `MouseY()` return the coordinates of the mouse at the given time.

After this, we determine if the player has clicked any mouse buttons. If so, the program creates a bullet. The tests for the left and the right mouse button begin in the same way: a new bullet is created with the coordinates of the player. This creates the bullet directly under the player, giving the illusion that the player's ship actually fired the bullet. The next line marks a difference between the left mouse test and the right mouse test. If the player clicked the left mouse button, the bullet type of the bullet is set to `NORMALBULLET`, whereas, if the player clicked the right mouse button, the bullet type is set to `LASER`.

The last section of each of the tests increments either the left mouse-click counter or the right mouse-click counter, depending on which button was clicked. You can see that the actions taken to increment the counter are different in each test, and if you need help understanding why, see the accompanying note.

note

Look at the end of each of the mouse input tests for both the left mouse button and the right mouse button: do you notice how each line is different? Both lines increment their respective counters that detail how many times a laser or bullet has been fired, but they do so in a different way. The first test, `MouseHit(LEFTMOUSEBUTTON)`, adds 1 directly to the left mouse-click counter, whereas the second test, `MouseDown(RIGHTMOUSEBUTTON)` adds the return value of a `MouseHit(RIGHTMOUSEBUTTON)` to its counter. Why can't we just add one to the right mouse-button counter?? Well, in the first test, we used `MouseHit()` to determine if the left mouse button was clicked. If you remember, `MouseHit()` always returns 1 when the key (here, the left mouse key) is clicked once. Because we are calling `MouseHit()`, we know for a fact that the key was clicked once, so we add one to the counter. On the other hand, we use `MouseDown()` for the right mouse button test. `MouseDown()` returns 1 as long as the button is being held down, not only if the button is being pressed (like `MouseHit()` does). In other words, a new bullet can be created even though the key was not released and then pressed again—the new bullet is created just because the key is being held down. Because of this fact, we add `KeyHit(RIGHTMOUSEBUTTON)` to the counter, which will add one if the right key is released and then pressed again, and zero if it is simply held down.

Anyway, we can now move on to the final function: `UpdateBullets()`.

```
;Function UpdateBullets() - Moves each bullet onscreen
Function UpdateBullets()

;For every bullet, move it up 5 pixels.
;If it goes offscreen, delete it, otherwise, draw it
For bullet.bullet = Each bullet
       ;If bullet moves offscreen, delete it, otherwise, draw it onscreen.
```

```
	;Draw laserimage if it is a laser, bulletimage if it is a bullet
	If bullet\y < 0
		Delete bullet
	ElseIf bullet\bullettype = NORMALBULLET
		bullet\y = bullet\y - 5   ;Move bullet up
		DrawImage bulletimage, bullet\x, bullet\y    ;Draw the bullet
	ElseIf bullet\bullettype = LASER
		If player\x <> bullet\x
			Delete bullet
		Else
			DrawImage laserimage, bullet\x, bullet\y
			  ;Draw the laser
		EndIf
	EndIf

Next  ;Move to next bullet

End Function
```

This function begins by moving each bullet upward five pixels. The function then determines if the bullet is on the screen or if it has moved offscreen. If the bullet's y coordinate is less than 0, the bullet is offscreen. When this happens, the bullet is deleted using the `Delete` function. If the bullet wasn't deleted, the function tests to see what type the bullet is, using `bullet\bullettype`. If the bullet is a normal bullet, the program draws the bullet at the proper coordinates. If the bullet is a laser, the program must do a few more tests.

Because the laser follows the player around, and it stretches to the end of the screen, we do not want the player's x coordinate to be any different from the laser's x coordinate. Therefore, we test the player's x against the bullet's x using the Not Equal To operator <>. If `player\x` and `bullet\x` are not equal to one another, the laser is deleted. If the player's x and the bullet's x are equal to one another, the laser is drawn on the screen.

That is it for demo10-09.bb. Figure 10.17 is a screenshot taken from the program.

All right, I hope you understand basic mouse input now. Before we move on to joystick input, I want to go over the middle mouse wheel.

The Middle Mouse Wheel

As you know, many mice have a middle mouse button in addition to the normal right and left mouse buttons. Often, the middle mouse button is a scrolling wheel, which can be used in programs such as Internet Explorer to scroll up and down. BlitzPlus provides support for the middle mouse wheel, both in clicking and in scrolling.

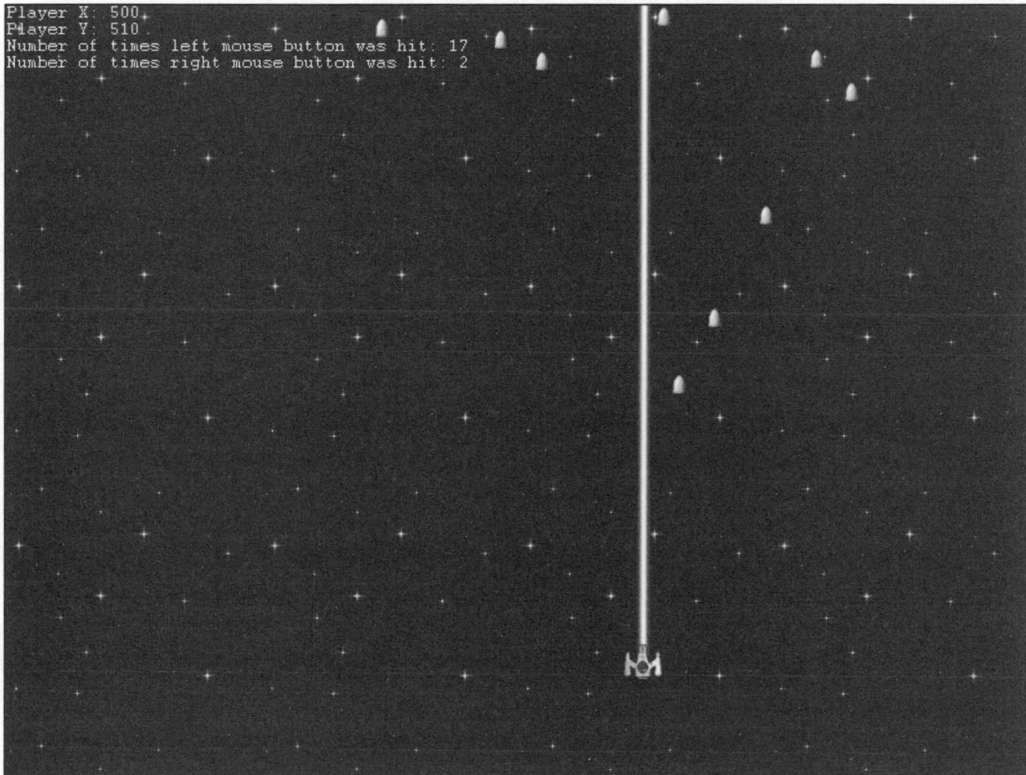

Figure 10.17 The demo10-09.bb program.

You already know how to determine if the middle mouse button was clicked. To do this, just call `MouseDown()` with `3` as its parameter. You would write something like this in your program:

```
If MouseHit(3)
       ;perform actions
EndIf
```

Not that difficult, eh? Determining if the mouse was scrolled is almost as easy.

Remember at the beginning of the mouse input section, where we used the two functions `MouseX()` and `MouseY()`? If you remember, `MouseX()` and `MouseY()` gave the coordinate position of the mouse. BlitzPlus provides the function `MouseZ()` that tests the mouse wheel to determine if it has scrolled.

caution

The BlitzPlus program on the CD does not allow the function `MouseZ()` to be used. This is very unfortunate, because you cannot determine if the mouse wheel has been scrolled on your demo program. The full version of BlitzPlus does allow the function `MouseZ()` to be used, however. You can buy the full version at http://www.blitzbasic.com.

The demo10-10.bb program will not work if you try to compile it from the BlitzPlus program. You will get a "Function not Found" error. The executable file however, does work, so just use that. This program shows you how you can use MouseZ() if and when you purchase the full version of BlitzPlus.

MouseZ() begins at 0 when your program begins. As you scroll the mouse wheel away from you (upward), MouseZ() increases. As you scroll the mouse wheel toward you (downward), MouseZ() increases. See Figure 10.18; it might help illustrate what scrolling the mouse "upward" and "downward" means.

Anyway, to test for what MouseZ() is, you simply call the function. There are no parameters or anything to look for. So, let's try a sample program, demo10-10.bb. This program scrolls the background 20 pixels as you scroll the mouse wheel.

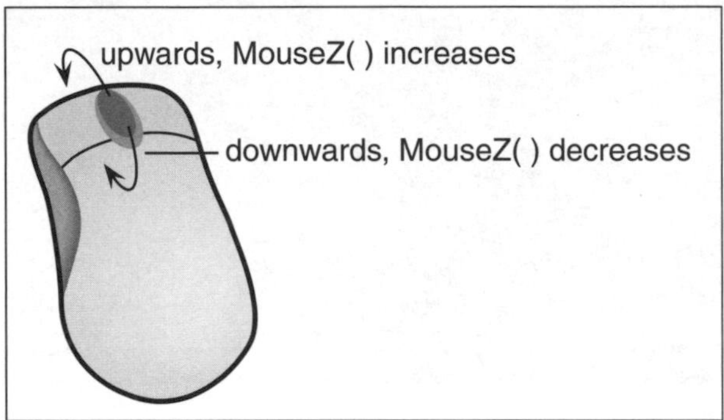

Figure 10.18 Scrolling a mouse wheel.

```
;demo10-10.bb - Demonstrates use of MouseZ()

;Set up graphics and backbuffer
Graphics 800,600
SetBuffer BackBuffer()
;Load images
backgroundimage = LoadImage("stars.bmp")
shipimage = LoadImage("ship.bmp")

;MAIN LOOP
While Not KeyDown(1)

;Scroll the background 20 pixels with each mouse wheel scroll
scrolly = MouseZ() * 20

;Tile the background
```

```
TileBlock backgroundimage,0,scrolly


;Draw the player
DrawImage shipimage, MouseX(), MouseY()

Flip
Wend
;END OF MAIN LOOP
```

note

Take note that, unfortunately, the demo does not support `MouseZ()`, probably because of some error in the coding. The actual program does support `MouseZ()`, however. If you try to compile this code with the demo version of BlitzPlus, it will not work correctly, but it will work with the full version.

As you can see, the program sets `scrolly` to `MouseZ() * 20`. Multiplying `MouseZ()` by 20 forces the scrolling variable to change by 20 pixels with each change in the mouse wheel. This means that the background will scroll faster and easier. Try changing 20 to a different number and see what happens. If you set 20 to a smaller number, you will notice that the background scrolls much slower, whereas making it larger makes the background scroll faster.

The following figure, Figure 10.19, is a screenshot directly from demo10-10.bb.

Okay, before we move on to the next section, there are a few miscellaneous mouse functions that you should know. Like `FlushKeys()`, BlitzPlus provides the function `FlushMouse()`. This function clears the computer's memory of keys that have been pressed on the mouse.

`WaitKeys()` is another function that has a keyboard counterpart, `WaitKeys()`. This function waits for the player to press a button on the mouse before resuming the program's execution.

`GetMouse()` can be used when you want to get a key that the player pressed, but do not know what it will be. `GetMouse()` has no parameters, but if a button is pressed, it returns the number of the pressed button. Therefore, if the left mouse button was pressed, 1 is returned; if the right mouse button was pressed, 2 is returned; and if the mouse wheel was pressed, 3 is returned.

Last, BlitzPlus provides the function `MoveMouse()`. This function has the declaration

```
MoveMouse x,y
```

This function moves the mouse to the coordinates you feed it. Therefore, if you type `MoveMouse(0,0)`, the mouse moves to the top-left corner of the screen.

All right, that is it for mouse input. Next up: joystick input.

Figure 10.19 The demo10-10.bb program.

Handling Joystick Input

As you know, mice and keyboards are the most common input devices for games. However, there are many other devices that are used, just not as commonly. Game pads and joysticks are used for many flying and racing video games.

BlitzPlus provides support for joysticks, much like its support for keyboards and mice. However, I do not want to go over joysticks entirely, because the subject is large and infrequently used. However, if you want to learn about joysticks, I have compiled a list (see Table 10.6) of the most useful functions, their parameters, and their return values.

Table 10.6 Joystick Functions

Function	Description
`JoyType ([port])`	This function determines if a joystick is currently connected to the given port. The function returns 0 if there is no joystick, 1 if the joystick is digital, and 2 if the joystick is analog.
`JoyDown (button,[port])`	This function returns 1 if the specified button is being held down.
`JoyHit (button, [port])`	This function returns the number of times the specified joystick button has been pressed.
`GetJoy ([port])`	This function returns the number of the button that was pressed.
`WaitJoy ([port])`	This function stops the program's execution until a joystick button is pressed.
`JoyX# ([port])`	This function returns the x coordinate of the joystick. The return value can range from −1 (far left) to 1 (far right), with 0 being directly in the center.
`JoyY# ([port])`	This function returns the y coordinate of the joystick. The return value can range from −1 (far up) to 1 (far down), with 0 being directly in the center.
`JoyZ# ([port])`	This function returns the z-axis of the joystick. Usually, the z-axis is a button. The value can range from 0 to 1 (none to max).
`JoyU# ([port])`	Depending on the joystick, this function can be used to detect a slider, a throttle, or a button; this is referred to as the u-axis. This function returns a value between −1 and 1.
`JoyV# ([port])`	Depending on the joystick, this function can be used to detect a slider, a throttle, or a button that is different than the one in `JoyU#`; this is referred to as the v-axis. This function returns a value between −1 and 1.
`FlushJoy`	This function flushes all of the commands in the joystick's queue, much like F`JoyType FlushKeys()`.

You probably noticed that only two parameters are used in all of the functions. The parameter `[port]` is used only when there is more than one joystick connected to the computer. A port is a number that refers to the place on your computer where the joystick is plugged in. Almost always, just leave `[port]` blank.

The parameter `button` refers to the buttons on your joystick. The first mouse button begins at one, and the last button depends on the make of the controller. Usually, there are at least three buttons total.

You can call `JoyX#` (and also `JoyY#`, `Z#`, `U#`, and `V#`) like this:

```
returnvalue = JoyX#()
```

`Returnvalue` will now contain a value between −1 and 1.

Summary

Whew, that was a long chapter. Hopefully, you now understand the basis of input. Mouse, keyboard, and joystick input are used in all games, and it is of the utmost importance that you have a firm grasp of these concepts. This chapter covered the following concepts:

- Receiving keyboard input with `KeyDown()` and `KeyHit()`
- Displaying a mouse cursor
- Handling mouse key presses with `MouseDown()` and `MouseHit()`
- Using the middle mouse wheel
- Handling joystick input

Even though BlitzPlus provides you with a large number of functions (I didn't even go over them all), only a few are absolutely necessary. You will almost definitely be using either `KeyDown()` or `MouseDown()` in your programs. Other functions, such as `FlushKeys()`, only occasionally.

Anyway, get ready for the next lesson. We are moving on to something really fun: sound. You will learn how to use sound in your games to give the effect of action!

Chapter 11

Sounds and Music

If you've played any games lately, you know the difference that sound can make. Sound not only makes you feel like you are part of the game, but it can also provide clues about what's around the corner. Many newer games even support *multi-channel sound*, which allows you to hear sound in more than one direction. In multi-channel sound, you have more than two speakers (many systems have as many as five, and sometimes even more located around the player). All of these speakers, or channels, can play different sounds at the same time. You can hear someone approaching from behind you (from the speakers that are located to your back), yet when you turn around to face him, the footsteps are emitted from your front speakers!

BlitzPlus provides a lot of support for both sound and music, and this chapter teaches you how to use both. First up, sound!

Sound

In the introduction, I said that we will learn about both sound and music in this chapter, and you might be thinking that they are the same. Nope! BlitzPlus refers to sounds and music as two different entities. Unlike music, sound is played dynamically. What does this mean? The game does not play sound files over and over. Instead, the sound is only played at specific times. Take, for example, a gun. You don't want a gunshot to ring over and over; you want it to make a sound only when the gun actually shoots.

For this book, we will be using the .WAV file format for the sound files. What is the .WAV file format, you might ask? It is a file format that represents a sound on the computer. This sound format does not have any quality loss like some other file formats (which we will discuss later), so the sound from a .WAV file is "cleaner." I have included a number of royalty-free sound files on the CD, most in .WAV format, that you can use in your programs. By the way, WAV stands for "Windows Audio Volume."

Anyway, let's get started. First off, we need to know how to load sounds.

Loading Sounds

Remember images? It was extremely easy to load them, right? We just used the `LoadImage()` function. Well, BlitzPlus makes loading sounds just as easy: we use the `LoadSound()` function. `LoadSound()` is declared as follows:

```
LoadSound (filename$)
```

Table 11.1 describes the parameter for `LoadSound()`.

Table 11.1 LoadSound()'s Parameter

Parameter	Description
`filename$`	The file name of the sound file you want to load.

You load sounds just like you load images.

```
soundfile = LoadSound ("soundfile.wav")
```

Change *`soundfile`* and *`soundfile.wav`* to the name of the variable and file of the sound you want to load into your program.

note

From this point on, I use a certain style for my sound files. Whenever I load them, I call the variable that holds the file, `xxxxxsound.wav`, where `xxxxx` describes the sound. For example, to load the sound of a laser, I would call the `sound lasersound`, and I would load it as follows: `lasersound = LoadSound (laser.wav)`.

By the way, there is something else you might want to know. The name of the variable that contains the sound (in the previous example, `soundfile`) is called a *handle*. Why is it called a handle? Well, basically, you use the handle variable as an address or reference to the object. So a "handle" helps you refer to something—in this case a sound file. When you want to manipulate a sound file, you need a handle to access it; it's like a key to a lock.

Okay, I hope you understand loading sounds thus far. Before I move on, I want to detail one little function. This function is `FreeSound`. `FreeSound` deletes a sound from the memory. After freeing the sound, you can use `LoadSound()` and load another sound file with the same handle name. Following is the function declaration for `FreeSound`.

```
FreeSound sound_variable
```

And, as you probably guessed, Table 11.2 explains the parameter.

Table 11.2 FreeSound's Parameter

Parameter	Description
`sound_variable`	The handle to the sound file you want to delete from memory.

You might use this function in a game with numerous levels, perhaps because you use different sounds from one level to the next. By freeing the sound, you are free to load another sound with the same handle that can then be used in place of the old sound.

Let's consider one more example of when you might use `FreeSound`. Say you were writing a game that uses a handgun. Maybe you named the sound that is played when the player's gun is fired `playergunsound`. Now, imagine that the player receives a silencer that can be placed on the gun. The gun with the silencer, of course, sounds much different than the gun without the silencer. The easiest way to do this is to delete the old non-silenced sound from memory and load the silenced sound into the same handle name. That way, the game will continue to play the sound that is loaded in `playergunsound`, even though the sound file has changed. Take a look at Figure 11.1. In the first frame, `playergunsound` contains gunshot.wav. This sound file is just the sound of a regular gunshot. In frame two, `FreeSound` has been called and `playergunsound` doesn't contain anything. In the third and final frame, `LoadSound()` was called again and `playergunsound` now contains silencer.wav.

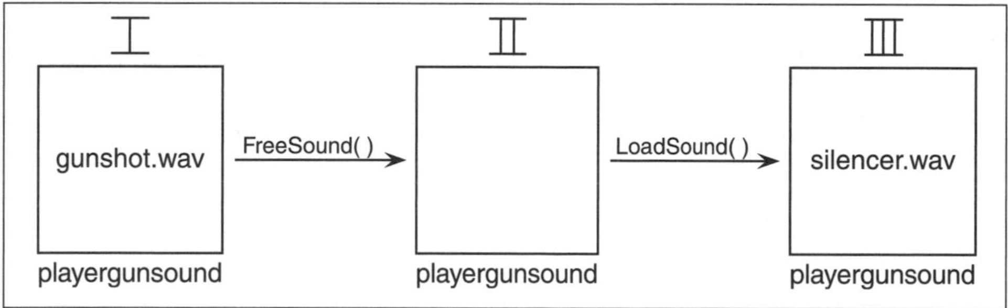

Figure 11.1 `Playergunsound`.

Let's try this in code. Your program might look something like this.

```
;Load the beginning sound for regular gunshot
Global playergunsound = LoadSound ("gunshot.wav")

;Begin MAIN LOOP
While Not KeyDown(1)
```

```
If GunshotOccurred()
       PlayGunshotSound()
Endif

If SilencerAttached()
       SwitchSoundFiles()
Endif

Wend ;END OF MAIN LOOP

;Function SwitchSoundFiles() switches regular gunshot sound file
;with silenced gunshot sound
Function SwitchSoundFiles()
FreeSound playergunsound
playergunsound = loadsound("silencer.wav")
End Function
```

This code sample, of course, will not work if you copy it straight into BlitzPlus. Most of the functions used are user-created functions that we haven't made, but you can probably figure out what they do. `GunShotOccurred()` would return `True` if a gunshot occurred; `PlayGunshotSound()` would play the `playergunsound` file; `SilencerAttached()` returns `True` if a silencer is attached to the gun; and `SwitchSoundFiles()` (which is also user-defined) deletes the old gun sound and attaches the new silenced gun sound.

With this technique, you can change sound files without disturbing the main section of your game.

All right, I hope you understand this. Let's move on to the next section, which teaches you how to actually play the sounds.

Listen Closely—Playing Sounds

You've gotten this far into the chapter, and you probably want to learn how to actually listen to those beautiful sounds that you just learned to load. BlitzPlus provides us with an easy way to play sounds.

This function is called `PlaySound`. (Predictable, huh?) It is declared as follows.

```
PlaySound sound_variable
```

Take a wild guess what `sound_variable` is. Yep, you got it: `sound_variable` is the handle of the sound file you loaded using `LoadSound()`. In other words, you can load a sound clip like this:

```
explosionsound = LoadSound("explosion.wav")
```

Then you play it like this:

```
PlaySound explosionsound
```

Crazy difficult, huh? Anyway, Table 11.3 summarizes `PlaySound`'s parameter.

Table 11.3 PlaySound's Parameter

Parameter	Description
`sound_variable`	The handle to the sound file (loaded with `LoadSound()`) you want to play.

Okay, let's use this function in a sample program. Let's begin with a scrolling background. (Why? Because it is easy and always fun to do.) Then we can add the nice-looking spaceship we use way too often. Then, and listen closely because this is the fun part, we allow the player to fire a bullet using the spacebar. The firing of a bullet creates a bullet-firing sound.

Let's also add an enemy spaceship to the mix. This enemy is like me: he moves in a random fashion, is never predictable, and has no self-defense capabilities whatsoever. Anyway, when the bullet hits this crazy mini-me, an explosion sound is played, and the enemy is destroyed. His ship is then reset.

Hey, I wanted to make this program a little weird, so I used a picture of myself for the enemy ship. Well, just watch.

Anyway, Table 11.4 explains the keys for the program.

Table 11.4 Demo11-01.bb's Keys

Key	Action
Esc	Exits the game
Up arrow	Moves ship up
Down arrow	Moves ship down
Right arrow	Moves ship right
Left arrow	Moves ship left
Spacebar	Fires bullet

I was going to show the entire source for the program, but I realized it takes up about five pages. I am in the mood to save some trees, so I will just display the important parts. The first code block I will show you is taken from the initialization section of demo11-01.bb.

```
;SOUNDS
;Load the sound that is played when the player fires a bullet
Global bulletsound = LoadSound("zing.wav")

;Load the sound that is played when the player destroys the enemy
Global explosionsound = LoadSound ("explode.wav")
```

I bet you can guess what this does! This code loads both of the sounds that are used in the program.

Let's move on to using those loaded sounds. The following source is the `UpdateBullets()` function.

```
;Function UpdateBullets() - Moves and tests each bullet for collision
Function UpdateBullets()

;Loop through every bullet
       For bullets.bullet = Each bullet

              ;Update the bullet's position by moving 5 pixels up
              bullets\y = bullets\y - 5

;Draw the bullet at its proper coordinates
              DrawImage bullets\image, bullets\x, bullets\y


;If the bullet hit the enemy, play the explosion and reset the level
              If ImagesOverlap(enemy\image,enemy\x,enemy\y,
                 bullets\image,bullets\x,bullets\y)
                     PlaySound explosionsound ;Play the explosion
                     Cls
                     Text 260,300, "You destroyed the enemy! How could you?"
                     Flip
                     Delay 4000
                     ResetLevel() ;Reset all variables of the level
                     Return ;Go back to main loop
              EndIf

;If the bullet goes offscreen, delete it
              If bullets\y < 0
                     Delete bullets
              EndIf


       Next  ;Move on to next bullet
End Function
```

As you probably guessed, this function updates all of the bullets onscreen. It begins by moving each bullet up five pixels, and then draws the bullet. The bullet then tests for a collision.

The collision test uses the function `ImagesOverlap()`. As you might remember, `ImagesOverlap()` tests two images, here `enemy\x` and `bullets\x`, to see whether they have overlapped one another. If they have, the explosion sound is played using the command `PlaySound`.

```
PlaySound explosionsound ;Play the explosion
```

The rest of the function clears the screen and displays some text. It then resets the level, and, using the `Return` command, returns back to the main loop.

caution

> You might be wondering why I used the `Return` command to go back to the main loop instead of just letting the function finish going through its instructions. Here is the reason why: Within the function `ResetLevel()` (which is called directly before the `Return` command), all of the bullets are deleted. This includes the bullet that was just being processed. Because the bullet no longer exists, how could we perform the actions of the next line, which tests to see whether the bullet has gone offscreen? There is no way, so in order to fix this situation, we just return back to the main loop and start from scratch.

The last part of the function just tests to see whether the bullet is offscreen. If it is, the bullet is deleted.

The `PlaySound` function is used once more in the program. The following block is ripped from the `TestKeys()` function.

```
;Create a new bullet if spacebar is hit
If KeyHit(SPACEBAR)
	bullets.bullet = New bullet	;Create the bullet
	bullets\x = player\x	;Assign bullet to player's x
	bullets\y = player\y	;Assign bullet to player's y
	bullets\image = LoadImage("bullet.bmp")	;Load the bullet image

	;Play the bullet sound
	PlaySound bulletsound
EndIf
```

What does this do? Well, it begins by testing to see whether the player has pressed the spacebar. If he has, the program then creates a new bullet. The program then assigns the bullet's starting coordinates to the player's starting coordinates. The bullet's image is then loaded.

The block ends by playing `bulletsound`. This sound is created every time a new bullet is created.

That's it for this crazy program. Figure 11.2 shows the program in its full glory. Wow, I look so bad in that photo. (You try finding a good picture of me in the last few years!)

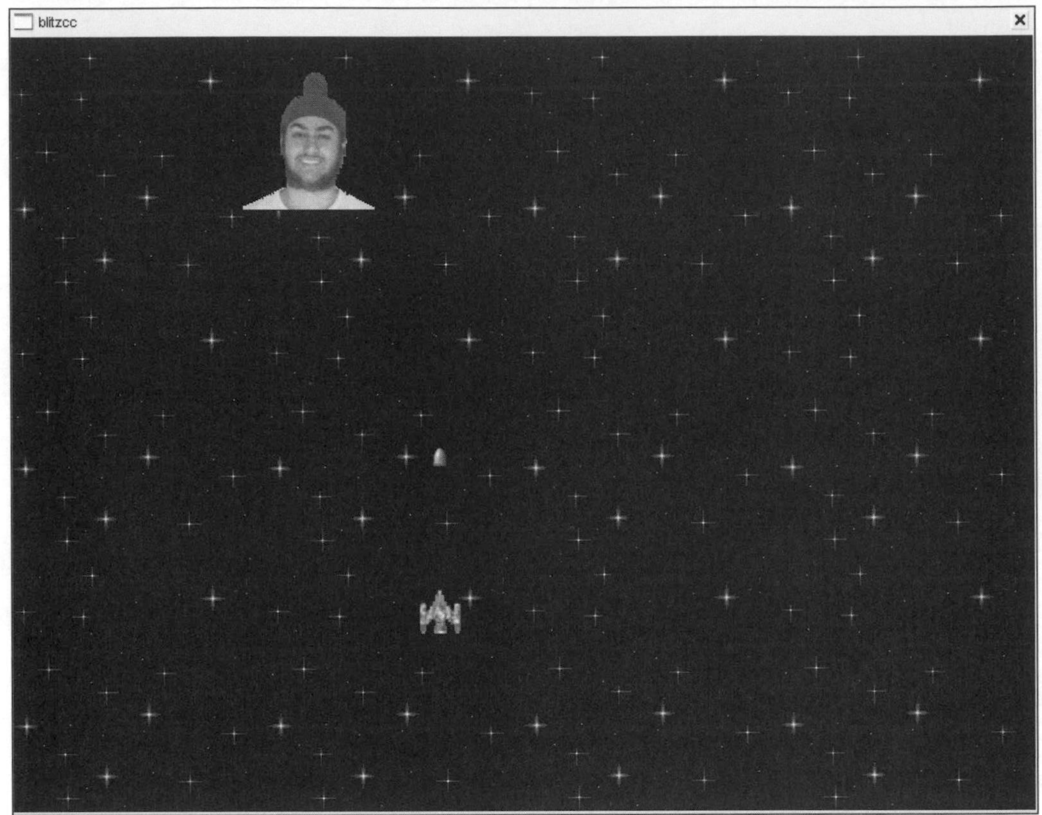

Figure 11.2 The demo11-01.bb program.

Okay, so we now know how to play a sound. We're not done yet, folks! BlitzPlus provides some really cool tools that make sounds a lot more fun to use.

BlitzPlus gives us three functions: `SoundPitch`, `SoundVolume`, and `SoundPan`. These three functions can be used in conjunction with each of your sound files to produce some absolutely sweet effects. Let's go over each of them in order, beginning with `SoundPitch`.

SoundPitch: Am I a Devil or a Chipmunk?

What is pitch? In essence, the pitch of a sound determines how high or low the frequency of the sound is. Take the guy at your school who has been held back six or seven years. He probably has a very deep voice. This guy's voice has a very low pitch. Now take that other kid who seems like he is still six years old. That kid has the voice of a chipmunk! His voice has a very high pitch.

Pitch is measured on a scale called hertz. The scale of hertz goes from 0 to infinity, but for humans, 44,000Hz is about the absolute max you could ever hear. (Actually, 22,000Hz is the max, but in computers, we have to use two times the max to be able to sample the sound properly.) That's a large scale, huh? The lower the number, the deeper the sound. Usually, the sound is slower as the pitch becomes lower, and the sound is faster as the pitch increases.

How might you use this in a program? Well, using hertz values in BlitzPlus is a lot different than using hertz values in real life. The values that I give are attributed to sounds in BlitzPlus, and not to sounds in reality.

Think of someone with a really deep, gruff voice. They would have an average hertz value of around 8,000Hz. Now take the should-be-in-third-grade-how-is-he-in-my-class boy with the high-pitched voice. He probably has an average pitch of 44,000Hz.

When you load a sound into your programs, you don't know what the hertz value is. To change the hertz value to a value of your choice, you use the `SoundPitch` function. `SoundPitch` is declared like this:

```
SoundPitch sound_variable, hertz
```

Table 11.5 details all of the parameters of `SoundPitch`.

Table 11.5 SoundPitch's Parameters

Parameter	Description
`sound_variable`	The handle to the sound file you want to change.
`hertz`	The hertz value you want to change `sound_variable` to (between 0 and 44000).

Anyway, let's write a program. This program allows you to create an explosion. If you press the spacebar, the explosion sound is played, and by pressing up or down, you change the hertz value by 1,000. We will also set the hertz of the variable to 22,000 to begin with (so we have a starting point for the tests).

Following is the source from demo11-02.bb.

```
;demo11-02.bb - Demonstrates SoundPitch

Graphics 800,600

;Make sure backbuffer is drawn on and automidhandle is true
SetBuffer BackBuffer()
AutoMidHandle True
```

```
;IMAGES
;load the player's ship image
playerimage = LoadImage ("spaceship.bmp")



;SOUNDS
;Load the bullet sound
explosionsound = LoadSound ("explode.wav")

;CONSTANTS
;The following constants are used for key codes
Const ESCKEY = 1,SPACEBAR = 57, UPKEY = 200, DOWNKEY = 208

;create hertz variable
hertz = 22000

;Make sure bullet has hertz value of hertz variable to begin with
SoundPitch explosionsound, hertz




;MAIN LOOP
While Not KeyDown(1)
;Clear the screen
Cls

;Make sure text is drawn in top left hand corner
Locate 0,0
Print "Current Hertz Value: " + hertz

;Play explosion sound if player hits spacebar
If KeyHit(SPACEBAR)
        PlaySound explosionsound
EndIf

;If up is hit, increment hertz variable
If KeyHit (UPKEY)
        hertz = hertz + 1000
EndIf

;If down is hit, decrement hertz variable
If KeyHit(DOWNKEY)
```

```
        hertz = hertz - 1000
EndIf

;Make the explosion have the same pitch as the hertz variable
SoundPitch explosionsound, hertz

;Draw the player
DrawImage playerimage, MouseX(), MouseY()

Flip
Wend
;END OF MAIN LOOP
```

Cool, huh? The program lets the player change the hertz by pressing up or down, and it also synchronizes the explosion sound with the hertz value by using the `SoundPitch` function.

```
SoundPitch explosionsound, hertz
```

Figure 11.3 is a screenshot from demo11-02.bb.

Figure 11.3 The demo11-02.bb program.

All right, that's it for pitch. Let's learn how to use SoundVolume now.

SoundVolume

I bet you can guess what SoundVolume does. Simply put, changing the volume of a sound adjusts how loud or quiet the sound is.

SoundVolume is used a lot like SoundPitch. Here is the declaration:

```
SoundVolume sound_variable, volume#
```

sound_variable is the handle to the sound that you want to change the volume of. Volume# is a floating-point variable between 0 and 1.000. The closer to 1 volume# is, the louder the sound is. Table 11.6 summarizes the parameters.

Table 11.6 SoundVolume's Parameters

Parameter	Description
sound_variable	The handle to the sound file you want to work with.
volume#	The volume you want to set sound_variable to. Can be between 0 and 1.000.

Cool? Let's make a program. Demo11-03.bb draws a randomly moving spaceship, and plays a laser sound every time you press the spacebar. The farther away the enemy ship is from your ship, the quieter the sound. If the ship is really close, the sound is played loudly.

This program is a long one, so I am just going to show two parts of it. The first is ripped from the user-defined function FindCurrentVolume().

```
;Function FindCorrectVolume - Sets volume# to the correct value
;depending on distance from player to enemy
Function FindCorrectVolume()

;Find distance between player and enemy
dist = Distance(player\x,player\y,enemy\x,enemy\y)

;Assign the volume number to volume# depending on how far the
;distance is. The farther the distance, the quieter the sound
If dist < 100
	volume# = 1.000
ElseIf dist < 200
	volume# = .700
ElseIf dist < 300
	volume# = .400
```

```
ElseIf dist < 400
        volume# = .1000
Else
        volume# = 0.000
EndIf
```

The first thing this function does is find the distance between the enemy and the player using the `Distance()` function we wrote in Chapter 9, "Collision Detection." (I copied the source from the `Distance()` function into this program.) It then assigns `volume#` to a number depending on how high `dist` is. If `dist` is higher, the spaceship is farther away; therefore, the sound should be quieter. The block of `If...ElseIf...Else` statements determines how loud the volume should be.

The next and last part of demo11-03.bb actually uses the `SoundVolume` function.

```
;Create a new bullet if spacebar is hit
If KeyHit(SPACEBAR)

        ;Find what volume# should be
        FindCorrectVolume()

        ;Assign bulletsound to volume#
        SoundVolume bulletsound, volume#

        ;Play the bullet
        PlaySound bulletsound
EndIf
```

This code is executed when you press the spacebar. It calls `FindCorrectVolume()`, which assigns `volume#` to its correct value. The code then adjusts the volume of `bulletsound` depending on the `volume#` variable. The block finally plays the sound clip of the bullet.

Figure 11.4 is a screenshot taken from demo11-03.bb.

All right, that's it for `SoundVolume`. We only have one more function to learn about before we move on to playing music!

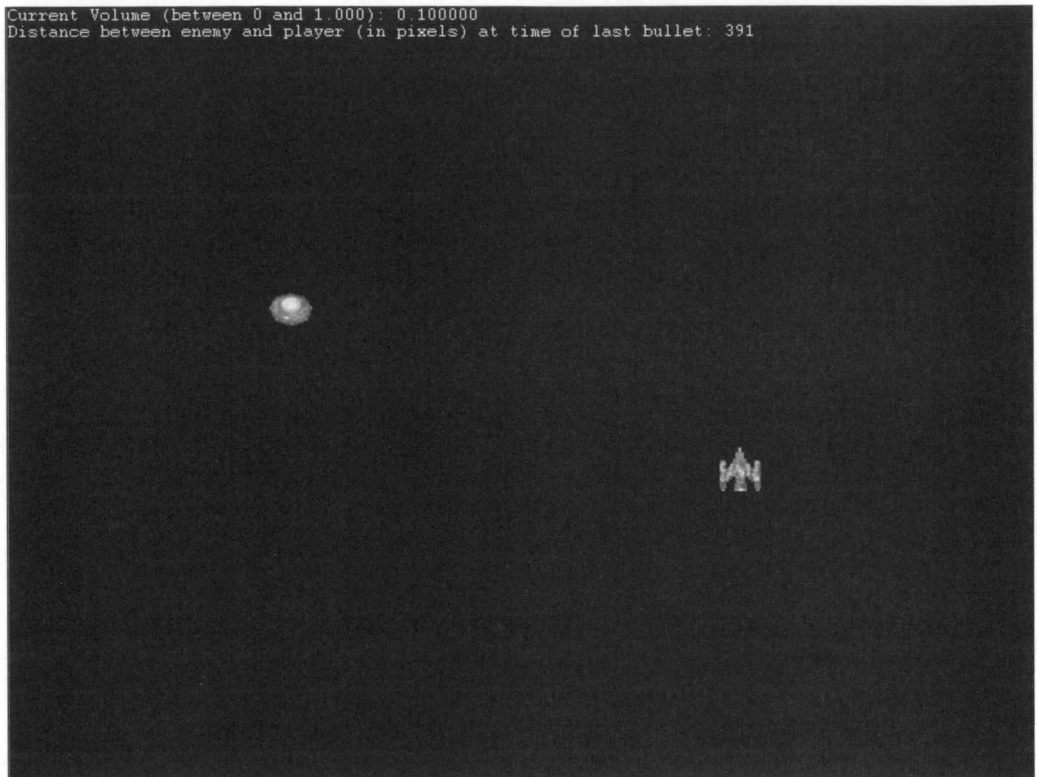

Figure 11.4 The demo11-03.bb program.

SoundPan

Good things always come in threes, huh? There are three major video game consoles, three months of summer, and three Pepsis on my desk that keep me up late. Well, there are also three sound-editing functions. We have already discussed two of them (`SoundPitch()` and `SoundVolume()`). `SoundPan` is the third and last one.

`SoundPan` offers a very cool effect: it allows you to create the illusion of moving sound by letting you pick which speaker the sound plays out of. You can have the program play sound out of the left speaker, the right speaker, or both. This allows you to make the players feel like the sounds are actually moving around them.

`SoundPan` is declared like this:

```
SoundPan sound_variable, pan#
```

Now this is the cool part: because `pan#` is a floating-point variable, you can have the sound panned a little to the left but still playing slightly on the right. What do I mean? Well, if you set `pan#` to −0.75, the sound would play 75% out of the left speaker and 25% out of the right speaker.

Sound_variable, as you probably know, is the handle to the sound you want to edit. Pan# contains the amount you want to pan the sound. Pan# can be between −1.000 and 1.000—if the number is negative, it will play predominantly out of the left speaker, and if it is positive, it will play mostly out of the right speaker.

Table 11.7 summarizes all of SoundPan's parameters.

Table 11.7 SoundPan's Parameters

Parameter	Description
sound_variable	The handle to the sound you want to pan.
pan#	The amount between −1.000 and 1.000 you want to pan the sound.

Cool? Let's write a program. This thing is going to be easy: an enemy ship moves left and right. When the player presses the spacebar, the sound is played. If the enemy is to the left of the player, the sound is played completely out of the left speaker. If the enemy is to the right of the player, the sound is played out of the right speaker. If the enemy is directly in front of the player, the sound is played out of both speakers. The following is the main loop that is taken from demo11-04.bb.

```
;MAIN LOOP
While Not KeyDown(ESCKEY)

;Tile the background
TileBlock backgroundimage, 0, scrolly
;increment the scrolling variable
scrolly = scrolly + 1

If scrolly > ImageHeight(backgroundimage)
        scrolly = 0
EndIf

;Print all text at top-left corner
Locate 0,0
Print "Panning variable: " + pan#

;set up player coordinates
player\x = MouseX()
player\y = MouseY()

;if enemy is to the left of player, make sound come out of left speaker
```

```
If enemy\x < player\x
       pan# = -1.000
       ;If enemy is to right of player, make sound come out of right speaker
ElseIf enemy\x > player\x
       pan# = 1.000
       ;If enemy is in front of player
Else
       pan# = 0
EndIf

;Pan the sound
SoundPan bulletsound, pan#



;If player presses spacebar, play the sound
If KeyHit (SPACEBAR)



       PlaySound bulletsound
EndIf

;Move the enemy according to his velocity
enemy\x = enemy\x + enemy\xv

;If the enemy goes offscreen, reflect his velocity
If enemy\x < 0 Or enemy\x > 800
       enemy\xv = - enemy\xv
EndIf

;Draw the player and the enemy
DrawImage player\image,player\x,player\y
DrawImage enemy\image,enemy\x,enemy\y

Flip

Wend
```

Not that bad, eh? The main part is finding what the `pan#` variable should be. `Pan#` is used as a parameter for `SoundPan`, and it determines how far to the left or right the sound should pan. To find what `pan#` should be, we use the following code block.

```
;if enemy is to the left of player, make sound come out of left speaker
If enemy\x < player\x
       pan# = -1.000
```

```
        ;If enemy is to right of player, make sound come out of right speaker
ElseIf enemy\x > player\x
        pan# = 1.000
        ;If enemy is in front of player
Else
        pan# = 0
EndIf
```

This code sets `pan#` to -1 (left speaker) if the enemy is to the left of the player, 1 if the player is to the right, and 0 if he is directly in front of the player. The last part of the main loop I want to show you actually uses the `SoundPan` function.

```
;Pan the sound
SoundPan bulletsound, pan#
```

Pretty cool, huh? This function synchronizes the bullet sound with the `pan#` variable.

Figure 11.5 is a screenshot taken from the program. By the way, this program does not work on everyone's speakers, so if it doesn't seem to pan out correctly, it might just be your speaker hardware.

Whew! That's it for sounds! Now we get to move on to using music in our games.

Figure 11.5 The demo11-04.bb program.

Music

You've gotten this far, but you might not quite understand the difference between music and sound, at least on a computer. Here's the thing, you have used sound so far to produce gunfire and explosion sounds. You can see that these sounds are played only at the time of the actual explosion or at the time when the bullet is actually fired. Music, however, is played in the background while your game is running. Therefore, it is much easier to use, because you can rig it up to play at the beginning of the game, and not worry about the music from then on.

For the music examples in this book, I use the .MP3 format. BlitzPlus also allows you to use the .WAV, .OGG, the .XMS, and the .MID formats for your games, but I won't be covering them to keep things simple. These are all special formats that are like the .WAV format, but have small differences that won't be explained. There's a lot of information out there if you want to learn about the other formats. Special thanks to Thomas Stenbäck and every one else at Interim Nation for letting me use their music on the CD. You can visit Interim Nation, the composers for the music on the CD, at http://www.interimnation.cin.

To begin understanding music in BlitzPlus, we first need to discuss *channels.*

Channels and PlayMusic()

What is a channel? Well, imagine you have a sibling who is talking to you. At that point, the only thing you can hear is your sibling. Now, imagine that a phone located near you begins to ring. Suddenly, you can hear two things at once, right? Well, at this moment, there are two channels playing: the sibling channel and the telephone-ringing channel.

Now, the cool thing about channels is that you can edit each channel independently. What does this mean? Well, for instance, say your sibling, who is currently on the sibling channel, begins to whisper to you. The volume of this voice has decreased. Using channels, you can change the volume of one channel while leaving another the same. If you take a look at Figure 11.6, you can see an example of how channels might work. There are two boxes, both emitting sounds. One is on the right and one is on the left; thus, using the magic of channels, the one on the left is panned far to the left and the one on the right is panned to the right.

All we need now is to learn how to get control of a channel. Unlike handles, which you retrieve by loading sounds, you must *play* a sound in order get access to a channel.

The most common way to get a channel is to use the function `PlayMusic()`. This function is declared as follows:

```
PlayMusic(filename$)
```

When playing music, you don't need to load the sound first. You just call `PlayMusic()` with the proper file name, and your sound is good to go!

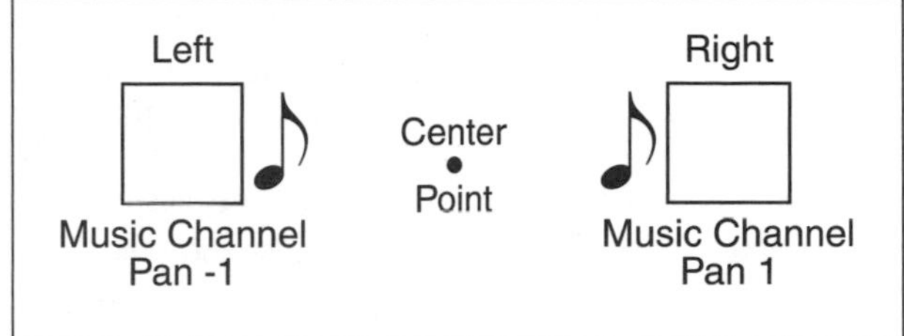

Figure 11.6 Channels and panning.

Say you wanted to load a techno song named technosong.mp3. This is what you would do:

```
technosong = PlayMusic("technosong.mp3")
```

As you can see, the function uses the `PlayMusic()` function and assigns the song to a channel variable. This variable can be used later for sound editing.

Notice that this line of code actually plays the music. That means that at the time of using this line of code, technosong.mp3 will begin to play. If you want to load the sound before using the sound file in the program, use the `LoadSound()/PlaySound()` functions. By the way, `PlaySound()` also returns a channel variable, which you can use just as you can with channel variables from music files.

Okay, now that we know how to load a music file, let's find out what we can do with those channels. By the way, Table 11.8 lists `PlayMusic()`'s parameter.

Table 11.8 PlayMusic()'s Parameter

Parameter	Description
`filename$`	The full path and file name of the file you want to play.

Messing With 'Da Channels

The last section taught you how to play music files and load channels, and this section teaches you how to use them. Following is a list of all the functions and their declarations that can be used with channels.

- `StopChannel channel_handle`
- `PauseChannel channel_handle`
- `ResumeChannel channel_handle`
- `ChannelVolume channel_handle, volume#`
- `ChannelPan channel_handle, pan#`
- `ChannelPitch channel_handle, hertz`

That's quite a few, but they are very easy to understand. Most of them don't even require parameters beyond the obligatory channel variable, and those that do aren't tough. Anyway, let me help you understand what these functions do.

The first half of the list (`Stop`, `Pause`, and `ResumeChannel`) can be separated into one group, and the second half (`ChannelVolume`, `Pan`, and `Pitch`) can be separated into another group. All of the functions within each group are related. The first group's functions work much like the Stop, Pause, and Resume buttons on a CD player. The `StopChannel` function stops a song immediately. The song is shut down and can only be restarted from the beginning. `PauseChannel` and `ResumeChannel`, however, allow you to pause and begin playing a music file anywhere within the song. `PauseChannel` pauses the song and `ResumeChannel` picks up the song from the same point that was left off.

You can use these functions in numerous situations. Say you have a game with a monster alien at the end. The music plays in the background, and when you get to the monster, you want the music to stop playing while the monster says or does something. What you do is call `PauseChannel` right when the monster appears onscreen, and after he finishes his speech or video or whatever, you call `ResumeChannel` to begin the music right from the starting point.

Anyway, Table 11.9 explains the parameters in the `StopChannel`, `PauseChannel`, and `ResumeChannel` functions.

Table 11.9 Stop/Pause/Resume Channel's Parameters

Parameter	Description
`channel_handle`	The channel you want to stop/pause/resume.

All right, cool. Next up is the second group, which consists of the functions `ChannelVolume`, `ChannelPan`, and `ChannelPitch`.

Do you remember the `SoundVolume`, `SoundPan`, and the `SoundPitch` functions? Well these work in the same way. `ChannelVolume` adjusts the volume of the music playing from the given channel. The `volume#` variable can be anywhere between 0 and 1.000, with 0 being the softest and 1.000 the loudest.

`ChannelPan` allows you to adjust the direction the sound is coming from. The value of the sound can be anywhere from −1.00 to 1.00. −1.00 is from the far left and 1.00 is on the far right, and of course, 0.00 is directly in the center.

The last function that can be used with music is `ChannelPitch`. `ChannelPitch` uses a hertz value between 0 and 44,000, with 44,000 being the highest-pitched sound and 0 being the lowest-pitched sound. (Actually 0 means no sound!)

The cool thing about these functions is that every change you make to them happens in real-time—you do not have to replay the music files every time you want to hear the changes. For example, if you had a program with music playing from the right and music playing from the left, and the player turns his character around 180 degrees, all you have to do is call `ChannelPan` and you're done, rather than playing the sound again.

Table 11.10 lists the parameters for `ChannelVolume`, `ChannelPan`, and `ChannelPitch`.

Table 11.10 ChannelVolume/Pan/Pitch's Parameters

Parameter	Description
`channel_handle`	The channel that contains the sound you want to edit.
`volume#`	The volume (between 0 and 1.00) you want to assign to the channel.
`pan#`	The panning value (between −1.00 and 1.00) you want to assign to the channel.
`hertz`	The hertz value (between 0 and 44,000) you want to assign to the channel.

Okay, I included a program, demo11-05.bb, that allows you to play with a music file. You can change its volume, pan it, and change its pitch. You can also pause, stop, and resume the song. Table 11.11 details all of the keys for demo11-05.bb.

Table 11.11 Demo11-05.bb's Keys

Key	Action
Up Arrow	Increases pitch by 100 hertz
Down Arrow	Decreases pitch by 100 hertz
Left Arrow	Pans music to left by −.1
Right Arrow	Pans music to right by .1
'A' key	Increases volume by .1
'Z' key	Decreases volume by .1
'P' key	Pauses sound
'R' key	Resumes sound
'S' key	Stops sound

The source for demo11-05.bb is very long, so it's not included in the book. Feel free to check it out on the CD. By the way, listen to the song included in the demo—it's very cool.

Figure 11.7 is a screenshot from demo11-05.bb.

There are a few more channels that you might want to know a bit more about. The first function, `ChannelPlaying()`, tests to see whether a channel is currently playing. If the music file is playing, `ChannelPlaying()` will return 1; if it is not playing, `ChannelPlaying() returns 0`.

You would use this function when you want your background music to play more than once, back to back. This is called *looping*, which is the action of playing the same music file over and over without a break in the middle. How would you do it? Maybe like this:

Figure 11.7 The demo11-05.bb program.

```
coolsong = PlayMusic("song.mp3")
;MAIN LOOP
While Not KeyDown(1)
If Not ChannelPlaying(coolsong)
       coolsong = PlayMusic ("song.mp3")
Endif
```

Sound files are easier to loop. BlitzPlus provides a function, `LoopSound`, which you can use to play a sound file over and over again. `LoopSound` is declared like this:

```
LoopSound sound_variable
```

All you do is pass the handle to the sound file to this function. After you do that, call `PlaySound` with the handle of the sound, and the file will play over and over.

Summary

BlitzPlus really makes it easy to use sound and music within games, and sound and music really make a difference in a game. They provide a nice tone and setting for the game. Using background music, you can give the player the feeling of a frenetic action mission or a slow searching mission.

To review, the main topics that we covered are:

- Loading sounds
- Playing sounds
- Using PlayMusic() and channels
- Editing channels

By the way, there are a lot of sounds and music files on the CD. Thomas Stenbäck provided all the music files, and they sound great.

In the next chapter, we are going to cover artificial intelligence. You will learn how to make computers think and act—well sorta!

Artificial Intelligence

As we near the end of this book, we get more to the heart of computer game programming. Unlike any other program that you will find on computers, games need to be able to actually make the computer think! Well, maybe not think, but at least appear as if it were thinking :). In games that have enemies that are not human-controlled, the computer has to take over and play against the player. This chapter provides you with the tools to make any enemy appear to act as a human would.

The art of artificial intelligence can be extremely complicated and tough to follow; therefore, this chapter is a very quick primer to some easier parts of artificial intelligence. There are many more interesting topics above and beyond what I'll teach you, and if you want to learn about some of them, I suggest you seek out other books on the topic.

I'm sure you're itchin' to get started, so I'm going to conclude the introduction right now. I mean, now. Seriously, the intro is over. I'm not joking.

Random Numbers

The first part of artificial intelligence we're going to learn is how to use random variables in programs. Using random variables in programs isn't really intelligent, but it's a first step, right?

Random Variables: Really Random?

Here is an interesting bit of information about random numbers in computers: finding a true random number is almost impossible. Computers only take input, process it, and produce output—they are not built to produce random numbers, for the most part. Therefore, computers can only produce pseudo-random numbers. What is a pseudo-random number? It is a number that, even though it might appear to be random, isn't truly random. For example, if you print out ten million random numbers, you shouldn't be able to detect any patterns, and there should be an equal distribution between the numbers. However, if you try this on a computer, you will see patterns and you will see slight unevenness in the numbers. For the purposes here, though, the pseudo-random numbers are close enough to random!

In order to generate random numbers, we need to call two functions. The first one we call is named `SeedRnd`.

SeedRnd is declared like this:

```
SeedRnd seed
```

What is a seed? Well, `SeedRnd` works like this: it feeds the computer a number that will be used later to create pseudo-random numbers. We need to make `seed` equal to a number that changes every time the game is played; otherwise, the "random" numbers will always be the same every time the game is played.

The function `MilliSecs()` is a function that changes every time the program runs. This function returns the number of milliseconds in the system timer (since the computer last started up). Because the time on the system timer changes continuously, `MilliSecs()` is a good choice for a value to feed `SeedRnd`.

At the beginning of a program that uses random variables, we call `SeedRnd` as follows:

```
SeedRnd MilliSecs()
```

Pretty cool, huh? After doing that, we can continue to use random numbers. Note that `SeedRnd` doesn't actually perform any noticeable functions in a program; it simply sets up the program to use random variables later in the program.

Now that we have set up the random generator (by calling `SeedRnd`), we are able to actually find those random numbers. There are two functions that are provided by Blitz Basic. These functions are `Rnd` and `Rand`.

Both of these functions have similar declarations.

```
Rand ([start], end)
Rnd (start#, end#)
```

As you can see, they are almost the same. First of all, let me help you understand what those parameters are.

The parameter names for both `Rand()` and `Rnd()` are the same. The `start|start#` parameter is the smallest possible value for the random number, and `end|end#` is the largest possible value for the random number. That was probably a little hard to comprehend, so let me explain it better. When using one of the random functions, you will usually feed it two parameters. For example, you might do something like this:

```
randomvalue = Rand (100,200)
```

Because you handed `Rand()` the parameters 100 and 200, `randomvalue` will now contain a number between 100 and 200. You can change the parameters slightly to see what I mean. If you changed the 100 to 50 in the previous call, `randomvalue` would contain a number between 50 and 100.

Also, one other thing. You might have noticed that the `[start]` parameter in `Rand()` is optional (as signified by the brackets). Because it is optional, you are only required to provide `Rand` with one parameter. If you neglect to include `[start]`, Blitz Basic will assume that you want the `[start]` parameter to equal to 1. Therefore, calling `Rand()` as follows

```
Rand (205)
```

returns a random number between 1 and 205.

Both `Rand()` and `Rnd()` have the same parameters, except `Rand()`'s are integers and `Rnd()`'s are floating points. Remember, an integer is a number without a decimal point (for example, 314), whereas a floating-point variable has a decimal attached (for example, 314.13, where ".13" is the decimal).

The fact that `Rnd()` allows you to provide it with floating-point parameters means that you can make your random variables contain numbers with decimal points. If you call `Rnd()` like this:

```
Rnd (1.000,14.000)
```

the function will return a number between 1.000 and 14.000. It could end up being a number such as 3.133 or something like that.

If you decided to call `Rand()` in the same way, the number would end up being only an integer, such as 4 or 9. Take a look at Figure 12.1 to see what happens when you call the `Rand()` function with floating parameters. As you can see, even if you provide `Rand()` with floating-point numbers as parameters, it will still return an integer. It does this by finding the random number and deleting the decimal point.

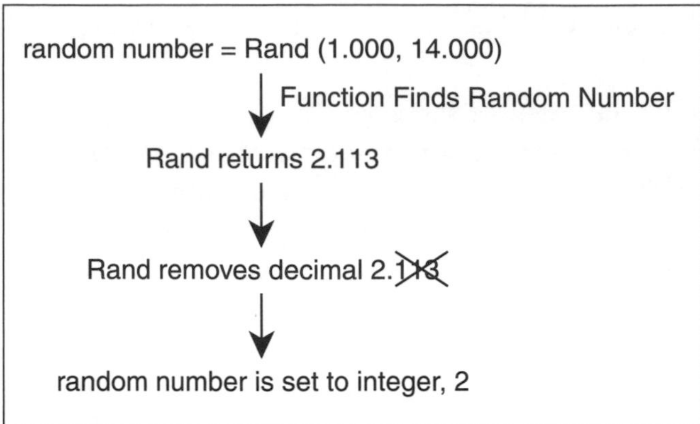

Figure 12.1 Using `Rand()` with floating-point parameters.

All right, excellent. Hopefully you understand how to determine random numbers. Now, let's put this into a program.

Following is the source to demo12-01.bb.

```
;demo12-01.bb - Demonstrates random variables
Graphics 800,600

;Set up automidhandle and backbuffer
AutoMidHandle True
SetBuffer BackBuffer()

;Make sure we seed the random generator
SeedRnd MilliSecs()

;Now we load the image that we will use.
flyimage = LoadAnimImage ("fly.bmp",64,64,0,4)
;create a starting frame value
frame = 0

;create the x and y values for the fly
flyx = 400
flyy = 300

;MAIN LOOP
While Not KeyDown (1)

;Clear the screen
Cls
```

```
Text 0,0,"Fly X: " + flyx
Text 0,20,"Fly Y: " + flyy

;move the fly a random amount
flyx = flyx + Rand(-15,15)
flyy = flyy + Rand(-15,15)

;Draw the fly onscreen
DrawImage flyimage,flyx,flyy,frame

;increment the frame
frame = frame + 1

;If frame gets too large or small, reset it
If frame > 3
        frame = 0
ElseIf frame < 0
        frame = 3
EndIf

;Flip the buffers
Flip

;Wait a little bit
Delay 25

Wend   ;END OF MAIN LOOP
```

Figure 12.2 is a screenshot taken from demo12-01.bb.

All right, the program is nice and all, but it's not smooth, is it? The fly is extremely jerky and looks terrible when drawn on the screen. The reason for this is that the fly's x and y variables are updated every single frame, which means his position changes drastically more than 30 times a second (because usually about 30 frames per second occur during games such as these).

Let's redo this program, but instead of changing the fly's coordinates 30 times every second, we will do it only once every few seconds. How are we going to do this? Well, first of all, we need to learn the art of making a timer using the `MilliSecs()` function.

Figure 12.2 The demo12-01.bb program.

Creating a MilliSecs() Timer

You have probably noticed the frequent use of `MilliSecs()`—we use it to seed our random generator with the `SeedRnd` command. If you remember, the reason we use milliseconds to seed the random generator is because `MilliSecs()` is never the same twice. So, if it is never the same twice, how can we use this to create a timer?

`MilliSecs()`'s value increases every millisecond that the computer is running. For example, if `MilliSecs()` is equal to 100123 right now, in exactly one millisecond, it will be equal to 100124. A millisecond is equal to one one-thousandth of a second (in other words, there are 1000 milliseconds in a second), so 101123 occurs exactly one second later than 100123. Now, we need to use `MilliSecs()` to create a timer. Even though `MilliSecs()` will never be called at the exact same time, this isn't a big problem. What we are going to do is create a variable that holds `MilliSecs()` at the starting time. We then check `MilliSecs()` every frame until its value is equal to or greater than the starting variable we created at the beginning plus the amount of time we want the timer to last.

So, let's put a timer into code. The following snippet shows how a three-second timer would work.

```
;Create timerbegin which holds the value of the starting timer
timerbegin = MilliSecs()

;We would begin the main loop here

;test if the current number of MilliSecs() is equal to the timerbegin + 3 secs
If MilliSecs() >= timerbegin + 3000
	;Do Something
EndIf
```

caution

If you happened to cut and paste this code into a program, it would not work correctly. The timer would never run out! The reason is that the timer would reset every frame because of the `timerbegin = MilliSecs()` line, and the If `MilliSecs() >= timerbegin + 3000` would never stray more than a few milliseconds from `timerbegin`. In order for the program to work, we need to separate the initialization of the timer and the timer test. If you need to use the timer only once, you can just place the initialization at the beginning of the program and insert the test in the main loop.

Let's go through this line by line. First of all, we created the timer.

```
;Create timerbegin which holds the value of the starting timer
timerbegin = MilliSecs()
```

This creates a timer with a value equal to the amount of `MilliSecs()` at the time of the creation of the timer.

Next, we need to test the timer to determine whether it has been in existence long enough.

```
;test if the current number of MilliSecs() is equal to the timerbegin + 3 secs
If MilliSecs() >= timerbegin + 3000
```

How does this work? Well, the function tests the current value of `MilliSecs()` against `timerbegin` plus three seconds (3000 milliseconds). If you remember, `timerbegin` is equal to the value of `MilliSecs()` at the time of creation of the timer. Because `MilliSecs()` increases every millisecond that the computer is running, the test will return true three seconds after the timer was created.

Pretty sweet, if I do say so myself. The following is the full source to demo 12-02.bb.

```
;demo12-01.bb - Demonstrates random variables
Graphics 800,600

;Set up automidhandle and backbuffer
AutoMidHandle True
SetBuffer BackBuffer()
```

```
;Make sure we seed the random generator
SeedRnd MilliSecs()


;CONSTANT
;this constant regulates how long it takes before the fly changes directions
Const CHANGEDIRECTIONS = 1500    ;the fly changes every 1.5 seconds

;The fly type
Type fly
        Field x,y  ;the coordinate position
        Field xv,yv   ;the fly's velocity
        Field image  ;The fly's image
End Type


;let's create the fly
fly.fly = New fly

;Start the fly in the center of the screen
fly\x = 400
fly\y = 300

;Give the fly a random velocity
fly\xv = Rand(-15,15)
fly\yv = Rand(-15,15)

;Now we load the fly image
fly\image = LoadAnimImage ("fly.bmp",64,64,0,4)

;create a starting frame value
frame = 0

;Create starting timer
timerbegin = MilliSecs()

;Create a variable that says the timer does not need to be reset
timeractive = 1

;MAIN LOOP
While Not KeyDown (1)
```

```
;Clear the screen
Cls

Text 0,0,"Fly X: " + flyx
Text 0,20,"Fly Y: " + flyy
Text 0,40, "Current time remaining on timer: " + ( CHANGEDIRECTIONS - MilliSecs() +
timerbegin )

;If the counter has run through, update the fly's velocities
If MilliSecs() >= timerbegin + CHANGEDIRECTIONS

	;move the fly a random amount
	fly\xv = fly\xv + Rand(-10,10)
	fly\yv = fly\yv + Rand(-10,10)

	;make sure timer is reset
	timeractive = 0
EndIf



;If the timer is inactive, reset the timer
If timeractive = 0
	timerbegin = MilliSecs()
	timeractive = 1
EndIf



;Move the fly
fly\x = fly\x + fly\xv
fly\y = fly\y + fly\yv

;Test if fly hit any walls
If fly\x <= 0 Or fly\x > 800
	fly\xv = -fly\xv
EndIf

If fly\y <= 0 Or fly\y >= 600
	fly\yv = - fly\yv
EndIf
```

```
;Draw the fly onscreen
DrawImage fly\image,fly\x,fly\y,frame

;increment the frame
frame = frame + 1

;If frame gets too large or small, reset it
If frame > 3
	frame = 0
ElseIf frame < 0
	frame = 3
EndIf

;Flip the buffers
Flip

;Wait a little bit
Delay 75

Wend   ;END OF MAIN LOOP
```

I only made a few small changes from the demo12-01.bb program, which I will address now.

First of all, I created a constant that determines how long the pause is between the changes in speed and direction for the ship. This constant is named `CHANGEDIRECTIONS`.

The next part of the program that I changed was the fly itself. I created a type around the fly and set up its starting variables. Following is the code from the source that creates and initializes the fly.

```
;The fly type
Type fly
	Field x,y  ;the coordinate position
	Field xv,yv   ;the fly's velocity
	Field image  ;The fly's image
End Type


;let's create the fly
fly.fly = New fly

;Start the fly in the center of the screen
fly\x = 400
```

```
fly\y = 300

;Give the fly a random velocity
fly\xv = Rand(-15,15)
fly\yv = Rand(-15,15)

;Now we load the fly image
fly\image = LoadAnimImage ("fly.bmp",64,64,0,4)
```

As you can see, the `fly` type makes it a lot easier to identify all of the variables that pertain to the fly. We start the fly in the center of the map, give him random coordinates, and load his image in the previous section.

The next thing I changed was directly before the main loop. I added a section that creates the timer.

```
;Create starting timer
timerbegin = MilliSecs()

;Create a variable that says the timer does not need to be reset
timeractive = 1
```

You already know what `timerbegin` does, but you might be wondering what `timeractive` is there for. `Timeractive` is equal to 1 when the timer is working correctly, but when the timer completes, `timeractive` is set to 0. The timer then resets, and `timeractive` is set to 1 again.

Next we move on to the main loop. We go through the usual process of clearing the background and drawing out the pertinent info on the screen. In this program, the x and y coordinates, as well as the time remaining on the timer, are written on the screen.

The following `If…EndIf` statement does the grunt work for the timer.

```
;If the counter has run through, update the fly's velocities
If MilliSecs() >= timerbegin + CHANGEDIRECTIONS

        ;move the fly a random amount
        fly\xv = fly\xv + Rand(-5,5)
        fly\yv = fly\yv + Rand(-5,5)

        ;make sure timer is reset
        timeractive = 0
EndIf
```

This block begins with a test to determine if the timer has finished. It does this by testing the current value of `MilliSecs()` against the value of `MilliSecs()` when the timer began (`timerbegin`), plus the length of the counter (`CHANGEDIRECTIONS`). If the test returns true, the timer has run through. That means that the commands within the block are executed.

When the timer runs out, the fly gets new random x and y velocities, which move the fly in a different direction at a different speed. The `timeractive` variable is then set to 0, which means that the timer is unusable and needs to be reset. The code that resets the timer occurs directly after the previous code. It looks something like this:

```
;If the timer is inactive, reset the timer
If timeractive = 0
       timerbegin = MilliSecs()
       timeractive = 1
EndIf
```

This section of the code resets the starting point of the timer to the current value of `MilliSecs()`. Because the timer no longer needs to be reset (at least until the new timer has completed), `timeractive` is set to 1.

There are two other changes from the first program to the second program of this chapter. The first is the addition of code that determines whether the fly has hit any walls. The code looks like this.

```
;Test if fly hit any walls
If fly\x <= 0 Or fly\x > 800
       fly\xv = -fly\xv
EndIf

If fly\y <= 0 Or fly\y >= 600
       fly\yv = - fly\yv
EndIf
```

This code tests if the fly has moved offscreen, and if it has, it reverses the direction the fly is traveling.

The other change was the addition of velocity values in the program. In the first program, we only changed the x and y coordinates of the fly, and in this program we used x and y coordinates along with x and y velocities. Figure 12.3 shows what the new demo looks like.

All right, that's the end of the first part of this chapter. The next section introduces you to some of the easiest things you will ever learn: chasing and evading.

Figure 12.3 The demo12-02.bb program.

Chasing and Evading

Well, now that we know how to use random variables and timers, we now need to learn how to create artificial intelligence that actually works for a reason. Chasing and evading are very good ways to demonstrate this. Both are easy and interesting: chasing makes one object follow another and evading makes one object run away from another.

Without further ado, chasing!

Chasing

Chasing entails finding the coordinates of one object and moving another based on where the first one is located. That might be a complex explanation, so let's break it down.

Let's say you have a spaceship following another spaceship; in fact, we will be writing a program that does this in a few minutes. Well, the program starts with the two ships onscreen in such a manner that ship A is following ship B. When ship B is to the left of ship A, ship A begins to move left. When ship B is to the right of ship A, ship A moves right. The same thing happens when ship B is above or below ship A: when above, ship A moves up; when below, ship A moves down. Figure 12.4 demonstrates chasing.

So, because everything we do in this book uses spaceships, let's make a chasing game in Blitz Basic.

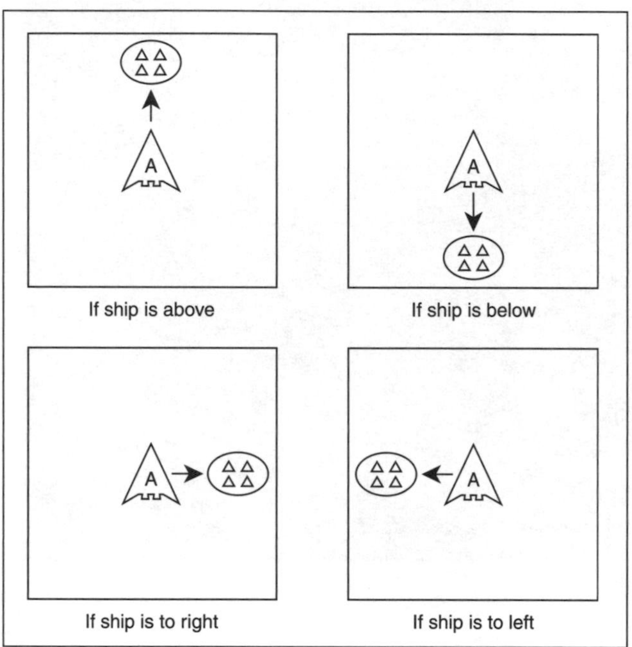

Figure 12.4 Following, chasing, tracking, or stalking? You be the judge.

```
;demo12-03.bb - Demonstrates chasing algorithms
Graphics 800,600

;Set up backbuffer and automidhandle
SetBuffer BackBuffer()
AutoMidHandle True

;IMAGES
;player and enemies ships
playership = LoadImage ("spaceship.bmp")
enemyship  = LoadImage ("enemyship.bmp")

;Load background
backgroundimage = LoadImage ("stars.bmp")
```

```
;CONSTANTS
;The following constants are used for testing key presses
Const ESCKEY = 1, UPKEY = 200, LEFTKEY = 203, RIGHTKEY = 205, DOWNKEY = 208

;the following constants define how fast the player and the enemy move
Const PLAYERSPEED = 10
Const ENEMYSPEED = 5

;position player on bottom center of screen
playerx = 400
playery = 400

;position enemy on upper center of screen
enemyx = 400
enemyy = 200

;set up scrolling variable
scrolly = 0

;MAIN LOOP
While Not KeyDown(ESCKEY)

;tile the background image
TileBlock backgroundimage, 0, scrolly

;move the background up a little
scrolly = scrolly + 1

;If scrolly gets too big, reset it
If scrolly > ImageHeight(backgroundimage)
	scrolly = 0
EndIf



;Test the keypresses of the player
;If the player hits up, we move him up
If KeyDown(UPKEY)
	playery = playery - PLAYERSPEED
EndIf
```

```
;If the player hits left, we move him left
If KeyDown(LEFTKEY)
	playerx = playerx - PLAYERSPEED
EndIf

;If player hits right, we move him right
If KeyDown(RIGHTKEY)
	playerx = playerx + PLAYERSPEED
EndIf

;If player hits down, we move him down
If KeyDown(DOWNKEY)
	playery = playery + PLAYERSPEED
EndIf



;Now, we move the enemy depending on where the player is
;If the player is above the enemy, move the enemy up
If playery > enemyy
	enemyy = enemyy + ENEMYSPEED
EndIf

;If the player is to the left of the enemy, move the enemy left
If playerx < enemyx
	enemyx = enemyx - ENEMYSPEED
EndIf

;If the player is to the right of the enemy, move the enemy right
If playerx > enemyx
	enemyx = enemyx + ENEMYSPEED
EndIf

;if the player is below the enemy, move the enemy down
If playery < enemyy
	enemyy = enemyy - ENEMYSPEED
EndIf

;draw the player and the enemy on the screen
DrawImage playership, playerx, playery
DrawImage enemyship, enemyx, enemyy
;delay for a bit
```

```
Delay 25

;Flip the front and back buffer
Flip

Wend
;END OF MAIN LOOP
```

As you can see, this program is a lot of fun to watch when it runs on the screen. No matter where you go, that tenacious spaceship won't go away! Check out Figure 12.5 for a screenshot from the program.

There is only one section of the program I want to discuss: the tracking section. The tracking code looks like this:

Figure 12.5 The demo12-03.bb program.

```
;Now, we move the enemy depending on where the player is
```

```
;If the player is above the enemy, move the enemy up
If playery > enemyy
       enemyy = enemyy + ENEMYSPEED
EndIf

;If the player is to the left of the enemy, move the enemy left
If playerx < enemyx
       enemyx = enemyx - ENEMYSPEED
EndIf

;If the player is to the right of the enemy, move the enemy right
If playerx > enemyx
       enemyx = enemyx + ENEMYSPEED
EndIf

;if the player is below the enemy, move the enemy down
If playery < enemyy
       enemyy = enemyy - ENEMYSPEED
EndIf
```

Let's start off with the first line, If `playery > enemyy`. What does this do? Well, this just checks the y coordinate of the player against the y coordinate of the enemy. Because the higher on the screen the object is, the lower the y coordinate is (remember that the top of the screen is y = 0), when `playery` is greater than `enemyy` (this is tested in the first `If…EndIf` statement), the player is below the enemy. Therefore, the enemy moves down a little bit.

The same thing happens in the following `If…EndIf` statements. When `playerx` is less than `enemyx`, the player is to the left of the enemy, and the enemy moves left. When `playerx` is more than `enemyx`, the player is to the right of the enemy, and the enemy moves right. Finally, when `playery < enemyy`, the enemy moves down.

Well, that's it for tracking. All that's left in this chapter is the extremely difficult concept of evasion.

Evading

A lot of times, when I tell a joke, my friends comment that they can't determine whether the statement I said was true or if I was simply kidding them. The final sentence of the last section would be an example of that. Just to let you know, evading isn't the "extremely" difficult concept I made it out to be. But you probably already knew that, right?

Either way, I'm sure you want to know all the ins and outs of evasion. Actually, you already do. Evasion is the opposite of chasing, because the enemy is running away from you. Check out Figure 12.6 to see how evasion works, with the player being the ship marked

"A." As you can see, the ship always moves away from the player.

Anyway, take a guess as to how you would use evasion. If you guessed that all you do is take the tracking algorithm and change the pluses to minuses and the minuses to pluses, you are right!

Demo12-04.bb shows evasion, and it is almost exactly the same as its predecessor, demo12-03.bb. In fact, I only made two changes. Here is the first one.

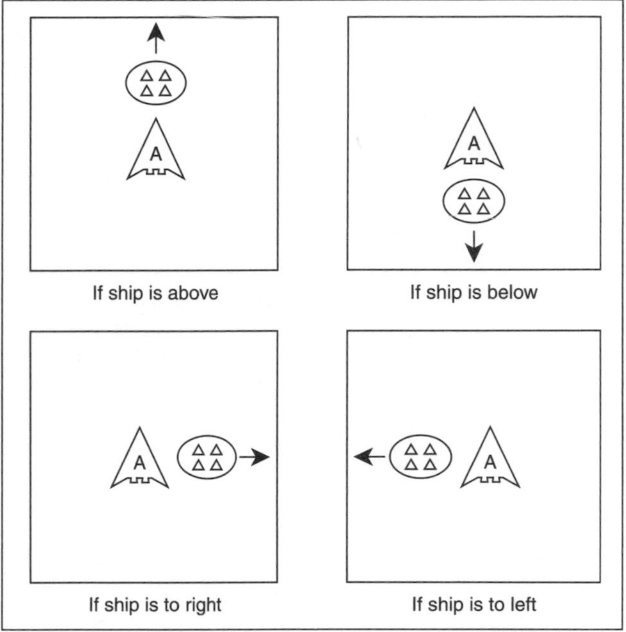

Figure 12.6 Evasion.

```
;Now, we move the enemy depending
on where the player is
;If the player is above the enemy, move the enemy down
If playery > enemyy
	enemyy = enemyy - ENEMYSPEED
EndIf

;If the player is to the left of the enemy, move the enemy right
If playerx < enemyx
	enemyx = enemyx + ENEMYSPEED
EndIf

;If the player is to the right of the enemy, move the enemy left
If playerx > enemyx
	enemyx = enemyx - ENEMYSPEED
EndIf
```

```
;if the player is below the enemy, move the enemy up
If playery < enemyy
       enemyy = enemyy + ENEMYSPEED
EndIf
```

Does this look familiar? As I said, it is exactly the same as demo12-03.bb, but the pluses and minuses have been flipped. Now, when the enemy is to the right of the player, it continues to move right. When the enemy is to the left, the player moves even farther left. When the player is above the enemy, the player moves up, and when the player is below the enemy, the player moves down.

I also added one new section to the program. This section makes sure that the enemy ship doesn't run offscreen, as you would expect it to because it is fleeing the player.

```
;if enemy goes offscreen, move him back onscreen
If enemyx <= 0
       enemyx = 0
ElseIf enemyx >= 800
       enemyx = 800
EndIf
If enemyy <= 0
       enemyy = 0
ElseIf enemyy >= 600
       enemyy = 600
EndIf
```

This code checks the enemy's coordinates to see if he is onscreen or offscreen. If he is offscreen, the code makes sure he cannot move any farther in that direction and keeps him onscreen.

Summary

Beautiful, ain't it? One more chapter and we will have created a real game.

In this chapter we lightly touched on the concepts of Artificial Intelligence. There are a lot (I mean A LOT) of other things that can be done with artificial intelligence, some of which are really interesting and exciting. Some programmers are coming up with ways to model the human genome (Genetic algorithms) and even the human brain (neural networks)!

Keep practicing artificial intelligence, and you will likely stumble upon some concepts of your own. Just keep in mind; it is impossible to actually make a computer think. Your job, as a programmer, is to make the computer appear to be thinking. If it seems to be doing the expected, that is all that is required.

In this chapter, we went over the following topics:

- Random variables
- Timers
- Chasing
- Evasion

Hopefully you will be able to put these topics to use in your upcoming games and programs! If you would like to learn more about artificial intelligence, check out *AI Techniques* by Mat Buckland (published by Premier Press, ISBN: 1-931841-08-X).

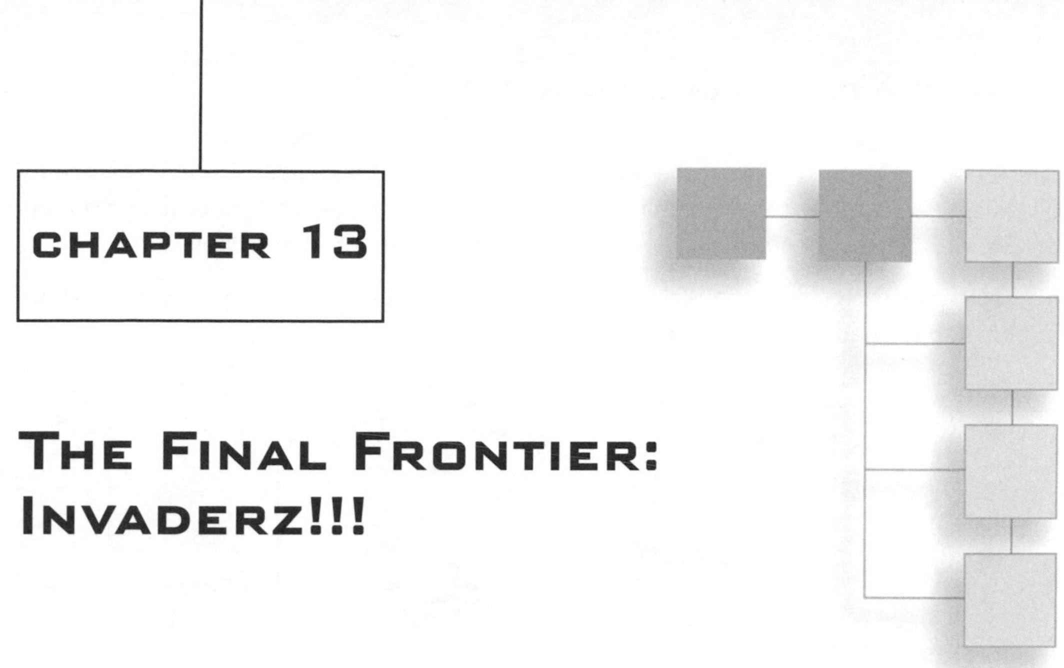

The Final Frontier: Invaderz!!!

Are you ready to finish this? Well guess what! It's the final game—the last demo!

When I wrote Invaderz!!!, I planned on copying and pasting the entire source into the book, and then I was going to explain all of the code to you step by step. Unfortunately, the code is 17 pages long. That's right, 17 pages! In other words, the full source is on the CD!

What we can do is go over the most important sections and algorithms of the code. I won't be explaining the easy sections, just the tough ones. The good thing though, is the code is heavily commented, and you can probably figure out most of what you want to just by reading through the source.

note

I'm going to make a recommendation right now. As you read this chapter, please, please, PLEASE keep a copy of the source code open! It's named invaderz.bb, and it's on the CD. It will be a heck of a lot easier to view the entire source from the file, and you will understand the major points a lot better.

Let's Bust It: Planning the Game

So, I knew I wanted to make a game for the final program in the book. What kind of game do you think I chose to make? You guessed it: a space shooter. I decided I wanted the game to be like *Space Invaders* (if you have ever played it before, you know what I am talking about). The point of the game is, as the player, to fire bullets at the enemy UFOs as they appear on the screen. The player is a human ship, and the enemy is alien ships. Now, I'll give you a little history on how I created it, and then we'll walk through the specifics together.

First of all, I planned out what the game would look like. I designed it so that the enemy UFOs appear from the top of the screen, and the player is on the bottom of the screen. As the enemies appear onscreen, the player shoots at the enemies, and they explode on contact.

My sketch for the game setup is shown in Figure 13.1. Well, actually my sketch was done in pencil, but I had it redrawn for this book.

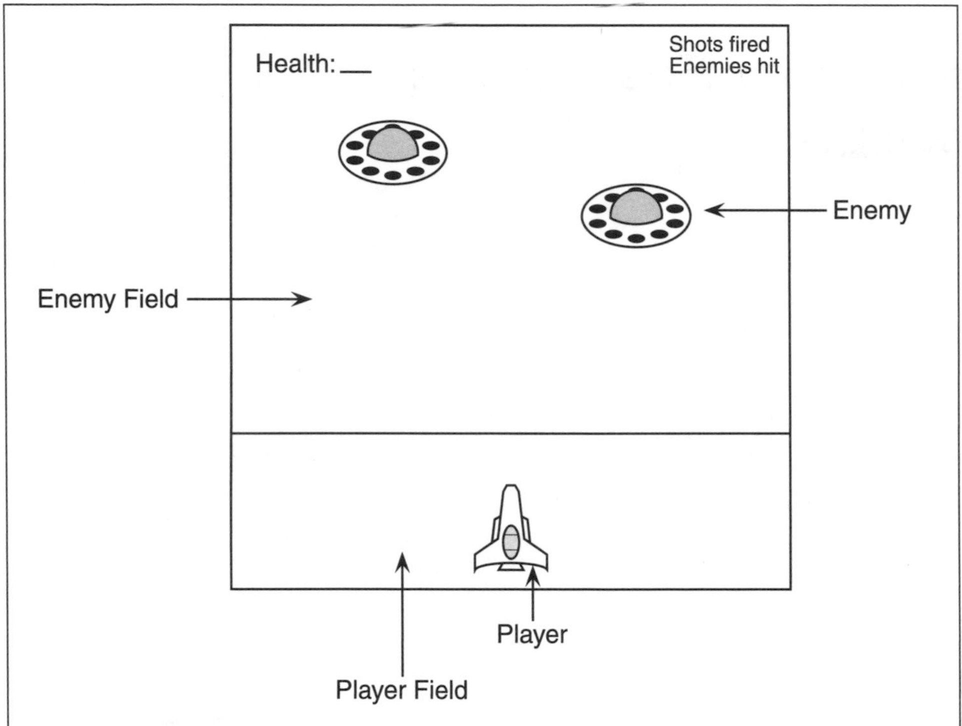

Figure 13.1 A sketch of the final game's playing field.

I then had a basis for how the game would look and feel. Notice that in the sketch, I created a HUD that displays the health and the shots fired/enemies hit totals. This allowed me to spend my time on the actual game, instead of thinking about how the HUD should look later when writing the game. Now that I had the game plan ready, I created the images I would be using for the game. The most important ones, of course, were the player and the enemy images. The enemy bitmap looks like Figure 13.2.

And the player looks like Figure 13.3.

These images are used in the game. As you can see, they are animated; however, they are animated in different ways.

The enemy bitmap has a rather straightforward animation style—it just loops from the first frame to the last frame. What I mean is that when the enemy ship moves around, it

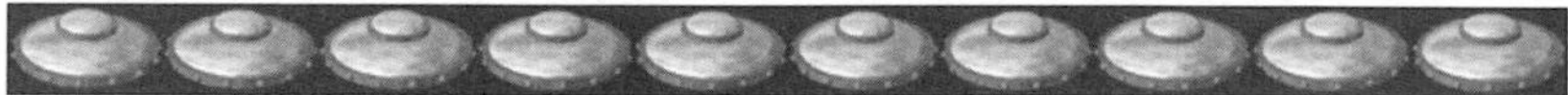

Figure 13.2 The enemy bitmap.

Figure 13.3 The player bitmap.

plays each frame in the bitmap consecutively. The first frame of the game loop is the first frame of the spaceship, the second frame of the game loop is the second frame of the spaceship, and so on, until you reach the final frame of the enemy spaceship (the 10th frame). The 11th frame of the game loop is then the first frame of the bitmap again, and so on.

The player bitmap reacts a little bit differently. We want the game to make the player tilt left when the spaceship is moving left and tilt right when the spaceship is moving right. It will remain flat when not moving at all.

We have to use some interesting code to get this to work. First of all, load the bitmap in, as you might expect, with the command `LoadAnimImage()`.

```
Global playerimage = LoadAnimImage("player.bmp",35,32,0,13)
```

This assumes that each frame of the player bitmap is 35×32 pixels (and so it is), and that there are 13 frames (and so there are). Well, as you can see, the first frame is not a flat position, but instead a view of the spaceship tilting left. We want the player spaceship to rest on the seventh frame, and have the frames increase (move toward tilting right) when the player presses right, and, conversely, have the frames decrease (move toward tilting left) when the player presses left. Set the frame to rest on frame 7 when no key is pressed, like this:

```
player\frame = 7
```

Then, when the player presses right, the code will do this:

```
;tilt player right
player\frame = player\frame + 1

;don't let frame get too high
If player\frame >= 12
	player\frame = 12
Endif
```

Can you see what is happening here? Note that this code occurs within the right key testing block, meaning this code is tested only when the right key is pressed. What is happening is that the frame is being incremented each frame, but only as long as the right key is pressed.

(The right-key testing code occurs around the previous code, and is not visible in the book.) The code limits how high `player\frame` can get, however, because there are only 13 frames in the player spaceship image.

Why does it check to see if the `frame` variable is greater than or equal to 12, instead of 13? Remember that frame counts begin at 0, therefore, the final frame is 13 − 1, or 12.

Okay, it's time to wrap up the planning section. There are a lot of other things you need to do, such as decide how to choose where the enemies come from, how many enemies are on each level, and the like. If you want to see how I did it, open up the invaderz.bb program from the CD. It contains the source, and the comments will help you understand what I was thinking when I wrote the game.

By the way, I chose the name Invaderz!!! for the name of my game. Why? It's a cool name. And you can tell it's important because there are not one, not two, but three exclamation points after the word!

Constants, Functions, and Types in Invaderz!!!

Let's take the time to go over each of the variables, constants, functions, and types used in Invaderz!!! First off, let's check out all of the constants.

There are only a few constants, but they are very important. Table 13.1 lists all of the constants and their descriptions.

Table 13.1 Constants in Invaderz!!!

Constant	Value	Description
ESCKEY	1	The key code for the Esc key.
SPACEBAR	57	The key code for the spacebar.
LEFTKEY	203	The key code for the left arrow.
RIGHTKEY	205	The key code for the right arrow.
CHANGEENEMYDIRECTION	700	The time (in milliseconds) between velocity changes for enemy UFOs.
TIMEBETWEENENEMYBULLETS	1200	The time (in milliseconds) between enemy bullet fire.

I am sure you understand how the first four key codes work (in case you need a refresher, they are used with `KeyDown()` and `KeyHit()`), but you might not know what `CHANGEENEMYDIRECTION` and `TIMEBETWEENENEMYBULLETS` do. Well, let's go over both of them.

In this program, the enemies' movement is random. We need to move those UFOs in a random direction at the beginning. We don't want it to appear random, however, so we need to adjust their direction variables every once in a while to make it appear that they are moving. CHANGEENEMYDIRECTION determines the time between those direction changes. Each UFO changes direction every 700 milliseconds (or every 7/10 of a second).

TIMEBETWEENENEMYBULLETS does the same sort of thing. This constant determines how long a break there is between the bullet shots by the enemy. Instead of 700 milliseconds like the CHANGEENEMYDIRECTION constant, this constant has the enemies fire bullets every 1,200 milliseconds (1 and 1/5 of a second, or every 1.2 seconds).

Cool? Let's examine the functions. There are a lot of them!

Table 13.2 lists each function in Invaderz!!!

Table 13.2 Functions in Invaderz!!!

Function	Description
InitializeLevel()	Resets the level with the proper amount of enemies and resets all the starting variables.
DrawHUD()	Draws the health points remaining and the bullets fired/hit displays in the top of the window.
CreateNewEnemy()	Creates a new enemy ship onscreen.
DrawShips()	Draws the enemy and player spaceships.
EnemyAI()	Updates the directions and bullet fires of the enemy spaceships.
CreateBullet()	Creates a new bullet onscreen.
UpdateBullets()	Moves bullets and checks to see if they collided against any opposing ships.
CreateExplosion()	Creates an explosion after a ship collision.
UpdateExplosions()	Rotates explosions through its frames and deletes the explosion when it is over.
GameOver()	Prepares the game for exit and quits to desktop.

Not all of these functions are called by the main loop, so I drew a function outline that explains how the functions interact with one another (see Figure 13.4).

That's all for functions. Last, we have the types used in Invaderz!!!

There are four types used in Invaderz!!! They are

- The ship type
- The user type
- The bullet type
- The explosion type

The ship type refers to all of the enemies that are created during the game, the user type is the player spaceship that is onscreen, the bullet type describes each bullet that is fired during the game (both enemy and player bullets), and the explosion type refers to explosions that occur after a ship dies for either enemy or player.

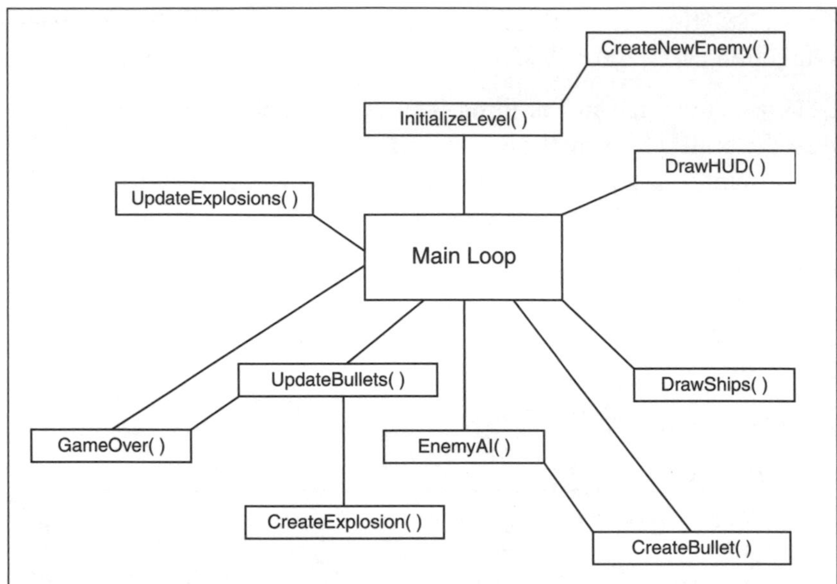

Figure 13.4 The function outline for Invaderz!!!

I am going to list tables with all of the types' fields, in order to give you a feel for the Invaderz!!! program.

Table 13.3 lists the `ship` type's fields.

Table 13.3 The Ship Type's Fields

Field	Description
`x`	The x coordinate of the ship.
`y`	The y coordinate of the ship.
`hits`	The hit points remaining on the ship.
`xv`	The x direction variable that governs how far left and right the ship moves per frame.
`yv`	The y direction variable that governs how far up and down the ship moves per frame.
`frame`	The frame of the animated image that will be drawn. (See Figure 13.2.)

Table 13.4 lists the `user` type's fields, which are used to make the player.

Table 13.4 The User Type's Fields

Field	Description
`x`	The x coordinate of the user.
`y`	The y coordinate of the user.
`hits`	The remaining hit points on the user.
`frame`	The frame of the animated image that will be drawn. (See Figure 13.3.)
`draw`	Determines whether the user should be drawn on the screen or not. The user should be drawn if set to 1 and should not be drawn if set to 0.

Notice, if you will, that the `ship` and `user` types are very similar to one another. This is because they are both spaceships, and although they are opposing forces, both of them have to move in the same way. Their similarities remind me of comic book heroes and super villains: the super villains are almost exactly the same as the hero, and in fact, they are often friends growing up.

Table 13.5 lists the `bullet` type's fields.

Table 13.5 The Bullet Type's Fields

Field	Description
`x`	The x coordinate of the bullet.
`y`	The y coordinate of the bullet.
`draw`	Determines whether the bullet should be drawn on the screen or not. The bullet should be drawn if set to 1 and should not be drawn if set to 0.
`from`	Determines who fired the bullet. This is set to 1 if it was fired by the user and set to 2 if it was fired by an enemy.
`c`	The frame of the animated image that will be drawn.

And last but not least, Table 13.6 lists the `explosion` type's fields.

Table 13.6 The Explosion Type's Fields

Field	Description
`x`	The x coordinate of the explosion.
`y`	The y coordinate of the explosion.
`from`	Determines who is exploding. This is set to 1 if the user exploded and set to 2 if the enemy exploded.
`from`	The frame of the animated image that will be drawn.

Woo hoo! Now, let's move on to actually playing the game.

Playing Invaderz!!!

We've gone through the motions of creating the game (or at least getting a feel for the game) and now we get to the fun part: playing the game!

Invaderz!!! is a very simple game to play. There are two ways to open it, but both require you to navigate to the Chapter 13 folder on the CD. Put the CD in your CD-ROM drive and find the Source folder, and then double-click Chapter 13. Once you have done this, you will see a bunch of files that relate to the Invaderz!!! game. To play the game directly, double-click the icon that looks like a rocket ship. This file is named invaderz.exe.

The other way to load Invaderz!!! is to run it from within the Blitz Basic compiler and compile the code straight away. Do this by finding the file named invaderz.bb and double-clicking it. It should load in the Blitz Basic compiler within a few seconds. Look near the top of the screen and you will find a toolbar with a number of menus starting with File. Select the menu named Program and click Run Program. Another way to do this is to press the F5 key on your keyboard (after you load the program in Blitz Basic).

note

If you want to run the game within the Blitz Basic compiler, you will need to have Blitz Basic installed on your machine. You probably already installed this program earlier in the book, but just in case you didn't, now is the time to do so. See Chapter 1 for instructions on installing the compiler.

You have just opened the game! You can now play it to your heart's content. There are only three functioning keys within the program, and Table 13.7 explains all of them.

Table 13.7 The Keys Used in Invaderz!!!

Key	Description
Left Arrow	Moves the player ship left.
Right Arrow	Moves the player ship right.
Spacebar	Fires a bullet.

Let me give you some tips for Invaderz!!! Note, by the way, that you can't "beat" the game. The game continually gets harder and harder until the player dies.

- Try to stay in one place and fire bullets as quickly as you can. When one of the enemies fires a bullet at you, however, get out of the way.
- Remember, the bullets not only hurt the enemy if it hits him head on, but also if the enemy runs into it.
- Try to judge how fast the enemy is moving when firing a bullet. Oftentimes, you can fire a bullet directly into the enemy's path simply by watching.

- On the contrary to the previous tip, remember that the velocities of each ship change every 7/10 of a second. If they are moving to the left quickly, their route might modify to move them up slightly. If they are moving right very slowly, they might reverse directions completely!

And that's it for the Invaderz!!! game. Take a look at the screenshots from the game, Figures 13.5 and 13.6.

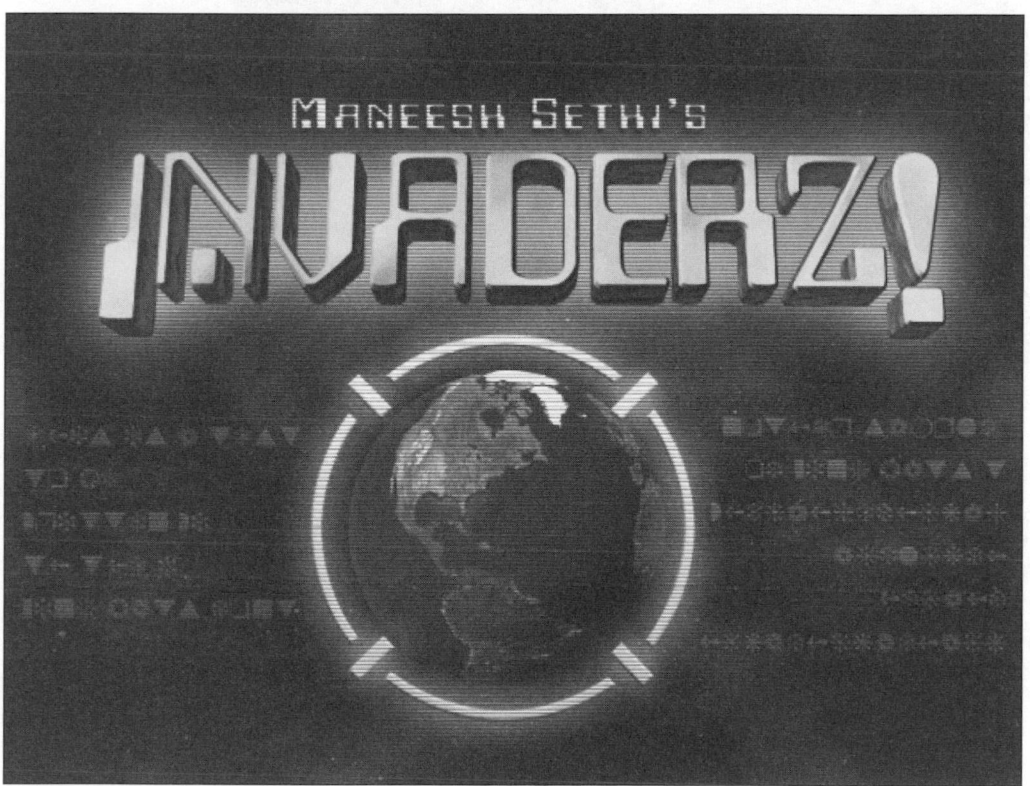

Figure 13.5 The Invaderz!!! title screen.

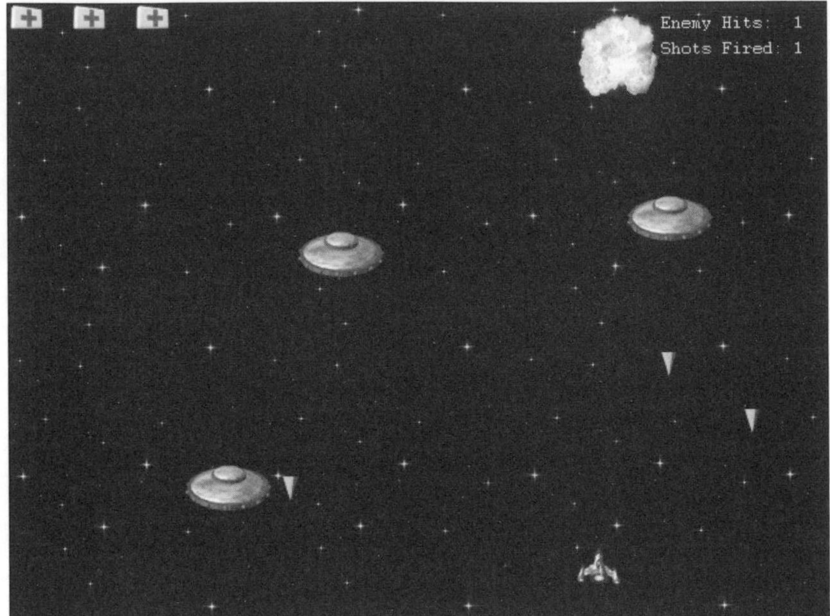

Figure 13.6 The Invaderz!!! game.

Epilogue

The game is over and the book is done. I've had a lot of fun traveling down this path with you, and I hope that what I have taught you will help you reach new limits in game programming and in life. I know this sounds clichéd, but really, I want you to use your new knowledge to make some new games!

Let's talk about the future of game programming—namely, yours. If you enjoyed what we have done with this book, you should know that there is a heck of a lot more out there to learn. Take a look at some of the sites listed in Appendix B to see what else you can learn. Play around with the compiler and the Blitz Basic language and create your own games. Believe me, the best way to get better is to practice.

Blitz Basic is an excellent language for learning programming. Now that you have the necessary skills of programming, you will understand a lot more if you choose to move on to other languages. Some concepts, such as loops and functions, have been hammered into your head in this book, and it won't be nearly as hard to understand them when doing the same in a different language.

Once you have reached the limits of Blitz Basic, there are two paths you might consider. The first is to move on to three-dimensional game programming using Blitz3d. This language is made by the same people who brought you Blitz Basic. It's a tough language, but the things you can do with Blitz3d are simply amazing. You can create entire game worlds with people and houses and the like. Amazing.

The other choice is to leave the Blitz language all together. There is a language called C (and its successor, C++) that is the most common language for producing and actually publishing games. The reason C is used over Blitz is because C is a much more powerful language; it can reach into the hardware to perform functions, and it is faster as well. You might think about picking up a book on C or C++ and studying the language (C was the first language I ever taught myself).

As you well know, life is simply a maze of paths, and each choice you make leads you down a path you have to follow. Choose to continue programming, choose to continue making games, choose to enjoy what you are doing, or don't. It's that simple.

Anyway, my tirade is over. I want to hear from you, however! I will gladly help with any games or programs that you make and want me to see or help you with. Simply e-mail me the program at:

maneesh@maneeshsethi.com

I want you to go to my Web site and join the community! You can find forums that talk about this book also.

http://www.maneeshsethi.com

Lastly, if you liked this book, make sure you review it on amazon.com! It really helps sales! (Tell your friends also.)

I will be organizing a contest on my Web site in the near future. Submit your best game, and you could win a free book or, if you are really lucky, a signed photo of me. ☺

Oh yeah, one more thing. Make sure you check out my other books. *Web Design for Teens* teaches you how to make Web sites and *How to Succeed As A Lazy Student* will help you learn how to beat school without doing any work. Keep your eye out for other things I will be putting out.

I would love to hear from you, so don't hesitate to e-mail me. Heck, just e-mail me and say hi, if you want.

"The greatest trick the devil ever pulled was convincing the world he didn't exist. And like that, *whoosh*, he's gone."

That's it from me. Maneesh Sethi, signing out.

PART IV

APPENDIXES

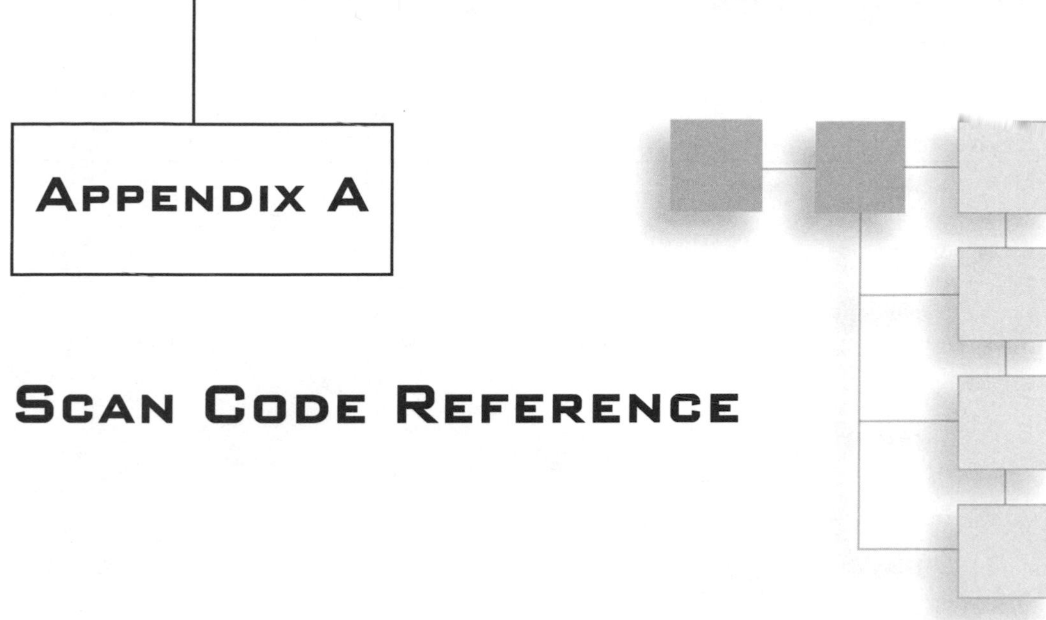

Appendix A

Scan Code Reference

This appendix contains a list of all the scan codes you can use for input in your programs. Scan codes are used in functions such as `KeyHit()` or `KeyDown()` like this:

```
KeyDown(scancode)
```

Input the scan code for the key you want to test for, and this function will return 1 if the key was pressed.

Many of the following keys won't appear on your keyboard; some of them are international keys (like the symbol for the Yen) and some of them only exist on advanced keyboards that have extra keys (like the Calculator key). Anyway, you can find any key that you would ever think of using on this list, shown in Table A.1.

Table A.1 The Scan Code Reference

Keyboard Key	Scan Code	Comments
ESCAPE	1	
1	2	
2	3	
3	4	
4	5	
5	6	
6	7	
7	8	
8	9	
9	10	
0	11	

continued

Keyboard Key	Scan Code	Comments
Minus (2)	12	On main keyboard
Equals sign (=)	13	
Backspace	14	Backspace key
Tab	15	
Q	16	
W	17	
E	18	
R	19	
T	20	
Y	21	
U	22	
I	23	
O	24	
P	25	
Left bracket ([)	26	
Right bracket (])	27	
Return/Enter	28	Return/Enter on main keyboard
Left control	29	
A	30	
S	31	
D	32	
F	33	
G	34	
H	35	
J	36	
K	37	
L	38	
Semicolon (;)	39	
Apostrophe (')	40	
Grave	41	Accent grave
Left shift	42	
Backslash (\)	43	
Z	44	
X	45	
C	46	
V	47	
B	48	
N	49	
M	50	
Comma (,)	51	

Keyboard Key	Scan Code	Comments
Period (.)	52	On main keyboard
Slash (/)	53	On main keyboard
Right shift	54	
Multiply (*)	55	On numeric keypad
Left Alt/menu	56	
Space	57	
Capitol	58	
F1	59	
F2	60	
F3	61	
F4	62	
F5	63	
F6	64	
F7	65	
F8	66	
F9	67	
F10	68	
NumLock	69	
Scroll Lock	70	
NumPad 7	71	
NumPad 8	72	
NumPad 9	73	
Subtract (−)	74	On numeric keypad
NumPad 4	75	
NumPad 5	76	
NumPad 6	77	
Add (+)	78	On numeric keypad
NumPad 1	79	
NumPad 2	80	
NumPad 3	81	
NumPad 0	82	
Decimal (.)	86	On numeric keypad
OEM_102	87	On UK/Germany keyboards
F11	87	
F12	88	
F13	100	(NEC PC98)
F14	101	(NEC PC98)
F15	102	(NEC PC98)
Kana	112	On Japanese keyboard

continued

Keyboard Key	Scan Code	Comments
ABNT_C1	115	/? On Portuguese (Brazilian) keyboards
Convert	121	On Japanese keyboard
NoConvert	123	On Japanese keyboard
Yen	125	On Japanese keyboard
ABNT_C2	126	Numpad on Portuguese (Brazilian) keyboards
Equals	141	Equals (=) on the numeric keypad (NEC PC98)
PrevTrack	144	Previous Track (DIK_CIRCUMFLEX) on Japanese keyboard
AT	145	(NEX PC98)
Colon (:)	146	(NEC PC98)
Underline	147	(NEC PC98)
Kanji	148	On Japanese keyboard
Stop	149	(NEC PC98)
AX	150	Japan AX
Unlabeled	151	(J3100)
Next track	153	Next Track
Enter	156	Enter on numeric keypad
Right control	157	
Mute	160	Mute
Calculator	161	Calculator
Play/Pause	162	Play/pause
Media stop	164	Media stop
Volume down	174	Volume –
Volume up	176	Volume +
Web home	178	Web home
Comma (,)	179	On numeric keypad (NEX PC98)
Divide (/)	181	On numeric keypad
SysReq	183	
Right Alt/menu	184	Right Alt
Pause	197	Pause
Home	199	Home on Arrow keypad
Up	200	Up Arrow on Arrow keypad
Page Up/Prior	201	Page Up on Arrow keypad
Left	203	Left Arrow on Arrow keypad
Right	205	Right Arrow on Arrow keypad
End	207	End Key on Arrow keypad
Down	208	Down Arrow on Arrow keypad
Next	209	Next Key on Arrow keypad
Insert	210	Insert Key on Arrow keypad
Delete	211	Delete Key on Arrow keypad
Left Windows	219	Left Windows key

Keyboard Key	Scan Code	Comments
Right Windows	220	Right Windows key
Apps	221	Apps Menu key
Power	222	System power
Sleep	223	System sleep
Wake	227	System wake
Web search	229	
Web favorites	230	
Web refresh	231	
Web stop	232	
Web forward	233	
Web back	234	
My Computer	235	
Mail	236	
Media select	237	

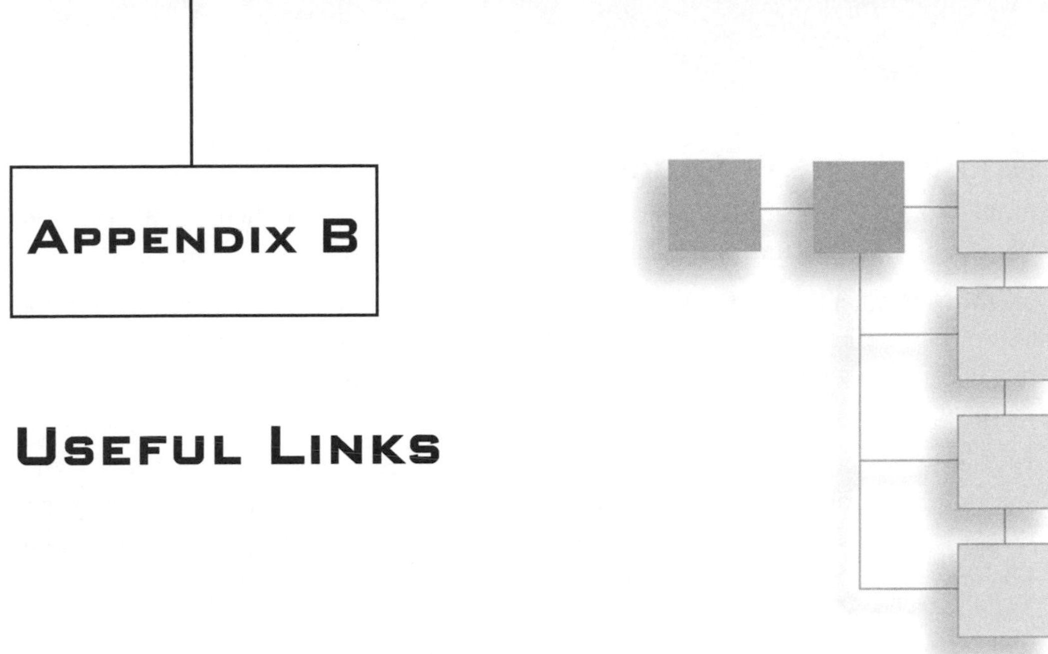

Useful Links

This appendix lists some links where you might be able to learn more about Blitz Basic game programming.

Blitz Basic Links

There are some extremely good sites for learning Blitz Basic programming. Check out the forums on each: they are active and helpful.

www.maneeshsethi.com is the official site for this book. You will find updates to this book and tutorials/programs on this site. You can also contact me directly from this site.

www.BlitzBasic.com is the official site of the BlitzPlus program. You can find the actual BlitzPlus program to download (this program is also included on the CD) along with some tutorials. The most updated version of the command reference is on this Web site. To get to the command reference, go to www.blitzbasic.com, click Community, and click Blitz3D Docs directly below. From there, you can choose to see the 2D command reference.

www.BlitzCoder.com is an excellent site run by John "Krylar" Logsdon. This site has numerous articles and tutorials about Blitz Basic and Blitz3D, along with a very active community. If you have any problems with Blitz, leave a message on the forums and you will get a response quickly. I promise.

General Game Programming Links

Although the number of Blitz Basic programming sites is limited, there are plenty more Web sites on general game programming. Following is one very useful one.

www.GameDev.net is one of the most widely known and most visited game programming sites on the Internet. The site boasts literally hundreds of articles and tutorials on game coding. This site can help introduce you to other languages, as well as provide theories and concepts that you can use in Blitz Basic programming.

http://www-cs-students.stanford.edu/~amitp/gameprog.html is the site of Amit's Game Programming Information site. This site is an introduction to game programming. It has answers to some questions you might have about furthering your game programming knowledge.

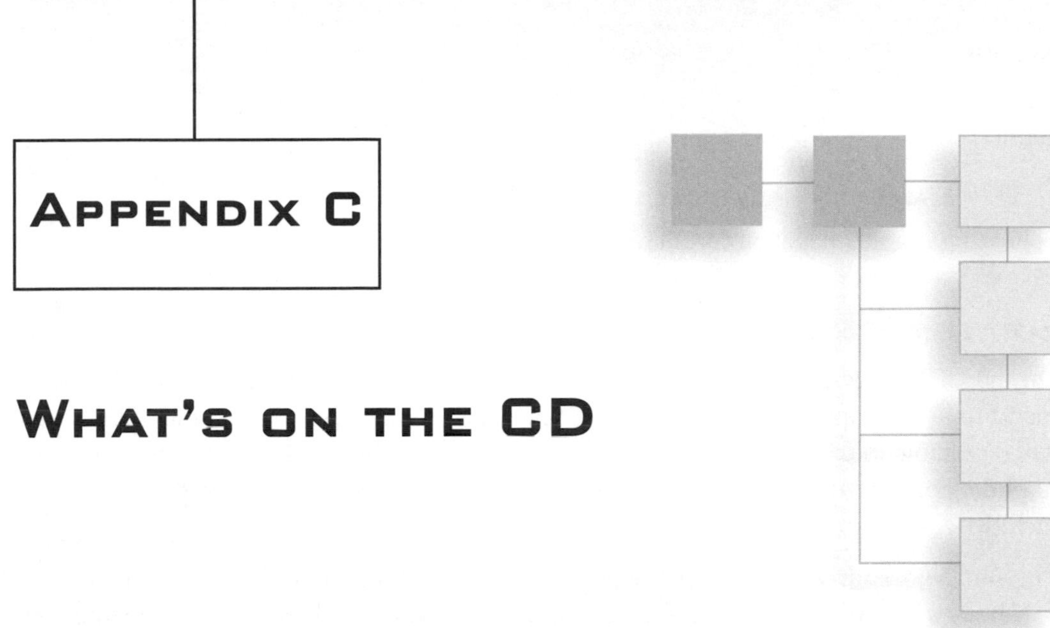

Appendix C

What's on the CD

The CD that is in the back of the book comes with a lot of useful programs and demos. Let me explain to you everything that you will find when you boot this baby up.

Check out the readme files in every directory! They will have instructions and updates to everything on the CD.

The directory structure for this CD should be pretty easy to follow. You will find everything arranged like this:

Source\

- Chapter01\
- Chapter02\
- ...
- Chapter13\
- BlitzMax Source\

Art\

- Book Art\
- Spritelib_Gpl\

Sounds\

- Sound\
- Music\

Games\

Programs\

Following is an explanation for all of these categories.

Source

On the CD, you will find all of the source code from the examples in the book. I recommend that you copy all of the code to your hard drive before playing around with it. You will be unable to compile the source if it is left on the CD, but moving it to the hard drive fixes the compilation errors. Also, executable files for each and every demo program are included.

The BlitzMax source directory is the ported source for Blitz's new program, BlitzMax. If you have a Macintosh, you can use the BlitzMax demo, which is included on the CD. Thanks Nicolas de Jaeghere for porting this code. Everything is ported except the final Invaderz!!! game.

Art

I have included a section that contains all of the art I have used in the book, along with a few other art libraries I have found. The main folder contains the art created by Edgar L. Ibarra for the book, and the subfolder named *Spritelib_Gpl* is a library of images made by Ari Feldman. The *Spritelib_Gpl* folder contains numerous subdirectories, each which contain different images. Special thanks to Edgar and Ari for the art.

Sounds

This section contains two subdirectories: Sound and Music. Inside the sound directory, you will find numerous sound effects that can be used in your programs, royalty free. The Music subdirectory has a few MP3 files and some MIDI music files that can be used in your programs also. If you want to use the MP3 files for anything other than personal use (if you decide to sell your game, for example), please contact Thomas Stenbäck of Interim Nation for licensing info. You can contact Thomas at interimnation@hotmail.com.

Games

This folder contains demos of a few games that were written in Blitz Basic. Have fun with them and try to learn from them. Special thanks to Jason Brasier, Edgar Ibarra, and Marcus "Eikon" Smith for these games.

Programs

This section contains a few programs that you can use to help you in your conquest of the gaming world. Included are the demo files for the following programs.

- **BlitzPlus**—The actual program that you will be writing and compiling the source of the book from. Make sure you install this program first.
- **Blitz3D**—The 3D version of BlitzPlus. Check it out, you may like the 3D capabilities.
- **Blitz Basic 2D**—This is the demo for the original 2D version of the program. Some files might work better with this version.
- **BlitzMax**—This is a modified version of BlitzPlus that works with Macintosh computers.
- **Jasc Paint Shop Pro**—An art program, much like Microsoft Paint, but much more robust.
- **MilkShape 3D**—A 3D modeler for more advanced techniques.
- **CoolEdit Pro**—A sound-editing program.

Okay, that's about it for the CD. Have fun with everything that is included!

INDEX

Symbols

A

B

Q

R

S

W

X

Y

Gamedev.net

License Agreement/Notice of Limited Warranty

By opening the sealed disc container in this book, you agree to the following terms and conditions. If, upon reading the following license agreement and notice of limited warranty, you cannot agree to the terms and conditions set forth, return the unused book with unopened disc to the place where you purchased it for a refund.

License:
The enclosed software is copyrighted by the copyright holder(s) indicated on the software disc. You are licensed to copy the software onto a single computer for use by a single user and to a backup disc. You may not reproduce, make copies, or distribute copies or rent or lease the software in whole or in part, except with written permission of the copyright holder(s). You may transfer the enclosed disc only together with this license, and only if you destroy all other copies of the software and the transferee agrees to the terms of the license. You may not decompile, reverse assemble, or reverse engineer the software.

Notice of Limited Warranty:
The enclosed disc is warranted by Thomson Course Technology PTR to be free of physical defects in materials and workmanship for a period of sixty (60) days from end user's purchase of the book/disc combination. During the sixty-day term of the limited warranty, Thomson Course Technology PTR will provide a replacement disc upon the return of a defective disc.

Limited Liability:
THE SOLE REMEDY FOR BREACH OF THIS LIMITED WARRANTY SHALL CONSIST ENTIRELY OF REPLACEMENT OF THE DEFECTIVE DISC. IN NO EVENT SHALL THOMSON COURSE TECHNOLOGY PTR OR THE AUTHOR BE LIABLE FOR ANY OTHER DAMAGES, INCLUDING LOSS OR CORRUPTION OF DATA, CHANGES IN THE FUNCTIONAL CHARACTERISTICS OF THE HARDWARE OR OPERATING SYSTEM, DELETERIOUS INTERACTION WITH OTHER SOFTWARE, OR ANY OTHER SPECIAL, INCIDENTAL, OR CONSEQUENTIAL DAMAGES THAT MAY ARISE, EVEN IF THOMSON COURSE TECHNOLOGY PTR AND/OR THE AUTHOR HAS PREVIOUSLY BEEN NOTIFIED THAT THE POSSIBILITY OF SUCH DAMAGES EXISTS.

Disclaimer of Warranties:
THOMSON COURSE TECHNOLOGY PTR AND THE AUTHOR SPECIFICALLY DISCLAIM ANY AND ALL OTHER WARRANTIES, EITHER EXPRESS OR IMPLIED, INCLUDING WARRANTIES OF MERCHANTABILITY, SUITABILITY TO A PARTICULAR TASK OR PURPOSE, OR FREEDOM FROM ERRORS. SOME STATES DO NOT ALLOW FOR EXCLUSION OF IMPLIED WARRANTIES OR LIMITATION OF INCIDENTAL OR CONSEQUENTIAL DAMAGES, SO THESE LIMITATIONS MIGHT NOT APPLY TO YOU.

Other:
This Agreement is governed by the laws of the State of Massachusetts without regard to choice of law principles. The United Convention of Contracts for the International Sale of Goods is specifically disclaimed. This Agreement constitutes the entire agreement between you and Thomson Course Technology PTR regarding use of the software.